Basic Estimating for Construction

SECOND EDITION

James A. S. Fatzinger, CPE, ME

American Society of Professional Estimators

Upper Saddle River, New Jersey
Columbus, Ohio

Library of Congress Cataloging-in-Publication Data

Fatzinger, James A. S.
    Basic estimating for construction / James A.S. Fatzinger.--2nd ed.
       p. cm
    Includes index.
    ISBN 0-13-111913-3
     1. Building--Estimates. I. Title.

TH435.F28 2004
692'.5--dc21

                                        2003042982

Editor in Chief: Stephen Helba
Executive Editor: Ed Francis
Development Editor: Linda Cupp
Production Editor: Holly Shufeldt
Production Coordination: Carlisle Publishers Services
Design Coordinator: Diane Ernsberger
Cover Designer: Ali Mohrman
Cover art: Superstock
Production Manager: Matt Ottenweller
Marketing Manager: Mark Marsden

This book was set in Stone Serif by Carlisle Communications, Ltd. It was printed and bound by Banta Book Group. The cover was printed by Phoenix Color Corp.

Pearson Prentice Hall™ is a trademark of Pearson Education, Inc.
Pearson® is a registered trademark of Pearson plc
Prentice Hall® is a registered trademark of Pearson Education, Inc.

Pearson Education Ltd.   Pearson Education Australia Pty. Limited
Pearson Education Singapore Pte. Ltd.   Pearson Education North Asia Ltd.
Pearson Education Canada, Ltd.   Pearson Educación de Mexico, S.A. de C.V.
Pearson Education—Japan   Pearson Education Malaysia Pte. Ltd.

10 9 8 7 6
ISBN 0-13-111913-3

Preface

Basic *Estimating for Construction* is intended to guide students through a set of construction plans to make a material quantity survey, convert the material quantities to a monetary value, and add the cost of labor and equipment. The text further instructs students how to apply overhead and profit to produce a total monetary value to be tendered to an owner.

It is imperative to know the reasons why an estimate is so critical to the construction industry. An estimator in construction has several skills. These skills include a strong knowledge of mathematics, how to apply that knowledge, and the ability to sell the owner, the architect, and/or the engineer of the project the cost of the construction. The estimator is responsible for identifying the objects noted on a plan, the material required to make the object a reality, and then determining the cost of the material, the labor to install the material on the project, and the equipment necessary to assist in its placement.

An estimator must know the meaning of a blueprint and how that blueprint pertains to a constuction project. The plans alone mean nothing without someone taking the drawings from the plans, picturing them in one's mind's eye, and applying them to some use. The estimator is the one who must accept the responsibility for the proper application.

In this text manual estimating is made as simple and as accurate as possible so that the student can learn how an estimate is made and how it is applied to the bidding process, the contract, and the follow-up procedures.

The estimate is laid out in the text so that the actual construction can be made following the standard construction specifications. All construction costs noted in this text are fictitious. If the instructor and the student wish to update the noted costs using a current construction cost book, as the material is presented, this will not be a problem. Such updating will make the student better understand construction costs.

The author also wishes to introduce a CD containing a set of drawings identical to the drawings supplied with the text. The plans on the CD are for the primary purpose of teaching the new technology of working with an internet (on-line) plan room.

ACKNOWLEDGMENTS

The author gratefully acknowledges the following reviewers for their insightful suggestions. They are Philip W. Johnson, The University of Alabama, and Kathy Klingman, Bates Technical College.

The author further wishes to acknowledge and thank Mr. Ed van der Bogert, chairman of the Construction Education Department, Edmonds Community College, Edmonds, Washington; and Mr. Ed Golembiewski, construction estimating consultant in Las Vegas, Nevada, who is a member of the American Society of Professional Estimators (ASPE), for the work that they have added to enhance the text.

Mr. Van der Bogert prepared the compact disc (CD) and the explanation of, and the directions for, its use in conjunction with the text.

Mr. Golembiewski, a Certified Professional Estimator (CPE), assisted in the upgrading of the text to a more professional level.

Contents

6 MASONRY 105

7 STRUCTURAL AND MISCELLANEOUS STEEL 127

8 WOOD AND PLASTICS; DOORS AND WINDOWS 139

9 THERMAL AND MOISTURE PROTECTION 173

10 FINISHES 197

11   SPECIALTY DIVISIONS   239

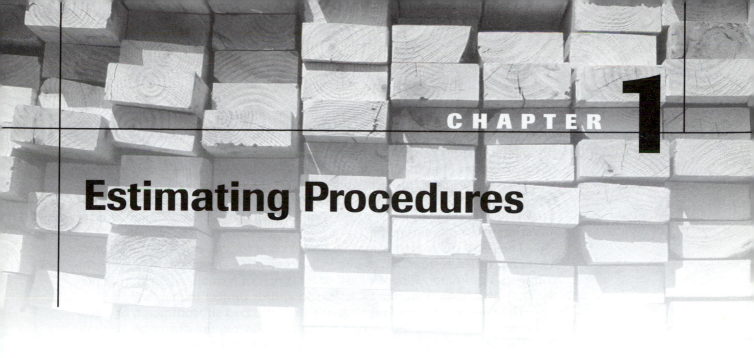

CHAPTER 1

Estimating Procedures

Welcome to the world of construction estimating! By definition estimating is *"the act of appraising or valuing the worth of something."* In construction, it is the *science of mathematics*, the *knowledge of materials*, and the *art of interpretation* of a blueprint. This combination produces an assessment of a construction project that becomes the bid package, or proposal, and the basis of the construction contract.

There are two basic prerequisites for wanting to learn these procedures:

1. A knowledge of blueprint reading
2. A strong mathematics background

If the student is depending solely upon a computerized estimating program, he or she must understand that such a program is only as good as the software program and the person supplying the information to the program. It is, therefore, important that the student know how to perform manual solutions for an estimate.

THE ESTIMATOR

The ability to understand and interpret a blueprint places the estimator in the position of a professional, on a par with the architect and engineer. Part of the estimator's role is to work in cooperation with both of these professionals and to maintain a good rapport with them. This rapport carries on throughout the estimating process as well as after the contract and through the period of construction.

For whom does an estimator work? The estimator may be an employee of an architectural or engineering firm, a general contracting firm, a subcontracting company, or a specialty contracting company. The estimator for an architectural or engineering firm may not only make a quantity survey but he or she is also seeking any possible construction errors that may need to be corrected, or suggest additions that will identify possible better construction techniques.

ENR Classifications

The Engineering News-Record (ENR) has established three classifications identifying the size of a company in construction. These are determined by the size of construction projects the contractor deals with. They are referred to as the **small-cap** company (projects under $500,000), **mid-cap** companies (projects from $500,000 to possibly $2,000,000), and **large-cap** companies (projects from $2,000,000 and up). The size of company determines the requirements for an estimator or estimators.

The *small-cap* company may be a subcontractor, a specialty contractor, or a general contractor/builder. In small-cap companies, the owner may act as the company's estimator. Where an estimator is part of a small-cap firm, that person may also be the company salesperson and/or project manager.

The *mid-cap* construction company may also be a subcontractor, or a general contractor/builder. A company of this size may require one or two estimators. The estimator(s) for a mid-cap company may also be the project manager(s).

In *large-cap* companies there may be a team of estimators to do a complete quantity survey on a project to make certain that materials, labor, and equipment are properly identified for their specific costs and quantities. The estimator may perform such positions as the office engineer, project administrator, assistant superintendent, or project manager. Over a period of time the individual may be involved with estimating in each position until reaching the position of full-time estimator or chief estimator.

Estimators are also an integral part of interior design firms, construction product manufacturers, and construction supply companies. Many experienced estimators have become independent, free-lance consultants working directly with the architectural and/or engineering firms.

The estimator is the "front man" for a contractor in most instances. He or she is frequently the first contact with an owner, developer, architect, engineer, or other contractor. It is the estimator that assists the contractor to seek projects in which the company is interested, qualified, or experienced. This information is explained in chapter 3.

Accuracy

The requirement for accuracy determines how well the estimator is able to understand a set of plans. *The accuracy of the quantity survey also determines whether or not a project will be successful.* The reputation and appreciation of the members of the industry are tantamount for the estimator. His or her performance within the company, as well as with the construction industry, enhances the industry's performance as a whole.

Concern for proper identification of materials, labor, and the necessary equipment for a project is the estimator's responsibility. The ensuing chapters of this text identify these responsibilities.

PREPARATION OF THE ESTIMATE

A good estimator constantly follows a well-organized program of procedures. When all of the procedures are followed, the chances of making errors are minimized. A good procedural guideline should be similar to the following:

1. Study legal documents and specifications.
2. Study the plans thoroughly before starting the quantity survey.
3. Mark the plans, sections, and details that pertain to the estimate.
4. Do the quantity survey making sure to mark all areas covered.
5. Always double-check the survey. This is especially important if there is interference during the survey.
6. Obtain material costs; extend those costs.
7. Add taxes where applicable.
8. Determine labor costs through the productivity process or from historical data (see chapter 3).
9. Determine equipment requirements and costs.
10. Add overhead and profit (see chapter 14).
11. Include bonding costs, if any.
12. Double-check all math and prepare to tender the bid.

A quantity survey, also called the takeoff, is a study of the amount of materials needed for a construction project. When doing the quantity survey, the estimator should think in terms of actual field procedures. By picturing these procedures, the estimator can develop an organized estimate that will be easily understood by all interested parties. For example, a carpentry estimator should prepare the survey the way the structure is built, by starting at the lowest level (basement, first floor, and so on) and finishing at the roof structure.

The Workshop.   The ideal setup for an estimator is a location that includes a room large enough for a desk, plan table, and files. The room should be separated from the traffic and noise of the rest of the office. The plan table should be capable of holding a complete set of plans. Other tools that are important to the estimator are a good calculator, drawing scales, and other small drafting tools. The latter should be available in the event that it is necessary to clarify a portion of the estimate.

Forms

See figure 1–1. The estimating procedures should definitely include completion of forms for a paper-trail audit. The estimator needs to compile information in an orderly manner so that those who need to see the estimate can readily understand it. Forms aid in this process. The forms may be standard types purchased from various office supply distributors or may be customized for the trade by the contractor or estimator.

A good form will include space for information such as the project owner's (an individual, a partnership, or a corporation) name and address, architect's name and telephone number, the project name, location, and size (area). The main portion of the form should include a description of the area being estimated (floor, roof, exterior walls, room number or name, and so on), the measurement used (units, lineal measure, square measure, or cubic measure), and the quantity of material required (pieces, sacks, gallons, and so on). Space for unit costs, cost extensions, and total costs of material, labor, equipment, taxes, permits, fees, and bonds, as well as the project total, should be available on the forms.

ESTIMATE SUMMARY

PROJECT: ____________________

ESTIMATE NO. ____________________

SHEET NO. ____________________

PREPARED BY: ____________________ DATE: __________

CHECKED BY: ____________________ DATE: __________

MAIN ACCOUNT	DESCRIPTION	QUANTITY	MATERIALS		LABOR				SUB-CONTRACT		TOTAL
			UNIT PRICE	AMOUNT	UNIT M.H.	TOTAL M.H.	RATE	AMOUNT	UNIT PRICE	AMOUNT	

FIGURE 1–1
Typical Manual Estimate Form

Computer Estimating Systems

A good computer-estimating program that fits the capabilities of the contractor is an asset. There are a number of computer software systems available to the estimator. Some programs are for specific trades such as the plumbing and electrical trades. The major systems available are set up to be usable by the architect, engineer, general contractor, and subcontractor.

These programs may or may not include a **digitizing system.** The **digitizer** is a stylus (pen) or mouse used in conjunction with a magnetic or sonic pad upon which the plans lay. The digitizer system works similar to "scaling" a drawing manually. The difference between manual and digitizer "scaling" is that the software program uses a built-in compensation system that produces the actual measurement noted on the plan. The digitizer relays the information directly to the computer and stores the data, thereby speeding up the estimating time and improving accuracy. The digitizer may even draw the item on the computer with measurements. The estimator and/or contractor must determine the estimating system that is most compatible with the company's needs.

See also appendix I, *The Plan Center Concept, Internet Communications*, and the CD included with the text. Study and work carefully with it so that the plans may be displayed on the computer screen and can be studied more carefully.

TYPES OF ESTIMATES

When an owner, architect, or engineer requests a determination of the cost of a construction project, the estimating process begins. The estimator may be asked to produce a **feasibility (conceptual) study, preliminary proposal,** or **construction proposal.** In all cases, the estimator is responsible for an accurate, competitive assessment of the project.

Feasibility Study

See figure 1–2. The feasibility study is the first step in the development of estimating project costs. The study determines whether or not the owner may wish to continue. It is usually done by the architectural or engineering firm with which the owner is dealing. The architect/engineer may have an in-house estimator or may look to an independent estimating professional for help. In either case, the estimate is done for the purpose of determining possible costs for a proposed project. It is this estimate that is the groundwork for all succeeding estimates. If the costs do not exceed the money set aside, financed through individuals or shareholders, the architect/engineer can proceed with the plans and seek other more accurate estimates. This initial estimate is calculated on the basis of "cost per square foot" and/or cost of materials and furnishings. The costs may be a lump-sum figure or may be broken down, with structural costs separated from the total estimate costs.

The estimator should have historical knowledge or backup from which to produce costs, starting from the feasibility estimates of previous projects through the costs incurred during completion of the projects. The initial sketches and presentation plans provided to the estimator may include such drawings as a site plan, a floor plan, and a structural section with very few dimensions given. It is the estimator's responsibility to be able to "see" the completed project from the information provided.

CHRISTLE Associates
500 Broad Street
Las Vegas, Nevada

April 1, 1996

Dr. Robin Stone
The Medical Associates
500 Main Street
Caliente, Nevada

Dear Dr. Stone:

The following information is a breakdown of the estimated construction costs:

Architectural Fees	$ 50,000.00	
Fees, Permits, etc.	$ 35,000.00	
Contingencies	$ 85,000.00	
		$170,000.00
Off-Sites:		
Excavating/Grading	$ 32,690.00	
Soils Investigation	$ 3,000.00	
Survey	$ 1,260.00	
		$ 36,950.00
On-Sites:		
Foundation	$ 3,970.00	
Structure	$160,650.00	
Furnishings	$ 50,000.00	
		$214,620.00
Taxes:		$ 8,585.00
TOTAL VALUE:		**$430,155.00**

These study figures are within the boundaries of a budget that you and your associates specified and we feel that this amount can be met with little change.

Respectfully,

(Signed) Steven Christle

FIGURE 1–2
Feasibility (Conceptual) Estimate

The estimator must also offer a study on the extent of time the project will take to complete. This is important since the time extensions determine how far "down the road" the owner will see any profit. This information gives the owner two options if the project term is too long: (1) cancel the project or (2) change the "dream" into something less expensive and time-consuming.

Preliminary Proposal

See figure 1–3. The owner accepts the results of the feasibility study and determines that the project is worth completing. The architect expands on the sketches and presentation drawings and prepares a set of preliminary

PHASE DESCRIPTION	PHASE QTY	LABOR AMOUNT	MATRL AMOUNT	SUB AMOUNT	EQUIP AMOUNT	OTHER AMOUNT	TOTAL AMOUNT
3000.00 CONCRETE							
3209.00 Rebar - Walls		7,190					7,190
CONCRETE		7,190					7,190
4000.00 MASONRY							
4105.00 Mortar - All Types			2,010				2,010
4221.10 Concrete Block 10"		2,161	2,572				4,733
4221.15 Concrete Block 8"		7,913	8,369				16,282
4221.65 Concrete Wall Caps			300				300
4731.00 Scaffolds - Tubular Steel					1,500		1,500
4731.50 Grout Fill Concrete			6,148		1,000		7,148
MASONRY		10,074	19,399		2,500		31,973
		Labor hrs: 49.195			**Equip hrs:**		**10.00**

Labor　49.195 crew hrs
Equipment　10.00 crew hrs

Labor	17,264	
Material	19,399	
Equipment	2,500	
		B
Surety Bond	476	T 7.00000%
Sales Tax	2,775	T 15.00000%
Overhead	6,362	T 10.00000%
Profit	4,878	C 960.00000$
Fees	960	
	39,163	
TOTAL ESTIMATE	54,614	

FIGURE 1–3
Computer Estimate Readout

drawings. The plans may include many of the architectural and structural drawings, but they are not complete. Some of the sections, details, and schedules may be missing. There may even be some specifications that are incomplete. The completed portion of the drawings are produced to scale with accurate dimensions.

Preliminary plans are submitted for bid for two reasons:

1. The selected major contractors such as the excavating, concrete, mechanical, and electrical contractors are asked for assistance in providing more specific information as to the best methods to use for the construction. The feedback from these contractors assists the architect/engineer in making a better, more complete set of plans.
2. There is a continuing *question of cost overruns*, which may have occurred as the result of delays in financing, governmental requirements, and so on.

Design/Build.   Plans similar to the preliminary plans may also be used as the basis for a "design-build" project, in which the contractors selected build according to all codes and supply the specifications along with those produced by the architect and engineer. The plans are produced as the actual production is in progress. This is a difficult way to complete a construction project because there are hidden costs that must be paid for by the owner "after the fact."

The Construction Proposal

See figure 1–3. Most estimators for the general contractor and the subcontractor work with a set of plans referred to as the **construction set.** Where required by law, these have been approved by the local building authorities. These plans reflect all changes in plans since the initial estimate. On them, details, sections, schedules, and the specifications have been completed. They are the blueprint by which the project is built unless additional plans, with approval, are developed during construction. The estimate is similar to the Preliminary Proposal shown in figure 1–3 except that it is much more detailed.

A general contractor may work specifically in one or two trades. The estimator produces a detailed analysis of these trades for the purpose of the bid. In most other cases, the general contractor requests an estimate from the subcontractors that will be required to complete the project. These subcontractors must each produce a detailed estimate of costs for their portions of the project. The general contractor accepts the subcontract bids, analyzes them, determines the best bid from each trade, and submits a proposal, using these bids to determine the total cost of the project.

THE CONTRACT DOCUMENTS

See appendix III, The Contract Documents. The estimator must be totally informed regarding the procedural requirements of a project. It is, therefore, mandatory that the estimator thoroughly read each and every document that is a part of the project. The estimator must study the information available, from the initial Invitation to Bid through the specifications and any addendum or addenda before any actual estimating is started. The estimator reviews the basic documentation stating requirements, dividing the responsibilities, and offering legal protection for all parties to be involved in the construction of a project. It is the estimator's responsibility to "weed out" all the pertinent information to determine if the company he or she is working for even qualifies to bid the project.

Included in the Contract Documents, also referred to as the Legal Documents, are the **Invitation to Bid** or **Advertisement to Bid,** the **Instructions to Bidders,** and the **Contract.** These documents contain pertinent information as well as the legal requirements regarding the project. All parties must adhere to such information and requirements, from the owner to the subcontractors selected to perform the work.

The Invitation to Bid or Advertisement to Bid

An owner, developer, architect, or engineer sends letters to known and qualified general contractors requesting them to tender bids on the proposed project. Only those parties who receive such a letter may bid the project. In turn, any subcontractors known to be qualified by the successful contractor may also be invited to bid in the same manner. The Invitation to Bid includes such information as the following:

1. Owner of project
2. Location of project
3. Bid time and date
4. Some minimal information regarding insurance
5. Plan availability and cost

The Advertisement to Bid requests general contractors to bid a project and is placed in a newspaper or other periodical widely read in construction circles. Such an advertisement is normally required for government bidding. This method may also be applied for private construction where there are insufficient qualified contractors or where the owner has no knowledge of any qualified general contractors. This method may also be used by the general contractors for subcontract bids.

Instructions to Bidders

The Instructions to Bidders describe in more detail what is expected of those bidding on the project. The information, if not stated in the invitation to bid, includes other instructions such as these:

1. The cost for the plans and specifications (if required)
2. The requirements for a bid security (bonds)
3. Material substitutions allowed (if any)
4. The manner in which the bid is to be handled (open or sealed bid)

Contract

The contract may be standard, or it may be customized for certain projects. There are a variety of such documents, including the military (army, navy, or air force), public works, Corps of Engineers, utilities, and private projects. Many private construction projects and some of the public works projects use documentation provided by the American Institute of Architects (AIA), such as form A401 (revised), or by the Engineering Joint Contractor Documents Committee (EJCDC).

The contract includes information on bid requirements, proposal (bid) forms to be used, bonding, sample contract, and so on, and they should be studied and used by all bidders tendering a proposal for the work. The documents may be standard types mentioned above or customized to fit the needs of the owner, architect, engineer, and/or contractor.

General and Special Conditions

The general and special conditions expand and explain the administrative procedures, setting forth the legal rights of all participants. These conditions may be included in the Contract Documents or the Project Manual.

The **General Conditions Documents** are the standard means for establishing legal rights of parties, and they include all of the administrative and procedural controls governing a project. Such information as release from injury or harm ("hold harmless" clause), rights of rejection or rescission of contract, specific insurance requirements, litigation rights, payment procedures, and accounting are thoroughly laid out. Instructions regarding addenda prior to acceptance of contract, as well as work authorizations and change orders after acceptance of contract, are also provided.

Special Conditions Documents are made by agreement between the owner, architect, and general contractor. The changes made in the Special Conditions may modify, delete, or supply additional instructions to or from the General Conditions that are related to the specific project.

Bid Forms

Refer to appendix III, The Contract Documents. Special bid forms may also be included with the documents. The form may require such information as the type of company bidding (sole ownership, partnership, corporation) and the signature of the party legally appointed to sign such documents. The general contractor may also be required to submit the list of subcontractors chosen to perform the work whose bids were used.

Bonds

There may also be a requirement for certification of qualification by demanding bonding of the contractor and all subcontractors. Bonds are submitted only if required. Most institutional and government projects insist upon them. Bonding may include a **bid, payment,** and **performance bond.** In most instances, the owner will not accept responsibility for the bond cost.

Bid Bond.   The bid bond is used to ensure that the contractor will enter into the contract if said contractor is the chosen bidder. The bond cost may be from 5% to 15% of the bid total. The dollar amount may be included in the total or may be submitted separately as an **add** to the bid. A bid bond is kept by the owner or the owner's representative for the chosen and next chosen bidder until the contract is signed. All other bonds submitted are returned to the unsuccessful bidders. If the bidder reneges on the contract, that is, fails to sign, the bond is forfeited to the owner and the next chosen bidder is given the opportunity to sign the contract.

Payment Bond.   A payment bond is required only if the contractor and/or subcontractor are selected to do the work. The cost of the bond may be from 1.2% to 5% of the total contract value depending on the contractor's record. It is used as an assurance that all material suppliers, labor wages, and subcontract work will be paid. If, after acceptance of the contract, the contractor cannot meet the obligations, the bonding company takes over. The forfeiting contractor must repay the bonding company the costs incurred. The costs could include additional payments made by the bonding company to the owner or the replacement contractor.

Performance Bond.   This bond is often used in tandem with, and is normally at the same percentage rate as, the payment bond. The purpose for this bond is identical to that of the payment bond. If the contractor is unable to complete the work specified in the contract, the bonding company has the right to complete the project and hire a new contractor. Again, the bonding company will demand repayment of the costs incurred.

The Project Manual

See appendix IV, Project Manual. As previously mentioned, the General and Special Conditions may be included in the Project Manual. Other information typically included in the Project Manual is the following:

1. General Project Information Sheet (Cover Sheet)
2. Index to the Specifications
3. List of support trade organizations
4. Specifications: Divisions 1 through 16

The Specifications, Division 1, referred to as the **General** and/or **Special Requirements,** contain information about the responsibilities and limitations of the general contractor and subcontractors, specific details for submitting product information sheets, alternate/alternative proposals, allowances for special equipment and materials, change orders and work authorizations, specific insurance requirements, payment procedures, quality control, temporary facilities, and so on.

Divisions 2 through 16 specify instructions for a trade or combination of trades included in each division, the material and installation requirements, code requirements, and standards of good construction practice. Each contractor and subcontractor bids the work according to the division and/or section of a division pertaining to the trade or trades in which the contractor is involved. For example, Division 7, Thermal and Moisture Protection, includes work pertaining to thermal insulation, below-grade moisture protection, roofing, sheet metal flashings, roof accessories, and sealants. Specialty contractors working in insulation or below-grade moisture protection, roofing, sheet metal, or painting will bid portions of this division. Manufacturers or suppliers specializing in roof accessories, such as prefabricated roof hatches or skylights, may bid these accessories separately as well.

SOURCES FOR STANDARDS

Architects, engineers, and specification writers get their information for establishing the rules of construction from code organizations and materials testing laboratories.

Codes are the rules, both safety and workmanship, by which the construction trades are required to work. They are established by government or private organizations using the expertise of insurance, manufacturing, architectural, engineering, and contracting professionals. A few of the organizations created for the establishment of uniform construction codes include, but not limited to, the Occupational Safety and Health Administration (OSHA), the American National Standards Institute (ANSI), the International Code Council (ICC), and the National Fire Protection Association (NFPA). Each of these organizations may make changes (deletions or additions) to national, regional, state, or local codes, or make recommendations to associations that write the codes.

The **materials testing laboratories,** approved by the code makers and other authorities, do testing of all types of materials of construction and submit findings on the material qualifications. The most widely known and accepted organizations include the American Society for Testing Materials (ASTM), the Factory Mutual (FM) testing laboratories, and Underwriters Laboratories (UL). The findings from these laboratories may become a part of the trade standards or are included in local, state, regional, or federal codes. The Federal Specifications (Fed Spec) listed in the Federal Register, a daily document published by the federal government, are followed for government projects.

Every item of material used in residential, commercial, industrial, and government work must meet the requirements of one or all of the above testing laboratories. The tests are made under conditions prevailing in the area of the country where the material is to be used. The findings are distributed to manufacturers and building officials as a guideline against poor material quality and workmanship.

Refer to Appendix IV, The Project Manual. A reference list of many organizations also involved with construction codes is found in the Project Manual in appendix IV. The regulations established by these and similar organizations are also used by local building, zoning, and inspection departments to ensure adherence to the codes, regulations, and resulting local ordinances, and to become the basis of the "the standards of the trade."

Construction Specification Institute (CSI)

One of the major organizations involved with specifications and codes is the Construction Specifications Institute. This group works very closely with the architects and engineers. They may be a part of the architectural or engineering team. The members of this organization are involved with establishing construction procedures to be used on a project.

THE PROPOSAL

So far, the initial procedures leading to a thorough, quantity survey have been presented. The work does not stop at this point, however. Once the survey has been completed, all of the information must be gathered together into one final summary. The material quantities, the labor, and the equipment must be correlated and placed in an organized system, such as used for each individual trade. In addition, the sum total with taxes, overhead, and profit needs to be determined. There are bid, contract, and production follow-ups that are a part of the estimator's responsibility. The completion of the proposal and the follow-ups will be discussed in chapter 14.

CHAPTER EXERCISES

Essay

1. In your own words define "ethic" and "ethics."

2. If you were employed by a contractor to do estimating, how should the company fit your definition?

3. By inference to the size of the projects, name the three categories of construction companies.

Completion

_____   1. The final set of plans with which the estimator is involved is the _____ set.

_____   2. A study made to determine if the project may continue is called the _____ or _____ study.

_____   3. The instructions given for a set of plans is called the _____.

_____   4. The search for a bid is called _____ where the owner has little knowledge of the available contractors.

_____   5. The _____ bond is required for protection of wages by contractor.

_____   6. All construction codes are under the jurisdiction of the _____.

_____   7. The General Conditions describe the _____ of all companies and individuals involved with a project.

_____   8. "Ethic" describes _____.

_____   9. The estimator is responsible for the knowledge of all _____.

_____   10. It is best to thoroughly study the _____ before starting the quantity survey.

True or False

T F   1. The quantity survey is the same as the take-off.

T F   2. An ethical estimator will trade off the secrets of a bid as he or she chooses.

T F   3. The Contract Documents refer to the actual contract only.

T F   4. The Instructions to Bidders is usually supplied with the plans upon pick-up.

T F   5. A professional estimator is on a par with the architect or engineer on a project.

T F   6. A mid-cap company is one that hires several estimators to work as a team on an estimate.

T F   7. Knowledge of the specifications is a must before starting the estimate.

T F   8. The Construction Specifications Institute is responsible for overseeing all codes.

T F   9. The preliminary set of plans is used for the feasibility study.

T F   10. An Advertisement to Bid is the same as the Instructions to Bidders.

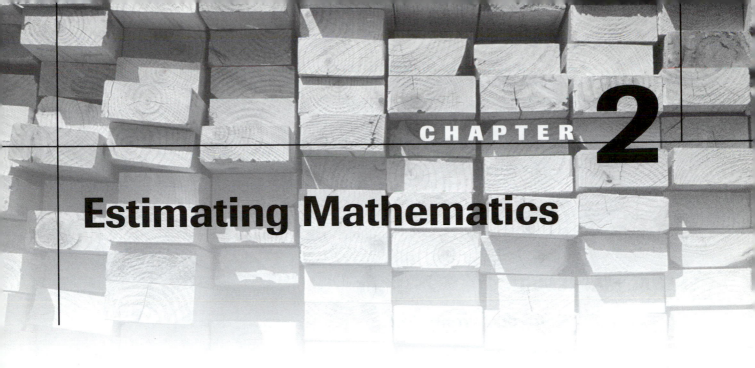

CHAPTER 2

Estimating Mathematics

Construction estimating includes calculations for four basic components in construction: lineal, square, cubic, and unit (bag, block, brick, and so on) measures. Many of the mathematical problems and solutions in this chapter represent common examples that construction personnel use everyday as a matter of course. Some of these problems become so ingrained from constant use that solving them becomes "second nature" for construction field personnel as well as for the estimator. The use of ratio and proportion and the Pythagorean theorem are examples of typical computations. This chapter deals with these and other mathematical problems and computations that the estimator is bound to encounter.

METRICS IN CONSTRUCTION

See appendix II, Metric Ratios and Metric to English Equivalents. Calculations for both English and metrics are covered in this chapter. This section on metrics is included to introduce the student to metric measure and calculations. In some areas of industry, the use of metrics is common. Construction plans of many federal- and state-owned projects along the Mexican border have been using metric plans for years. The purpose behind this change is to make plans uniform throughout the world. The system that has been accepted as the worldwide metric system is called the Système International (European) or Standard International (American), abbreviated "SI." Both systems are identical.

An organization called The Construction Metrication Council made up of many of the trade organizations is also making changes to the metric system. These organizations are making changes converting "hard metrics" to "soft metrics." This means that the actual calculations from English pound/inch measurements are converted to a *nominal* metric size. For example, #3 and #4 rebar are combined into *one metric size, 40 mm*. The metric measurements shown in the text are the "hard metrics."

Measurement Scales

The larger the plan, the larger is the ratio. The ratios vary with usage (see the chart in appendix II). A plat or plot plan uses a much larger ratio than a detail drawing. The millimeter size is reduced to match the scale.

In English measure, the plat or plot drawings use engineering scales, 1″ = 10 lf, 20 lf, and so on. The architectural scales, 1/16″ = 1′-0″, 3/32″ = 1′-0″ and 1/8″ = 1′-0″, are also used for plot measurements. Where a detail is required the metric ratio ranges from 1:5 up to 1:20. The architectural equivalents for details range from 3/8″ = 1′-0″ to 3″ = 1′-0″.

The ratios in the metric table are the same as those found on the drawings and are used in the same manner as the English scales. For example, the ratio 1:5 means that 1 millimeter on the scale is equal to 200 millimeters, 5 × 200 millimeters, or 1,000 millimeters, is equal to 1 meter on the drawing.

GENERAL MATHEMATICS

Ratio and Proportion

The dictionary defines a **ratio** as "a fixed relation in degree, number, etc., between two similar things; proportion; in mathematics, the quotient of one quantity divided by another of the same kind, and usually expressed as a fraction." When two such ratios, or fractions, are placed in a format forming an equation, they become one of the common simple algebraic expressions expressed in any of the following ways:

$$a{:}b = c{:}d; \text{ or } a/b = c/d; \text{ or } a \div b = c \div d$$

See figure 2–1 and chart 2–1.   When three of the four parts of the equation are known, the fourth part can be determined. One of the most common uses of proportion equations is found in framing and roof structure calculations for

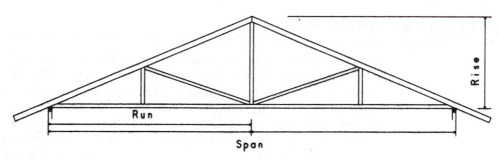

FIGURE 2–1
Rise and Run

CHART 2–1
Sample Proportion Calculations

Rise and run (figure 2–1):	Scale-to-scale changes:	
$a \div b = c \div d$	$3\frac{1}{2}″ = {}^{28}\!/_{8}″$	$3\frac{1}{2}″ = {}^{14}\!/_{4}″$
$5 \div 12 = c \div 20$	${}^{28}\!/_{8} = {}^{c}\!/_{20}$	${}^{14}\!/_{4} = {}^{c}\!/_{20}$
$12c = 5 \times 20$	$28 \div 8 = c \div 20$	$14 \div 4 = c \div 20$
$c = 100 \div 12$	$8c = 20 \times 28$	$4c = 20 \times 14$
$c = \mathbf{8.33}$ **lf or 8′-4″**	$c = 560 \div 8$	$c = 280 \div 4$
	$c = \mathbf{70\ lf}$	$c = \mathbf{70\ lf}$

rise and run. For example, the **span** in a transverse section of a 5/12 gable is 40 lf. The **run** of a true gable is one half (1/2) the distance of the span. With the proportion formula, the **rise** of the gable at the ridge can be determined. The rise is determined as 8'-4", as shown in *chart 2–1*.

Proportional calculations can be used in other situations as well. For example, a plot plan in a blueprint is the only place that indicates a masonry retaining wall along one of the property lines. The information on the plan indicates that the height of the wall is 6.0' above grade. No length is indicated. How can the length be determined? There are two solutions to the problem. The best possible solution is to get an answer from the engineer or architect. Verify that the wall exists and, if so, ascertain if there is any other information that is needed.

Where time may be of the essence and the information is not available, the alternative is to use the proportion formula. *This is one of the rare times when the estimator is allowed to "scale" a plan.* The architectural, engineering, and estimating professions frown on this procedure except in this type of situation. The measurements indicated on a plan will otherwise take precedence over "scaling" in all instances.

Refer to chart 2–1. The plan is scaled at 1" = 20.0'. The wall measures 3 1/2" on the plan as determined by use of a ruler or tape measure. The inches can be converted into any desired increments (for example, 1/8", 1/4") to produce a fraction. This fraction is used in the proportion calculation. In the examples in chart 2–1, the inches are converted into 1/8" and 1/4" increments.

The following are part of the proportion formula: the fractional value calculated in the conversion and the scale of the plan (in this case 1" = 20.0'). The 20 is the **denominator** (lower half) of one of the fractions. The 8 or 4 is the denominator of the other fraction in the proportion. The denominator becomes the **divisor** in the calculation. The length of the wall is determined to be 70 lf.

Lineal Measure

Lineal foot measurements, for determining perimeters (length around), heights, and depths of properties, buildings, rooms, and so on, are basic to construction calculations. To obtain square measure two lineal measurements are required; for volume, three lineal measurements are required.

See chart 2–2. For example, an architect is preparing a conceptual estimate for an owner. Part of the information to be determined includes the size of the slab and the exterior wall framing for "shell" construction (exterior walls only). The rectangular building footprint measures 100 lf by 73 lf. The slab area and volume, the quantity of plate stock, sill plate, and studs are estimated by a quick method. All of the measurements start with the lengths of four sides, or walls.

Lineal measure—slab:	Lineal measure—"shell" framing estimate:
100 lf + 100 lf + 73 lf + 73 lf = 346 lf	Plate stock: **346 lf** – 2 × 6 treated DF, sill plate, R/L **692 lf** – 2 × 6 HF, utility plate, R/L Studs – 92⅝" precut: **346 pc** – 2 × 6 × 92⅝", DF, SG

CHART 2—2
Lineal Measure

Example 1: 2,500 pieces of 2 × 10 × 18 lf joists are needed for a project. Because there are specific quantities indicated, formula 1 is used.

BF = (2 × 10 ÷ 12") × 18 lf × 2,500 pc

BF = 1.67 × 18 lf × 2,500 pc

BF = **75,150**

Example 2: 14,880 lf of 2×4 utility plate are needed. The number of pieces of material is not required because this type of lumber is usually purchased in random lengths; therefore, formula 2 is used.

BM = (2 × 4 ÷ 12") × 14,880 lf

BM = 0.67 × 14,880 lf

BM = **9,969.6**

CHART 2–3
Board Measure

Board Measure

Board measure (BM), or board foot (BF) measure, is used by lumber mills and brokers for the purpose of determining the quantity of lumber, regardless of size or length, that can be properly loaded onto a truck or railroad car. The measurement assists the mills to identify the volume and weight of a shipment. It is the weight with which the brokers and mills are primarily concerned. A variety of lengths and sizes of lumber can be safely shipped to the lumber yards or directly to a project site. Projects such as multifamily complexes (apartments, hotels, motels, and so on) and large commercial or industrial complexes (shopping malls or multiple office/warehouse projects) are typical examples of where such shipments may be made.

The mathematical measurement of 1 **board foot** is defined as a piece of lumber 12″ long, 12″ wide, and 1″ thick. Board measure may be determined in two separate formulas calculated from lineal measure.

See chart 2–3. Formula 1 is used where specific lumber sizes, lengths, and quantities are known. The formula is the following:

BF or BM = (nominal size ÷ 12") × length(ft) × number of pieces

Formula 2 is used where the lumber sizes are known and only the total quantity of material required is given. The lumber may be of **random lengths (R/L)** or all one length. The formula is the following:

BF or BM = (nominal size ÷ 12") × total lineal feet

Chart 2–3 shows two examples of the use of the board measure formulas. Example 1 uses formula 1 and example 2 uses formula 2.

ADVANCED MATHEMATICS

Advanced mathematics includes algebra, geometry, and trigonometry.

Algebraic equations have already been shown in the proportion and board measure calculations in this chapter. Like lineal measure, algebra is basic to geometric and trigonometric calculations.

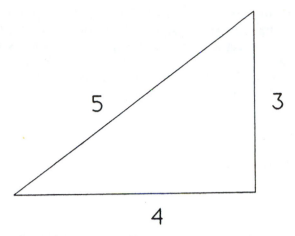

FIGURE 2–2
Pythagorean Theorem (3-4-5)

Rafter/chord length (figure 2–1):
$c^2 = (20 \text{ lf} \times 20 \text{ lf}) + (8.33 \text{ lf} \times 8.33 \text{ lf})$
$c^2 = 400 \text{ sq ft} + 69.39 \text{ sq ft}$
$c^2 = 469.39 \text{ sq ft}$
$c = \sqrt{469.39}$
$c = \mathbf{21.67}$ or **22 lf**

CHART 2–4
Pythagorean Theorem: Rafter/Chord Length

Geometric calculations are of two types:

1. **Plane geometry** is the study of flat planes (squares, circles, triangles, and so on). The solutions include **lineal measure** (lineal feet) and **square measure** (area).

2. **Solid geometry** is the study of solids (cubes, spheres, and so on) or the space they occupy. The solutions are in **cubic measure** (volume).

   Plane trigonometry is a combination of algebra and plane geometry and is only a small part of estimating because it is used only occasionally. However, it is one of the many facets of mathematics found in computer estimating programs.

   The following sections focus on calculating areas of figures and volumes—calculations that are basic for construction estimating and that involve algebra and geometry.

The Pythagorean Theorem and Right Triangles

See figure 2–2 and chart 2–4. The Pythagorean theorem relates to **right triangles** (triangles with one 90° angle). The theorem states that the sum of the square of the two sides (legs) of a right triangle is equal to the square of the hypotenuse (diagonal). The algebraic formula is the following:

$$c^2 = a^2 + b^2$$

This equation is in use daily by many trades for which it is important to make sure that corners are square. The workers in these trades use what is referred to as the **3-4-5 system.** The system states the same thing as the theorem; namely, if the length of one leg of a right triangle is 3 units and the other leg is 4 units, the diagonal must be 5 units. The same is true for multiples of these values, where the same multiplication factor is used for each; for example, 6, 8, and 10; 9, 12, and 15; and so on. This theory is proven as follows:

$$5^2 = 3^2 + 4^2$$
$$(5 \times 5) = (3 \times 3) + (4 \times 4)$$
$$25 = 9 + 16$$
$$25 = 25$$

Refer to figure 2–1 and *chart 2–4.*   Another of the primary uses of the theorem in construction is the determination of the roof rafter (conventional framing) or top chord (truss framing). The rise and run are the horizontal and vertical measurements used to determine the length or height of a gable. They are also the legs of a right triangle. The rafter or top chord represents the hypotenuse. For example, from the previous rise and run calculation (figure 2–1 and chart 2–1), the rafter length from ridge to plate can be determined.

The Nonright Triangle

See figure 2–3 and *chart 2–5.* The figure shows a triangle with a base of 94 lf (28.65 m) and legs of 59.01 lf (17.98 m) and 46 lf (14.02 m). A perpendicular drawn from the apex to the base cuts the base into measurements of 39.73 lf (12.10 m) and 54.27 lf (16.54 m). The base measurements are determined from a trigonometric calculation. (Trigonometry is discussed later in this chapter.) The length of the vertical (perpendicular) and the area of the triangle can be calculated from these measurements, as shown in chart 2–5. The lineal and area measurements can be determined by formulas as long as a right triangle is formed (a triangle with one 90° angle) and the lengths of two sides are known. The area of a right triangle is determined using the following formula:

$$A = 1/2 \; ab \; \text{or} \; A = ab/2$$

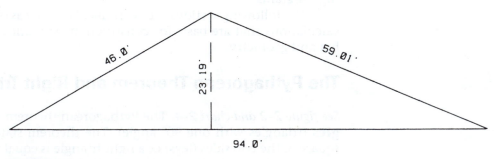

FIGURE 2–3
Nonright Triangle

Triangle height and area (figure 2–3)

Length of side of a (vertical):
(using left-half triangle)

$c^2 = a^2 + b^2$
$a^2 = c^2 - b^2$
$a^2 = (46 \text{ lf})^2 - (39.73 \text{ lf})^2$
$a^2 = 2116 \text{ sq ft} - 1578.47 \text{ sq ft}$
$a^2 = 537.53 \text{ sq ft}$
$a = 23.19 \text{ lf}\pm$

Area of left-half triangle:
$A = \frac{1}{2}ab$
$A = \frac{1}{2}(23.19 \text{ lf} \times 39.73 \text{ lf})$
$A = \dfrac{921.34 \text{ sq ft}}{2}$
$A = \textbf{460.67 sq ft}$

Area of right-half triangle:
$A = \frac{1}{2}ab$
$A = \frac{1}{2}(23.19 \text{ lf} \times 54.27 \text{ lf})$
$A = \dfrac{1258.52 \text{ sq ft}}{2}$
$A = \textbf{629.26 sq ft}$

Area of large triangle
$A = 460.67 \text{ sq ft} + 629.26 \text{ sq ft}$
$A = \textbf{1089.93 sq ft}$

Metric

Length of side a (vertical)
(using right-half triangle)

$c^2 = a^2 + b^2$
$a^2 = c^2 - b^2$
$a^2 = (17.98 \text{ m}^2) - (16.54 \text{ m}^2)$
$a^2 = 323.28 \text{ m}^2 - 273.57 \text{ m}^2$
$a^2 = 49.71 \text{ m}^2$
$a = 7.05 \text{ m}$

Area of left-half triangle:
$A = \frac{1}{2}ab$
$A = \frac{1}{2}(7.05 \text{ m} \times 16.54 \text{ m})$
$A = \dfrac{116.61 \text{ m}^2}{2}$
$A = \textbf{58.31 m}^2$

Area of right-half triangle:
$A = \frac{1}{2}ab$
$A = \frac{1}{2}(7.05 \text{ m} \times 12.1 \text{ m})$
$A = \dfrac{85.31 \text{ m}^2}{2}$
$A = \textbf{42.66 m}^2\pm$

Area of large triangle
$A = 42.66 \text{ m}^2 + 58.31 \text{ m}^2$
$A = \textbf{100.97 m}^2\pm$

CHART 2–5
Obtuse Triangle: Height and Area

Squares and Rectangles

See figure 2–4 and chart 2–6. A large office/manufacturing plant is shown in figure 2–4. The structure is 537 lf (163.68 m) wide by 2,375 lf (723.9 m) long. A rectangle and square (four-sided figures with opposite sides parallel and equal in length and the angles all right angles) are formed in the drawing. The office portion is square and the manufacturing/warehouse area is rectangular. Two perpendicular sides in the example in chart 2–6 are multiplied together to determine the area occupied by the whole structure. A further breakdown can be made by separating the office area from the manufacturing/warehouse area

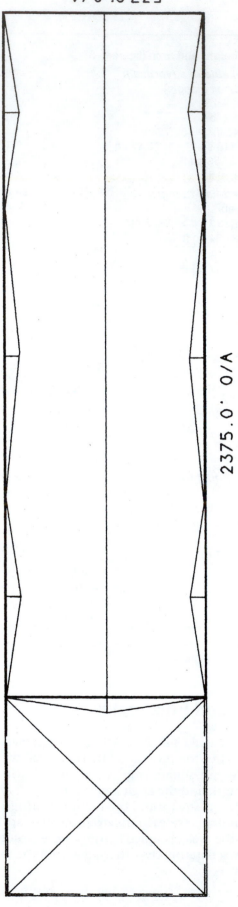

FIGURE 2–4
Office/Warehouse (Square and Rectangle)

537.0 O/A

2375.0˙ O/A

22

Area of a square and a rectangle (figure 2–4):

Area of a square (office):

$A = ab$

$A = 537 \text{ lf} \times 537 \text{ lf}$

$A = \textbf{288,369 sq ft}$

Area of a rectangle (manufacturing/warehouse):

$a = ab$

$A = 537 \text{ lf} \times (2375 \text{ lf} - 537 \text{ lf})$

$A = 537 \text{ lf} \times 1838 \text{ lf}$

$A = \textbf{987,006 sq ft}$

Total area:

$A = 288,369 \text{ sq ft} + 987,006 \text{ sq ft}$

$A = \textbf{1,275,375 sq ft}$

Metric

Area of a square (office):

$A = ab$

$A = 163.68 \text{ m} \times 163.68 \text{ m}$

$A = \textbf{26,791.14 m}^2$

Area of a rectangle (manufacturing/warehouse):

$a = ab$

$A = 163.68 \text{ m} \times (723.9 \text{ m} - 163.68 \text{ m})$

$A = 163.68 \text{ m} \times 560.22 \text{ m}$

$A = \textbf{91,696.81 m}^2$

Total area:

$A = 26,791.14 \text{ m}^2 + 91,696.81 \text{ m}^2$

$A = \textbf{118,487.95 m}^2$

CHART 2–6
Area of Squares and Rectangles

and determining the area of each. The formula for both the area of a square and the area of a rectangle is as follows:

$$A = ab$$

Parallelogram

See figure 2–5 and chart 2–7.   The figure shows a parallelogram whose horizontal parallel sides are 143.5 lf (43.74 m) and perpendicular height is 65.25 lf (19.89 m). The height is again determined by trigonometric calculation. There is a quicker, simpler way of calculating the area of a parallelogram when this height is known. Instead of figuring the area of the triangle, transfer it to the opposite side of the parallelogram, thus forming a rectangle, and calculate the rectangular area.

Trapezoid

See figure 2–6 and chart 2–8.   This drawing indicates a footprint of a structure placed in a corner of a property with unusual boundaries. No two sides are the same length, but two sides are parallel. Because there are parallel sides, a quick calculation called the **averaging method** may be used. This is accomplished by adding the measurements of the parallel lines, dividing by 2, and multiplying the answer by the vertical height. The vertical measurement is 146 lf

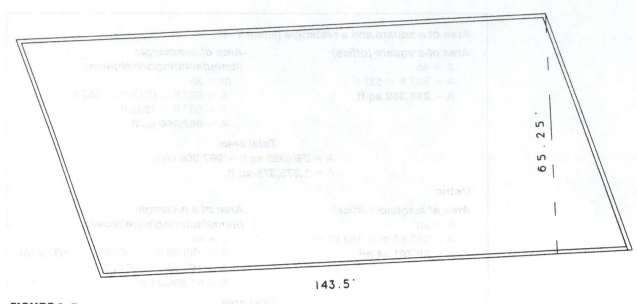

FIGURE 2–5
Parallelogram-Shaped Roof

CHART 2–7
Area of Parallelograms

Area of a parallelogram (figure 2–5):

A = ab	A = ab
A = 65.25 lf × 143.5 lf	A = 19.89 m × 43.74 m
A = 9363.38 sq ft	**A = 869.99 m²**

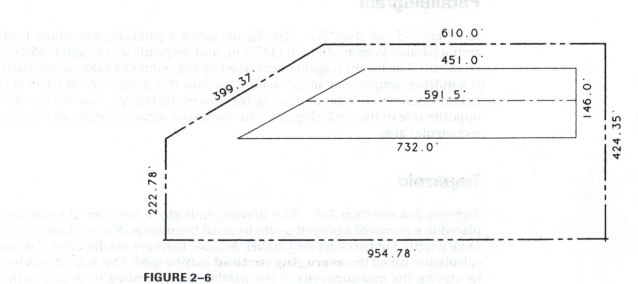

FIGURE 2–6
Trapezoid Footprint

Area of a trapezoid (figure 2–6):

$$A = 146 \text{ lf} \times \frac{(732 \text{ lf} + 451 \text{ lf})}{2}$$

$$A = 146 \text{ lf} \times \frac{1183 \text{ lf}}{2}$$

$$A = 146 \text{ lf} \times 591.5 \text{ lf}$$

$$A = \mathbf{86{,}359 \text{ sq ft}}$$

$$A = 44.50 \text{ m} \times \frac{(223.1 \text{ m} + 137.46 \text{ m})}{2}$$

$$A = 44.50 \text{ m} \times \frac{360.57 \text{ m}}{2}$$

$$A = \frac{16{,}045.37 \text{ m}^2}{2}$$

$$A = \mathbf{8022.69 \text{ m}^2}$$

CHART 2–8
Area of Trapezoids

(44.50 m), the shorter parallel side is 451 lf (137.46 m), and the longer side is 732 lf (223.11 m). The formula is as follows:

A = ([parallel base + parallel opposite side] ÷ 2) × height
A = ([b + b'] ÷ 2) × h

Regular Polygon

A figure with four or more sides is normally referred to as a polygon and the sides are called chords. Polygons include those studied above. As in a circle, a polygon has a **radius,** an imaginary line drawn from the center to a point at the junction of two chords. In a regular polygon, these surfaces are *equal and equidistant from the center.*

See figure 2–7 and chart 2–9. A community has decided to build a large gazebo in the shape of a regular octagon in the town square. The floor plan indicates one chord, 11.5 lf (3.51 m), and the radius, 15 lf (4.57 m). The perimeter and area occupied by the gazebo can be determined. The area is determined by configuring a triangle in one segment of the octagon made up of two radii and the intersecting chord. A line perpendicular to the chord is drawn from the center of the octagon. The length of two sides of the triangle are immediately known: the radius, 15 lf (4.57 m) and one half of the length of the chord, 5.75 lf (1.75 m). The area of the triangle is determined and multiplied by the number of triangles formed. The formula for the calculation of a right triangle is used.

Trapezium

See figures 2–8 and 2–9. The configuration shown in the figures is a site plan. A four-sided figure with no sides parallel and no equal angles is called a trapezium. To calculate the area of a trapezium, the estimator must apply many of the previously explained calculations plus some plane trigonometry. The estimator has two alternatives: (1) average the area or (2) determine the area of each plot.

Method 1: Averaging Method. *Refer to figure 2–8 and chart 2–10.* The lengths of each side of the property are known: North property line (P/L), 180 lf

FIGURE 2-7
Octagonal Gazebo

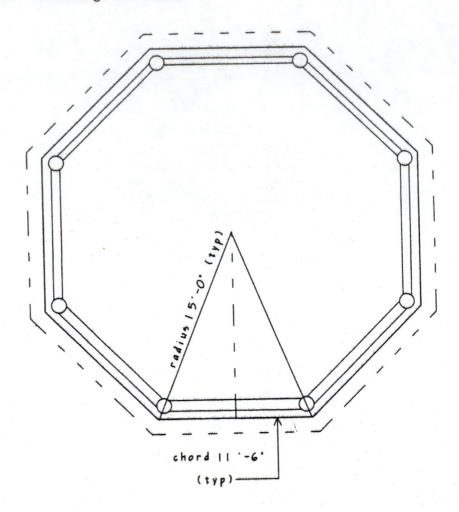

Perimeter and area of gazebo (figure 2–7):

Perimeter:	*Perimeter:*
11.5 lf × 8 (chords) = 92 lf	3.51 m × 8 = 28.08 m

Area:

A = ½ × (15 lf × 5.75 lf)   A = ½ × (4.57 m × 1.75 m)

A = ½ × 86.25 sq ft   A = ½ × 8.00 m²

A = 43.125 sq ft   A = 4.00 m²

A = 43.125 × 16 = **690 sq ft**   A = 4.00 m² × 16 = **64 m²**

CHART 2–9
Perimeter and Area of Octagons

(54.86 m); South P/L, 170 lf (51.82 m); East P/L, 160 lf (48.77 m); West P/L, 103 lf (31.39 m). When opposite sides are averaged, an approximate area can be determined, as shown in chart 2-10.

Method 2: Geometric and Trigonometric Calculation. *Refer to figure 2–9 and chart 2–11.*   The first step to be taken is to break the trapezium down into as few right triangles as possible. There are four right triangles formed

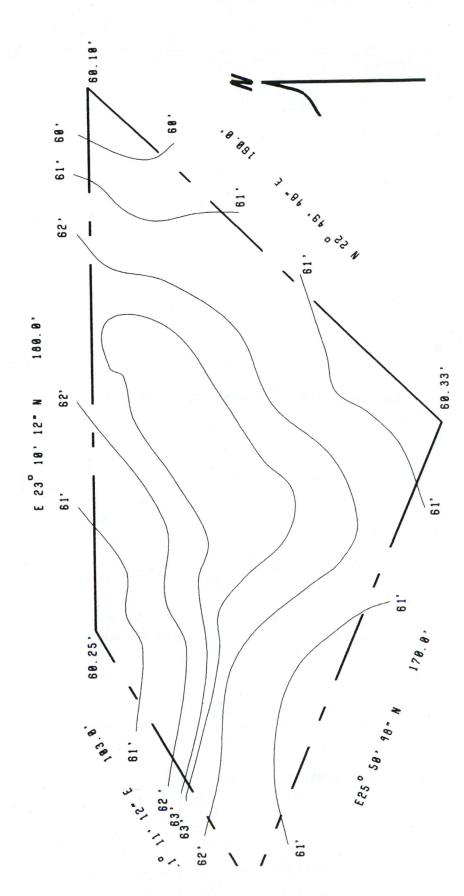

FIGURE 2–8
Trapezium (Plot Plan)

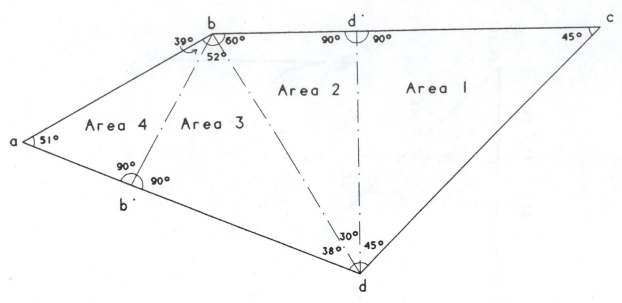

FIGURE 2–9
Trapezium (Geometric Breakdown)

Area of Trapezium-Shaped Property (figures 2–8 and 2–9):

Method 1, Averaging:
A = ([180 lf + 170 lf] ÷ 2) × ([160 lf + 103 lf] ÷ 2)
A = (350 lf ÷ 2) × (263 lf ÷ 2)
A = 175 lf × 131.5 lf
A = 23,012.5 sq ft

CHART 2–10
Area of Trapeziums (by Averaging)

in figure 2–9, referred to here as plots 1 through 4. The lengths of each side of the property and the corner angles are the following:

North P/L - 180 lf (54.86 m)	Northeast ∠ bcd - 45°
East P/L - 160 lf (48.77 m)	Southeast ∠ adc - 113°
South P/L - 170 lf (51.82 m)	Southwest ∠ bad - 51°
West P/L - 103 lf (31.39 m)	Northwest ∠ abc - 151°

The breakdown of the sides and angles drawn and the areas are determined as shown in chart 2-11. The total area determined from the breakdown in method 2 is the following:

Plot 1 =   6,400.00 sq ft (594.58 m^2)

Plot 2 =   3,782.23 sq ft (351.38 m^2)

Plot 3 =   4,189.52 sq ft (389.22 m^2)

Plot 4 =   2,687.83 sq ft (249.71 m^2)

Total = 17,059.58 sq ft (1,584.89 m^2)

Area of Trapezium-Shaped Property (figures 2–8 and 2–9)

Method 2, Breakdown:

Plot 1: Known: 3 angles: ∠dcd' = 45°; ∠cdd' = 45°; ∠ cd'd = 90° ; 1 side:
East property line, cd = 160 lf

Length of sides cd' and dd':

a and b each = the $\sqrt{\ }$ of ½ c²	½ c² = 25,600 sq ft ÷ 2
c = 160 lf	½ c² = 12,800 sq ft
c² = (160 lf)²	a and b each = $\sqrt{12,800}$
c² = 25,600 sq ft	a and b each = 113.14
	sides cd' & dd' = **113.14 lf**

Area:

A = ½ab
A = ½ × (113.14 lf × 113.14 lf)
A = ½ × 12,800 ft²
A = 6,400 ft²

Plot 2: Known: 1 angle: ∠bd'd = 90°; 2 sides: bd' = 180 lf - 113.14 lf = 66.86 lf;
dd' = 113.14 lf

Length of side bd is:

c² = a² + b²	c = $\sqrt{17,270.26}$
c² = (113.14 lf)² + (66.86 lf)²	c = 131.42
c² = 12,800 sq ft + 4,470.26 sq ft	side bd = **131.42 lf**
c² = 17,270.26 sq ft	

∠ bdd' is:	Area:
sin of ∠ = opposite side ÷ hypotenuse	A = ½ab
sin ∠ bdd' = bd' ÷ dd'	A = ½ × (113.14 lf × 66.86 lf)
sin ∠ bdd' = 66.86 lf ÷ 131.42 lf	A = ½ × 7,564.54 ft²
sin ∠ bdd' = 0.5088	**A = 3,782.23 ft²**
∠ bdd' = 30°, therefore, ∠ bdd' = 60°	

Plot 3: Known: 3 angles: ∠ bdb' = 113° - 85° = 38°; ∠ b'bd = 90° - 38° = 52°;
∠ bb'd = 90°; 1 side: side bd = 131.42 lf

Side b'd is:	Side bb' is:
cos of ∠ = adjacent side ÷ hypotenuse	a² = c² − b²
0.7880 = b'd ÷ 131.42 lf	a² = (131.42 lf)² − (103.56 lf)²
b'd = 131.42 lf × 0.7880	a² = 17,271.22 ft² − 10,724.67 ft²
side b'd = **103.56 lf**	a² = 6,546.55 ft²
	a = $\sqrt{6,546.55}$
	a = 80.91 lf
	side bb' = **80.91 lf**

Area:

A = ½ab
A = ½ × (80.91 × 103.56 lf)
A = ½ × 8,379.04 ft²
A = 4,189.52 ft²

Plot 4: Known: 3 angles: ∠ abb' = 151° - (52° + 60°) = 39°; ∠ bab' = 51°;
∠ ab'b = 90°; 3 sides: ab = 103 lf; ab' = 170 lf - 103.56 lf = 66.44 lf;
bb' = 80.91 lf

Area:

A = ½ab	A = ½ × 5,375.66
A = ½ × (80.91 lf × 66.44 lf)	**A = 2,687.83 ft²**

CHART 2–11
Area of Trapeziums (by Breakdown)

FIGURE 2–10
Stage

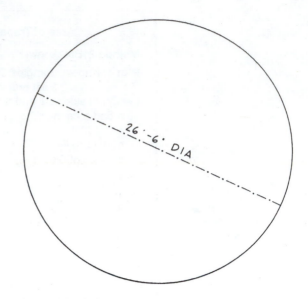

Circumference of stage (figure 2–10):

$C = \pi d$ $C = 2\pi r$

$C = 3.14 \times 26.5$ lf   or $C = 2 \times 3.14 \times 13.25$

$C = 83.21$ lf or 83'-3" $C = 83.21$ lf or 83'-3"

Area of stage (figure 2–10):

$C = \pi r^2$

$C = 3.14 \times (13.25 \text{ lf})^2$

$C = 3.14 \times 175.56$ sq ft

$C = 551.26$ sq ft

CHART 2–12
Circumference and Area of Circles

The difference between method 1 and method 2 is as follows:

Method 1   =   23,012.50 sq ft (2,137.93 m²)
Method 2   =   −17,059.58 sq ft (1,584.89 m²)
Difference =   5,952.92 sq ft (553.04 m²)

Circle.   *See figure 2–10 and chart 2–12.* A "theater-in-the-round" needs a new stage area. The engineer designed the stage in a circle as shown in the figure. The stage has a diameter of 26.5 lf (8.08 m). From this measurement alone, both the circumference (lineal feet of perimeter) and the area of the stage can be determined. The formula for calculating the circumference of a circle is $C = \pi d$ or $C = 2\pi r$. The formula for determining the area of a circle is $A = \pi r^2$. The calculations for the stage are shown in chart 2–12.

Solid Geometry

Volume is calculated by multiplying the area of one plane by the true height or depth (perpendicular) of a three-dimensional object. The basic formula for calculating volume is $V = Ah$. Volume can be determined for any object occupying space such as a room or warehouse. The following sections demonstrate the calculations of volume of various objects or spaces.

Cube. *See figure 2–11 and chart 2–13.* The most common solid is the cube. The term **cubic measure** is derived from the calculation of a cube. The basic cube used for many measurements is the 3 lf × 3 lf × 3 lf (0.91 m × 0.91 m × 0.91 m) cube. The calculations for excavating, grading, and concrete are based on 27 cu ft, or 1 cu yd.

Rectangular Solid (Space). *See figure 2–12 and chart 2–14.* An excavation for a rectangular-shaped culvert, 36 lf (10.97 m) long by 16 lf (4.88 m) wide, and 10 lf (3.05 m) deep is to be made for drainage under a highway from a wash on one side of the highway to a retention basin on the other. The culvert is installed 36″ (91.44 cm) below natural grade. The excavation must be cut 24″

FIGURE 2–11
Cube

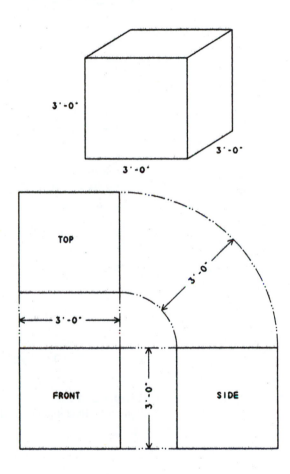

CHART 2–13
Calculations for Cubic Yard

Cubic yard (figure 2–11):
$$V = Ah$$
$$V = (3\ \text{lf})^2 \times 3\ \text{lf}$$
$$V = 9\ \text{sq ft} \times 3\ \text{lf}$$
$$V = 27\ \text{cu ft}$$
$$V = 27\ \text{cu ft} \div 27\ \text{cu ft}$$
$$\mathbf{V = 1\ cu\ yd}$$

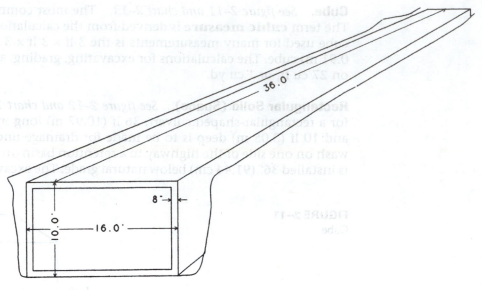

FIGURE 2–12
Rectangular Culvert

Volume of rectangular culvert in cubic feet, cubic yards, and cubic meters (figure 2–12):

Area of end:

A = ab	A = ab
A = 16 lf × 10 lf	A = 4.88 m × 3.05 m
A = **160 sq ft**	A = **14.88 m²**

Volume:

V = Ah	V = Ah
V = 160 sq ft × 36 lf	V = 14.88 m² × 10.97 m
V = 5760 cu ft	V = **163.23 m³**
$V = \dfrac{5760 \text{ cu ft}}{27 \text{ cu ft}}$	
V = **213.33 cu yd**	

CHART 2–14
Volume of Rectangular Solid/Area

(60.96 cm) wider than the culvert for working space. Chart 2–14 shows the calculations to determine the total volume of earth to be removed.

Cylindrical Solid (Space).   *See figure 2–13 and chart 2–15.*   Included in cylindrical configurations are the *round column (solid or hollow), tank (hollow),* and *prism (a multisided figure similar to the cylinder).* These configurations require a variation of the formula for the volume. The formula for calculating volume of cylinders, columns, or prisms is $V = \pi r^2 h$.

A cylindrical corrugated steel tube (shown in figure 2–13) is used for a culvert under a driveway for drainage to the nearest retention area. The culvert measures 175 lf (53.34 m) in length by 4 lf (1.22 m) in diameter. The calculations for determining the volume of the culvert are given in chart 2–15.

By inspection of the formula, it can be seen that the area of a circle and the height are multiplied together to obtain the volume. The same formula could be written V = Ah, as long as the estimator remembers the formula for the area of a circle.

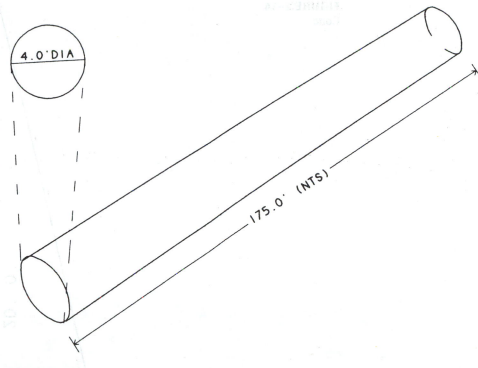

FIGURE 2–13
Tubular Culvert

Volume of a circular culvert (figure 2–13):

V = πr²h	V = πr²h
V = 3.14 × (2 lf)² × 175 lf	V = 3.14 × (0.61 m)² × 53.34 m
V = 3.14 × 4 sq ft × 175 lf	V = 3.14 × 0.37 m² × 53.34 m
V = 3.14 × 700 cu ft	V = 3.14 × 19.74 m³
V = $\dfrac{2198 \text{ cu ft}}{27 \text{ cu ft}}$	**V = 61.98 m³**
V = 81.41 cu yd	

CHART 2–15
Volume of Cylindrical Solid/Space

Cones and Pyramids.   *See figures 2–14 and 2–15.*   Although cones and pyramids are included in the study of solids, they are rarely ever used in construction. The formula for these figures is similar to the cylinder with one exception. The volume of a cone (figure 2–14) or a pyramid (figure 2–15) is equal to 1/3 that of a full cylinder. The formula is V = 1/3πr²h for a cone and **V = 1/3 Ah** for a pyramid. Examples of calculations of volumes are shown in *charts 2–16 and 2–17.*

Spheres.   *See figure 2–16 and chart 2–18.*   The surface area and volume of a sphere are calculated by cutting four planes through the sphere. The surface area formula is A = 4πr². The formula for determining the volume is V = 4/3πr³. A sphere with a diameter of 10 lf (3.04 m) is used in the sample calculations in chart 2–18.

FIGURE 2-14
Cone

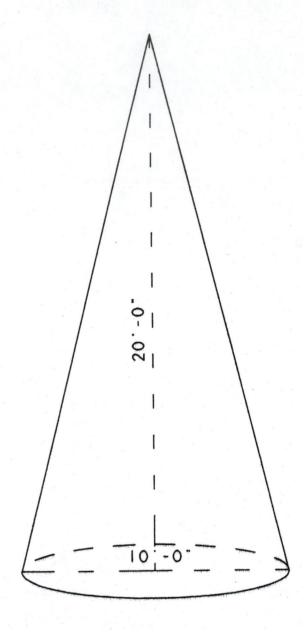

20´ - 0˝

10´ - 0˝

Volume of a cone (figure 2-14):

$$V = \frac{1}{3}\pi r^2 h$$

$$V = \frac{3.14 \times (5\ lf)^2 \times 20\ lf}{3}$$

$$V = \frac{3.14 \times 500\ cu\ ft}{3}$$

$$V = \frac{1570\ cu\ ft}{3}$$

$$V = \frac{523.33\ cu\ ft}{27\ cu\ ft}$$

$$V = \textbf{19.38 cu yd}$$

$$V = \frac{1}{3}\ \pi r^2 h$$

$$V = \frac{3.14 \times (1.52\ m)^2 \times 6.10\ m}{3}$$

$$V = \frac{3.14 \times 14.09\ m^3}{3}$$

$$V = \frac{44.24\ m^3}{3}$$

$$V = \textbf{14.75 m}^3$$

CHART 2-16
Volume of Cones

34

FIGURE 2–15
Pyramid

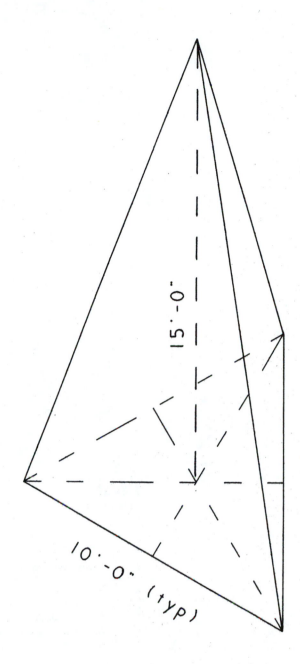

15'–0"

10'–0" (typ)

Volume of a pyramid (figure 2–15):

$V = Ah$

$V = (10 \text{ lf} \times 10 \text{ lf}) \times 15 \text{ lf}$

$V = 100 \text{ sq ft} \times 15 \text{ lf}$

$V = \dfrac{1500 \text{ cu ft}}{27 \text{ cu ft}}$

$V = \textbf{55.56 cu yd}$

$V = Ah$

$V = (3.04 \text{ m} \times 3.04 \text{ m}) \times 4.57 \text{ m}$

$V = 9.24 \text{ m}^2 \times 4.57 \text{ m}$

$V = \textbf{42.23 m}^3$

CHART 2–17
Volume of Pyramids

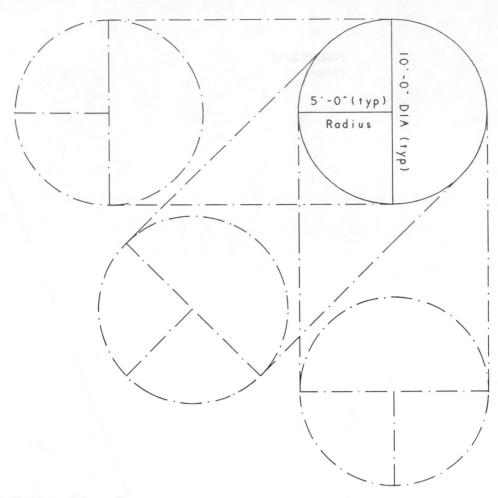

FIGURE 2–16
Sphere

Area and volume of a sphere (figure 2–16):

Area:

A = 4πr²
A = 4 × 3.14 × (5 lf)²
A = 3.14 × 100 sq ft
A = 314 sq ft

A = 4πr²
A = 4 × 3.14 × (1.52 m)²
A = 4 × 3.14 × 2.31 m²
A = 29.01 m²

Volume:

V = ⁴⁄₃ πr³
V = ⁴⁄₃ × 3.14 × (5 lf)³

$$V = \frac{4 \times 3.14 \times 125 \text{ ft}^3}{3}$$

$$V = \frac{1570 \text{ ft}^3}{3}$$

$$V = \frac{523.33 \text{ ft}^3}{27 \text{ ft}^3}$$

V = 19.38 yd³

V = ⁴⁄₃ πr³
V = ⁴⁄₃ × 3.14 × (1.52 m)³

$$V = \frac{4 \times 3.14 \times 3.51 \text{ m}^3}{3}$$

$$V = \frac{44.09 \text{ m}^3}{3}$$

V = 14.70 m³

CHART 2–18
Area and Volume of Spheres

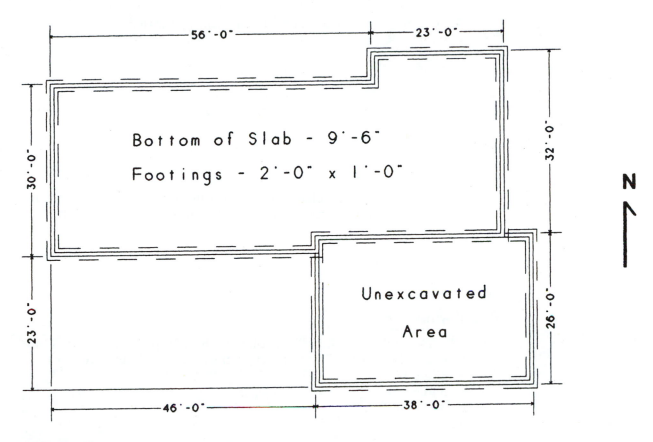

FIGURE 2–17
Residential Foundation

CHAPTER EXERCISES

■   PART 1

Lineal Measure

See figure 2–17. Figure 2–17 illustrates a residential foundation plan with an attached garage. The garage is located at the unexcavated area on the southeast corner. The following questions are in reference to this drawing.

1. The west side of the residence measures
    a. 17'-9"
    b. 30'-0"
    c. 25'-0"
    d. 23'-9"

2. The perimeter of the residence less the unexcavated area is
    a. 314 lf
    b. 324 lf
    c. 295 lf
    d. 228 lf

3. The perimeter measurement of the unexcavated area is
    a. 90 lf
    b. 96 lf
    c. 92 lf
    d. 94 lf

4. The north side of the residence is shorter than the overall measurement by
    a. 15 lf
    b. 20 lf
    c. 5 lf
    d. none of the above

5. A drawing of the same plan is in metric scale. The ratio used is 1:80. Determine all of the lengths in millimeters, and then convert all of the lengths to meters.

■ PART 2

Board Measure

1. A lumber order contains 30 pcs of 2×4 × 8 lf, 10 pcs of 2×4 × 16 lf, and 12 pcs of 2×4 × 10 lf. The mill determines the board measure to be
    a. 375.60 BF
    b. 346.67 BF
    c. 322.22 BF
    d. 355.67 BF

2. A lumber bill of lading includes 4,500 lf of 2×4, HF Utility; 1,500 lf of 3×6 DF#1; 200 lf of 4×4, DF#2; and 6,000 lf of 2×8, DF, CG. All lumber is to be R/L. The board measure is
    a. 15,001.33 BM
    b. 21,233.67 BM
    c. 25,320.33 BM
    d. 13,516.67 BM

3. Another load of lumber includes 20,000 lf of 2×6, DF, CG; 4,000 lf of 1×12, Select Pine; 14,000 lf of 3×4, DF#2; and 17,350 lf of 2×12, DF#2. The board measure is
    a. 72,700 BM
    b. 85,350 BM
    c. 61,575 BM
    d. 125,150 BM

4. A lumber yard sends an order to a lumber mill. The bill of lading shows 376 lf of 1×12, Select Pine, R/L; 621 pcs of 2×4 × 92 5/8"; 56 pcs of 2×4 × 12 lf studs, DF, CG; 295 pcs of 2×6 × 8 lf, DF, CG; 34 pcs of 2×8 × 18 lf, DF#2; 90 pcs of 2×10 × 22 lf, DF#2; 10 pcs of 4×4 × 18 lf, DF#1; 14 pcs of 4×8 × 8 lf, DF#1; and 6 pcs of 4×10 × 10 lf, DF#1. The mill determined the board measure to be
    a. 9,919.00 BF
    b. 9,445.67 BF
    c. 11,234.75 BF
    d. 11,498.42 BF

■ PART 3

Area and Volume

Refer to figure 2–17. Questions 1, 2, and 3 refer to that drawing.

1. Calculate the area of the residence less the unexcavated area.
   a. 2,369 sq ft
   b. 2,329 sq ft
   c. 2,386 sq ft
   d. 2,332 sq ft

2. The volume of earth to be removed (no slope or additional work space included) for the basement area is
   a. 1,150.20 cu yd
   b. 625.42 cu yd
   c. 739.56 cu yd
   d. 856.41 cu yd

3. The volume of earth to be removed in cubic meters is
   a. 563.12 m³
   b. 654.75 m³
   c. 879.36 m³
   d. 478.15 m³

4. Calculate the lengths of the two equal sides of a triangular-shaped property if the base measures 150'-0" and the perpendicular from the apex to the base is 60'-0".
   a. 110'-8" each
   b. 96'-0 1/2" each
   c. 101'-5" each
   d. 104'-9 1/2" each

See figure 2–18. Questions 5, 6, and 7 refer to that drawing.

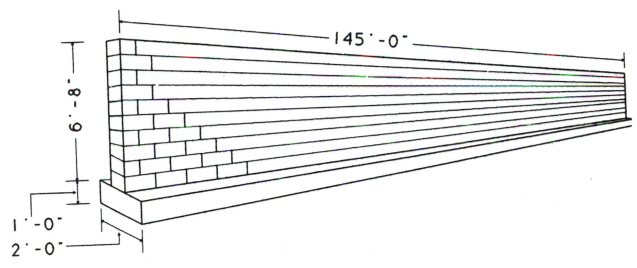

FIGURE 2–18
Masonry Wall

5. A masonry wall 145′ long by 6.67′ deep has an area of
   a. 967.15 sq ft
   b. 870.25 sq ft
   c. 1,257.15 sq ft
   d. 780.33 sq ft

6. Convert the wall measurements to metrics. The area of wall in m² is
   a. 90.69 m²
   b. 72.47 m²
   c. 116.80 m²
   d. 89.83 m²

7. The footing for the wall in question 5 is 2′-0″ wide by 1′-0″ deep by 145 lf. The volume of concrete necessary (rounded to the nearest whole cu yd) to complete the footing is
   a. 6 cu yd
   b. 11 cu yd
   c. 9 cu yd
   d. 7 cu yd

8. A trapezoid has a base, b, 25′-0″ long and a base, b′, is 15′-0″. The perpendicular length is 7.67′. The area is
   a. 175.2 sq ft
   b. 192.5 sq ft
   c. 212.8 sq ft
   d. 153.4 sq ft

See figure 2–19. Questions 9, 10, 11, and 12 refer to that drawing.

FIGURE 2–19
Storage Tank

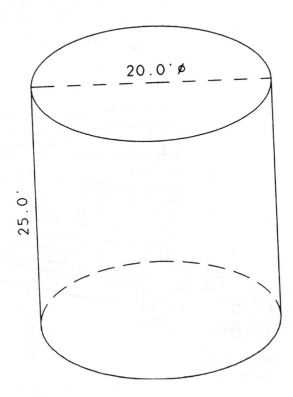

9. A storage tank has a base diameter of 20'-0". Determine the area of the base.
   a. 314 sq ft
   b. 256 sq ft
   c. 413 sq ft
   d. 216 sq ft

10. The tank in question 9 is 25'-0" tall. Determine the area of the tank wall.
    a. 1,335 sq ft
    b. 1,978 sq ft
    c. 1,561 sq ft
    d. 1,570 sq ft

11. Determine the volume of space in cubic feet that this same tank occupies.
    a. 7,420 cu ft
    b. 7,850 cu ft
    c. 7,200 cu ft
    d. 7,000 cu ft

12. Determine the volume of the tank in cubic meters.
    a. 729.34 m^3
    b. 666.68 m^3
    c. 889.17 m^3
    d. 222.29 m^3

13. A plastering contractor estimates an 8'-1" high wall at 1,008 sq ft. The length of the wall is
    a. 124'-9"
    b. 130'-6"
    c. 128'-3"
    d. 126'-7"

14. A precast manufacturer has an order for 50 columns. Each column is 16 lf tall by 3 lf in diameter. Determine the total volume, in cubic yards, of concrete required for the columns.
    a. 219.67 cu yd
    b. 209.33 cu yd
    c. 200.89 cu yd
    d. 213.56 cu yd

15. A warehouse measures 132.5' long by 63.67' wide and is 20' high. Calculate the volume of space occupied by the building.
    a. 168,725.5 cu ft
    b. 168,835.6 cu ft
    c. 168,366.5 cu ft
    d. 170,366.5 cu ft

16. The floor area of the warehouse in question 15, in square meters, is
    a. 783.81 m^2
    b. 788.31 m^2
    c. 837.18 m^2
    d. 387.18 m^2

See figure 2–20. Questions 17 and 18 refer to that drawing.

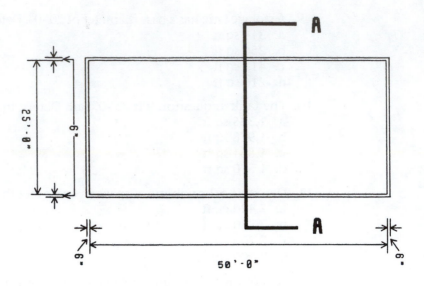

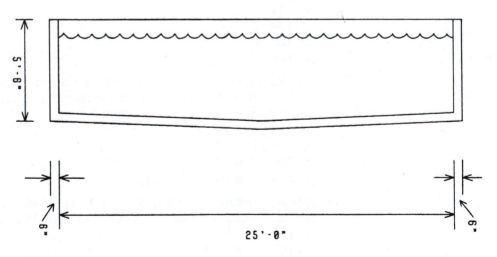

FIGURE 2–20
Swimming Pool

17. The inside measurements of a pool are 50 lf × 25 lf × 5 lf. The walls and bottom of the pool are 6″ thick. Determine the volume of concrete necessary for the walls and bottom of the pool to the next larger whole cubic yard.
   a. 36 cu yd
   b. 52 cu yd
   c. 48 cu yd
   d. 39 cu yd

18. The pool in question 17 is filled to within 6″ of the top. Calculate the volume of water required to fill the pool. (1 cu ft = 7.48 gal)
    a. 42,075 gal
    b. 55,683 gal
    c. 35,186 gal
    d. 75,420 gal

    See figure 2–21. Questions 19 and 20 refer to that drawing.

19. Determine the volume of earth to be removed for a wall and footing. The footing is 2′-0″ wide by 1′-0″ deep. The wall is 400′-0″ long, 3′-6″ high, and 10″ thick. The top of the footing is 3′-0″ below natural grade. The excavation is made with 1:4 slope all around and the specifications require a minimum of 1′-0″ completely around the wall for working space.
    a. 183.33 cu yd
    b. 211.50 cu yd
    c. 360.89 cu yd
    d. none of the above

20. From the information given in question 19 determine the quantity of concrete to be ordered from a ready-mix supplier for the footing and wall. Indicate each quantity separately. Round off to the nearest cubic yard.
    a. 43 cu yd, wall, and 30 cu yd, footing
    b. 22 cu yd, wall, and 28 cu yd, footing
    c. 30 cu yd, wall, and 43 cu yd, footing
    d. 28 cu yd, wall, and 22 cu yd, footing

21. A room is 25′-0″ long by 25′-0″ wide by 10′-0″ high. An air-handling unit is to be purchased capable of moving 25 cubic feet per minute (CFM) of air. Calculate the volume of air in the room.
    a. 5,260 cu ft
    b. 5,620 cu ft
    c. 2,650 cu ft
    d. 6,250 cu ft

22. Determine the amount of air changed in the room in one hour.
    a. 2,000 cu ft
    b. 1,500 cu ft
    c. 2,500 cu ft
    d. 1,000 cu ft

23. Determine the length of time it will take to completely change all the air in the room.
    a. 4 hr 10 min
    b. 4 hr 25 min
    c. 4 hr 15 min
    d. 4 hr 20 min

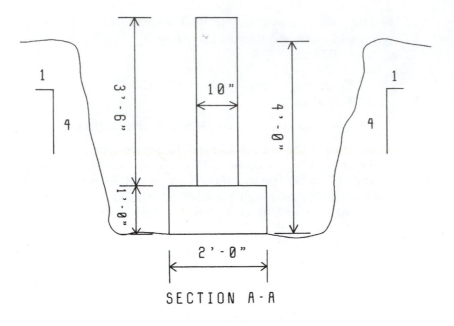

SECTION A-A

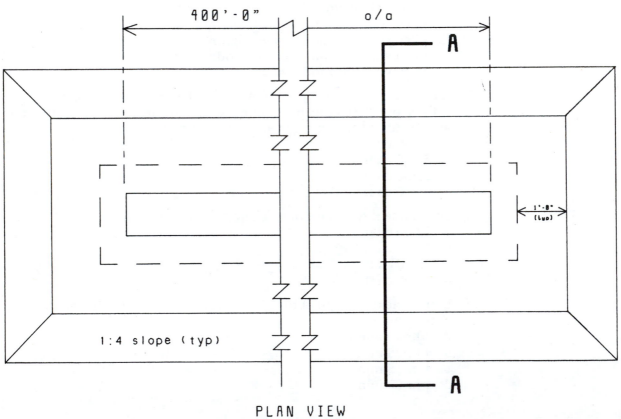

PLAN VIEW

FIGURE 2–21
Footing and Stem Wall

CHAPTER 3

Efficiency and Productivity

A thorough study of the company's performance and abilities must be made before any estimate is produced. Once the contract/legal documents have been understood, time must be taken to determine whether the company can actually complete the work and is qualified to tender a bid. The major concerns of the company should be the following:

1. Is the company capable enough to properly *control* the work?
2. Is the *workload* of the company such that the timetable of the project will fit into the schedule of work for the contractor?
3. Does the company have a sufficient number of *experienced personnel* available?
4. Does the company have the *proper equipment* available?

Control and the workload must be considered simultaneously. The company must have a sufficiently large employee pool and financial reserves to ensure both quality control and work performance when the contract demands it. These requirements must be met first. Only then can the company look at the remaining two issues, regarding personnel and equipment. If the personnel are extended to their maximum or the equipment has not been properly maintained or is getting old, a choice must be made. The workload must be reduced, the company must hire additional personnel, or equipment must be repaired or replaced. If none of these three actions will be taken, the company will have to forego the contract assignment.

If the company is three or more years old, there should be a good solid historical background to indicate its capabilities. The company probably would not be in business after three years if it had not established a solid efficiency base. This historical background makes determining efficiency and productivity much simpler. Checking previous estimates, contracts, and job cost analyses of projects of similar size makes it easier for the estimator to determine efficiency and, thus, productivity.

If the company is new (under three years old), there would be little historical information. A new company can attempt to make an investigation into the practices of more experienced contractors who may be willing to give such assistance.

A thorough study of the following efficiency factors can give some indication as to the capabilities of the company.

EFFICIENCY

What is efficiency? By dictionary definition, "efficiency is . . . the ability to complete work correctly in the least amount of time and at the least expense."

Factors in Efficiency

There are six factors that affect efficiency. The factors, individually or collectively, have a direct bearing on the ability of a company to manage itself properly. All of the factors may or may not be important at all times. This must be determined by the person doing the study. The six major factors to be considered are the following:

1. General efficiency
2. Project supervision
3. Job conditions
4. Tools and equipment
5. Weather
6. Labor relations

General Efficiency.   General efficiency encompasses a company's ability to perform in such a manner that little time is wasted. As the definition of efficiency states, all activities are geared to perform the maximum amount of work in the least amount of time. This means that not only the field personnel must perform efficiently, but also the management team and the nonconstruction personnel must work efficiently.

Project Supervision.   How well do the owner and supervisory personnel know the employees? How does a supervisor get along with individual crew members? How well does the project superintendent know the subcontractors and their supervisory personnel? The willingness of the contractor and supervisory personnel to get to know and understand the needs and desires of the field personnel increases the desire for the employees to want to stay with the company and, thereby, aids in increasing the company efficiency. A company that has been in business for an extended period of time will have a better grasp of the need to maintain this communication and cooperation than will a new company with inexperienced administration and employees. The longer the length of employment of a supervisor with the same company, typically the better will be the working relations among the contractor, management, and employees. More work with fewer problems can be accomplished as personnel become better acquainted with one another, with the type of work to be performed, and with the company's work policies.

In many cases, an older, more experienced supervisor will receive more respect than someone younger with less experience in supervision. An older supervisor has more experience in handling various types of personnel and problems, which would give an advantage.

Job Conditions.   Is the job site safe? Is the work area clean? Are the work areas easily accessible? Are materials delivered in a timely manner, and are they ready to use upon arrival on the job site? Efficiency is immediately reduced when crews are required to work in areas where other trades are also working, where debris is strewn about, and where equipment and materials are constantly in the way. As a result of these conditions, work is slowed and morale breaks down. This, in turn, reduces efficiency.

Efficiency is also greatly reduced if there is poor access to the work area because of uncovered trenches. If the crews cannot easily or safely reach their work areas and if materials cannot be properly supplied, there is again cause for a slowdown and reduced efficiency. It is also important that a proper delivery schedule be kept so that the crews can continue to work continuously and efficiently.

Tools and Equipment.   Is the equipment well maintained? Hand tools (personal and company supplied) and the heavier company-owned (or rented) equipment must be kept in good repair so that the work can flow smoothly. Poorly maintained equipment reduces the efficiency and productivity of a crew and will also cause problems within the crew and with the surrounding trades.

Weather.   This is the one area over which no one has control, but becomes a constant problem for everyone. Weather affects the types of work being scheduled, as well as what can be done at the job site at certain times of the year. For example, in the northern parts of the country, the trades working outdoors can work for only six to nine months of the year. Through the late fall, winter, and early spring months, the work available is greatly reduced. As the colder weather approaches and work slows down, so may the crews, trying to prolong the work as much as possible, again, causing a loss of efficiency.

Normally, in the southern, midwestern, and extreme northwestern portions of the country, the primary concern is the possibility of very rainy conditions through a great portion of the year. Under these conditions, care must be taken as to the type of work scheduled to avoid moisture problems. Again, the weather slows down work and causes a less efficient operation.

The southwest and western part of the country have more consistent working conditions because of the generally fair and warm climate. Still, these areas face another weather problem—the extreme summer heat. For example, in mid-summer, the work schedules in the desert areas must be shifted to night work or to very early morning hours to avoid the health hazards and construction problems that could result from the intense heat.

Labor Relations.   A high level of efficiency results when a contractor has good working relations with employees as a result of good supervision and when the contractor's workforce has a good record of employment. However, efficiency is reduced when there are problems with union labor agreements, poor management, or low wages.

A crew of employees that has been together for some time is more efficient than a newly organized crew. An experienced crew accomplishes more work with fewer personnel in less time as a result of the knowledge each member has of the responsibilities of the others as well as their own. Because of this understanding, the crew members are better able to support one another and work faster and better. Steady employment also increases crew experience and the efficiency level, as well as helping to provide a comfortable working relationship between management and employees.

A company that pays better wages than the competition will attract better personnel, who will be likely to stay with the company longer. The problem that the employer faces with higher wages is that too high a wage can reduce the competitiveness of the company in the market place.

If the management team of a company becomes overly aggressive and tries to force an additional workload without some sort of compensation for the crews, there will be a major drop in efficiency. Similarly, if management does not properly delegate work among all the field personnel, a drop in efficiency will occur.

Even where there has been a long record of employment but the chances of continued employment appear to be dwindling because there is no work in the near future, crews will automatically slow down to prolong their employment for as long as possible, producing another cause for a reduction in efficiency.

Morale.   As each of the six efficiency factors has been discussed above, its effect on morale has been noted. Good management, experienced personnel, and good wages produce a high morale which, in turn, increases the efficiency level of any labor force. Problems from low morale can result from any of the above causes of poor efficiency. In merit shop companies, as well as in the union hierarchies, politics and favoritism can also play a large part in low morale among workers and can be a major cause of reduced efficiency.

The Efficiency Schedule

See figure 3–1, Efficiency Rating: Six Factors. The question is, How does the estimator make use of knowledge about efficiency? This is the one "gray" area of estimating, often referred to as the "guesstimate," because there is no scientific or mathematical rule to govern the calculations relating to efficiency. The knowledge gained from the company work history and from the six factors above helps to determine if it is worth taking the time to do an estimate and offer a bid on a project. Not all of the efficiency factors may be important in determining labor costs. Labor relations, for example, may have no effect on a situation. Assuming that all six factors are of equal weight, the estimator must first establish an **efficiency schedule.**

Efficiency Schedule 1	
If	**Then**
General Efficiency is fair	Productivity is 75%
Supervision is good	Productivity is 85%
Job Conditions are fair	Productivity is 70%
Weather is unseasonable	Productivity is 75%
Equipment is maintained	Productivity is 80%
Labor Relations are poor	Productivity is 65%
Total Efficiency Percentage	450%

FIGURE 3–1
Efficiency Rating: Six Factors

Efficiency Schedule 2	
If	**Then**
General Efficiency is good	Productivity is 80%
Supervision is good	Productivity is 85%
Weather is excellent	Productivity is 90%
Equipment is poorly maintained	Productivity is 70%
Total Efficiency Percentage	325%

FIGURE 3–2
Efficiency Rating: Four Factors

The experience of many contractors and estimators has determined that a *minimum 65% efficiency* is necessary to produce a profit. Figure 3–1 gives an example of a typical efficiency schedule using all six factors. The total percentage (450%) is divided by the number of factors:

$$450\% \div 6 = 75\%$$

See figure 3–2. Efficiency review: Four factors. If any of the factors mentioned in the schedule have no bearing on the company's work position, then only those that might have an effect should be used. Assume that labor relations and job conditions have no effect on a situation. Figure 3–2 is an example of an efficiency schedule using only four factors. The total percentage (325%) is divided by the number of factors:

$$325\% \div 4 = 81.25\%$$

These efficiency schedules are produced by research on the part of the estimator, contractor, and the follow-up team that makes project analyses. As mentioned previously, the company that has a historical background can determine figures based on previous projects. Experience with the labor force, weather conditions, and so on, are the prime sources for determining these factors.

PRODUCTIVITY

Efficiency determines the productivity of the company and the size of the labor force. In turn, the size of the labor force determines the labor and equipment costs. **Productivity** is defined as "the maximum capability to produce," referring to both work and profit. More specifically, in construction terms, productivity is the amount of work that can be accomplished by one person or one crew in one hour. The final percentages in the above calculations are examples of the **percentage of productivity.** Productivity ratings can serve a twofold purpose:

1. They can help determine the present efficiency of a company.
2. They can help improve a company's capabilities (productivity) by pinpointing the weak spots, which the company can then work to improve.

The productivity determined above means little without its application to some value. The value to which it is applied is referred to as the **productivity factor** and is determined by a combination of the **composite crew** and the **percentage of productivity.**

Productivity Factor

Although the percentage total of the composite crew is considered to equal 100%, in reality, only *70% of the time is spent in productive work*. The remaining 30% is "free" time, which the contractor knows must be paid for labor. This time includes regular breaks and lunch periods, time spent in personal care, material delays, and equipment breakdowns. The 70% figure is included in the calculations of the productivity factor. The norm of 70% is always the numerator, while the denominator is the percentage of productivity. The result is known as the productivity factor.

When the percentage of productivity *is more* than the norm, the productivity factor *decreases*. For example, if a 75% percentage of productivity is calculated, the productivity factor is as follows:

$$70\% \div 75\% = 0.93$$

When the percentage of productivity *is less* than the norm, the productivity factor *increases*. For example, if a productivity percentage of 66% is determined, the productivity factor is as follows:

$$70\% \div 66\% = 1.06$$

This change in productivity factor indicates that the *poorer the efficiency rating of the crew, the greater is the labor cost*, to compensate.

Using these calculations, the contractor can maintain a comparative cost as conditions fluctuate in the labor market or crew abilities change. The use of the productivity calculations is discussed later in this chapter, including their use with the composite crew rate.

LABOR

The labor costs used throughout the text are for the purpose of example only. Many of the costs shown in the following discussion and problems are fictional and are not necessarily based on current costs. Each contractor and estimator must become familiar with up-to-date standard merit shop, union, prevailing, or other wage scales that apply to the company and the locale.

Burden

A portion of wages paid to an employee includes items that are referred to as the **labor burden.** The labor burden includes all costs incurred by the contractor that are not direct labor costs but are a part of the individual hourly cost and have a direct effect upon the labor cost of a project. Below are listed examples of the burden and burden costs for a boilermaker (union scale).

Personal and property liability insurance (company paid)	= $0.10/hr
Medical insurance benefits (company program)	= $2.00/hr
Worker's compensation insurance (state insurance)	= $0.24/hr
F.I.C.A. (federal insurance)	= $0.34/hr
Vacation and apprenticeship fees	= $1.10/hr
Pension funding	= $1.40/hr
Total	$5.18/hr

The base wage for the boilermaker is $21.60 per hour. The percentage of burden is as follows:

$$\$5.18/hr \div \$21.60/hr = 0.2398 \text{ or } 24\%$$

For a contractor just starting in business and with no work history, these costs are determined by projecting the monthly costs for all employees, multiplying by 12 months, and dividing that amount by the **projected annual gross revenues**. For example, a new company projects $1,000,000 worth of work for the year. The monthly burden is projected at $20,000 per month. The percentage of burden is as follows:

$$\$20,000/mo \times 12 \, mo = \$240,000/yr$$
$$\$240,000 \div \$1,000,000 = 0.24 \text{ or } 24\%$$

The contractor with a good historical background can determine the actual costs for the burden by breaking the costs down into hourly rates and applying them to the labor wage.

The burden is added to the base wage as shown in the Composite Crew Schedule (see figure 3–3a and 3–3b) by multiplying the base wage by the percentage of burden determined. For example, a foreman's wage is $19.25. The burden is as follows:

$$\$19.25 \times 0.24 = \$4.62$$

The labor cost for the foreman is as follows:

$$\$19.25 + \$4.62 = \$23.87$$

CREW	HOURLY WAGE + BURDEN	% TIME ON JOB/HR	HOURLY RATE
Foreman	$16.65 + $ 5.20	10%	= $ 2.19
Oper. Engr	$16.45 + $ 3.40	7%	= $ 1.39
Ironworker	$16.15 + $ 5.20	45%	= $ 9.61
Oiler	$13.24 + $ 3.40	3%	= $ 0.50
Laborer	$11.75 + $ 3.74	35%	= $ 5.42
Composite Crew Rate:		100%	$19.11

FIGURE 3–3a
Composite Crew Schedule

CREW	HOURLY WAGE + BURDEN
Foreman	$16.65 + $ 5.20
Oper. Engr.	$16.45 + $ 3.40
Ironworker	$16.15 + $ 5.20
Oiler	$13.24 + $ 3.40
Laborer	$11.75 + $ 3.74
	$74.24 + $20.94 = $95.18
Composite Crew Rate:	$95.18/5 = $19.04

FIGURE 3–3b
Composite Crew Schedule

The contractor with historical information on a yearly basis can determine the burden for employees by breaking costs down into hourly rates from historical data and applying them to the labor wage. For example, here is an estimate for a crew of five workers:

Personal liability insurance	$ 4,000 annually
Medical benefits	$20,000 annually
Worker's compensation	$10,000 annually
Vacation and apprenticeship	$ 5,000 annually
Pension fund	$12,000 annually
Total	$51,000

Divide the total by 52 weeks and then by 40 hours/week, as follows:

$$\$51,000 \div 52 \text{ weeks} = \$980.77/\text{week}$$

$$\$980.77 \div 40 \text{ hours} = \$24.52/\text{hr}$$

$$\$24.52/\text{hr} \div 5\text{-worker crew} = \$4.90/\text{MH}$$

The percentage of burden can then be determined for the crew:

$$\$4.90/\text{MH} \div \$24.52/\text{MH} = 0.199, \text{ or } 20\% \text{ burden}$$

The exact wage and burden per employee would be best, but the average burden, as calculated here, may be used.

Further caution must be taken because of the variations between the trades. The actual burden will vary from trade to trade in the same locale. This is because of the increasing burden costs placed on the contractor by union contracts, governmental fees, and taxes. The prevailing wages for government work are similar. It is, therefore, mandatory that the same caution and care must be taken to ensure that the burden is properly identified and the costs kept up to date.

Many of the merit shop contractors reduce the burdens considerably since they are not required to meet the demands of the unions. Still other merit shop contractors will use the prevailing wage standards to remain competitive and, thus, keep in step with the union contractor. Such choices are dependent upon the local market demands.

For overtime work, the hourly wage and consumption of time on the job are the only increases considered. This, in turn, changes the hourly rate. The overtime rate is the hourly wage multiplied by the overtime rate (time and one half or double time). The labor burden remains the same.

Composite Crew

The composite crew is the number of employees assigned to work on a project. The composite crew schedule includes employees from the foreman to the lowest-paid laborer. The superintendent is not included as field personnel and is, therefore, not included in a schedule. The composite crew calculation includes the base hourly wage of each member of the crew and the burden paid by the contractor for each crew member.

Caution must be taken when estimating labor costs. There are two ways in which to calculate a composite crew schedule. *See figure 3–3a, Composite Crew Schedule.* This composite crew calculation uses the base wage and burden. In addition, the percentage of time spent on each project must be included.

See figure 3–3b, Composite Crew Schedule. A second, more common method also uses the base wage and burden. The time on the job is not included. It is used to calculate the total hourly rate for each member of the crew.

Man Hour (MH).   One **man hour** is the rate used to determine the cost for one worker for a period of one hour. It is the basis for the average rate of labor for each member of a crew. The calculation for the man-hour rate is shown in figures 3–3a and 3–3b. The total ironworker composite crew cost per hour in 3–3a is $20.57/hr. The cost per hour in figure 3–3b is $19.04/hr. The productivity factor determines the true man-hour rate. The productivity factor calculated above is 0.93. The **man-hour** rate is:

Figure 3–3a: $20.57/hr $\times$ 0.93 = $19.13/MH
Figure 3–3b: $20.47/hr $\times$ 0.93 = $19.04/MH

Man Day (MD).   The man day is based on the man-hour rate. It is the labor cost for one (1) man for a period of one (1) day. The **man-day** rate is calculated as follows:

Figure 3–3a: $19.13/MH $\times$ 8 hr/day = $153.04/MD
Figure 3–3b: $19.04/MH $\times$ 8 hr/day = $152.32/MD

Crew Hour (CH).   The total man-hour rate multiplied by the number of crew members is the **crew-hour rate.** The crew hour determined from the crew in Figures 3–3a and 3–3b and the productivity factor is as follows:

Figure 3–3a: $19.13/MH $\times$ 5 men = $95.65/CH
Figure 3–3b: $19.04/MH $\times$ 5 men = $95.20/CH

Crew Day (CD).   A **crew day** is determined in the same way as the man day using the crew-hour rate. The crew day is calculated as follows:

Figure 3–3a: $95.65/CH $\times$ 8 hr/day = $765.20/CD or $765.00/CD
Figure 3–3b: $95.20/CH $\times$ 8 hr/day = $761.60/CD or $762.00/CD

Note that the combination of the man-day rate multiplied by the number of workers also equals the same as the crew-day rate. The crew-day rate and the term labor day rate are identical. The crew-day rate, or day rate, is calculated as follows:

Figure 3–3a: $153.04/MD $\times$ 5 members = $765.20 or $765.00/day rate
Figure 3–3b: $152.32/MD $\times$ 5 members = $761.60 or $762.00/day rate

CONTROLLING LABOR COSTS

Beyond the quantity survey and the labor calculations as shown above, there are other materials that can be used as background information for estimating a project. These include information from previous work using the Critical Path Method (CPM), the daily reports, and inventory control records.

The Critical Path Method (CPM)

See figure 3–4. Most concerns regarding productivity could be cleared up by proper supervision. One method of control is to improve coordination of work schedules; for example, coordinating the work schedules of the various trades with utility company schedules. A bar chart (similar to figure 3–4) of organization can help direct "traffic" and correct many of the coordination problems. The individual subcontractors can make use of the same chart or produce a simpler **linear CPM,** describing the work expected of a crew each day, and coordinate it with the bar chart.

Cost Analyses

There are other analyses used by the experienced contractor. One is a day-to-day check on costs as the project is ongoing. Another tool is the follow-up analysis, which is the work of the estimator, project manager, project superintendent, and the company bookkeeper or accountant in determining profit and loss once the project is complete. The job-cost analysis process is discussed in chapter 14.

Many contractors and estimators fail to understand the importance of these analyses. Analyzing the costs of material, labor, and equipment can have a major effect on the outcome of any project. The analyses are used to keep tabs on the material costs and labor progress, and used effectively, it can help reduce overall costs. A company can estimate labor costs on future work by doing the following:

1. Projecting performance (for a new company) and trying to apply the strictest surveillance on each project. In this manner, a historical record can be built.

2. Using past history as a reference by analyzing performance on projects of similar construction and comparing the records with the project being estimated and/or in progress

3. Using daily reports to assist in day-to-day operations and making use of these reports for investigation of problems with contractors and subcontractors, as well as for verification of work authorizations or change orders and the ways they are handled

4. Constant updating of material costs

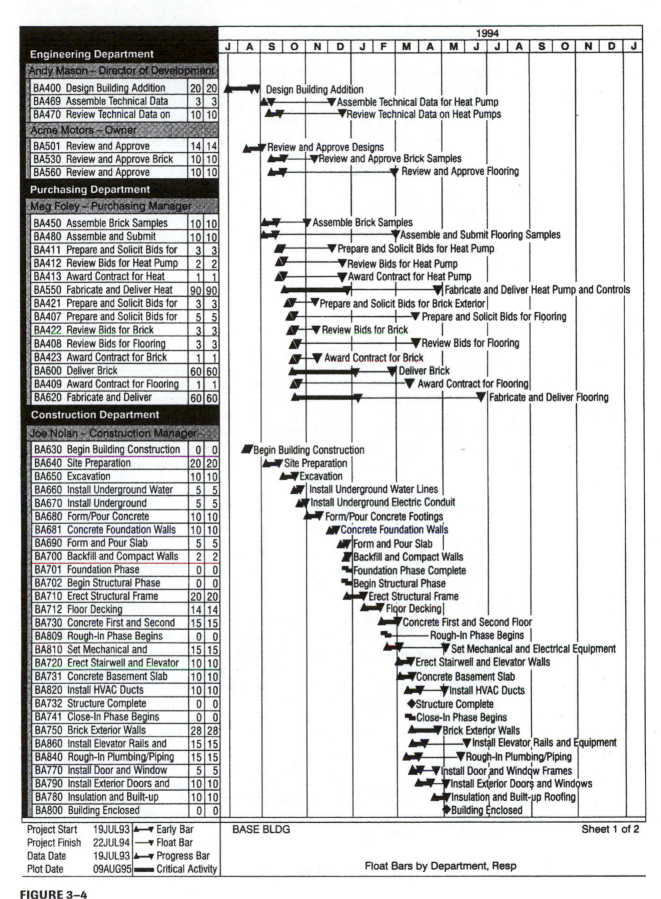

FIGURE 3–4
Critical Path Method (CPM) Chart

Daily Report. *See figure 3–5.* The control of a project is of prime importance if any profit is to be made. A daily report form filled out by a supervisor on a job is of prime importance to the contractor for several reasons. The written word regarding happenings between the employees of the contractor and other trades gives insight as to how well that supervisor is controlling the work. Without such information, the contractor and/or estimator can only continue to "guesstimate" the labor costs.

This information may also save the contractor problems in the future. In the event a problem is raised after the fact or some form of litigation is being attempted, information relating to the situation is immediately available in the daily report. Because the report stated what happened at the particular time of the incident or work phase, the contractor can stand firmly and probably be exonerated of any costs or damages in either case.

EQUIPMENT

As with materials, there is no flat rate for equipment costs. Each trade uses different types of equipment for specific purposes on a project. There are two calculations for determining equipment costs. In one case, the equipment is *owned*. In the other case, equipment is *rented or leased*. The cost of owned or rental equipment must be included and identified during the survey or in the summary. Equipment should never be "buried" under other costs such as overhead. "Burying" makes it impossible to trace equipment costs for historical cost data, accounting, tax deductions, or other purposes.

Owned Equipment

A contractor must be careful in acquiring equipment, especially if the equipment costs are very large ($35,000/unit and up). When money is available or a credit line is established and the contractor can afford to make a purchase, several things must be considered. Additional workers are necessary to run the equipment, such as drivers, mechanics, oilers, and so on. Storage facilities must be available with security to prevent theft. Each of the above factors must be determined on an hourly or daily cost basis and included in the estimate for owned equipment. Some of the costs of maintaining company-owned equipment that must be broken down into an hourly rate include insurance premiums, licenses and fees, taxes, repairs, preventive maintenance, depreciation, and pickup and delivery charges.

Estimating Owned Equipment. *See figure 3–6.* All the above factors must be considered in estimates of equipment costs. For example, a bulldozer is needed for 3 days for doing some grading. The cost for the operator, equipment use, and equipment maintenance is $73.00/hr. The wages (including all costs) for the operator are $39.89/hr. There is a cost of $120 for delivery and pickup of the equipment and a $22.32/hr cost for a maintenance oiler. The oiler is on the job for 2 hours per day.

Equipment Rental (Leasing)

A contractor may rent equipment. When or if this occurs, the operator labor cost is included as a separate item only with heavy equipment such as graders,

DAILY REPORT

TRADE	JOB #	JOB NAME	DATE
Delta Electric Co.	1234-92	Medical Clinic	5/08/92

DAY of WEEK	Temperature	Weather Conditions (fair, rain, etc.)
Thursday	84°	cloudy and humid

Crew	# Employees	WORK PERFORMED
Forman	1	Installed 200 lf or 1 1/2" IMC conduit
Electrician	2	Pulled 220 lf - 3-#4 RHW
Apprentice	2	Connected same to 3Ø. 400A disconnect for 30 HP motor
Laborer	1	control panel.
		Meggered circuit - tested clear.

SUBCONTRACTOR	# Employees	WORK PERFORMED
The Digger	1	Bob Digger cut 40 long by 48" deep trench for main feeder
		from utility transformer to entrance switchgear panel.
		Time - 4 hours. 30 minutes.

DELAYS

COMPANY RESPONSIBLE	TIME of DELAY	REASON for DELAY
Woods Framing and	8:30 AM to 9:45 AM	Loading and installing
ABC Crane Company		trusses

INSTRUCTIONS - AUTHORIZATIONS - REQUESTS

NAME	COMPANY	How Communicated	TYPE of COMMUNICATION
Steve C.	Christle Arch.	personal	Work Authorization #005 (attached)
Jim Fatzinger	JM Land Co.	phone	Change Order #2 - start work on new
			emergency generator system
			(CO to be mailed this date to office)
Topper McKay	Carson Const.	personal	Subcontractor complaint -
			remove our material from present location
			it is in the way of drywallers.
(signed) Mike Hennessey			

Authorized Signature (Forman, Superintendent)

FIGURE 3-5
Daily Report

Equipment Cost Schedule			
Equipment	**Use Time**	**Unit Cost**	**Total**
Bulldozer depreciation	3 days	$ 5.65/hr	= $135.60
Oil and fuel	3 days	$12.50/hr	= $300.00
Insurance, fees/taxes	3 days	$ 4.38/hr	= $105.12
Freight (pickup and delivery)	3 days	$ 5.00/hr	= $120.00
Total		$27.53/hr	$660.72

The oiler's wages are:	
$22.32/hr x 2 hr x 3 days =	$ 133.92
The operator's wages are:	
$39.89/hr x 8 hr x 3 days =	$ 957.36
Total labor costs:	$1,091.28
Total equipment costs (from schedule):	$ 660.72
Subtotal	$1,752.00
Taxes @ 7%	$ 122.64
The total cost (labor and equipment):	$1,874.64 or $1,875.00

FIGURE 3–6
Labor and Equipment Costs for Owned Equipment

bulldozers, cranes, and so on. Small equipment rentals, such as forklifts and bobcats, normally do not include operator labor. Rental costs also include all, or a major portion of, the costs associated with owning the equipment, such as delivery and pickup charges, license costs, insurance costs, and depreciation.

Estimating Rental Equipment.   *See figure 3–7.* Here is an example of estimating cost of equipment rental: A contractor needs to rent a hoe-ram to break up the caliche and rock for a trench that is being dug. The company requests an estimate for services from a trenching specialty contractor that owns several pieces of such equipment. The estimate, similar in form to that shown in figure 3–7, includes delivery and pickup, machine rental, and the operator costs. If the contractor makes use of the services, the specialty contractor submits an invoice on completion of the work.

QUANTITY SURVEY

The most tedious and time-consuming aspect of estimating is making the quantity survey (the takeoff). There are two types of surveys that are used, the quick estimate and the detailed estimate.

"Quick" Method

The so-called "quick" estimate is the easiest and most tempting to use. This method uses calculations of lineal, square, and cubic measures without considering details.

Refer to chart 3–1. The lineal calculation of a rebar takeoff from a slab plan can serve as an example of just such a survey. The slab is 735 lf (224.03 m) ×

```
                          I N V O I C E

   FROM:   Eagle Equipment Rentals
           25 Mountain Avenue
           Elko, Nevada

                                          Date:  2/16/92
   ═══════════════════════════════════════════════════════════
   TO:    ABC Excavating                 │ Invoice #  ABC-1
          200 Phoenix Drive              │    Due and payable
          Las Vegas, Nevada              │         upon
                                         │   Receipt of Service
   ═══════════════════════════════════════════════════════════

   Estimate (  ) Billing (X) for Equipment Rental:


      Compactor                 1 ea │ per mo. │ $   500.00

      Bulldozer                 1 ea │ per mo. │ $4,500.00

      Delivery to and from project   │ ea way  │ $   275.00
```

FIGURE 3–7
Equipment Rental

Takeoff for rebar—"quick method":

Slab is 735 lf (224.03 m) × 1735 lf (528.8 m)

2–#4 rebar, continuous in the footing:

(735 lf × 2) + (1735 lf × 2) =
1470 lf + 3470 lf = 4940 lf
4940 lf × 2 = **9880 lf total**

(224.03 m × 2) + (528.83 m × 2) =
448.06 m + 1057.66 m = 1505.72 m
1505.72 m × 2 = **3011.44 m total**

With 15% waste factor added:
9880 lf × 1.15 = **11,362 lf** or **11,360 lf**

3011.44 m × 1.15 = **3463.16 m**

Material cost is $0.30/lf:
11,360 lf × $0.30 = **$3,408.00**

Material cost is $0.30/0.3 m:

$$\frac{3463.16 \text{ m} \times \$0.30}{0.3048 \text{ m}} = \mathbf{\$3408.46}$$

CHART 3—1
Quick Estimate for Footing Rebar

1,735 lf (528.83 m). There are two #4 rebar, continuous, in the footings. A quick estimate for footing rebar is shown in chart 3–1.

Note that to cover the waste factor for laps and corner pieces, the contractor can add a waste factor of 15%, as shown in the chart.

What has been left out of the quick estimate? Such items as cross rebar, loops, or chairs have been excluded. Each of these items adds to the cost. Calculated in detail, these items can dramatically increase costs.

The architect and general contractor normally use the quick estimate method. The architect uses this method for the feasibility study or for a quick check on the estimated costs of a preliminary or construction estimate. If the general contractor is "brokering" a project (one in which all the estimating is done by subcontractors and submitted for bid), the quick estimate is used for double-checking the subcontractors bidding the work.

The subcontractor attempting to do a quantity survey using the quick method can easily lose money because of failure to incorporate all the necessary information. This method is definitely *not* recommended for the new company. After a period of years, where a solid historical background has been developed, a contractor may use the quick method for a bid when a bid is needed on short-term notice. However, where possible, the quick estimate should be avoided by all contractors, not just new ones.

Detail Method

The contractor should do a detailed survey, where a portion of the project work is a company craft, such as concrete or framing. Subcontractors should always use the detailed survey for two reasons:

1. The subcontractor needs to study the specifications and plans thoroughly to ensure that all the work is properly covered.
2. By doing a detailed survey, the subcontractor has no need to "redo" if a contract is awarded. The material and equipment quantities have already been estimated.

Computer programs may be built to calculate either the quick or the detail method of estimating. The major software programs available have detailed data bases for accurate estimating of materials and costs. The detail quantity survey is the method used throughout the text for the Medical Clinic estimate, which is the principal example used throughout this book. Each chapter will include a partial estimate on a manual form and/or a computer readout.

CHAPTER EXERCISES

1. The factors of efficiency determined by the estimator include the following information:

General Efficiency—fair	75%
Project Supervision—good	80%
Job Conditions—fair	70%
Tools and Equipment—good	85%

Weather Conditions—moderate   70%

Labor Relations—good   85%

Determine the productivity factor for the above percentages.

2. An ironworker crew consists of the following personnel:

Foreman	@ $22.50/hr	15% time on the job
Carpenter (3)	@ $17.15/hr	39% time on the job
Helper (2)	@ $13.42/hr	39% time on the job
Welder	@ $16.79/hr	5% time on the job
Equipment Operator	@ $18.05/hr	2% time on the job

The percent of burden to be added is 27%. The percentage of time on the job per hour is shown in the column at the right. Determine the composite crew total and, using the productivity factor in question 1, determine the MH rate, the MD rate, the CH rate, the CD rate, and the day labor rate. The project takes ten days to complete. From the composite crew cost, calculate the total labor cost.

3. A grading contractor owns three large graders valued at $75,000 each, two 40 cu yd trucks valued at $35,000 each, two payloaders valued at $45,000 each, and a compactor valued at $25,000. The depreciation is estimated at 7% per annum. Break the depreciation down to an hourly value.

4. Equipment is rented at $75.00/hr. The operator is charged at $22.74/hr. All of the equipment listed in question 3, with an operator for each, will be used for three weeks (fifteen working days) to complete a project. The oiler labor rate is $20.00/hr, and the oiler is on the job three hours per day, three times a week during the project. Oil and fuel, insurance, fees, taxes, and freight are the same as in the example in the chapter in figure 3–6. Estimate the total equipment costs.

Earthwork

Division 2

GENERAL INFORMATION

Earthwork starts with the soils report and finishes with landscaping. Included in between are demolition, clearing and grubbing, excavating and grading, and paving. All **on-site, off-site,** and **site improvements** pertaining to earthwork are included in this division.

On-site work usually includes all construction on a project, including the structure and work within a 5 lf (1.52 m) wide perimeter surrounding it. **Site improvements** includes any and all other construction within the boundaries of the property, but beyond the 5 lf (1.52 m) on-site perimeter. **Off-sites** refer to items such as street improvements, easement work, driveway entrances (approaches), curb and gutter, and sidewalk construction outside the property lines. Local governing agencies may demand that these improvements be a part of the project. Otherwise, they hire the work done and back-charge the costs to the owner.

The Soils Report

See Excerpts of a Soils Report, appendix IV. The building and safety department of a community may insist on an investigation of the soil properties on a construction project. A soils engineering firm takes samples of the surface soil and makes test borings. The two primary pieces of information being sought are the type and stability of the soil. A **soils report** states the conditions of the earth on, and immediately adjoining, the property. The report is submitted to the owner or owner's representative upon completion of the investigation. The soils engineer is also responsible for information regarding hazardous materials that may be present. Civil and structural engineers involved with the development of the grading plan and the structure make a careful study of this report to determine proper construction procedures and design.

Site Preparation

Demolition.   A specialty contractor or the excavating contractor may be contracted for structure and debris removal. The demolition crew dismantles structures or parts of structures and removes or caps existing utilities. It is also the demolition crew's responsibility to see that all hazardous wastes are completely removed from the site. Demolition costs include labor and equipment, as well as transportation and disposal of the materials. The demolition is sometimes accomplished by a salvage company; the company recoups some of the expense of the demolition by reselling the salvageable materials.

Clearing and Grubbing.   Clearing and grubbing may be included with demolition. Like demolition, **clearing** entails removal of structures and debris. The costs involved in clearing are the same as those considered for demolition. **Grubbing** refers to removal of the vegetation. The work includes removal of trees, shrubs, and other vegetation. The costs involved for grubbing include labor, equipment, and transportation.

The owner or architect determines which form of vegetation is to be saved, moved, or removed. The contractor responsible for clearing and grubbing or the landscape contractor takes the responsibility for the trees and vegetation to be saved. The items to be saved are tagged and listed on some form of log or invoice, with a value given to each item.

Excavating and Grading (Earthwork)

The bulk of the work in Division 2 deals with excavating and grading. There are little or no materials required for earthwork, with the exception of stakes or flags for identifying grade levels and carpentry materials for mass or trench excavation. The major costs in the excavating and grading estimate are labor and equipment, of which the equipment makes up the largest part. The equipment necessary is dependent on the size of the project and the type of soil encountered. The contractor may need only a small bulldozer or may require a large earthmover and grader.

The estimator must have an equipment cost breakdown by the hour, day, week, or month. The cost is determined by using the original value of the equipment, the deductible annual amortization, maintenance costs, and the number of times that the equipment is used on an annual basis. These costs are made available from historical records from accounting and past projects for existing companies. A company without any historical backup can use rental companies for equipment costs.

Soil treatment against termites and rodents, as well as revegetation, is included in the work of the excavating contractor. The location of the treatment and the quantities of chemicals are determined by the soil conditions, by the chemical manufacturer's recommendations, and by local codes and ordinances. The treatment is usually confined to the area under and immediately adjacent to the structure.

Shoring.   Shoring is required for any excavation that is *5'-0" (1.52 m) or more in depth or where specified by an engineer.* In the case of very unstable or sandy soils, there may be an engineering requirement for shoring and additional care at levels less than 5'-0" (1.52 m). Shoring may be eliminated only where the soil is stable enough to support itself and when the excavation is designed by a civil engineer. The design of the excavation may be sloped or stepped and is determined by the physical properties of the soil being excavated. Where an excavation uses the sloped design, the recommended minimum slope is a 1:1 ratio.

See figure 4–1. Large trenches and mass excavations requiring shoring use either **wood planking, plywood, rolled plate steel,** or **steel boxes.** Each

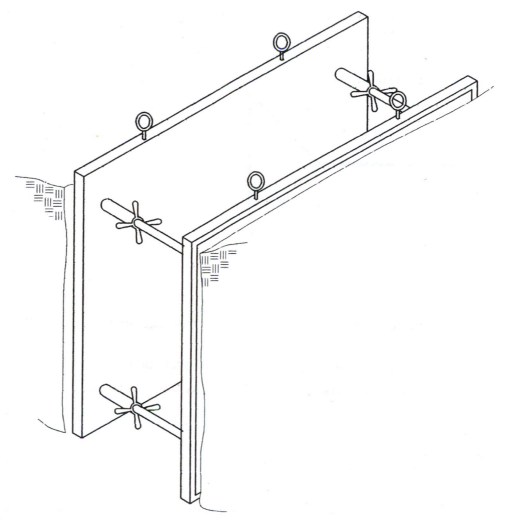

FIGURE 4–1
Steel Box Shoring

shoring system requires manually or hydraulically operated jacks as spacers between the sides, placed at mid-height and at the top of the excavation, to keep the supporting walls rigid. Steel plates or box systems can be used for excavations of any depth but must be used in areas where the depth is greater than 8'-0" (2.44 m). Cranes are used to move the plates or boxes from section to section as the work progresses.

Wood plank or sheet plywood systems may be used if the excavation is not deeper than 8'-0" (2.44 m). Planking and plywood are moved by carpenters and laborers in advance of the crews working in the excavation. The plank system is constructed with 2 × 12 (5.08 cm × 30.48 cm) planks placed vertically and supported with 2 × 4 (5.08 cm × 10.16 cm) or 2 × 6 (5.08 cm × 15.24 cm) single or double **walers** and bracing. The plywood system uses minimum 1" (2.54 cm) thick plywood supported by walers and bracing in the same manner as the plank system.

Swales and Basins.   *See figure 4–2.* Both swales and retention basins may be included under the heading of excavations or they may be a part of paving. A

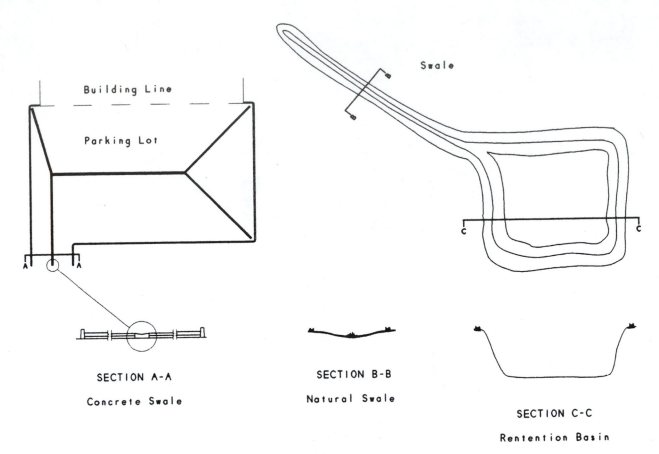

FIGURE 4–2
Swales and Retention Basin

swale may be a natural dip or shallow sloped area in the earth, a shallow sloping of paved parking areas and driveways, or a concrete trench through the center of such areas used to direct the drainage away from any structure located on the property. A (detention) basin is an area, on or off the property, that is either a natural basin or an excavated one and that is several feet lower than the surrounding area. The swale may be a part of a flood control system, and a basin is part of the system. Some so-called "green belts" in residential areas which are lower than the surrounding properties may actually be flood control swales or retention basins.

Paving and Landscaping

After the grades have been completed and established, the finished surfaces for traffic are constructed. The materials required include a **subbase,** an **aggregate base,** and the **surfacing material** with a **seal coat.** The surfacing materials used may either be of **concrete** or a **bituminous product (asphalt).**

Landscaping includes everything within the site improvements and, possibly, off-sites on a project. The paving may be shown on landscape plans. The identification of paving, sidewalks, patios, plazas, and so on in these plans is called the **hardscape.** The remaining areas—lawns or other ground cover, shrubbery, or trees—are the **softscape.** The drawings and specifications may be either under separate contract or a part of the base contract. The designer/engineer may also be the landscape contractor. All design work, estimating, negotiations, bidding, and so on are usually done by the landscape contractor in direct contact with the owner.

SCOPE OF WORK

The first step in an estimate is to study the project specifications carefully to ascertain project size and what materials (if any), equipment, and labor costs are involved. The following specifications for the Medical Clinic are taken from the Project Manual in appendix IV. They will be used for making the estimate in the next section in this chapter.

Division 2: Earthwork

02000 Scope of Work

Division 1 and the General Conditions are to be considered a part of this division. All labor and equipment for a complete installation are also a part of this division.

02010 Subsurface Investigation

The owner shall provide for subsurface exploration to be conducted by a qualified soils engineering firm. The soils testing and results shall be made available, in writing, to the owner or owner's representative and the contractor and shall become a part of these Specifications.

   The report shall include the type of surface soil, the type, or types, of soil for a minimum of ten (10) feet (3.05 m) below grade, obtained by test borings or core drillings, and shall make recommendations, if any, for correcting substandard soils conditions.

   During excavation and grading, soils testing shall be performed to ensure the soils meet a minimum of 3,000 psf (1,360.71 kg/0.929 m^2) design strength.

02100 Site Preparation

The contractor shall make certain that certain vegetation is marked to remain intact or to be removed, saved and transplanted. This shall be accomplished in cooperation with the owner, contractor and clearing and grubbing contractor. When all vegetation to be saved is so marked, all remaining vegetation, debris and refuse is to be cleared and removed.

02200 Earthwork

Excavate as required to achieve proper grade levels, for the mass excavation of the crawl space and for working room required for laying of foundation walls and footings surrounding the mass excavation. Excavation for all footings to be on undisturbed earth or minimum 95% compacted soil with a minimum depth as shown on drawings or otherwise governed by local codes.

Should the contractor contact caliche or large rock conditions which would require blasting, the owner will reimburse the contractor for the cost of such work.

Backfill at exterior walls shall be Type II soil, well compacted, to a subgrade 8″ (20.32 cm) below top of foundation wall. Backfill over utilities shall conform with the utility company requirements of sand and Type II soil. The remainder of the site shall be graded to assure proper drainage away from the building. Remove all excess soils from the site.

Grades not otherwise indicated on the plans shall be of uniform levels or slopes between points where elevations are given.

Contractor is to notify owner immediately if any excavation reveals fill or ground water.

02500 Paving and Surfacing

All paving is to be of asphaltic materials. All paving shall be installed in areas indicated on plans. Pavement design shall meet ten (10) year minimum design criteria for local areas as established by the Asphalt Institute. The following guide should be used as a **minimum** thickness required:

Soil Class	Minimum Pavement
Poor-CBR = 3.5-type, plastic when wet such as clay, fine silt, sandy loam	6″ (15.24 cm) coarse asphalt base binder (1½″ [3.81 cm] asphalt aggregate) and 1½″ (3.81 cm) asphalt topping (maximum ½″ [1.27 cm] aggregate)
Medium-CBR = 7.0-type, hard, silty sands or sand gravels containing clay or fine silt	4′ (10.16 cm) coarse asphalt base binder (1½″ [3.81 cm] asphalt aggregate) and 1½″ (3.81 cm) asphalt topping (maximum ½″ [1.27 cm] aggregate)
Good-CBR = 12-type, clean sand and sand gravel free of asphalt topping clay, silt or loam	3″ (7.62 cm) coarse asphalt base material (1½″ [3.81 cm] asphalt aggregate) and 1½″ (3.81 cm) asphalt topping (maximum 12″ [1.27 cm] aggregate)

or

6″ (15.24 cm)(compacted thickness) stone base plus 2½″ (6.35 cm) asphalt topping (maximum ¾″ [1.91 cm] aggregate)

Finish paving shall be 4″ (10.16 cm) asphalt mix at all light-trafficked areas over a 6″ (15.24 cm) cementitious base over 10″ (25.40 cm) compacted base aggregate or sand at all paved areas. The aggregate base shall be compacted to maintain an 80% compaction rate. Base shall be tested for compaction prior to application of asphalt finish. All paving surfaces shall be properly sealed from weather deterioration as per local codes and accepted workmanship of the trade.

Precast concrete parking blocks, 6′-0″ (1.83 m) long and 5″ (12.70 cm) high, shall be as shown on plans, or one for each two (2) parking places, spanning one half (1/2) per parking space, except at handicapped parking where the concrete block shall be

4'-0" (1.22 m) long and 5" (12.70 cm) high, one (1) per parking space, if not indicated otherwise on plans.

Curbs shall be 6" (15.24 cm) machine-formed asphaltic curbs of the same material as the heavily trafficked topping. Any curbing which becomes defective within a ninety (90) day period after final certificate of occupancy shall be replaced at no cost to owner.

02900 Landscaping

Provide all labor, material and equipment necessary to complete the seeding, sodding, landscape planting, earthwork and edging as shown on plans. Landscape bidder shall submit a proposal and drawings for approval by the owner. Proposal shall include size, type and number of plantings, and exact area to be sodded.

Landscape contractor shall be responsible for the installa-tion of the topsoil to finish grade at all the rough grading. The area shall be free of all debris and well drained prior to any planting. Total proposal shall include all taxes where applicable.

End of Division

THE ESTIMATE

Procedures for estimating excavating and grading, as well as paving, are ex-plained in this section. The examples include the use of a grid technique for a better quantity survey of a large property, the meaning of "cut" and "fill," a paving materials survey, as well as examples of labor and equip-ment calculations.

See figure 4–3. The form shown in figure 4–3 is one of several excavating/ grading survey spreadsheets common to the industry. Already included are spaces for identifying quantities (Qty, the length, width, depth, and D'). Note that Depth and D' indicate the highest and lowest points of an area, which are to be averaged, as shown in the following estimate.

The spaces on the left of the items may be used for accounting codes and descriptions of the area being estimated. The remaining columns on the right may be used for extensions of the calculations; material, labor, and equipment costs; and total estimating costs.

Demolition

The portion of the estimate for demolition and clearing and grubbing normally involves only labor and equipment. Materials that may be required are for these activities—such as the root protection for the saving of trees, fertilizer, burlap cloth for wrapping, and wood crating for easier handling—are not included; nei-ther are costs for storage and transportation. Except for the possibility of removal of hazardous waste materials, there is no demolition included in this estimate.

The demolition estimate includes clearing and grubbing of trees and veg-etation. The original trees, shrubs, and vegetation on the property of the Med-ical Clinic includes four maple trees and twelve juniper shrubs. The owner, architect, and/or general contractor makes a survey of the property. The owner

QUANTITY SURVEY

PROJECT:
ACCOUNT:

ESTIMATE NO.
SHEET NO.
PREPARED BY: DATE:
CHECKED BY: DATE:

Qty	Length	Width	Depth	D'											

FIGURE 4-3
Excavating Estimate. (Typical Form)

FIGURE 4–4
Vegetation Report

Save	Remove
1 maple tree	3 maple trees
12 juniper shrubs, replant all	All other vegetation

decides that only one maple tree and the twelve junipers are in good enough condition to save. The remainder is unwanted vegetation and debris. The survey may appear on paper as in figure 4–4.

Excavating and Grading

See Plans, Sheet C–1, Site Plan. See also figure 4–5. The calculation for excavating and grading is determined in cubic feet (cu ft or ft^3), cubic yards (cu yd or cu^3), or cubic meters (m^3). The calculations also need to show whether soil is to be removed or added. Soil that is to be removed is called **cut.** Cut areas are always positive quantities in calculations. Soil that has to be added is referred to as **fill.** When a negative quantity is calculated, it is identified with the symbol (< >). *This symbol appears in the calculations, and it indicates that average grade level is lower than the finished rough grade.*

A large property with many contour changes is difficult to estimate without the use of some form of reduction of area. The simplest technique for reducing areas is through the use of a **grid system.** Dependent upon the size of the property, grids are drawn in squares of 50 lf (15.24 m) or 100 lf (30.48 m). The grids may be drawn directly on the site plan or on an overlay. The overlay must be drawn to the same scale as the plan and aligned over the site plan. The grid layout for the Medical Clinic property is 50 lf (15.24 m) squares, as noted in the upper right-hand corner of the plan in figure 4–5.

There are two grid estimating procedures: (1) the **grid averaging** (cross section) method, which is the more commonly used method, and (2) the breakdown method of **geometric configurations.** The geometric breakdown is accomplished by forming geometric configurations along the contour lines and a cross section of each. The form in figure 4–3 should be used for the estimate backup for both systems of estimating.

Method 1: Grid Averaging Method.   *See figure 4–6; see also chart 4–1.* The averaging method uses the cross sectional view of the whole grid and the elevations noted on the four corners of the grid. The section should cut through the grid in as nearly a perpendicular line to the contours as possible. The section shown in figure 4–6 diagonally cuts through the grid from station 1A to B2. The stations will be explained more thoroughly in the next section. When the average depth is calculated, the rough elevation must be determined. The footprint on the site plan indicates that the top of the wall is 95'-0" (28.96 m). The finish grade is 4" (10.16 cm) below the top of the wall (T.O.W.). There are 4" of topsoil to be placed to that level. Therefore, the rough grade is 8" (20.32 cm) below the T.O.W. See chart 4–1 for the estimating procedure.

Method 2: Geometric Grid Breakdown.   *See figure 4–7 and 4–5; see also chart 4–1.* The drawing in figure 4–7 indicates a geometric configuration for each contour in grid 1. The grid is identified by numbers and letters, shown in each corner. These are called the primary "stations"; they identify the grid. The four

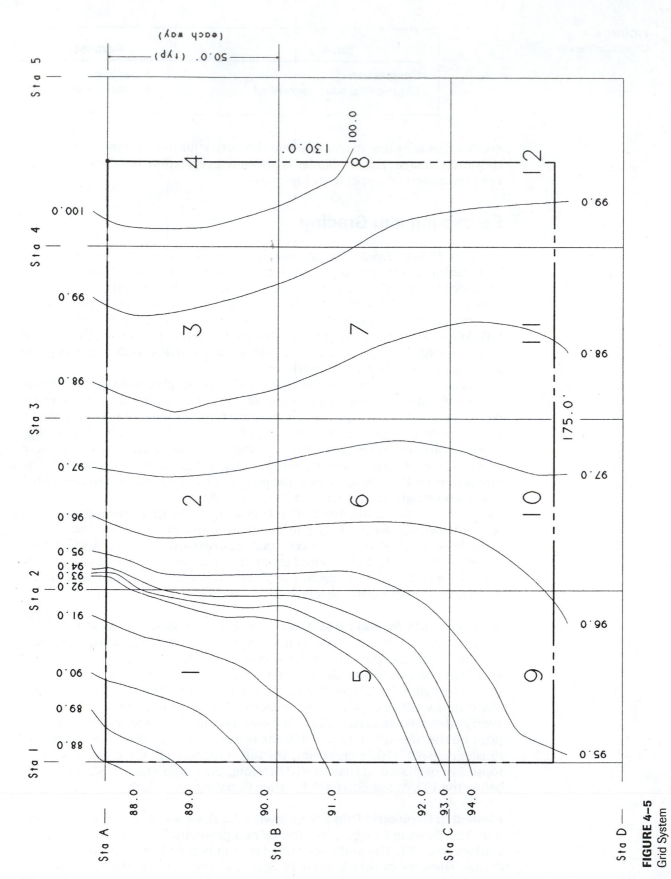

FIGURE 4–5
Grid System

72

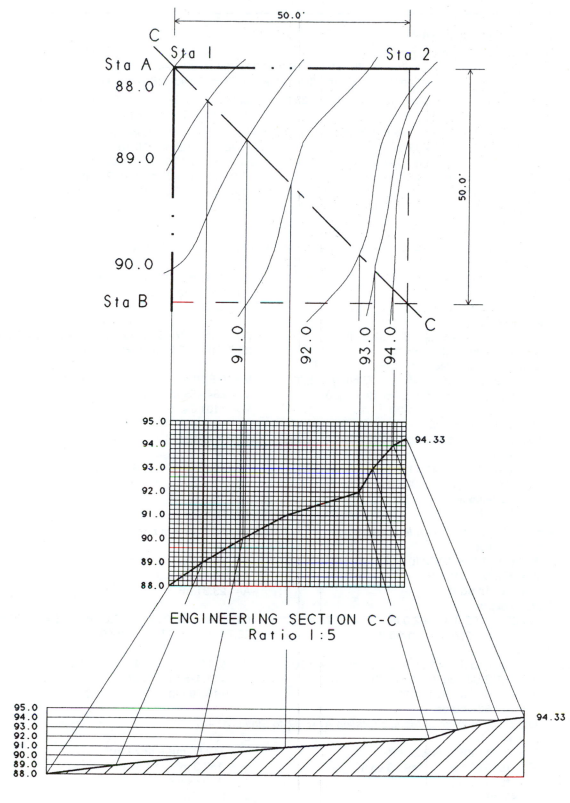

ENGINEERING SECTION C-C
Ratio 1:5

ARCHITECTURAL SECTION C-C
Ratio 1:1

FIGURE 4–6
Averaging Cross Section

Grid Averaging (figure 4-6):

Elevations of 4 corners, grid 1:

Station 1A—88.00'; Station 2A—91.75'; Station 1B—90.33'; Station 2B—94.25'
Station 1A—26.82 m; Station 2A—27.97 m; Station 1B—27.53 m; Station 2B—28.73 m

88.00 ft + 91.75 ft + 90.33 ft + 94.25 ft = 364.33 ft   26.82 m + 27.97 m + 27.53 m + 28.73 m = 111.05 m
364.33 ft ÷ 4 = 91.08 ft   111.07 m ÷ 4 = 27.76 m

T.O.W. is 95.0 ft (28.96 m); the rough grade is 89″ (0.2 m) below the T.O.W., therefore:

95.0 ft − 0.67 ft = 94.33 ft   28.96 m − 0.2 m = 28.76 m
94.33 ft − 91.08 ft = <3.25> ft   28.76 m − 27.76 m = <1.0> m
<3.25> ft × (50 ft × 50 ft) =   <1.0> m × (15.24 m × 15.24 m) =
<3.25> ft × 2500 sq ft × 1.20   <1.0> m × 232.26 m² × 1.20 = **<278.71> m³**
<8125> cu ft ÷ 27 cu ft × 1.20 = **<361.11> cu yd**

Geometric Breakdown (figure 4-7):

Area 1 and 2. Known legs of triangle: 28.89 lf and 41.11 lf (8.81 m and 12.53 m).

Area of triangle:

A = (28.89 ft × 41.11 ft) ÷ 2   A = (8.81 m × 12.53 m) ÷ 2
A = 1187.67 sq ft ÷ 2   A = 110.39 m² ÷ 2
A = 593.84 sq ft   **A = 55.20 m²**

Average depth:

(90 ft + 90 ft + 88 ft) ÷ 3 = 89.33 ft   (27.43 m + 27.43 m + 26.82 m) ÷ 3 = 27.23 m
94.33 ft − 89.33 ft = **<5> ft**   28.76 m − 27.23 m = **<1.53> m**

Volume (fill × swell factor):

V = ([593.84 sq ft × <5> ft] ÷ 27 cu ft) × 1.20   V = (55.20 m² × <1.53> m) × 1.20
V = (<2969.20> cu ft ÷ 27 cu ft) × 1.20   V = <84.45> m³ × 1.20
V = <109.97> cu yd × 1.20   **V = <101.34> m³**
V = <131.96> cu yd

Length of hypotenuse of triangle (Station 1A+28.89' to Station A1+41.11'):

c² = a² + b²   c² = a² + b²
c² = (28.89 ft)² + (41.11 ft)²   c² = (8.81 m)² + (12.53 m)²
c² = 834.63 sq ft + 1690.03 sq ft   c² = 77.62 m² + 157.0 m²
c² = 2524.66 sq ft   c² = 234.62 m²
c = 50.25 ft   **c = 15.32 m**

Areas 5,6, and 7. Known legs of triangle: 41.11 lf and 12.22 lf (12.53 m and 3.72 m).

Area of triangle:

A = (41.11 ft × 12.22 ft) ÷ 2   A = (12.53 m × 3.72 m) ÷ 2
A = 502.36 sq ft ÷ 2   A = 46.61 m² ÷ 2
A = 251.18 sq ft   **A = 23.31 m²**

Average depth:

(94.25 ft + 92.0 ft + 92.0 ft) ÷ 3 = 92.75 ft   (28.73 m + 28.04 m + 28.04 m) ÷ 3 = 28.27 m
(94.33 ft − 92.75 ft = **<1.58 ft>**   28.76 m − 28.27 m = **<0.49 m>**

Volume:

V = ([251 sq ft × <1.58 ft>] ÷ 27 cu ft) × 1.20   V = (23.31 m² × <0.49 m>) × 1.20
V = (<396.58> cu ft ÷ 27 cu ft) × 1.20   V = <11.42> m³ × 1.20
V = <14.69> cu yd × 1.20   **V = <13.70> m³**
V = <17.63> cu yd

Length of hypotenuse of triangle (Station A1+8.89' to Station 1B+37.78):

c² = a² + b²   c² = a² + b²
c² = (41.11 ft)² + (12.22 ft)²   c² = (12.53 m)²+ (3.72 m)²
c² = 1690.03 sq ft + 149.33 sq ft   c² = 157.0 m² + 13.84 m²
c² = 1839.36 sq ft   c² = 170.84 m²
c = 42.89 lf   **c = 13.07 m**

CHART 4—1
Excavating and Grading: Grid Averaging and Breakdown

Areas 3 and 4:

Area of triangles (Station 1A+28.89' × Station A2+8.89' and Station 1B+37.78' × Station A1+41.11'):

A = ([21.11 ft × 8.89 ft] + [17.77 ft × 8.89 ft]) ÷ 2	A = ([6.43 m × 2.71 m] + [5.42 m × 2.71 m]) ÷ 2
A = (187.67 sq ft + 157.98 sq ft) ÷ 2	A = (17.43 m² + 14.69 m²) ÷ 2
A = 345.65 sq ft ÷ 2	A = 32.12 m² ÷ 2
A = **172.83 sq ft**	A = **16.06 m²**

Length of hypotenuse each triangle:

Station 2A:

$c^2 = a^2 + b^2$	$c^2 = a^2 + b^2$
$c^2 = (21.11\text{ ft})^2 + (8.89\text{ ft})^2$	$c^2 = (6.43\text{ m})^2 + (2.71\text{ m})^2$
$c^2 = 445.63$ sq ft + 79.03 sq ft	$c^2 = 41.34$ m² + 7.34 m²
$c^2 = 524.66$ sq ft	$c^2 = 48.68$ m²
c = **22.91 ft**	c = **6.98 m**

Station 1B:

$c^2 = (17.77\text{ ft})^2 + (8.89\text{ ft})^2$	$c^2 = (5.42\text{ m})^2 + (2.71\text{ m})^2$
$c^2 = 315.77$ sq ft + 79.03 sq ft	$c^2 = 29.38$ m² + 7.34 m²
$c^2 = 394.80$ sq ft	$c^2 = 36.72$ m²
c = **19.87 ft**	c = **6.06 m**

The 4 sides of the trapezium: 50.25 ft, 42.89 ft, 22.91 ft, and 19.87 ft (15.32 m, 13.07 m, 6.98 m, and 6.06 m).

Area of trapezium:

A = ([50.25 ft + 42.89 ft] ÷ 2)	A = ([15.32 m + 13.07 m] ÷ 2)
× ([22.91 ft + 19.87 ft] ÷ 2)	× ([6.98 m + 6.06 m] ÷ 2)
A = (93.14 ft ÷ 2) × (42.78 ft ÷ 2)	A = (28.39 m ÷ 2) × (13.04 m ÷ 2)
A = 46.57 ft × 21.39 ft	A = 14.20 m × 6.52 m
A = **996.13 sq ft**	A = **92.58 m²**

Average depth:

Triangle 2A:

(90.0 ft + 91.67 ft + 92.0 ft) ÷ 3 = 91.22 ft	(27.43 m + 27.94 m + 28.04 m) ÷ 3 = 27.80 m
94.33 ft − 91.22 ft = **<3.11> ft**	28.76 m − 27.80 m = **<0.96> m**

Triangle 1B:

(90.33 ft + 90 ft + 92 ft) ÷ 3 =	(27.53 m + 27.43 m + 28.04 m) ÷ 3 = 27.67 m
94.33 ft − 90.78 ft = **<3.55> ft**	28.76 m − 27.67 m = **<1.09> m**

Trapezium:

(90.0 ft + 92 ft) × 2 ÷ 4 = 91.0 ft	(27.43 m + 28.04 m) × 2 ÷ 4 = 27.74 m
94.33 ft − 91.0 ft = **<3.33> ft**	28.76 m − 27.74 m = **<1.02> m**

Average of areas 3 and 4:

(<3.11> ft + <3.55> ft + <3.33> ft) ÷ 3 = **<3.33> ft**	(<0.96> m + <1.09> m + <1.02> m) ÷ 3 = <1.02> m

Volume of areas 3 and 4:

V = (996.13 sq ft + 172.83 sq ft) × <3.33> ft	V = (92.58 m² + 16.06 m²) × <1.02> m
V = (1168.96 sq ft × <3.33> ft) × 1.20	V = (108.64 m² × <1.02> m) × 1.20
V = (<3892.64> cu ft ÷ 27 cu ft) × 1.20	V = <110.81> m³ × 1.20
V = <144.17> cu yd × 1.20	V = **<132.97> m³**
V = **<173.00> cu yd**	

Total volume all areas of grid 1:

<131.96> cu yd + <173.00> cu yd	<101.34> m³ + <132.97> m³
+ <17.63> cu yd > = **<322.59> cu yd**	+ <13.70> m³ = **<248.01> m³**

Difference between averaging and geometric calculations:

<361.11> cu yd − <322.59> cu yd = <38.52> cu yd	26.82 m + 27.97 m + 27.53 m + 28.73 m = 111.05 m
	28.96 m − 0.2 m = 28.76 m
	28.76 m − 27.76 m = <1.0> m
	<1.0> m × (15.24 m × 15.24 m) =
	<1.0> m × 232.26 m² × 1.20 = **<278.71> m³**
	<278.71> m³ − <248.01> m³ = <30.70> m³

CHART 4–1
Excavating and Grading: Grid Averaging and Breakdown

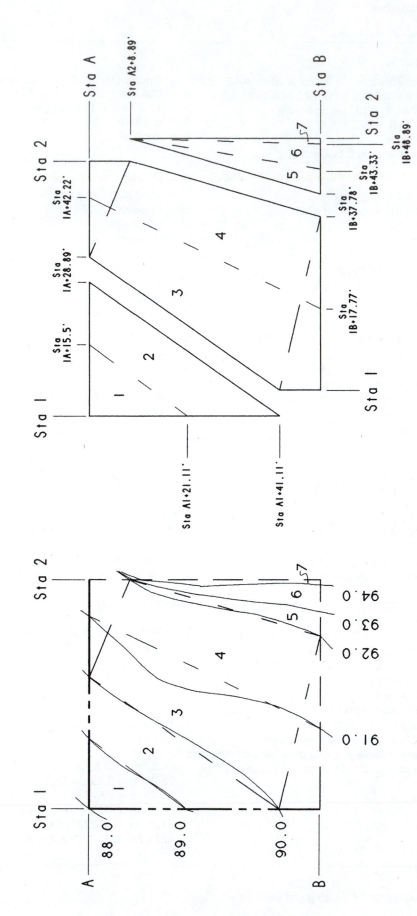

FIGURE 4–7
Geometric Grid Breakdown

identifying grids 1 are 1A, 1B, 2A, and 2B. These are the stations used for the averaging method calculation. The contours that cross the horizontal and vertical lines of the grids are also called stations. The horizontal stations are indicated with the number first, as Sta 1A+15.5′, Sta 1A+28.89′, and Sta 1A+42.22′ (these stations are along the top, line A, of the grid). The vertical points are identified with the letter first, as Sta A1+21.11′, Sta A1+41.11′, and Sta A2+8.89′ (along grid lines 1 and 2). The purpose for the reversal of numbers and letters is so that anyone studying the estimate can pick the proper stations without difficulty. The choice of numbers or letters first is up to the estimator.

When straight lines are drawn from the horizontal points to the vertical points on the grid, geometric planes are shown. In figure 4–7, there are seven figures. Some of the figures can be combined in the estimate because calculating them separately would be time-consuming and make little practical difference in the estimate. For example, areas 1 and 2 can be calculated together as a single unit since combined they make up a right triangle. The same is done for areas 3 and 4, and for 5, 6, and 7. See chart 4–1.

See appendix V, Swell Factors; see also chart 4–1. Included in the calculations is the number 1.20 (120%), which is the **swell factor.** This is a multiplier used to determine the actual quantity of fill required. The swell factor in chart 4–1 includes the original quantity (100%) plus the factor (20%) found in the appendix for the type of soil with which the contractor is working.

This variation in soil quantities is called "loose" soil and results from expansion caused by breaking the soil up and its mixing with air. The loss varies with the type of soil and the compaction requirements. A swell, or expansion, factor must be added to account for the "loose" soil variance. This is especially important for imports and fill soils. For example, the chart in appendix V indicates that dry, sandy loam expands by 20% when cut loose from its virgin origins. This *20% soil expansion* shall be used for all remaining grading and excavating calculations in this chapter.

Difference in Accuracy.   The difference between method 1 and method 2 is the following:

361.11 cu yd − 322.59 cu yd = <38.52cu yd>
278.71 m³ − 248.01 m³ = <30.70 m³>

This difference should cause concern for the estimator since this is only one of twelve grids (approximately the equivalent of 9 grids with the partial grids) to be calculated. Assuming this is the average difference for the whole project, the amount of earth to be moved that could be lost in the estimate is as follows:

9 × <38.52 cu yd> = <346.68 cu yd> or <347 cu yd>
(9 × <30.70 m³> = <276.3 m³>)

The variation in values is due to at least two factors:

1. The averaging method (method 1) does *not* give a true picture of the section.
2. The rounding of numbers can increase or decrease the mathematical values.

Depending upon the computer estimating system used, either method of calculation, that is, averaging or detailed breakdown, may be a part of the program.

The Foundation (Mass) Excavation

See Plans, Sheet S–1, Foundation Plan; also refer to the Specifications. The excavating contractor must also include the additional mass excavation for the 3'-0" crawl space over which the structure is built. In accordance with the Specifications, the contractor must maintain an additional 1'-0" (30.48 cm) around the perimeter of the foundation for working space. When there is no shoring used, a slope of 1:1 is cut to prevent cave-ins. Backfill of a Type II, or equivalent, soil shall be installed against the exterior side of the foundation walls upon completion of the work of all trades.

Labor: Excavating and Grading.   The quantity of material to be moved and the efficiency of the crews and equipment determine both the labor and equipment costs. The efficiency is reduced if the work includes breaking up large boulders or blasting. Special labor and/or equipment such as hoe-rams or blasting crews may be required. Caliche (hard scrabble) is more difficult to work with than sandy loam or clay soils. All of these points of information must be picked up by the estimator from the soils report and/or a job-site visit. Without these facts, a viable estimate of excavating costs cannot be made. According to the Soils Report and the Specifications for the Medical Clinic, the soil is good and there are no problems foreseen with rock or water.

   See figures 4–8a and 4–8b. The composite crew needed for excavating and grading for the Medical Clinic consists of a foreman, 2 equipment operators,

CREW	HOURLY + BURDEN WAGE		% TIME ON JOB/HR	HOURLY RATE
Foreman	$18.32 + $ 2.03		10%	= $ 2.04
Operator (2)	$18.05 + $ 1.80	× 2	45%	= $17.87
Truck Driver (2)	$14.21 + $ 1.58	× 2	22%	= $ 6.95
Grade Checker	$18.32 + $ 2.03		23%	= $ 4.68
Composite Crew Rate:			100%	$31.54/MH

FIGURE 4–8a
Composite Crew Schedule

CREW	HOURLY WAGE + BURDEN
Foreman	$18.32 + $2.03
Operator (2)	($18.05 + $1.80) × 2
Truck Driver (2)	($14.21 + $1.58) × 2
Grade Checker	$18.32 + $2.03
	$86.95 + $10.82 = $97.77
Composite Crew Rate:	$97.77/4 = $24.44

FIGURE 4–8b
Composite Crew Schedule

FIGURE 4–9
Excavating Equipment Costs

EQUIPMENT	USE TIME	UNIT COST	TOTAL
Pickup Truck	3 days	@ $50/wk	= $ 150.00
Water Truck	3 days	@ $192/day	= $ 576.00
CAT Bulldozer	3 days	@ $776/day	= $2,328.00
Compactor	1 day	@ $368/day	= $ 368.00
Equipment Total:			$3,422.00

2 truck drivers, and a grade checker. The productivity rate is 68.33%. The productivity factor is calculated as follows:

$$70\% \div 68.33\% = 1.02$$

Calculating the labor as per the method shown in figure 4–8a, the MH rate for the composite crew is:

$$\$31.54 \times 1.02 = \$32.17/MH$$
$$\$32.17/MH \times 6 \text{ crew members} \times 8 \text{ hr} = \$1,544.16/CD$$

The work takes 3 days to complete. The total labor cost is:

$$\$1,544.16 \times 3 \text{ days} = \$4,632.48 \text{ or } \$4,632.00$$

Per figure 4–8b, the composite crew rate and labor total are:

$$\$27.9 \times 1.02 = \$28.55/MH$$
$$\$28.55/MH \times 6 \text{ crew members} \times 8 \text{ hr} = \$1,370.40/CD$$

The work takes 3 days to complete. The total labor cost is:

$$\$1,370.40 \times 3 \text{ days} = \$4,111.20 \text{ or } \$4,111.00$$

Equipment: Excavating and Grading. *See figure 4–9.* The equipment estimated for the rear parking lot work includes a pickup truck for transportation, a watering truck, a CAT bulldozer, and a self-propelled compactor.

The total cost for labor and equipment is calculated as follows:

$$\$4,633.00 + \$3,422.00 = \$8,055.00$$

(Note: The value or the higher labor cost is used in all instances.)

Paving

See Plans, Sheet C–2, Plot Plan; also see Specifications and chart 4–2. In making estimates for paving, the estimator must note the following: the type and thickness of the base material, the cementitious aggregate, and the surfacing. Finally, the estimator should determine the slope, possibly including any small swale. The finish grades given on a plot plan will indicate the slope, if any. For the Medical Clinic, the finish grade at the structure and the top of the

(Refer to Plans, Sheet C–2.)

Area calculation:

A = 103 lf × 56 lf

A = **5,768 sq ft**

A = 31.39 m × 17.07 m

A = **535.83 m²**

Volume of base material and asphalt (using a dry sand base):

(All calculations include the 20% expansion factor.)

10" (25.4 cm) base:

V = ([5,768 sq ft × 0.83 lf] ÷ 27 cu ft) × 1.20

V = (4,787.44 cu ft ÷ 27 cu ft) × 1.20

V = 177.31 cu yd × 1.20

V = **212.77 or 213 cu yd**

V = (535.83 m² × 0.25 m) × 1.20

V = 133.96 m³ × 1.20

V = **160.75 or 161 m³**

6" (15.24 cm) cementitious base:

V = ([5,768 sq ft × 0.5 lf] ÷ 27 cu ft) × 1.20

V = (2,884 cu ft ÷ 27 cu ft) × 1.20

V = 106.81 cu yd × 1.20

V = **128.17 or 128 cu yd**

V = (535.83 m² × 0.15 m) × 1.20

V = 80.37 m³ × 1.20

V = **96.44 or 97 m³**

4" (10.16 cm) asphalt surfacing:

V = ([5,768 sq ft × 0.33 lf] ÷ 27 cu ft) × 1.20

V = (1,903.44 cu ft ÷ 27 cu ft) × 1.20

V = 70.5 cu yd × 1.20

V = **84.6 or 85 cu yd**

V = (535.83 m² × 0.10 m) × 1.20

V = 53.58 m³ × 1.20

V = **64.30 or 65 m³**

Material breakdown:

(Note: 1 short ton [2,000 lb] = 907.19 kg or .91 metric ton)

Base, ton	= 1.35 ton/cu yd; 1.23 metric ton/0.76 m³
Asphalt, ton	= 1.35 ton/cu yd; 1.23 metric ton/0.76 m³
Aggregate, ton	= 1.35 ton/cu yd; 1.23 metric ton/0.76 m³
Sealer 1 gal covers 50 sq ft; 1 gal	= 1.89 liter

10" base:

213 cu yd × 1.35 = **287.55 or 288 ton**

161 m³ × 1.23 = **198.03 or 198 ton**

6" cementitious aggregate:

128 cu yd × 1.35 = **172.8 or 173 ton**

97 m³ × 1.23 = **119.31 or 120 ton**

4" asphalt surfacing:

85 cu yd × 1.35 = **114.75 or 115 ton**

65 m³ × 1.23 = **79.95 or 80 ton**

Sealer:

5,768 sq ft ÷ 50 sq ft = **115.36 gal**

115.36 gal ÷ 2.2 gal/liter = **52.44 or 53 liter**

CHART 4–2

Asphalt Paving: Rear Parking Lot of Medical Clinic

paving is 94.67′ (28.86 m). The finish grade at the perimeter of the property is 94.33′ (28.75 m). The swale in the paved areas starts at 94.5′ (28.80 m) and slopes to 94.33′ (28.75 m) at the entry approach.

For the Medical Clinic, asphalt concrete paving is specified for all driveways, parking areas, and sidewalks. The Specifications state that all paving areas are to have a 4″ (10.16 cm) surface with a sealer over a 6″ (15.24 cm) cementitious aggregate base over a 10″ (25.40 cm) compacted Type II soil or sand base.

Labor: Paving. *See figure 4–10a and 4–10b, Paving Composite Crew.* The estimated composite crew includes a foreman, 2 equipment operators, 2 truck drivers, and 2 hand laborers. The productivity factor is 1.02, thus:

Method 4–10a:

$32.98 × 1.02 = $33.64/MH

CREW	HOURLY + BURDEN WAGE	% TIME ON JOB/HR	HOURLY RATE
Foreman	$18.45 + $ 1.90	11%	= $ 2.24
Operator (2)	$18.05 + $ 1.80 × 2	35%	= $13.90
Truck Driver (2)	$14.21 + $ 1.58 × 2	19%	= $ 6.00
Hand Labor (2)	$13.42 + $ 2.07 × 2	35%	= $10.84
Composite Crew Rate:		100%	$32.98/MH

FIGURE 4–10a
Paving Composite Crew

CREW	HOURLY WAGE + BURDEN
Foreman	$18.45 + $1.90
Operator (2)	($18.05 + $1.80) × 2
Truck Driver (2)	($14.21 + $1.58) × 2
Grade Checker	($13.42 + $2.07) × 2
	$109.81 + $12.80 = $122.61
Composite Crew Rate:	$122.61/4 = $30.65

FIGURE 4–10b
Composite Crew Schedule

Method 4–10b:

$30.65 × 1.02 = $31.27/MH$

The paving contractor estimates 2 days to complete the work of paving the rear parking lot. The total labor cost for the job is as follows:

Method 4–10a:

$33.64/MH × 8 hr × 7 members × 2 days = $3,767.68 or $3,768.00$

Method 4–10b:

$31.27/MH × 8 hr × 7 members × 2 days = $3,502.24 or $3,502.00$

Equipment: Paving.   *See figure 4–11.* The contractor estimates the necessity for a pickup truck, a grader, a spreader box, a roller, a dump truck, and a seal coat truck. The total labor and equipment cost for the rear parking lot is as follows:

$3,768.00 + $2,640.00 = $6,408.00$

Refer to figures 4–10a and b, figure 4–11, and Chart 4–2. The information in these figures and the chart make up a sample paving estimate of the rear parking lot. Information in them can be combined to make an estimate. The materials are found in the chart, the labor and equipment in the figures. Adding taxes, overhead, and profit would result in a complete estimate. Where taxes are required, the amount taxed may be for materials only or for materials and labor. Local requirements need to be checked.

FIGURE 4–11
Paving Equipment Costs

EQUIPMENT	USE TIME	UNIT COST	TOTAL
Pickup Truck	2 days	@ $76/day	= $ 152.00
Cat 613B	1 day	@ $632/day	= $ 632.00
Layton Box	1 day	@ $120/day	= $ 120.00
Roller, Hyster C350B	2 days	@ $256/day	= $ 512.00
Dump Truck	10 hr	@ $92/hr	= $ 920.00
Oil/Seal Coat Truck	1 day	@ $304/day	= $ 304.00
Equipment Total:			$2,640.00

Landscaping

Costs for all new vegetation, as well as for removal and transplanting of trees and shrubbery, are included in this portion.

See Plans, Sheet C–2, Plot Plan; also see the Specifications. The area to be covered with landscape soil is determined by deducting all structures, paving, and concrete from the project including the site improvement areas along the sidewalk and berms at the street. The quantity (depth) of topsoil required is indicated in the Specifications.

CHAPTER EXERCISES

1. Following the example in chart 4–1 for the Medical Clinic, estimate the quantity of cut and/or fill required for Grid 6 on figure 4–5 and Plans, Sheet C–1, using the averaging method

2. Estimate the quantity of cut and/or fill required for Grid 6 using the geometric configurations formed by the contours. The station-to-station measurements can be to the nearest whole foot.

3. Indicate the difference in quantities between the answers found in questions 1 and 2.

4. Determine the cubic yards of earth to be removed for the mass excavation of the crawl space area under the Medical Clinic structure. See Plans, Sheet S–1, and the Specifications.

5. Estimate the quantities of material required for the *side parking area* and driveway included in the area. *Do not estimate the whole driveway or the sidewalks.* Break down the quantities as shown in the chapter. See Plans, Sheet C–2.

6. Per the specifications in appendix III and the plot plan (Plans, Sheet C–2), estimate the quantity of topsoil required for the Medical Clinic.

7. The productivity factor is 0.89. Determine the crew labor cost for excavating, grading, and paving for the Medical Clinic. The work takes 5 weeks to complete. The excavating and grading takes 3 1/2 weeks. The paving takes 1 1/2 weeks. Use the composite crew rates given in the chapter, in figures 4–8 and 4–10.

8. Determine the materials required for installation of the alternate pad placed under a concrete slab. The slab is 58'-8″ × 41'-4″ (17.88 m × 12.60 m). The specification, per appendix IV, Project Manual, Division 1, Section 01030, for this alternate is as follows:

Alternate 1.

An alternate concrete slab and footing per drawings, identified as S-1A, shall be included with the bid. The concrete specifications shall read:

02100 Site Preparation. A base pad is to extend 5 lineal feet beyond the length and width of the slab and shall be 8″ (20.32 cm) thick. The pad shall be with the Federal DOT Specification type E aggregate soil mix (Type II) or a sand base compacted to 95% (ASTM standard).

CHAPTER 5

Concrete

Division 3

GENERAL INFORMATION

Types of Concrete

Concrete is one of the major, and most widely used, materials found in construction today. It is so widely used because of its durability, strength, watertightness, and resistance to abrasion. Concrete is the foundation material for masonry units, mortar, grout, precast concrete units, and many specialties, some of which will be discussed in this chapter.

Concrete is divided into two major classifications, structural and nonstructural. These two classifications are further broken down by weight per cubic foot and compressive strength.

Structural concrete installations include areas such as footings and foundation walls, slabs-on-grade, concrete pilings, columns, above-grade floor structures, wall and roof structures, and highway and bridge construction. Such installations are controlled by rigid codes and regulations. Specifications are provided regarding compressive strength, reinforcement, and use. Regular inspections are performed by the owner and/or the local building authorities. Tests are made daily to check material quality, strength, and content, which are laid out in the specifications for a project.

Nonstructural concrete is usually lightweight. Lightweight concrete is used for decorative plant-ons such as arabesques, exterior window and door trim, sonotube columns, balusters, railings, above-grade lightweight floors, stairwells, and specially formed and designed concrete such as statuary, corbels, and cornices. Nonstructural concrete does not require the rigid codes, regulations, or specifications of structural concrete.

Regular (normal) weight concrete, used in all structural installations below, on, and/or above grade, weighs approximately 150 lbs/cu ft (68.04 kg/0.28 m^3).

Lightweight concrete ranges from 20 lbs/cu ft (9.07 kg/0.28 m^3) to 70 lbs/cu ft (31.75 kg/0.28 m^3) for insulating lightweight concrete, 115 lbs/cu ft (52.16 kg/0.28 m^3) for structural lightweight concrete, and 115 lbs/cu ft (52.16 kg/0.28 m^3) to 130 lbs/cu ft (58.97 kg/0.28 m^3) for semilightweight concrete installations.

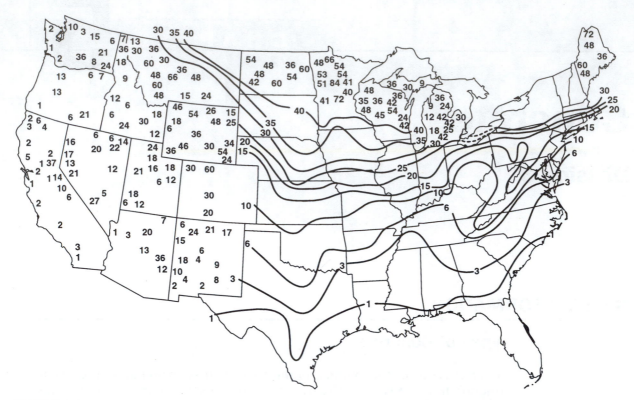

FIGURE 5–1
Footing Depths, in inches, in the United States

Compressive strength determines how much weight or impact concrete can withstand before cracking or breaking. The minimum compressive strength for residential construction is 2,000 psi (907.18 kg/6.45 cm^2); for light commercial construction, 2,500 psi (1,113.98 kg/6.45 cm^2) to 3,000 psi (1,360.77 kg/6.45 cm^2); and for major commercial, high-rise, or industrial construction, 3,500 psi (1,587.57 kg/6.45 cm^2) or more. The strength of concrete can be increased with the use of additives or reinforcement. This topic will be covered in more detail later in this chapter.

Footing Depth

See figure 5–1. Weather conditions, together with local codes and ordinances, determine the depth of concrete footings. A study of the map in figure 5–1 shows that footings in the northern areas of the country must be considerably deeper than those located in the southern and southwestern areas. In warmer climates, exceptions to the footing depths occur in higher altitudes. In northern climates and mountainous areas, full basements or under-floor crawl spaces are built to compensate for the frost-line requirements.

Formwork

Requirements for below-grade concrete construction and excavation shoring are very similar. Building and safety codes require that formwork in excavations be installed where the soil is too soft to support itself regardless of depth,

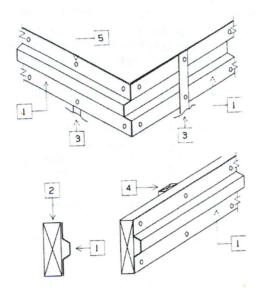

KEYNOTES:
1. Key screed form
2. 2x backing - continuous
3. Lt ga metal stake @ 2'-0" o.c.
4. 2x stake @ 2'-0" o.c
5. Knock-out for fastening
   stakes @ 6" o.c.

FIGURE 5–2
Flatwork Forms

where the excavation is 5'–0" (1.52 m) or more deep, or where the excavation may interfere with the foundation or wall support of another structure. For these reasons, concrete forms within such excavations must conform to local building safety codes and regulations.

See figure 5–2. Forms used for on-grade work such as curbs, gutters, and sidewalks and for on-grade slab construction are referred to as the **flatwork** forms. There are three types of flatwork forms:

1. Heavy-gauge steel for curb, gutter, and sidewalk construction
2. Light-gauge steel for slab construction
3. All wood, such as redwood bender board or a combination of wood and light-gauge steel

Wooden forms are initially the least expensive and can be used four or five times, if handled carefully, before requiring replacement. Metal forms are much more expensive but will last for many installations and are repairable. The type of work the contractor does dictates the material that would be the best suited to the company's needs.

Gang forms for below-grade construction may be made from wood planking, plywood, plyform, rolled steel sheets (boxes), or combinations of these materials. Trenching or mass excavations requiring shoring commonly use steel sheets or portable steel "boxes." Either one requires manually or hydraulically operated jacks, placed at mid-height and at the top of the excavation, to keep the supporting walls rigid.

Wood plank systems, constructed with 2 × 12 (5.08 cm × 30.48 cm) planks placed vertically and supported with 2 × 4 (5.08 cm × 10.16 cm) or 2 × 6 (5.08 cm × 15.24 cm) single or double walers and bracing, are used primarily for on-grade applications and may extend for a maximum height of 8' (2.44 m). This system may also be installed around the perimeter of mass excavations or on both sides of trenches or concrete walls.

The **plyform** system, used primarily for concrete wall construction, is made from perforated 4 × 8 sheets of treated plywood, 3/4" (1.91 cm) or 1" (2.54 cm)

thick. The perforations are spaced at 1'-0" (30.48 cm) or 2'-0" (60.69 cm) intervals horizontally and vertically, and are sized to allow the installation of
1/2" (1.27 cm) or 5/8" (1.59 cm) DIA threaded boltlike rods, called **formties**
or **snap-ties.** The formties are available in lengths of 12" (30.48 cm), 16"
(40.64 cm), 18" (45.72 cm), or 24" (60.96 cm), with nuts and washers. The
length used is dependent upon the thickness of the wall. They are installed
through the holes in the plyform and tightened on the inside and outside of
the wall form. Like the plank system or regular plywood, the plyform is supported with walers and bracing.

The ties may also serve as part of the reinforcement within the finished,
cured concrete wall. The rods are malleable steel and can be broken off. The
holes left in the concrete when the forms are removed are repaired with a
quick-curing plastic concrete mix or left exposed for aesthetic reasons.

High-rise concrete construction makes use of the **slip gang form** (also
called the **flying form**). The form, made of wood and steel construction, is
braced and bolted to a structure so that all reinforcement, other embeds, and
concrete may be placed inside the form. After a cure period, the braces are loos-
ened and the slip form is raised to the next level by crane and the bracing reinstalled. This procedure is repeated until the work has been completed.

Built-in Controls

The purpose of controls in concrete is for the prevention of buckling, cracking, curling, and spalling. The built-in controls considered here include expansion joints, contraction joints, steel reinforcement, and concrete
additives.

Joints.   Expansion joints are installed as separations between adjoining
sections of a concrete slab to allow for movement caused by the coefficient of
expansion of unlike materials. Expansion joints include the control joint,
keyed joints, isolation joints, and moisture-control joints. No expansion joints
should be separated by more than 400 sq ft (37.16 m^2) of slab area.

1.   A **control joint** is a separation of concrete such as found in sidewalk
or large slab construction. The joint extends the complete depth of the concrete and may or may not include a separation strip. The strip may be a redwood bender board (sidewalks), asphalt or pitch poured into the joint, a
foam-rubber filler and weatherproof sealant, or a neoprene strip.

2.   The **keyed joint,** also known as a key-cold joint, allows the concrete
to form so that concrete placed adjacent to an existing slab, foundation wall,
or footing "keys" (locks) onto the existing concrete. A thin strip of asphalt-
impregnated polystyrene foam, polyethylene sheet material, light-gauge
building paper, or foam rubber filler may be inserted between the existing and
new concrete immediately prior to the adjoining placement.

If the key joint is placed in the top of a footing upon which a foundation
wall is placed along with a barrier (polyethylene, neoprene, and so on), the
joint is referred to as a **water stop.**

3.   **Isolation joints** are used in the same manner as the standard control joints except that they are installed to separate differing thicknesses of
concrete or differing materials, such as a masonry wall, immediately adjacent
to the concrete. Isolation joints are used as seismic control joints to prevent

breaking of the concrete as a result of differential movement, such as earthquakes can produce. A 1/2″ (3.81 cm) neoprene strip or foam rubber filler and sealant is installed in the joint.

4.   A **moisture-control joint** is similar to the isolation joint. The joint, like the water stop, prevents moisture from penetrating into a structure from the exterior. The moisture-control joint is installed where an adjoining concrete surface such as a sidewalk abuts the structure. Where isolation and moisture control are required at the same point, the moisture-control joint may be used. Like the other control joints, this type is also filled with neoprene strips or foam rubber filler and sealant.

Steel plates and galvanized, cold-rolled steel strips are used as control joints where there is a separation of materials, where there is a change in exposure to the earth or atmosphere, or where dissimilar materials abut. Examples of such joints may be found where the ends of a bridge adjoin the highway approach or on roof structures where seismic control or variations in structures exist.

The **contraction joint** is better known as the **saw-cut.** It is a groove cut into a concrete surface to create a weakened plane, which aids in controlling cracking as the result of imposed loads. An imposed load may be heavy industrial machinery fixed to the concrete or moving vehicular traffic such as forklifts or trucks. The joint is made in the concrete the width of the saw blade(s) to a depth of from 3/8″ (0.95 cm) to 1″ (2.54 cm), dependent upon the concrete thickness. A foam rubber filler and sealant may be used to smooth the surface on the wider cuts (more than 1/2″ [1.27 cm]). The saw-cuts are usually made perpendicular to the expansion joints in smaller slabs similar to the alternate slab for the Medical Clinic, as shown in Sheet S–1A of the plans for the Medical Clinic. Saw-cuts may be parallel to the expansion joints in both directions in larger multiple placement slab construction. As with expansion joints, no contraction joints should be separated by more than 400 sq ft (37.16 m^2) of slab area.

Reinforcement.   *See appendix V, Reinforcement Bar and Welded Wire Fabric.* Use of reinforcement is also a control for concrete construction. **Reinforcement steel** and certain concrete **additives** can both be used for reinforcement. Reinforcement steel is installed prior to the concrete placement. An additive used to increase the compressive strength of the concrete is a chemical material included in the concrete mix.

Rebar.   Reinforcement steel includes a steel bar, called rebar. Rebar is available in varying sizes and shapes. #2 and #3 rebar, the smallest sizes, are normally a smooth finish. #4 through #11 rebar are deformed (having knobs or ridges) shapes. Sizes #14 and #18 are also available in deformed shapes. Any in-between or larger sizes are available only upon special order.

Another identifying characteristic of rebar is its **tensile strength.** This refers to how much stress a piece of rebar can resist before it breaks. The stress-point break is measured in kilopounds per square inch (1,000 psi or 453.59 kg/6.54 cm^2), abbreviated as kps (nicknamed "kips"). The four common strengths of rebar are 40 kps (40 grade), 60 kps (60 grade), 75 kps (75 grade) and 80 kps (80 grade). Rebar may be installed in a pattern similar to welded-wire fabric, where unusually heavy traffic conditions exist such as heavy equipment parking areas, industrial fixed machinery locations, loading docks, multistory parking structures, highways, bridges, and tunnels.

Welded-Wire Fabric (WWF).   Installation of welded-wire fabric (WWF) is recommended wherever continuous traffic of 3,000 lbs (1,360.77 kg/6.54 cm^2) or more is present. Although WWF is used primarily with on-grade concrete slabs, it may be used in lieu of rebar in some areas such as for warehouse or loading dock construction. WWF is cheaper and easier to install than rebar because the wire is lighter in weight than the smallest rebar and is available in rolls or sheets, depending on size, spacing, and quantities required.

Embeds.   Rebar, WWF, anchor bolts, framing hold-downs, anchor straps, and any other such items placed in the concrete are embeds. Some items are supplied by other trades to be installed by the concrete contractor during the layout or placement. Still others, such as plumbing pipes and electrical conduit within the slabs or foundation walls, are installed by the responsible trade prior to the concrete placement.

Additives.   **Additives** are chemicals or minerals added to the concrete mix for various purposes. The materials may be added at a ready-mix plant, an on-site batch plant, or by hand on site. A chemical additive can change the texture, strength, rate of curing time, or finish of concrete; can stabilize the reaction between destructive water conditions (e.g., salt water) and concrete; or can "plasticize" or "liquefy" the concrete mix. Mineral mixtures used for texturing such as a heavy aggregate or terrazzo are also considered additives.

The location of the project and the time of year determine whether or not an additive (chemical) may be required to achieve the proper strength and finish of concrete. Frost conditions require additives, such as an accelerator like calcium chloride. In desert regions, a retarder, such as calcium lignosulfonate, is likely to be used to slow the curing process. Care must be taken in the choice of additive so as not to harm the concrete. The wrong choice of additive or quantity of additive can cause problems, which arise from conditions about which the engineer may not have been aware.

Concrete

A mixture of cement, sand, and/or aggregate and water is used to produce concrete. The most commonly used cement for construction is known as Portland cement. It is made from limestone and clay that have been intensely heated (2,700° F or 1,500° C). Portland cement in itself can have some of the desired characteristics of concrete that can otherwise be obtained with additives, such as high early strength, sulfate-resistance, and low-heat, or slow, cure. These characteristics result from the materials used in the manufacture of Portland cement.

The mixture of cement to sand and aggregate and the water-cement ratio determine the compressive strength and curing time of concrete. The normal material mixtures range from a 1:2:4 (one [1] part cement, two [2] parts sand, and four [4] parts aggregate) to a 1:2:6 (one [1] part cement, two [2] parts sand, and six [6] parts aggregate). The water-cement ratio is determined by the quantity of water per unit (bag) of cement. One bag of cement weighs approximately 94 lbs (206.8 kg). The compressive strength of concrete is inversely proportionate to the water ratio: the more water used, the lower the compressive strength of the concrete.

Cast-in Place (CIP) Concrete.   Concrete that is neither prefabricated nor cured prior to delivery to a project is referred to as **cast-in-place (CIP).** CIP may be supplied by a ready-mix concrete company or mixed in a batch plant on the job. The concrete may be placed from a ready-mix truck, from a spreading machine such as used for highway construction, pumped hundreds of feet into the air using special pump equipment, or lifted by crane in containers with 2 to 5 cu yd (1.53 m^3 to 3.82 m^3) capacity to the top of tall structures. Bridges, above-grade floor, and roof concrete construction also use CIP concrete according to the type of construction.

Concrete used to encase steel beams and columns, sprayed-on concrete fire protection, or concrete installed in normally inaccessible places may be classed as CIP concrete. The procedures, setup time, and materials required for installing concrete in these difficult areas must be considered more carefully than for normal concrete placement.

Precast Concrete.   Concrete that is formed, placed, and cured in a concrete manufacturing plant prior to shipment to a project is referred to as **precast concrete.** Precast products, like all other concrete, may be either structural or nonstructural.

Precast beams or decking for bridges, parking structures, above-grade floor and roof hollow core, "T" (tee), double "T" (double tee), or plank slabs are examples of structural precast concrete products often used in lieu of CIP concrete placed on steel decking. The concrete decking can be grouted, caulked, or otherwise sealed and finished. The decorative, lightweight, nonstructural products previously mentioned are also manufactured, cured, and sold as a finished product directly by the manufacturer.

Concrete Tensioning.   *See figure 5–3.* Two special processes are used for reinforcement of precast concrete beams or planks for bridge or other elevated locations. These are called **pretensioning** and **posttensioning.** Pretensioning is the process of applying tension to the embedded reinforcement so that the unit acquires a specific stress on the unit prior to its shipment or use. Posttensioning is the same process, but it is done after the unit is in place on a project.

Tilt-up Walls.   Tilt-up walls are actually a combination of CIP and precast concrete construction. The walls may be formed at a precast plant and shipped to the project or may be constructed at the project on a cured on-grade slab or on treated plywood forms laid out and leveled on the ground. The on-site process uses a nonadherent additive applied to the slab and/or plywood forms so that the concrete may be placed and cured without adhering to the base materials. All reinforcement and embeds are installed prior to the concrete placement. When the concrete is cured, the forms are removed, and the wall is lifted by crane and set into place. The walls are braced with adjustable steel braces, which remain in place until the main roof structure is properly fastened. While awaiting the roof structure, carpenters and welders work to place the walls in proper position, set ledgers and fasteners, and prepare for caulking and sealing. The edges of the on-grade slab are then prepared for the remaining concrete and for the addition of moisture-control or isolation joints.

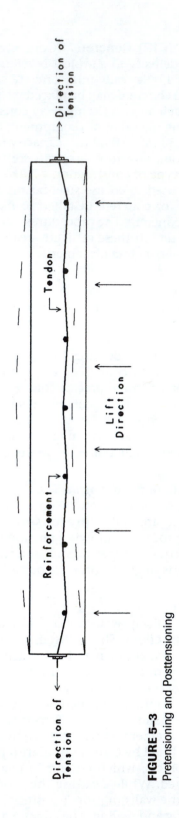

FIGURE 5-3
Pretensioning and Posttensioning

SCOPE OF WORK

From appendix IV, Project Manual, Division 3, Concrete, the Specifications for the Medical Clinic are as follows. This information will be used in the estimate in the next section of this chapter.

Division 3: Concrete

03000 Scope of Work

Division 1 and the General Conditions are considered a part of this division. All labor, material and equipment necessary to complete all concrete work including formwork, reinforcing and cement finish shall be furnished by the concrete contractor.

03100 Concrete Formwork

All labor materials and equipment necessary for the installation of footing and foundation wall formwork shall include steel stakes, 3'-0" (0.91 m) long for footing form support, 2× treated lumber or 1" (min) (2.54 cm) treated plywood for footing forms, 3/4" (min) (1.91 cm) plyform for wall forms, formties and any other accessories necessary for proper construction of the foundation walls and footings.

03200 Reinforcement

All rebar shall be grade 60 (60 kps). Rebar shall be 2-#4 laid horizontally and continuous in footings with 48 bar diameters at all laps. Rebar shall be installed on chairs 3" (7.62 cm) from bottom of footing. Corners shall have 2-#4 rebar, 4'-0" (1.22 m) long, bent 90° at the center, and shall extend 2'-0" (0.61 m) each way from the corner. 1-#5 rebar shall be installed vertically in foundation walls at 4'-0" O/C (1.22 m) horizontally with 6"(15.24 cm) hook tied to footing rebar. Bar length shall extend to 3"(7.62 cm) below top of wall. No rebar shall be heat bent. All rebar shall be installed and inspected prior to placement of concrete.

03300 Cast-in-place Concrete

Footings and foundation walls are to be 3,000 psi (1,360.77 kg/6.45 cm^2) ready-mix concrete per ASTM C94. Type III cement shall be used. Concrete shall be tested at the expense of the owner at 3 days, 7 days and 28 days in accordance with ASTM C31 and ASTM C150. If any of the tests fail, the contractor shall, at its own expense, make all necessary repairs and/or replacements.

Concrete components shall be Portland cement, one brand; aggregate-fine sand and maximum 3/4" (1.91 cm) DIA coarse gravel free from other deleterious substances; potable water.

Admixtures permitted shall be:

1. air-entrained agent per ASTM C260
2. hardener and dustproofer—Lapodith or equal
3. nonslip additive—Durafax or equal
4. nonshrink additive—Sika Set or equal

03400 Precast Concrete

Piers and pier pads are to be precast concrete products that are
supplied by the manufacturer to be installed by the concrete
contractor. Pier pads shall have 2-#4 rebar each way. The rebar
shall have a clearance of 2″ (5.08 cm) from each end of the pad
and shall be embedded 1 1/2″ (3.81 cm) below surface of concrete.
The vertical rebar shall be so placed so as to be perpendicular
to the horizontal rebar. The rebar height shall end 3″ (7.62 cm)
below top of pier. The 6″ (15.24 cm) hook shall be tied to the
horizontal pier pad rebar at each vertical rebar. Piers and pier
pads shall be aligned to support the beams as shown on the plans.

The concrete contractor shall build into the concrete all
materials furnished by others and shall secure same: including
plumbing, electrical conduit, concrete inserts, anchors, hangers,
hold-downs, sleeving for piping, etc., when and where required by
the other trades.

End of Division

THE ESTIMATE

The estimate for concrete includes all formwork, reinforcement, and both precast and concrete piers and CIP concrete for a portion of the foundation of the
Medical Clinic. There are alternates that affect the structural beam supports, as
well as an alternate for slab construction.

See figure 5–4. The form in figure 5–4 is a quote sheet requesting material
costs relating to concrete. The sample is for the Medical Clinic foundation wall

BASIC ESTIMATING, LTD	Estimating Plus Bill of Matl's Concrete	8-13-96 10:42 am	Page 1
DESCRIPTION	TAKEOFF QTY	ORDER QTY	UNIT PRICE
Conc: Concrete Prod			
Regular Concrete 3000 psi	7.00 cuyd	7.00 cuyd	_____
Conc: Form Material			
2 × 8 Random Length	168.00 lnft	168.00 lnft	_____
2 × 6 Random Length	516.00 lnft	516.00 lnft	_____
Forms–Patent System	264.00 sqft	264.00 sqft	_____
Steel Stakes At Forms ¾″	45.00 each	45.00 each	_____
Nails–16d common	2.00 keg	2.00 keg	_____
Conc: Rebar/WireMesh			
Rebar #4 Grade 60	141.00 lnft	148.05 lnft	_____
No. 4 × 5' Long Dowel	12.00 each	12.00 each	_____
Conc: Snapties			
Snaptie 12 in. (Generic)	240.00 each	240.00 each	_____

FIGURE 5–4
Bill of Materials (Quote Sheet)

and footing at the east wall only. The spreadsheet from which this quote sheet is derived is a regular computerized estimate, which includes materials, labor, and equipment.

See Plans, Sheet S–1, Foundation Plan; see also the specifications in Division 3, above. The foundation plan is the base plan for the Medical Clinic. Included are footings, foundation walls, concrete piers, and concrete pier pads. The piers and pier pads are precast concrete products made according to the specifications and plans.

Note that the concrete sidewalks, entry approaches, curb, and gutter are shown on the plot plan, Sheet C–2. These are site improvements to be installed by others or that are already existing. These site improvements are not a part of the bid. There is no trenching included in this estimate. The excavating contractor has completed the mass excavation for the foundation.

Materials

The materials for the estimate include all formwork, reinforcement, concrete, and the accessories necessary for a complete job. To perform the estimate in the best manner, follow the guidelines provided in chapter 3.

Formwork.   *See Plans, Sheet S–1, Foundation Plan, Detail 10–F/S–1; see also chart 5–1.* In accordance with the details in the drawing and the specifications for the Medical Clinic, the foundation wall extends 8" (20.32 cm) above rough grade; there is to be a 4" (10.16 cm) landscape fill over rough grade, starting 4" (10.16 cm) below T.O.W. The overall depth from the bottom of the footing to the top of the wall is 4"-0" (1.22 m). There are two ways the installation may be done:

1. As per detail 10-F/S-1, the normal footing and wall forms are used. This is the construction specified.
2. If the excavation is exposed for too long a period, or the earth is unstable, shoring must be used.

Footing Forms and Blocking.   The footing is 1'–0" (30.48 cm) deep. The estimate may include either 2—2×6 (2—5.08 cm × 15.24 cm) planks (random lengths) stacked on end or 1—2×12 (1—5.08 cm × 30.48 cm) plank (random lengths). The planks are fastened to 3'-0" (0.91 m) long wood or steel stakes spaced at 2'-0" O/C (0.61 m). Horizontal braces are installed to increase the stability of the footing forms. Blocking is also spaced at 2'-0" O/C (0.61 m).

Wall Forms and Formties.   *See Plans, Sheet S–1, Foundation Plan, Detail 10-F/S-1.* The plyform system is used for wall forms. In accordance with the keynotes in the plan, the perforations and formties are spaced 1'-0" O/C (30.48 cm) each way.

Walers and Bracing.   Detail 10-F/S-1 on Sheet S–1 shows two walers (or wales) required. One is installed with the top row of formties (snapties), and the other is installed with the lower row of formties. Although not shown, there is a 2× diagonal bracing, a maximum of 6'-0" (1.83 m) long (maximum), at 4'-0" (1.22 m) O/C on each side of the wall.

Making a Choice.   Detail 10-F/S-1 on Sheet S–1 indicates the wall and footing are formed at the same time. The contractor may choose to install the forms

Footing forms, 41'-0" (12.5 m) east wall, no shoring required
(Refer to Plans, Sheet S-1, Detail F/S-1. Calculations have a 5% waste factor.)

Length of 2'-0" (0.61 m) wide footing w/10" (0.25 m) thick wall:

2 lf − 0.83 lf = 1.17 lf

41 lf + 1.17 lf = 42.17 lf or 42'-2"

0.61 m − 0.25 m = 0.36 m

12.5 + 0.36 m = 12.86 m

2×8 (5.08 cm × 20.32 cm) planks:

(42.17 lf + [42.17 lf - 4 lf]) × 2 =

(42.17 lf + 38.17 lf) × 2 =

80.34 lf × 2 = 160.68 lf

160.68 × 1.05 = **168.71 or 170 lf**

(12.85 m + [12.85 m − 1.22 m]) × 2 =

(12.85 m + 11.63 m) × 2 =

24.48 m × 2 = 48.96

48.96 m × 1.05 = **51.40 or 52 m**

4'×8' (1.22 m × 2.44 m) plywood forms in lieu of 2×8 (5.08 cm × 20.32 cm) planks:

80.34 lf × 1.33 lf = 106.85 sq ft

106.85 sq ft ÷ 32 sq ft = 3.34 sheets

3.34 × 1.05 = **3.51 or 4 sheets**

24.5 m × 0.41 m = 10.04 m²

10.04 m² ÷ 2.97 m² = 4.38 sheets

3.38 × 1.05 = **3.54 or 4 sheets**

2×4 (5.08 cm × 10.16 cm) wood stakes or steel stakes @ 2 lf (0.61 m) OC:

(42.17 lf ÷ 2 lf) + 1 = 22 stakes

(38.17 lf ÷ 2 lf) + 1 = 21 stakes

(12.85 m ÷ 0.61 m) + 1 stake = 22 stakes

(11.63 m ÷ 0.61 m) + 1 stake = 21 stakes

21 stakes + 22 stakes = **43 stakes**

3'-0" (0.91 m) wood stakes only:

43 × 3 lf × 1.05 = **135.45 or 136 lf**

43 × 0.91 m × 1.05 = **41.09 or 41 m**

**Wall forms for 10" (20.32 cm) thick × 41'-0" × 3'-4" (0.25 m × 12.5 m × 1.01 m) east wall,
w/4'×8' (1.22 m × 2.44 m) plywood or plyform (including 4" [10.16 cm] for spacers at top of wall):**

Area of wall (both sides):

(41.0 lf + [41.0 lf − 1.67 lf]) × 3.33 lf =

(41.0 lf + 39.33 lf) × 3.33 lf =

80.33 lf × 3.33 lf = 267.5 sq ft

267.5 sq ft ÷ 32 sq ft = 8.36 sheets

8.36 × 1.05 = **8.78 or 9 sheets**

(12.5 m + [12.5 − 0.51 m]) × 1.01 m =

(12.5 m + 11.99 m) × 1.01 m =

24.49 m × 1.01 m = 24.73 m²

24.73 m² ÷ 2.98 m² = 8.30 sheets

8.30 × 1.05 = **8.72 or 9 sheets**

Formties for plyform @ 1 lf (30.48 cm) ea way starting 6" (15.24 cm) from ends and top and bottom:

39.33 lf − 1 lf = 38.33 lf or 38 spaces

38 + 1 = 39 ties horizontally

3.0 lf − 1 lf = 2 spaces

2 + 1 = 3 ties vertically

39 × 3 = **117 ties**

11.99 m − 0.30 m = 11.69 m

11.69 m ÷ 0.30 m = 38.97 or 39 ties horizontally

0.91 m − 0.30 m = 0.61 m

0.61 m ÷ 0.30 = 2 spaces + 1 = 3 ties vertically

39 × 3 = **117 ties**

2×4 (5.08 cm × 10.16 cm) spacers @ 4 lf (1.22 m) OC (@ top of footing and top of wall):

Top of footing:

40.17 (avg) ÷ 4 lf = 10.04 or 10 spaces

10 + 1 = 11 pcs

11 × 2 lf × 1.05 = 23.1 or 24 lf

Top of wall:

39.33 lf ÷ 4 lf = 9.83 or 10 spaces

10 +1 = **11 pcs**

11 × 0.83 lf × 1.05 = **9.59 or 10 lf**

12.24 m (avg) ÷ 1.22 m = 10.03 or 10 spaces

10 + 1 = 11 pcs

11 × 0.61 m × 1.05 = **7. 04 or 8 m**

11.99 m ÷ 1.22 m = 9.83 or 10 spaces

10 + 1 = **11 pcs**

11 × 0.25 m × 1.05 = **2.89 or 3 m**

2×6 (5.08 cm ×15.24 cm) wales top and bottom both sides:

80.33 lf × 2 × 1.05 = **168.69 or 170 lf**

24.49 m × 2 × 1.05 = **51.43 or 52 m**

2×4 (5.08 cm × 10.16 cm) diagonal bracing 6 lf (1.82 m) long @ 4 lf (1.22 m) OC:

80.33 lf ÷ 4 lf = 20 spaces

20 + 1 = 21 pcs

21 × 6 lf × 1.05 = 132.3 or 133 lf

24.49 m ÷ 1.22 m = 20 spaces

20 + 1 = 21 pcs

21 × 1.83 m × 1.05 = 40.35 or 41 m

CHART 5–1
Concrete Forms: East Wall Footing

Footing forms:
2×8 (5.08 cm × 20.32 cm) footing **planks** (interior side of footing only):
    38.17 lf × 2 × 1.05 = **80.15 or 80 lf**   11.63 m × 2 × 1.05 = **24.42 or 25 m**
2×4 (5.08 × 10.16) wood or steel footing **stakes** @ 2 lf (0.61 m) O.C.:
    38.17 lf ÷ 2 lf = 19.08 or 19 spaces   11.63 m ÷ 0.61 m = 19.06 or 19 spaces
    19 + 1 = 20 stakes   19 + 1 = 20 stakes
    20 × 3 lf × 1.05 = **63 or 64 lf**   20 × 0.91 m × 1.05 = **19.11 or 20 m**

Wall forms, wall + footing + 2×4 (5.08 cm × 10.16 cm) spacer size = 4.33 lf (1.32 m) high:
2×12 (5.08 cm × 30.48 cm) **planks** placed vertically (exterior wall facing only):
    42.17 lf ÷ 1 lf = 42.17 or 42 spaces   12.85 m ÷ 0.30 m = 42.83 or 42 spaces
    42 + 1 = 43 planks   42 + 1 = 43 planks
    43 × 4.33 lf = **186.19 lf**   43 × 1.32 m = **56.76 m**
2×12 (5.08 cm × 30.48 cm) **planks** placed vertically—footing excluded (interior wall facing only):
    39.33 lf ÷ 1 lf = 39.33 or 39 spaces   11.99 m ÷ 0.30 m = 39.97 or 39 spaces
    39 + 1 = 40 planks   39 + 1 = 40 planks
    40 × 3.33 lf = **133.2 lf**   40 × 1.01 m = **40.4 m**

Total planking:
    (186.19 lf + 133.2 lf) × 1.05 = **335.36 or 336 lf**   (56.76 m + 40.4 m) × 1.05 = **102.02 or 102 m**
4'×8' (1.22 m × 2.44 m) treated **plywood** (exterior wall facing only):
    42.17 lf × 4.33 lf = 182.6 sq ft   12.85 m × 1.32 m = 16.96 m²
    182.6 sq ft ÷ 32 sq ft × 1.05 = **5.99 or 6 sheets**   16.92 m² ÷ 2.98 m² = **5.68 or 6 sheets**
4'×8' (1.22 m × 2.44 m) treated **plywood** (interior wall facing only):
    39.33 lf × 3.33 lf = 130.97 sq ft   11.99 m × 1.01 m = 12.11 m²
    130.97 sq ft ÷ 32 sq ft × 1.05 = **4.30 or 5 sheets**   12.11 m² ÷ 2.98 m² × 1.05 = **4.27 or 5 sheets**

Total plywood:
    6 + 5 = **11 sheets**

2×4 (5.08 cm × 10.16 cm) spacers - footings and top of wall:
    same as in chart 5-1

2×4 (5.08 cm × 10.16 cm) wales (interior side only):
    39.33 lf × 2 × 1.05 = **82.59 or 83 lf**   11.99 m × 2 × 1.05 = **25.17 or 26 m**

2×4 × 6 lf (5.08 cm × 10.16 cm × 1.83 m) diagonal bracing @ 4'-0" (1.22 m)
O.C. (required on 1 side only):
    39.33 lf ÷ 4 ft = 9.83 or 9 spaces   11.99 m ÷ 1.22 m = 9.83 or 9 spaces
    9 + 1 = 10 pcs   9 + 1 = 10 pcs
    10 × 6 lf × 1.05 = **63 or 64 lf**   10 × 1.83 m × 1.05 = **19.20 or 20 m**

CHART 5–2
Shoring: East Wall

in one operation as per the drawing or install the wall forms after the footing is placed and cured. Which is more cost effective? Will time be saved by doing all the forms at one time? Is the carpenter available to return to do the forms after the footing is cured? The decision is the responsibility of the estimator and/or contractor. In either case, the concrete for the footing must be placed and left to cure before the concrete for the wall can be placed.

See Plans, Sheet S–1, detail G 9; see also chart 5–2. An alternate installation procedure may be required using shoring along the perimeter of the mass excavation to maintain straight and solid wall construction. Treated plywood or planking is used. Treated plywood is used in lieu of the plyform for the interior side of the wall and at the footing. Formties cannot be used for this installation. As a result, wood 2×4 (5.08 cm × 10.16 cm) spacers are installed at a minimum 4'-0" O/C (1.22 m) along the top of the forms to hold the wall rigid

(Refer to Plans, Sheet S–1, Detail 10-H/S-1.)

Footing (2-#4 rebar - continuous w/48 DIA laps):

(42.17 lf + 38.17 lf) ÷ 2 = 40.17 lf	(12.85 m + 11.63 m) ÷ 2 = 12.24 m
40.17 lf × 2 = 80.34 lf	12.24 m × 2 = 24.48 m
80.34 ÷ 20 lf = 4.01 or 4 lengths	24.48 m ÷ 6.10 m = 4.01 or 4 lengths
4 lengths × 2 lf = 8 lf or 1 length	4 lengths × 0.61 m = 2.44 m or 1 length
4 + 1 = **5 lengths** - #4 rebar	4 + 1 = **5 lengths** - #4 rebar

Footing @ shored wall (3-#4 rebar - continuous w/48 DIA laps):

5 lengths × 2 lf (lap) = 10 lf
10 lf × 3 rebar = 30 lf = 2 lengths
2 + 5 = 7 lengths
Add 2 lengths for a total of **7 lengths** - #4 rebar

#5 rebar dowels @ 4'-0" (1.22 m) O.C. per detail 10-H/S-1:

40.17 lf ÷ 4 lf = 10.04 or 10 spaces	12.24 m ÷ 1.22 m = 10.03 or 10 spaces
10 + 1 = **11 lengths** - #5 rebar dowels	10 + 1 = **11 lengths** - #5 rebar dowels

Length of #5 rebar dowels:

3.00 lf high wall	0.91 m
<0.10 lf> (1.25")	<0.03 m>
0.75 lf deep into footing	0.23 m deep into footing
0.75 lf hook	0.23 m hook
4.40 lf (4.42 lf or 4'-5")	**1.34 m**

#5 rebar dowel @ shored wall:
same quantity and length as the standard wall detail 10-H/S-1

CHART 5–3
Concrete Reinforcement: East Wall

for concrete placement. Therefore, the forms must be 4" (10.16 cm) higher than the finished concrete wall. The footing position is also changed so that it extends 1'-2" (0.36 m) beyond the inside of the wall along the whole perimeter. Bracing and staking are installed only on the inside face of the wall to help keep the forms rigid.

Footing and Wall Reinforcement (Rebar). *See chart 5–3.* For reinforcement, two #4 horizontal rebars and #5 dowels are required. The length of the east footing is used to determine the length of the reinforcement. The smaller rebar (#2 through #6 at least) is available in lengths of 20 lf (6.10 m). The #5 rebar dowels are purchased in precut lengths. Vertical dowels are usually placed so that the bottom of the dowel is tied to the horizontal rebar in the footing. The rebar is installed on supports, called chairs, which help to maintain a uniform height from the bottom of the trench allowing the concrete to flow under the rebar.

Concrete. *See chart 5–4.* Ready-mix CIP is specified for the Medical Clinic project. There are also several additives indicated that are to be used. The quantity of each additive must be determined per cubic yard and included in the total per-cubic-yard cost. The costs of these additives vary depending upon supplier and manufacturing freight costs. In most cases, the additives are supplied by the contractor on the job and placed in the ready-mix at the job site. When these additives are noted, the estimator must know where and how the additives are to be used and seek the cost for each. The additive per-cubic-yard costs are then added to the basic ready-mix costs.

(Refer to Plans, Sheet S–1, Detail 10-H/S-1.)

Footing—42'-2" × 1'-0" × 2'-0" (12.85 m × 0.30 m × 0.61 m):

V = (42.17 lf × 1 lf × 2 lf) ÷ 27 cu ft   V = 12.85 m × 0.30 m × 0.61 m

V = 84.34 cu ft ÷ 27 cu ft   V = **2.35 m³**

V = **3.12 cu yd**

Wall—41'-0" × 3'-0" × 10" (12.5 m × 0.91 m × 0.25 m):

V = (41 lf × 3 lf × 0.83 lf) ÷ 27 cu ft   V = 12.5 m × 0.91 m × 0.25 m

V = 102.09 cu ft ÷ 27 cu ft   V = **2.84 m³**

V = **3.78 cu yd**

Total concrete required:

3.12 cu yd + 3.78 cu yd = **6.9 or 7 cu yd**   2.35 m³ + 2.84 m³ = **5.19 m or 6 m³**

CHART 5—4
Concrete Materials: East Wall

Here is an example. The materials for the walls are to include air-entrainment, Lapodith hardener, and Sika Seal for smoothness. The cost of the concrete supplied by a ready-mix supplier is $47.50/cu yd (0.76 m³). The estimator is informed that air-entrainment costs $0.50/cu yd (0.76 m³) extra, and one pound of Sika Seal costs $9.00/lb/cu yd (0.76 m³). Ten pounds (4.54 kg) of Lapodith hardener and dustproofer are required. The Lapodith costs $59.00/50 lb (22.68 kg) a container, or $11.80/cu yd (0.76 m³). The cost per cu yd (0.76 m³) of the additives is as follows:

$0.50 + $9.00 + $11.80 = $21.30/cu yd (0.76 m³)

When the additive cost is added to the CIP ready-mix cost, the total is as follows:

$47.50 + $21.30 = $68.80

The cost is 45% more than the original CIP cost. This is one situation where a considerable amount of money can be lost as a result of negligence and/or misunderstanding of the specifications. Estimators need to remember to include the cost of additives in estimating concrete costs.

Precast Piers.   See Plans, Sheet S–1, Foundation Plan, Keynote 12. There are two pier sizes to consider dependent upon the construction which they support, the steel (base bid) or the wood (alternate bid) girder beam. In either case, the pier design remains the same; only the height differs. The total height of the foundation wall is 3'-0" (0.91 m); the beam depth for both the steel and wood is 8" (20.32 cm). There is a 2× plate on the pier on which either the steel or the wood beam rests. The steel beam has a 2×6 (5.08 cm × 20.32 cm) wood plate on top to make it easier to connect the wooden floor joists. The height of the pier supporting the steel beam is as follows:

3 lf − (0.67 lf + 0.16 lf + 0.17 lf) =

(0.91 m − [0.2 m + .05 m + .05 m] =)

3 lf − 1 lf = 2 lf

(0.91 m − 0.3 m = 0.61 m)

CREW	HOURLY + BURDEN WAGE	% TIME ON JOB/HR	HOURLY RATE
Carpenter Foreman	$16.90 + $ 3.32	5%	= $ 1.01
Carpenter	$16.40 + $ 3.32	20%	= $ 3.94
Concrete Finisher	$14.65 + $ 3.95	33%	= $ 6.14
Laborer Foreman	$12.25 + $ 3.74	9%	= $ 1.44
Laborer	$11.75 + $ 3.74	33%	= $ 5.11
Composite Crew Rate:		100%	$17.64/MH

FIGURE 5–5a
Composite Crew Schedule

CREW	HOURLY WAGE + BURDEN
Carpenter Foreman	$16.90 + $3.32
Carpenter	$16.40 + $3.32
Concrete Finisher	$14.65 + $3.95
Labor Foreman	$12.25 + $3.74
Laborer	$11.75 + $3.74
	$71.95 + $18.07 = $90.02
Composite Crew Rate:	$90.02/5 = $18.00

FIGURE 5–5b
Composite Crew Schedule

The wood girder beam rests directly below, and supports, the floor joists. The pier height for this *alternate* is as follows:

3 lf − (0.66 lf + 0.17 lf) =
(0.91 m − [0.2 m + .05 m] =)
3 lf − 0.83 lf = 2.17 lf or 2′- 2″
(0.91 m − 0.25 m = 0.66 m)

Labor

See figure 5–5a and 5–5b, Composite Crew Refer Schedule. The work on the east wall of the Medical Clinic is estimated to take 2 days to set the formwork, 2 days to install the horizontal rebar and dowels, and 1/2 each for the placement of the concrete for a total of 5 days. The productivity rate is 78%. The productivity factor is as follows:

70% ÷ 78% = 0.9

FIGURE 5–6
Equipment Schedule

EQUIPMENT	USE TIME	UNIT COST	TOTAL
Portable Saw	1 day	@ $ 75/day	= $ 75.00
Vibrator	2 days	@ $ 25/day	= $ 50.00
Pump (placement)	1 day	@ $125/day	= $125.00
Equipment Total:			$250.00

The total labor cost is as follows:

Method 5–5a

$17.64 \times 0.9 = \$15.88/MH$

$\$15.88/MH \times 8\ hr \times 5\ members = \$635.20/CD$

$\$635.20 \times 5\ days = \$3,176.00$

Method 5–5b:

$18.00 \times 0.9 = \$16.20/MH$

$\$16.20/MH \times 8\ hr \times 5\ members = \$648.00/CD$

$\$648.00 \times 5\ days = \$3,240.00$

Equipment

See figure 5–6. There is no excavation required for the concrete work on the Medical Clinic; therefore, no heavy equipment is necessary. The equipment needed is for the concrete placement only. The pump may or may not be necessary. With careful handling, the concrete can be placed directly from the ready-mix unit. The cost for equipment is summarized in figure 5–6.

CHAPTER EXERCISES

1. Shoring is required around the mass excavation for the Medical Clinic. Estimate the quantity of materials required for the shoring and the wall forms. The footing extends 1′-2″ (35.56 cm) on the inside of the wall along the whole perimeter.

2. Using the estimate for the east wall of the Medical Clinic, determine the materials required for the complete footing and foundation wall. Include both English and metric measurements where applicable.

   Walers   =
   Formties   =
   Concrete   =
   Rebar #4   =
   Rebar #5   =
   Forms   =

See appendix III, Addendum #1; appendix III, Division 3, Concrete, and Division 1, Section 1030, Alternate #1; and Plans, Sheet S-1A Foundation/Slab Plan, Foundation Plan (Alternate). The alternate is necessary only in the event the Medical Clinic is to be constructed on a concrete slab in conjunction with masonry exterior wall construction. The Specifications read as follows:

Alternate #1. An alternate concrete slab and footing per drawings, identified as S-1A, shall be included with the bid. The concrete specifications shall read:

03200 Concrete Reinforcing. Horizontal footing reinforcement shall be 2-#4 rebar, continuous, with 48 diameter laps at all end joints.

#5 rebar dowels shall be installed horizontally at 4'-0" O.C (1.22 m), extending 2'-0" (60.96 cm) A.F.F. Dowels shall start a minimum 1'-0" (30.48 cm) each way from the corners and from each side of exterior openings. Dowels shall have a 9" (22.86 cm) hook. Dowels shall be placed not more than 3" (7.62 cm) nor less than 1 1/2" (3.81 cm), above the bottom of the footing.

#4 rebar tie hooks, 4'-0" (1.22 m) long w/1'-6" (45.72 cm) hook turned down into footings, shall be placed horizontally along perimeter of slab starting 1'-0" (30.48 cm) from the corners each way at 48" O.C (1.22 m).

03250 Concrete Accessories. Admixtures permitted include:

1. Air-entrained agent per ASTM C260
2. Hardener and Dustproofer additive—Lapodith or equal
3. Nonslip additive—Durafax or equal
4. Nonshrink additive—Sika Set or equal
5. Cure Seal additive per ASTM C309

03300 Cast-in-Place Concrete Concrete slab, 4" (10.16 cm) thick, as per plans, with 6×6 W1.4×W1.4 WWF (15.24 cm × 15.24 cm W1.4×W1.4 WWF) embedded 1 1/2" (3.81 cm) below finish concrete surface. WWF to be lapped 6" (15.24 cm), minimum, at all sides, ends and turndowns along perimeter.

Questions 3, 4, and 5 refer to Sheet S–1A in the Plans and the specification above.

3. Determine separately, and then summarize the amount of concrete necessary for the footings, the slab, and the turndown in cubic yards (concrete only—no formwork). Calculate both English and metric measurements.

Footing   =
Slab   =
Turndown   =
Total   =

4. The horizontal rebar hook on the perimeter of the slab is 48" (1.22 m) long with an 18" (45.72 cm) hook placed as specified on the plan. Calculate the number of pieces and the total length of rebar required.

5. Determine the quantity, in sheets, of 6×6 W1.4 × W 1.4 WWF. The material is available in 7 lf (2.13 m) × 20 lf (6.10 m) sheets.

6. Determine the total hard costs for the base bid if the material costs are as follows:

Concrete @ $60.00/cu yd (0.76 m³)   =

#4 rebar @ $0.17/lf (0.305 m)   =

#5 rebar dowels @ $ 0.55/lf (0.305 m)   =

2×4 (5.08 cm × 10.16 cm) lumber @ $ 0.30/lf (0.305 m)   =

Formties @ $1.75 ea   =

Plyform @ $17.79/sheet   =

2×12 lumber (5.08 cm × 60.96 cm) @ $0.65/lf (0.305 m)   =

7. Total the hard costs for the *alternate bid* per the Specifications and Addendum #1 (see appendix II) if all the material costs are the same as in question 6 above plus: WWF @ $30.00/sheet, #4 rebar dowels @ $0.33/lf (0.305 m).

CHAPTER 6

Masonry

Division 4

GENERAL INFORMATION

Brick, concrete masonry units (CMU), and **stone** are the three basic categories of masonry. Brick and stone have been used for centuries. The technology of recent years has improved on traditional brick as well as having created new brick types and concrete masonry units.

Both brick and CMU are categorized as either **solid-core** or **hollow-core** units. **Solid-core** units contain 25% or less core space (air space). **Hollow-core** units contain from 25% to 75% core space (air space). Brick and CMU are also grouped into categories of **structural** and **nonstructural** strengths.

Hollow-core brick and CMU are used where reinforcement and grout installations are required. Solid-core units are used for trim or specialty work where reinforcement is unnecessary: for decorative finishes such as corbels, for filling voids around other structural materials, and for veneers and pavers.

A term referring to the thickness of a wall is the **wythe.** A single wythe wall is one unit thick, whereas a double wythe wall is two units thick, and so on. Each of the terms briefly mentioned above will be discussed more fully as the chapter progresses.

Masonry Materials

Concrete Masonry Units. *See figure 6–1.* A concrete masonry unit (CMU) is made of concrete mixed with fine aggregates such as crushed rock, cinders, iron filings, or combinations of them, to achieve the desired strength or color (for example, natural gray, tinted aggregates, or a glaze finish). CMU is also available in a variety of textures such as **smooth-face, split-face, fluted, scored, raked,** or **brushed.** The names of the textures may vary throughout the country but the styles are all similar to those shown in figure 6–1.

CMU sizes range from *2" (5.08 cm) high to 12" (30.48 cm) high,* from *4" (10.16 cm) wide to 16" (40.64 cm) wide,* and from *4" (5.08 cm) long to 16" (40.64 cm) long.* The smaller units are the solid-core bricklike units such as a 4"×2"×8" (10.16 cm × 5.08 cm × 20.32 cm) concrete brick. The larger sizes are usually of the hollow-core variety such as an 8"×8"×16" (20.32 cm × 20.32 cm × 40.64 cm) block. The actual size of an 8"×8"×16" CMU is 7⅝"×7⅝"×15⅝". The nominal size includes a 3/8" (0.95 cm) thick mortar bed (bottom and one end).

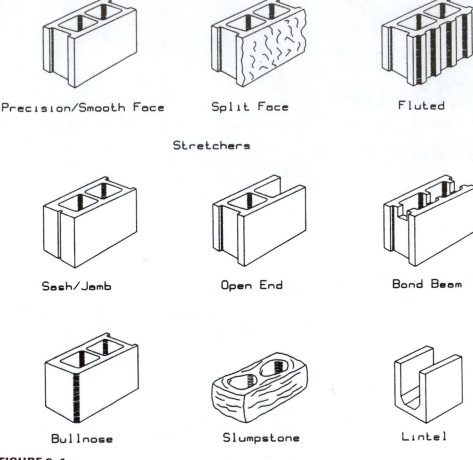

FIGURE 6–1
Concrete Masonry Units

Structural, or **load-bearing,** units are usually referred to as regular weight or heavyweight. Such units are classified by their ability to resist stress and are rated at approximately 1,530 lb (694 kg) $f'm$ (flexural measure) or more. This means that the block is able to withstand 1,530 pounds (694 kg) of **bending** (horizontal and vertical) pressure (stress) before cracking or breaking. The CMU is also classified according to its compressive strength, which varies with the style and flexural strength of the block. Do not confuse either of the above-mentioned strengths with *impact resistance*. A brick or block will break readily under impact because of its brittleness.

Nonstructural, or **non-load-bearing,** CMU is rated at approximately 1,500 lb (680.39 kg) $f'm$. Such units are used primarily for one-story structures, partition walls, and fences. The masonry walls of a building are normally considered structural bearing walls. The term *nonstructural*, as used in the sense of a one-story structure (a residence or small commercial building), implies only that there are no additional loads other than those applied by the roof structure and materials. Local codes and ordinances in many areas of the country require structural CMU for all exterior and interior bearing wall construction.

Brick. *See figure 6–2.* Clay brick is the most common masonry unit in existence. Most people refer to the clay brick as a "red" brick. As mentioned pre-

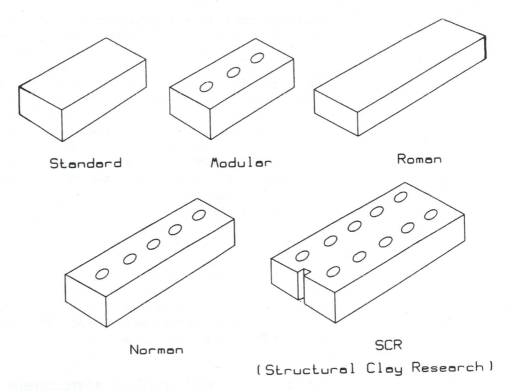

FIGURE 6–2
Brick Masonry Units

viously, brick may be solid-core or hollow-core and is available in sizes ranging from *4" (10.16 cm) to 6" (15.24 cm) wide, 2¹/₄" (5.72 cm) to 5¹/₄" (13.33 cm) high, and 8" (20.32 cm) to 12" (30.49 cm) long.* Brick is graded as SW, MW, or NW per ASTM standards. The grade definitions are as follows:

1. **Grade SW,** manufactured for high resistance to frost or wet locations
2. **Grade MW,** commonly used in dry locations such as the desert and southwestern portions of the country
3. **Grade NW,** used for veneer or the interior wythe on combination walls where frost or moisture problems are minimal

Brick is available in many varieties of color from the standard red brick to brick with variegated tinting and glazing. Brick, too, has a variety of textures, which gives it a different look, such as **cut, scored, scratched, broomed, or otherwise roughened surfaces.**

Structural clay tile may be classed as a brick or block. The difference between normal clay brick and structural clay tile is that the standard type brick is compressed in molds, whereas the clay tile brick is extruded. The remaining manufacturing processes are the same as for brick. Sizes, shapes, and styles are more in the range of CMU.

Refractories, more commonly known as **fire-brick,** are especially prepared materials with a calcium-aluminum base compound that does not break down under intense heat. The brick may be applied with or without a mortar bed and bond. The mortar, if used, also has the same base as the brick to prevent breakdown under heat. Refractory brick is used for residential, commercial, and industrial applications such as fireplaces, kilns, blast furnaces, and open hearths. The brick is available in sizes from 4″×4″×8″ (10.16 cm × 10.16 cm × 20.32 cm) to 8″×8″×16″ (20.32 cm × 20.32 cm × 40.64 cm).

Stone.   Granite, river rock, marble, slate, strata rock, limestone, and **sandstone** are all examples of natural stone used in masonry construction. One or more may be available in any area of the country. Stone may be used as structural or nonstructural. **Structural** use of stone may be found in exterior bearing walls for a building, especially in older buildings of the northeastern part of the country. **Nonstructural** use would be found in perimeter property walls or as a veneer over another material such as around fireplaces. Stone is estimated at 35 lb/sq ft (15.88 kg/0.0929 m^2).

Marble is primarily used as a facing over other materials because of its aesthetic appearance. **Slate** and **strata rock** may also be used as a veneer on walls, as well as a surface for decks, plazas, patios, or entry floors, because they are available in flat sections.

Cultured stone is a synthetic rock manufactured in a panel form. It is made from a mix of crushed rock and cement compressed and molded to look like natural stone. The panels vary in size from 2′×2′ (0.61 m × 0.61 m) to 4′×8′ (1.22 m × 2.44 m) and are adhered to the backup wall material. Cultured stone is estimated by the square foot or by the panel.

Mortar, Grout, and Steel Reinforcement

A complete masonry installation includes mortar, grout, and reinforcement steel added to the masonry units to make the units adhere together or to strengthen the masonry structure.

See appendix V, Mortar and Grout Tables. **Mortar** is a concrete mix with a fine aggregate or sand and may include a fluidifier additive used to bind the masonry units together. The need for the fluidifier is dependent upon weather conditions. Hot, dry areas of the country may require its use. In more moderate and cooler temperatures, the fluidifier may not be necessary. Mortar is applied 3/8″ (0.95 cm) thick to the bed (bottom of the unit) and one head (end of the unit). Special applications may be as little as 1/4″ (0.64 cm) or as much as 1/2″ (1.27 cm) thick.

Grout is another concrete mix, similar to regular concrete, with a 3/8″ (0.95 cm) aggregate and a plasticizer or other additive. Grout is used to fill the cavities of hollow-core units containing reinforcement (horizontal and vertical). *Where a four-hour fire wall* is required, the grout is placed in *all* cavities of the hollow masonry units.

Grout is placed in either a 4′-0″ (1.22 m) or an 8′-0″ (2.44 m) lift. A **lift** is the height of the wall allowed before grout is added. A four-foot lift has no additional requirement other than that the rebar be properly installed. The grout should be "rodded" or vibrated to remove any air pockets. "Rodding" means using some material smaller than the cell, such as a small wooden pole or piece of rebar, to be "pumped" up and down to relieve the air pockets and set the grout. A vibrator is a lightweight electrically or air-driven rotary stem that may "pump" and rotate simultaneously.

An 8′-0″ (2.44 m) lift requires the same treatment except that the vertical cell at the bottom course (grade or slab level) is opened to allow air to escape. This ensures that the grout has completely filled the cells from the eight-foot level to the grade or slab level. The removed piece of block is then reinstalled to finish the wall. The rebar requirements also change with the lift heights.

There are two types of **steel reinforcement** used in masonry construction, **rebar** and **horizontal joint reinforcement.** Rebar has already been introduced in chapter 5. **Horizontal joint reinforcement** is a 9-gauge wire system in the shape of a ladder or in the shape of an open-web **truss.** Both are available in 10′ (3.05 m) lengths. The width of the material varies according to the size of unit with which it is placed. The size is approximately 1/2″ (1.27 cm) to 1″ (2.54 cm) less than the overall width of the unit. The reinforcement is placed in the mortar bed between blocks *every 16″ (40.64 cm) vertically with an 8″ (20.32 cm) high block or brick,* or *12″ (30.48 cm) vertically with a 4″ (10.16 cm) or 6″ (15.24 cm) high block or brick.*

Accessories

There are specially formed masonry units such as lintels, sill block, keystones, or other nonstandard brick or block that are referred to as **masonry accessories.** There are also **nonmasonry accessories.** These are the embeds such as rebar, horizontal joint reinforcement, wall ties, beam supports, anchor bolts, and expansion bolts. As in concrete installations, many of the embeds are supplied by others and installed by the mason.

Masonry Fill Insulation

See figure 6–3. The four (4) major types of masonry insulation are inorganic fiber, vegetable fiber, mineral fiber, and liquefied polystyrene foam.

Inorganic-fiber loose-fill materials are made from molten rock, glass, or slag and blown by a jet of air into fine fibers. These fibers are packed into bags and may be blown or poured into wall cavities or attic spaces. This material is often referred to as **rock wool** or **mineral wool.** It is best suited for horizontal applications such as attic spaces.

Vegetable-fiber loose-fill materials are made from woody products shredded into lightweight, fleecy insulation. The materials are treated against moisture and termite infestation, as well as made fire-retardant. The materials are either blown or poured into wall cavities and attic spaces. Like inorganic fiber, it is best suited for horizontal applications but may be placed into the wall cavities.

Mineral loose fill is made of perlite or vermiculite. **Perlite** is a non-metallic mineral called **siliceous volcanic rock** containing *combined water* (which is chemically different from regular water). The rock is intensely heated until it expands and turns white in color. The combined water fuses with the softened rock and forms a honeycomb sealed structure. **Vermiculite** is manufactured from the mineral **mica** (hydrated magnesium-aluminum-iron silicate). It, too, is intensely heated until all moisture is evaporated, and the material expands into small pairs of sealed air pockets.

Liquefied polystyrene foam is another type of cavity fill used in masonry wall applications. It is a liquefied material that, when applied under pressure, expands into sealed multicell air pockets forming a honeycomb that is more durable and moisture-resistant than the loose-fill insulations. When dried or cured, the foam is similar to a sponge in appearance.

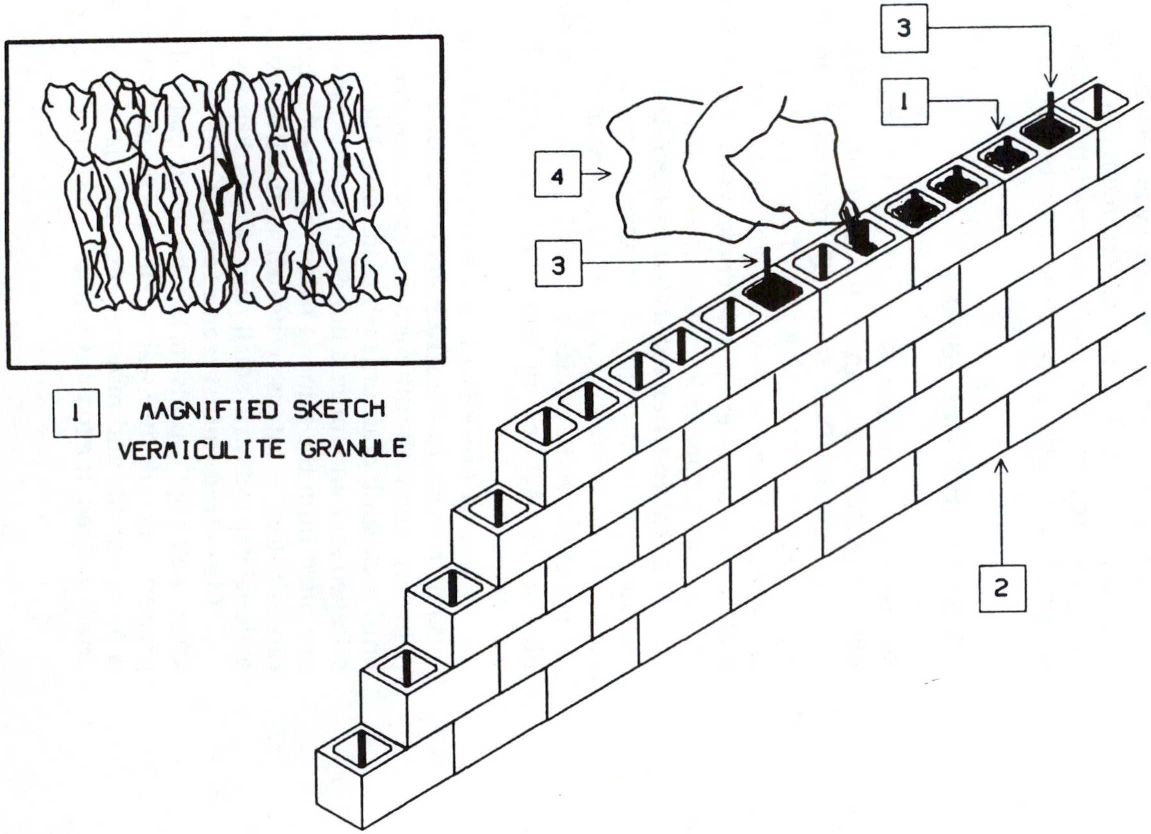

KEYNOTES:

1. Loose fill insulation vermiculite or perlite (see inset)
2. Masonry wall
3. Vertical rebar in grouted cell
4. Insulation sock

MAGNIFIED SKETCH
VERMICULITE GRANULE

FIGURE 6-3
Loose Fill Insulation

110

SCOPE OF WORK

The specifications for masonry for the Medical Clinic are found in appendix III, Addendum 1, and Appendix IV, Section 01030, Division 1, the Project Manual. These specifications are used as the basis for the estimate in the next section of the chapter. Section 01030, Alternate #2 reads as follows:

Alternate #2. The work included in this alternate shall be for masonry exterior wall construction and masonry wall insulation in lieu of the exterior base bid. The Specifications shall read:

DIVISION 1 General Requirements. The General and Special Conditions and Division 1 shall be considered a part of this alternate.

04100 Mortar and Grout. Mortar and grout shall meet specifications as indicated by the Masonry Institute of America and local codes. Solid grout shall attain a minimum strength of 2,000 psi (907.18 kg/6.45 cm^2).

04150 Masonry Accessories. All masonry accessories shall include, but are not limited to, corner units, halves, lintel block and sill block. Knock-out or deep-cut ("U") bond beam block may be used in lieu of lintel block.

04200 Unit Masonry. Concrete Masonry Units include split-face one side, load-bearing, 8×8×16 (20.32 cm × 20.32 cm × 40.64 cm), f'/m 1530, natural gray, on the East, North and South elevations. Standard (smooth face) load-bearing, f'/m 1530, natural gray, shall be on the West elevation only.

   The wall height is 9'-4" (2.84 m) from the top of slab to top of masonry. 2-#4 continuous rebar to be installed horizontally in first course, 1-#4 each course 2'-0" (0.61 m) vertically, 2-#4 rebar above all openings and 2-#4 rebar at the top course. No rebar shall be heat bent.

   #9 gauge truss-type horizontal joint reinforcement at 16" O.C (40.64 cm) vertically may be used in lieu of the #4 rebar except at the 4'-0" (1.22 m) level, above openings and at the top course.

   1-#5 vertical rebar shall be placed at 4'-0" O/C (1.22 m) horizontally in all walls to match dowel spacing. 1-#5 rebar shall be placed vertically on each side of wall openings and 2-#4 rebar horizontally over openings in bond beam extending a minimum 1'-0" (30.48 cm) beyond each side of opening.

   #4 rebar to be lapped 48 diameters and #5 rebar to be lapped 40 diameters. Rebar is lapped 2'-0" (60.96 cm) each way at all corners.

The Addendum

The architect has made note of the fact that not all of the information required for the masonry installation is included in the Alternate #2 Specification. Addendum #1 is an addition to the instructions. The addendum reads as follows:

Addendum #1   November 9, 1992
A Medical Clinic   Re: Alternates
Caliente, Nevada

This addendum shall become a part of the plans and specifications for the project known as the Medical Clinic, Caliente, Nevada.

This addendum supersedes any references or changes in the plans previously considered for said structure. The Specifications for Alternate #2, Masonry, shall prevail with the following additions and/or changes:

Masonry Reinforcement. All masonry shall be placed on-slab. There are no masonry stem walls. The first course placed on the slab shall be a bond beam course with 2-#4 reinforcement bars, continuous, lapped 48 diameters per code and local ordinances.

A #4 rebar horizontal hook shall be placed in the perimeter of the concrete slab and shall extend 4'-0" (1.22 m) into the slab with a 9" (22.86 cm) hook extending into the footing. The horizontal rebar shall also be placed at 4'-0" O/C (1.22 m).

Masonry. All materials, labor and equipment necessary to install a complete masonry system shall be included. The installation shall be to the best of the workmanship standards of the trade.

Masonry rough openings for windows:

East wall, Northeast and Southeast corners shall be
4'-0" × 5'-0" ea (1.22 m × 1.52 m)
Southwest corner shall be 6'-0" × 4'-8" (1.83 m × 1.42 m)
Northwest corner shall be 6'-0" × 3'-8" (1.83 m × 1.12 m)

All other window openings on North and South walls shall be
3'-4" × 3'-8" ea (1.01 m × 1.12 m)

Masonry rough openings for doors:

North and South openings shall be 3'-4" × 7'-4" ea (1.01 m × 2.23 m)
East wall opening shall be 6'-0" × 7'-4" (1.83 m × 2.23 m)

THE ESTIMATE

See Plans, Sheet S1–B, Masonry Wall Plan. The construction for the Medical Clinic is **modular** including the openings. Modular construction is based on 4" × 4" (10.16 cm × 10.16 cm) grids for details and 4'-0" × 4'-0" (1.22 m × 1.22 m) grids for larger areas such as floor plans. The 4" (10.16 cm) and 4'-0" (1.22 m) grids are geared to fit standard masonry measurements.

The Spreadsheet

See figure 6–4. The simplest spreadsheet form to use is the 13-column accounting pad. The spreadsheet should show the length, width, and square-foot area of the portion of the drawing being estimated. A list of each type of masonry, rebar, mortar, and grout is indicated. The list should include the following:

1. Smooth face 8×8×16 (20.32 cm × 20.32 cm × 40.64 cm) and 8×8×8 (20.32 cm × 20.32 cm × 20.32 cm) and bond beams (BB)
2. Split face (S/F), 1 side (1/s), 8×8×16 (20.32 cm × 20.32 cm × 40.64 cm) and 8×8×8 (20.32 cm × 20.32 cm × 20.32 cm) and bond beams (BB)
3. Split face (S/F), 1 side (1/s), 1 end (1/e), 8×8×16 (20.32 cm × 20.32 cm × 40.64 cm) and 8×8×8 (20.32 cm × 20.32 cm × 20.32 cm) and bond beams (BB)
4. 9×4×8 (22.86 cm × 10.16 cm × 20.32 cm) sill block
5. 8×8×8 (20.32 cm × 20.32 cm × 20.32 cm) lintel block ("U" block) (Split face 8×8×16 [20.32 cm × 20.32 cm × 40.64 cm]) and 8×8×8 [20.32 cm ×

Medical Clinic
Main Street & Broadway
Caliente, NV
Christie & Assoc. - Architect

Bid date: 10/10/95
Estimate survey date: 8/15/96
Plan Date: 1/27/96

Estimate by: JB
Checked by: JF
Date checked: 8/20/96

Description Wall L x H	Area	8816 regular	888 regular	8816 s/f l/s	888 s/f l/s	8816 s/fl/s/e/s/fl/s/e	888 s/fl/s/e/s/fl/s/e	8816 BB regular	8816 BB regular	888 BB regular	8816 BB s/f l/s	888 BB s/f l/s	8816 BB s/fl/s/e	888 BB s/fl/s/e
East 41.33'x9.33'														
West 41.33'x9.33'														
North 58.67'x9.33'														
South 58.67'x9.33'														
Openings:														
East wall:														
4 x 4.0' x 5.0'														
6.0' x 7.33'														
North wall:														
3 x 3.33' x 3.33'														
6.0' x 3.33'														
3.33' x 7.33'														
South wall:														
3 x 3.33' x 3.33'														
6.0' x 3.33'														
3.33' x 7.33'		948 Sill	888 Lintel	488 Glass Blk							Mortar cy/bags	Grout cy	#4 rebar	#5 dowel

FIGURE 6–4
Masonry Spreadsheet

113

20.32 cm × 20.32] bond beam [BB] block may be used in lieu of lintel block.)

6. 4×8×8 (10.16 cm × 20.32 cm × 20.32 cm) glass block, "Decor," by PPG

7. #4 and #5 rebar

8. Mortar (cu yd)(m³)

9. Grout (cu yd)(m³)

Materials

Rebar Estimate.   *See chart 6–1 and figure 6–5.* Both the east and west walls of the Medical Clinic are 41'-4" (12.60 m) long by 9'-4" (2.84 m) high. #4 hori-

---

(Refer to Plans, Sheet S1–B; figure 6–5)
West wall—41'-4" × 9'-4" (12.6 m × 2.84 m):

#4 horizontal rebar w/48 DIA lap:

9.33 lf ÷ 2 lf = 4.67 or 5 spaces	2.84 m ÷ 0.61 m = 4.66 or 5 spaces
Add:	Add:
1 + 3 for 1st, @ 4'-0", and top course	1 + 3 for 1st, @ 1.22 m and top course
5 + 1 + 3 = 9 places	5 + 1 + 3 = 9 places
9 × 41.33 lf = 371.97 or 372 lf	9 × 12.60 m = 113.41 m
372 lf ÷ 20 lf = 18.6 or 19 lengths	113.41 m ÷ 6.10 m = 18.59 or 19 lengths
19 × 2 lf = 38 lf or 2 additional lengths	19 × 0.61 m = 11.59 m or 2 additional lengths
19 + 2 = 21 lengths	19 + 2 = 21 lengths

Total #4 rebar:

21 × 20 lf = **420 lf**	21 × 6.10 m = **128.10 m**

#5 vertical rebar @ 4'-0" (1.22 m) O.C. w/40 DIA laps:

41.33 lf ÷ 4 lf = 10.33 or 11 spaces	12.60 m ÷ 1.22 m = 10.33 or 11 spaces
Add 1 for the end = 12 lengths	Add 1 for the end = 12 lengths

1st lift - 4'-0" (1.22 m) w/2'-0" (0.61 m) lap:

4 lf + 2 lf = 6 lf	1.22 m + 0.61 m = 1.83 m

2nd lift - 5'-4" (1.62 m) to top of wall:

5.33 lf	1.62 m

Length of #5 rebar:

6 lf + 5.33 lf = 11.33 lf	1.83 m + 1.62 m = 3.45 m

Total #5 rebar:

12 × 11.33 lf = **135.96 or 140 lf**	12 × 3.45 m = **41.40 m or 42 m**

East wall (see figure 6–5):

#4 horizontal rebar—same as west wall less 1 6-lf opening + 4 4-lf openings; 3 rebar through window openings, 5 rebar through door opening:

<16 lf> × 3 = <48 lf>	<4.88 m> × 3 = <14.64 m>
<6 lf> × 5 = <30 lf>	<1.83 m> × 5 = <9.15 m>
420 lf − 78 lf = 342 lf	128.10 m − 23.79 m = 104.31 m

Add full length over openings for bond beam:

41.33 lf + 2 lf lap = 43.33 lf	12.60 m + 0.61 m = 13.21 or 14 m
Add 3 lengths or 60 lf	Add 3 lengths or 18.29 m
342 lf + 60 lf = **402 or 400 lf**	104.31 m + 18.29 m = **122.60 or 123 m**

#5 vertical rebar — same as west wall plus openings:

Openings require 1 #5 rebar each side of opening, maximum 7'-4" (2.23 m):

12 lengths × 7.33 lf = 87.96 or 88 lf	12 lengths × 2.23 m = 26.76 or 27 m
140 lf + 88 lf = **228 or 240 lf**	27 m + 42 m = **69 m**

CHART 6–1
Masonry Reinforcement: East and West Walls

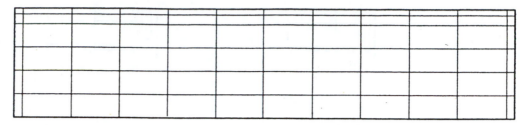

VEST ELEVATION

NOTE: #4 rebar horizontally @ 2'-0" o/c w/ 2-#4 @
and @ top course. #5 rebar at vertically as indicated.

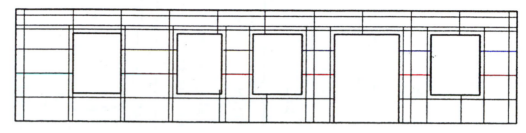

EAST ELEVATION

FIGURE 6–5
East/West Structural Wall Elevations

zontal rebar is required every 2 lf (0.61 m) vertically. The Specifications state that there are two (2) rebar laid at the 4'-0" (1.22 m) level and the top course. Addendum #1 states that the first course is also to be a bond beam with two (2) rebar. The estimator may include the 4'-0" (1.22 m), 90° returns at each end. They are included in the survey at this time.

The vertical #5 rebar is placed at 4'-0" O/C (2.44 m) to match the dowels in the concrete slab. The Specifications require a 4'-0" (1.22 m) lift for the grout placement. The vertical rebar must also be long enough to expose the 40 diameter laps for attachment of the next vertical piece.

The second lift is at 8'-0" (2.44 m). This means that there is another 6'-0" (1.83 m) section required, but there is only 1'-4" (0.41 m) left above the 8'-0" (2.44 m) height. The normal procedure here is to allow the length to be cut to the size necessary. There is also a gap of 1 1/2" (3.81 cm) left from the top of the wall to cover the rebar with grout.

The rebar estimate in chart 6–1 is for both the east and west wall. The estimator may wish to use the openings in the east wall for additions and deductions. Where there is a deduction for the openings, there is also an addition for horizontal rebar over the openings and vertical rebar on each side of the openings. When a wall has openings that are close together, as are those in the Medical Clinic (figures 6–5 and 6–6), it is best to estimate 2 additional horizontal rebar the complete length of the wall in lieu of pieces placed over the openings.

Masonry. *See chart 6–2 and figure 6–7.* Three methods of estimating masonry are commonly in use. In all instances, it is necessary to know the area (square feet). The area aids in determining not only the masonry materials

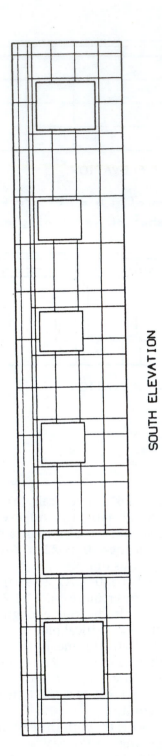

SOUTH ELEVATION

NOTE: #4 rebar horizontally w/2-#4 @
#5 rebar vertically as indicated.

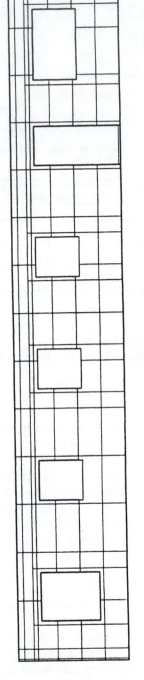

NORTH ELEVATION

FIGURE 6–6
North/South Structural Wall Elevations

116

(Refer to figure 6–7)

Square-foot method:

41.33 lf × 9.33 lf = 385.61 sq ft

385.61 sq ft × (cost/sq ft)

12.60 m × 2.84 m = 35.78 m²

35.78 m² × (cost/m²)

Quick-check method:

41.33 lf × 9.33 lf = 385.61 sq ft

385.61 sq ft ÷ 0.8888 = **433.85 or 434 pc**

12.60 m × 2.84 m = 35.78 m²

35.78 m² ÷ 0.083 = **431.08 or 431 pc**

Count-up piece method (horizontal and vertical combined):

41.33 lf × 12" ÷ 16" = 30.99 or 31 pc

9.33 lf × 12" ÷ 8" = 13.99 or 14 pc

31 × 14 = **434 pc**

12.60 m ÷ 0.41 m = 30.71 or 31 pc

2.84 m ÷ 0.20 m = 14.20 or 14 pc

31 × 14 = **434 pc**

Deduct split face CMU from west wall:

14 courses = {7 courses of 8×8×8 each end
{7 courses of 8×8×16 each end

434 units − (14 units + [14 units ÷ 2])

434 units − (14 units + 7 units)

434 units − 21 units = **413 units regular (precision) 8×8×16 CMU**

Separate precision CMU and bond beam CMU:

(9.33 lf ÷ 2 lf) + 1 = 4.67 or 5 levels

(2.84 m ÷ 0.61 m) + 1 = 4.66 or 5 levels

(5 × 31 pc) − 9 pc =

155 pc − 9 pc = **146 pc 8×8×16 precision BB**

9 pc 8×8×16 split face 1/s, 1e BB

CHART 6–2
Masonry Estimate: West Wall

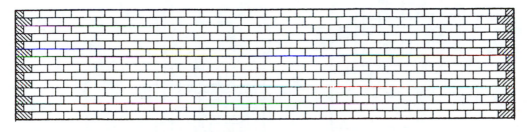

WEST ELEVATION

NOTE: East elevation - split face 8×8×16 CMU.

West elevation - smooth face 8×8×16 CMU (UNO).

EAST ELEVATION

 Split face return   ⊠ Lintel block   ▭ Sill block

FIGURE 6–7
East/West Architectural Wall Elevations

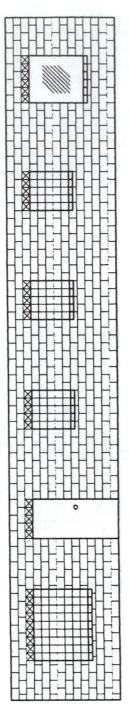

SOUTH ELEVATION

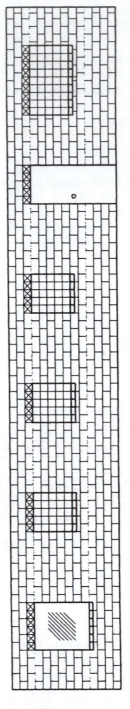

NORTH ELEVATION

FIGURE 6–8
North/South Architectural Wall Elevations

but also the reinforcement, mortar, and grout. The three methods are described below.

1.   *Square-Foot Method.* The Medical Clinic includes two types of block plus special masonry accessories, such as lintel and sill block, to be added to the installation. The reinforcement is not a standard application. Finally, taxes and fees may not be included. Any one of these items can cost the contractor a great deal more than the standard price/sq ft estimate. The estimate is based on the assumption that the wall is installed in a **common,** or **running, bond.** Unknowns in this calculation include the fact that there may be soldier courses, or other designs. These changes affect quantities of materials considerably. This method is not recommended for inexperienced contractors because of the above-mentioned issues.

2.   *Quick-Check Method.* This method is a very good check on quantities of masonry. *See appendix IV, Masonry Unit Factors.* The area of wall divided by a factor can give a very close count of the quantities required. The factor is determined by dividing the area of the face of a stretcher brick or block in square inches by 144 sq in, or if in square centimeters by 929 cm². A stretcher is the standard unit of masonry used.

The major problem with the quick-check method is that the quantities of each type of masonry is not known. Because of this, a second estimate must be made to determine the count. Again, the estimate is based on the assumption that the wall is installed in a common, or running, bond.

The "quick check" is appropriate for estimates of much larger structures (three stories or more). It is recommended that only an experienced masonry contractor/estimator should attempt such an estimate. Experience provides some tricks that make it easier to do a breakdown count of the materials required.

3.   *Count-up Piece Method. See Plans, Sheet S-1B, and figure 6–7.* This is the most difficult and time-consuming method. The count-up is the most accurate way to estimate masonry for smaller structures such as the Medical Clinic.

The West Wall Estimate. See chart 6–2 and figure 6–7. Caution should be taken for the estimate on the west wall for the Medical Clinic. The elevation shows that there is split-face block on each end of the wall. These units are "returns" from the north and south walls and are to be deducted from the west wall total.

Every third course is equal to 2 lf (0.61 m) vertically and is, therefore, a bond beam. The base course is also a bond beam (BB). The split-face half block (8×8×8) indicated in figure 6–7 does not represent additional blocks. They are the 8" (20.32 cm) return face of the 8×8×16 s/f, 1/s, 1/e, on the north or south walls. This is also true of the halves on the north and south walls at the corners of the west wall. Because of these split-faced CMU, there are no precision (smooth face) halves. The difference is in the number of block in each course. This is where the count-up procedure is used.

Glass Block.   *See Plans, Sheet S-1B, Masonry Wall Alternate. See also chart 6–3 and figure 6–8.* The architectural elevations and the Specifications indicate window sizes and locations containing 4×8×8 (10.16 cm × 20.32 cm × 20.32 cm) glass block. Glass block is calculated in the same manner as other masonry units. The number of glass blocks required in each direction is determined by dividing the width and height measurements by 8" (20.32 cm) and multiplying the results.

Southwest corner window glass block
(Refer to figure 6–8, south elevation. The block is 4 × 8 × 8 (10.16 cm × 20.32 cm × 20.32 cm) glass block; southwest corner window is 6" -0' × 4" -0' (1.83 m × 1.22 m).

(6 lf × 12") ÷ 8" = 9 pc   1.83 m ÷ 0.20 m = 9.15 or 9 pc
4.67 lf × 12" ÷ 8" = 7 pc   1.42 m ÷ 0.20 m = 7.10 or 7 pc

Total pieces of glass block:

9 pc × 7 pc = **63 pc**

Accessories for glass block:
Weatherstripping:

(6 lf × 2) + (4.67 lf × 2) + 0.17 lf (lap)   (1.83 m × 2) + (1.42 m × 2) + 0.05 m
12 lf + 9.34 lf + 0.17 lf = **21.5 lf**   3.66 m + 2.84 m + 0.05 m = **6.55 m**

Horizontal reinforcement (ladder or truss):

7 courses ÷ 2 courses = 3.5 or 3 lengths   3 × (1.42 m + 0.10 m) = **4.56 m**
3 × (4.67 lf + 0.33 lf [fastening]) = **15 lf**

Edge block spacers: *Interior block spacers (between units):*

(9 pc × 2) + (7 pc × 2) − 4 pc   6 pc × 8 pc = **48 pc**
(18 pc + 14 pc) − 4 pc = **28 pc**

Corner block spacers:
4 pc

CHART 6–3
Estimate for Glass Block

Accessories commonly used with glass block include weatherstripping (asphalt building paper or polyester foam strips), mortar, horizontal reinforcement, and plastic spacers. The spacers are used to aid in setting the glass block uniformly. The weatherstrip is placed so as to completely surround the glass block at the perimeter. Specially sized horizontal reinforcement, like other masonry units, is installed every other course. A white mortar is used to seal and adhere the glass block. When the mortar cures, the plastic spacers are broken off and the mortar is repaired.

Waste Factor.   To this point in the estimate, no waste factor has been added. There may be no necessity for a waste factor for two reasons:

1.   The masonry manufacturer/supplier usually allows a 3% waste factor for breakage. This is already included in the unit cost.

2.   The masonry contractor usually purchases the units by the pallet or by the carton. The quantity on a pallet varies with the material. Each supplier or manufacturer establishes the number of units per pallet. This information must be known prior to making a purchase once the contract is signed. The estimate for each item of masonry should be carried to the next full pallet or carton of stock unless the total quantity of material needed is less than half a pallet. These steps have not been included in the estimates in this chapter.

Mortar and Grout.   *See appendix V, Masonry Mortar and Grout Tables.* The quantity of mortar is *inversely* affected by the size of the masonry unit. The smaller the unit, the more mortar is necessary. The quantity of grout required is *directly proportional* to the size of the masonry unit and the reinforcement requirements. The larger the unit and the more reinforcement used, the greater the quantity of grout necessary.

(See appendix IV, Mortar and Grout tables.)
Mortar (8×8×16 [20.32 cm × 20.32 cm × 40.64 cm] CMU):

By the piece:
434 pc ÷ 112.5 pc = **3.86 or 4 cu yd**

By the square foot:	*By the square meter:*
41.33 lf × 9.33 lf = 385.61 sq ft	12.60 m × 2.84 m = 35.78 m²
385.61 sq ft ÷ 100 sq ft = **3.86 or 4 cu yd**	35.78 m² ÷ 9.29 m² = **3.85 or 4 m³**

Grout (8× 8× 16 [20.32 cm × 20.32 cm × 40.64 cm] CMU):

Solid grout:
385.61 sq ft ÷ 90 sq ft = **4.28 or 5 cu yd**   35.78 m² ÷ 8.36 m² = **4.28 or 5 m³**

Cell grout:

385.61 sq ft × 33.33% = 128.52 sq ft (vertical)	35.78 m² × 33.33% = 11.93 m²
385.61 sq ft × 16.67% = 64.28 sq ft (horizontal)	35.78 m² × 16.67% = 5.96 m²
128.52 sq ft + 64.28 sq ft = 192.8 sq ft	11.93 m² + 5.96 m² = 17.89 m²
192.8 sq ft ÷ 90 sq ft = **2.14 or 3 cu yd**	17.89 m² ÷ 8.36 m² = **2.14 or 3 m³**

CHART 6—4
Mortar and Grout Estimate: West Wall

Expanded loose fill (68 sq ft/sack or 6.31 m²/sack):	
192.81 sq ft ÷ 68 sq ft = **2.84 or 3 sacks**	17.91 m² ÷ 6.31 m² = **2.84 or 3 sacks**
Granulated loose fill (45 ft²/sack or 4.18 m²/sack):	
192.81 sq ft ÷ 45 sq ft = **4.28 or 5 sacks**	17.91 m² ÷ 4.18 m² = **4.28 or 5 sacks**

CHART 6—5
Insulation: West Wall

Mortar.   See chart 6–4.   According to the information in the table in appendix IV, 1 cu yd of mortar is necessary to properly install 112.5 units or 100 sq ft (9.29 m²) of 8×8×16 (20.32 cm × 20.32 cm × 40.64 cm) block.

Grout.   See chart 6–4.   All horizontal units (bond beam and lintel) and vertical cells containing rebar must be grouted. Per the table in appendix IV, 1 cu yd (0.76 m³) of grout will fill 90 sq ft (8.36 m²) of an 8″ (20.32 cm) CMU wall. The Specifications for the Medical Clinic state that the walls shall be fully grouted for a four-hour fire protection as required by local code.

If only the rebar cells were to be grouted, the amount would be much less than that required for a full-grouted wall. Since the rebar is installed at 2′-0″ O/C (0.61 m) vertically and 4′-0″ O/C (1.22 m) horizontally, the percentages from the table to use are 33.33% and 16.67%, respectively.

Insulation.   *See chart 6–5.* Both perlite and vermiculite are available in sacks. One (1) sack will fill approximately 68 sq ft (6.32 m²) for an 8″ (20.32 cm) wide wall. Both materials are also available as granular fill. The **granular insulation** fills approximately one-third less area than the expanded material, or 45 sq ft/sack (4.18 m²).

Summarizing the Takeoff.   *See figure 6–9.* Since there is so much information scattered over the estimate sheets, it is always a good idea to make a summary

SUMMARY

PROJECT **Medical Clinic**
Caliente, Nevada

Estimate # **42-92**
Sheet **1** of **4** Sheets
Estimate By: **Jim F.**   Date **10/12/92**
Checked by: _____   Date _____

DESCRIPTION	QUANTITY	MATERIALS		LABOR			SUB-CONTRACT		TOTAL
		UNIT PRICE	AMOUNT	M/H RATE	TOTAL M/H	AMOUNT	UNIT PRICE	AMOUNT	
West wall only:									
8x8x16 precision	239 pc	$0.85	$203.15	$18.39	46	$845.94			$1,049.09
8x8x16 precision bond beam	174 pc	$0.86	$147.90	$18.39	34	$625.26			$ 773.16
8x8x8 precision	0								
8x8x8 precision bond beam	0								
mortar	4 cy	$45/cy	$180.00						$ 180.00
grout	5 cy	$45/cy	$225.00						$ 225.00
#4 rebar	400 lf	$0.10/lf	$40.00	$0.25/lf install		$140.00			$ 228.00
#5 rebar - 12 ea @ 13'-4" O/A	160 lf	$0.30/lf	$48.00						
TAX (materials only)			$844.05			$1,611.20		Sub-total:	$2,455.25
Equipment total			$ 42.20						$ 42.20
									$ 400.00
(Note: all split-face units are included w/North-South walls)									

Hard Costs		$2,897.45
Overhead (15%)		
Sub-total		
Profit (10%)		
Sub-total		
Bonds		
Fees		
GRAND TOTAL		

FIGURE 6-9
Estimate Summary Sheet

of the materials. A summary sheet similar to the one in figure 6–9 is ideal for this purpose because it enables any interested party to be able to read the quantities of material, labor, equipment, and extensions of the costs to prepare a complete proposal.

Labor

Estimating Masonry Labor.   The best and most accurate method for calculating labor is the **piece method.** From experience, each contractor can closely determine the amount of brick or block a mason can normally install in one day. From the study on productivity, it is noted that the ability of a crew varies as the result of several factors. An additional factor that must be considered in masonry is the type and weight of the brick or block. The productivity factor will vary from contractor to contractor.

It is not unusual for a mason to install 185 pc of split-face block per day and 250 pc of precision (smooth face) block per day. These measures of productivity will be used for the summary in this chapter. From the masonry breakdown (chart 6–2), there are 413 pc of 8×8×16 (20.32 cm × 20.32 cm × 40.64 cm) precision units. The 14 pc of 8×8×16 (20.32 cm × 20.32 cm × 40.64 cm) and 14 pc of 8×8×8 (20.32 cm × 20.32 cm × 20.32 cm) split face, 1/s, 1/e, units exposed to the west wall are not included. *In calculations of labor costs, a half block is the same as a full size block.*

Sample Labor Estimate.   *See figures 6–10a and 6–10b, Composite Crew Schedule.* The contractor uses a 3-person crew to install the masonry on the Medical

CREW	HOURLY + BURDEN WAGE	% TIME ON JOB/HR	HOURLY RATE
Foreman	$16.90 + $ 3.32	30%	= $ 6.07
Mason	$16.40 + $ 3.32	35%	= $ 6.90
Hodman	$11.75 + $ 3.74	35%	= $ 5.42
Composite Crew Rate:		100%	$18.39/MH

FIGURE 6–10a
Composite Crew Schedule

CREW	HOURLY WAGE + BURDEN
Foreman	$16.90 + $3.32
Mason	$16.40 + $3.32
Hoddie	$11.75 + $3.74
	$45.05 + $10.38 = $55.43
Composite Crew Rate:	$55.43/3 = $18.48

FIGURE 6–10b
Composite Crew Schedule

FIGURE 6–11
Equipment Schedule

EQUIPMENT	USE TIME	UNIT COST	TOTAL
Truck	2 days	@ $10/day	= $ 20.00
Forklift	2 days	@ $80/day	= $160.00
Pump (2 lifts per wall)	2 lifts	@ $85/lift	= $170.00
Miscellaneous (mortar boards, hoses, etc.)			= $ 50.00
Equipment Total:			$400.00

clinic. The productivity factor for the crew is established at 1.0, therefore, there is no change in the crew rate and man-hour (MH) rate. The total labor cost would be:

Method 6–10a:

$18.39/MH $\times$ 8 hr $\times$ 3 workers = $441.36/CD

$441.36/CD $\times$ 2 days = $88.72 or $883.00

Method 6–10b:

$18.48/MH $\times$ 8 hr $\times$ 3 workers = $443.52/CD

$443.52/CD $\times$ 2 days = $887.04 or $887.00

Equipment

See figure 6–11. The primary piece of equipment required for installing the masonry for the Medical Clinic is the scaffold. The cost of the scaffold is determined by the square foot area and the height of the wall. It is not necessary until the crew has reached a height of four feet (1.22 m). The scaffold is moved as needed from wall to wall. The crew will also need transportation, a forklift, mortar boards, a mixing tub, water hoses, and a grout pump.

The scaffold quantity required is determined by calculating the length, width, and height of the scaffold. The number of frames is calculated as follows:

(Length of scaffold $\times$ Width of scaffold) = Square feet (m^2) of planking

([Length $\div$ 10 lf] + 1) $\times$ (Width $\div$ 4 lf) $\times$ (Height $\div$ 6.5 lf) = Quantity of frames

([Length $\div$ 3.05 m] + 1) $\times$ (Width $\div$ 1.22 m) $\times$ (Height $\div$ 1.98 m) = Quantity of frames)

This calculation is based on the length of each section at 10 lf (3.05 m), the width of the scaffold at 4 lf (1.22 m), and the height of one frame at 6.5 lf (1.98 m). The estimator must be aware that there are several sizes of scaffolding and should be certain to insert the proper sizes where appropriate. The planking is a nominal 2×12 (5.08 cm × 30.48 cm) DF #2 or better with no splits and as few knots as possible. The plank length varies with the frame size.

CHAPTER EXERCISES

1. Estimate the quantity of rebar required for the north and south walls of the Medical Clinic.

2. Estimate the quantity of split-face CMU required for the north and south walls, using the quick-check method. Do not deduct for openings.

3. Break down the quantities of materials for the north and south walls as follows:

   8×8×16 (20.32 cm × 20.32 cm × 60.64 cm) Split face, 1/s   =
   8×8×16 (20.32 cm × 20.32 cm × 60.64 cm) Split face, 1/s, 1/e =
   8×8×8 (20.32 cm × 20.32 cm × 20.32 cm) Lintel   =
   9×4×8 (22.86 cm × 10.16 cm × 20.32 cm) Sill block   =
   4×8×8 (10.16 cm × 20.32 cm × 20.32 cm) Glass block   =
   Mortar (cu yd)(m^3)   =
   Grout (cu yd)(m^3)   =

4. Estimate the total labor cost for the north and south walls using the information in the chapter.

5. Using the estimate of amounts of rebar from question 1 and the cost information below, estimate the cost of the rebar for the north and south walls.

   #4 rebar @ $0.13/lf (0.305 m) =
   #5 rebar @ $0.33/lf (0.305 m) =

6. Total the hard costs for the north and south walls, using the same labor and equipment costs as in the chapter. The masonry unit costs are as follows:

   Precision, 8×8×16 (20.32 cm × 20.32 cm × 40.64 cm) (and BB) @
       $0.90/unit =
   Precision, 8×8×8 (20.32 cm × 20.32 cm × 20.32 cm) (and BB) @
       $0.68/unit =
   S/F, 1/s, 8×8×16 (20.32 cm × 20.32 cm × 40.64 cm) (and BB) @
       $1.05/unit =
   S/F, 1/s, 8×8×8 (20.32 cm × 20.32 cm × 20.32 cm) (and BB) @
       $0.90/unit =
   S/F, 1/s, 1/e, 8×8×16 (20.32 cm × 20.32 cm × 40.64 cm) (and BB) @
       $1.11/unit =
   S/F, 1/s, 8×4×16 (20.32 cm × 10.16 cm × 40.64 cm) @ $0.78/unit =
   Lintel, 8×8×8 (20.32 cm × 20.32 cm × 20.32 cm) @ $0.57/unit =
   Sill Block, 9×4×8 (22.86 cm × 10.16 cm × 20.32 cm) @ $1.75/unit =
   Glass Block, 4×8×8 (10.16 cm × 20.32 cm × 20.32 cm) @ $4.50/unit =
   Mortar @ $55.00/cu yd (0.76 m^3) =
   Grout @ $55.00/cu yd (0.76 m^3) =
   Rebar =

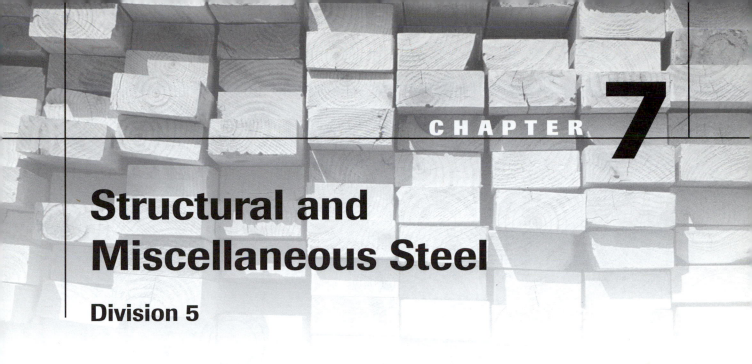

Structural and Miscellaneous Steel

Division 5

GENERAL INFORMATION

Structural steel has replaced much of the structural concrete and masonry construction in multistory buildings. Also, it is commonly employed to give additional support to buildings with concrete and masonry construction. Structural steel has made it possible to increase the size of multistory structures and has become an integral part of them.

Types of Steel

There are three structural categories referred to in Division 5, **heavy structural steel, light-gauge structural steel,** and **miscellaneous steel.**

Heavy Structural Steel. *See figure 7–1.* Heavy structural steel is a minimum 1/4" (0.64 cm) thick. Included in this category are wide-flange structural steel beams (W, WF), structural narrow-flange beams (I, S), miscellaneous or junior structural beams (M), channel steel (C), and angle iron. Materials of construction from concrete to plumbing, HVAC (heating, ventilation, and air conditioning), and electrical are frequently anchored to, or cover, structural steel.

See figure 7–2. Structural steel shop drawings are referred to as "detailing." These drawings are supplied by the steel fabricator for approval and use. They are pictorial descriptions of the manner in which the fabricator proposes to install and support the structural steel members. The approved drawings become part of the construction drawings and are used for the estimate.

Light–Gauge Structural Steel. *See appendix V, Structural Light-Gauge and Light-Gauge Metal Stud Framing.* Structural light-gauge steel refers to metal studs and joists ranging in thickness from 18-gauge to 12-gauge cold-rolled steel. The smaller the number of the steel gauge, the thicker the steel.

There are two types of studs in structural light-gauge metal framing: punched and unpunched. **Punched studs** are used in areas where it may be necessary to install other materials such as tie rods and turnbuckles for rigidity. They are also used for electrical and/or plumbing installations within the walls. An **unpunched stud,** more commonly called a joist, is more rigid than

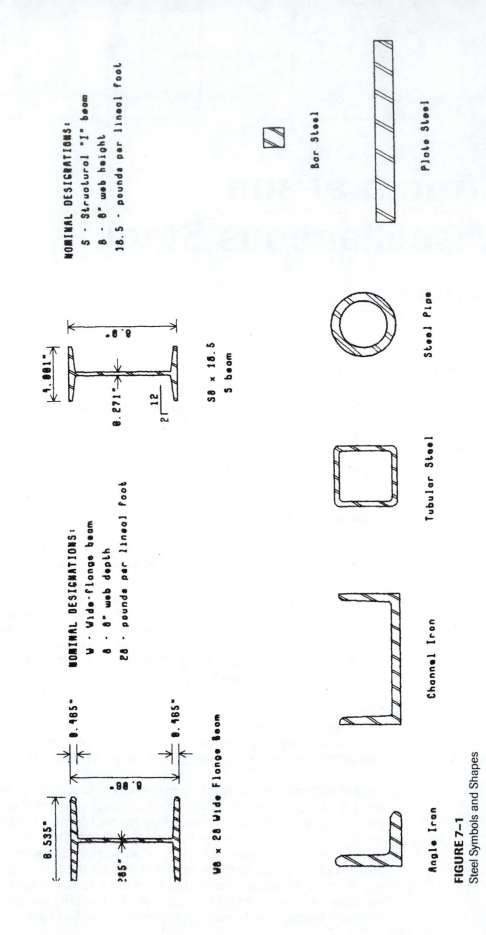

FIGURE 7–1
Steel Symbols and Shapes

NOMINAL DESIGNATIONS:
S - Structural "I" beam
8 - 8" web height
18.5 - pounds per lineal foot

S8 × 18.5
S beam

NOMINAL DESIGNATIONS:
W - Wide-flange beam
8 - 8" web depth
28 - pounds per lineal foot

W8 × 28 Wide Flange Beam

Bar Steel

Plate Steel

Steel Pipe

Tubular Steel

Channel Iron

Angle Iron

128

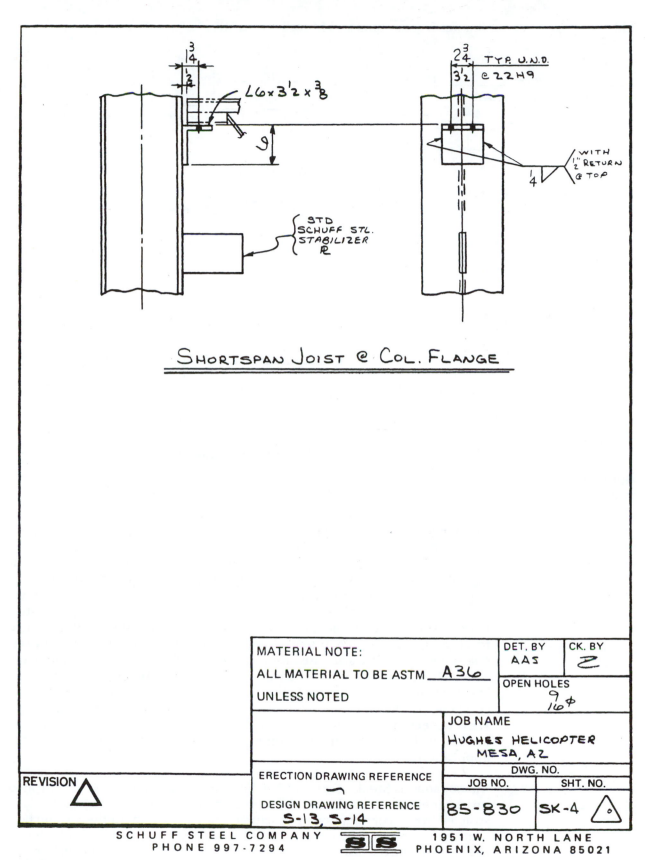

SHORTSPAN JOIST @ COL. FLANGE

MATERIAL NOTE:		DET. BY AAS	CK. BY Z
ALL MATERIAL TO BE ASTM A36		OPEN HOLES $\frac{9}{16}\phi$	
UNLESS NOTED			
	JOB NAME HUGHES HELICOPTER MESA, AZ		
ERECTION DRAWING REFERENCE	DWG. NO.		
	JOB NO.	SHT. NO.	
DESIGN DRAWING REFERENCE S-13, S-14	85-830	SK-4	

REVISION △

SCHUFF STEEL COMPANY
PHONE 997-7294

1951 W. NORTH LANE
PHOENIX, ARIZONA 85021

FIGURE 7-2
Sample of a Structural Steel Shop Drawing

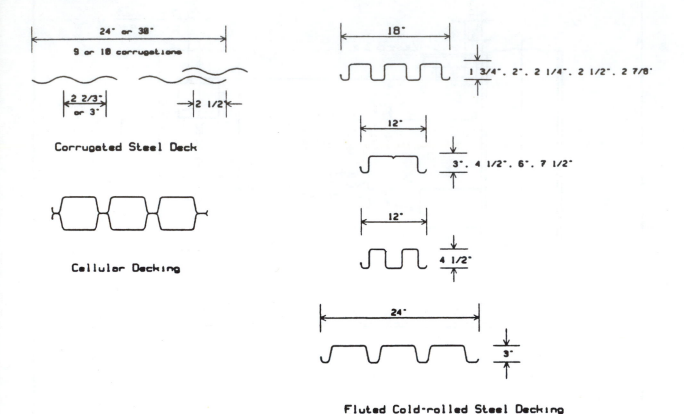

FIGURE 7–3
Steel Deck Shapes and Sizes

the punched stud and is used for structural floor, ceiling, and roof framing where no penetrations are required.

Interior bearing wall construction may be constructed with structural light-gauge steel. Its use is only necessary where extra support is required for large open areas such as found in retail store spaces, hotel lobbies, and so on.

See figure 7–3. Steel decking is also a part of the structural light-gauge steel materials used in construction. Prefabricated, cold-rolled steel from 22 gauge to 16 gauge, is available in several patterns and combinations: **corrugated** cold-rolled steel sheets are used for roofing or siding on nonresidential structures; **fluted** cold-rolled steel sheets and **fluted cellular** cold-rolled steel sheets are used as support for lightweight concrete floor decks, for wood and concrete roof decks, or for rigid roof insulation installations. A **cellular type fluted decking,** called "Walker Duct," is often used as a raceway (conduit) for under-floor wiring in large commercial office buildings and retail store applications.

Miscellaneous Steel. *See figure 7–4.* The **open-web steel joist,** a fabricated miscellaneous steel product, is the most common of the metal joists. It is constructed from a combination of structural gauge angle iron for the top and bottom chords and solid bent steel or tubular steel pieces welded and/or bolted to the chords. The open-web steel joist is common in large flat-roof construction for industrial and some commercial applications. The structural strength of an open-web steel joist makes it possible to span as much as 48'-0" (14.63 m) without additional support.

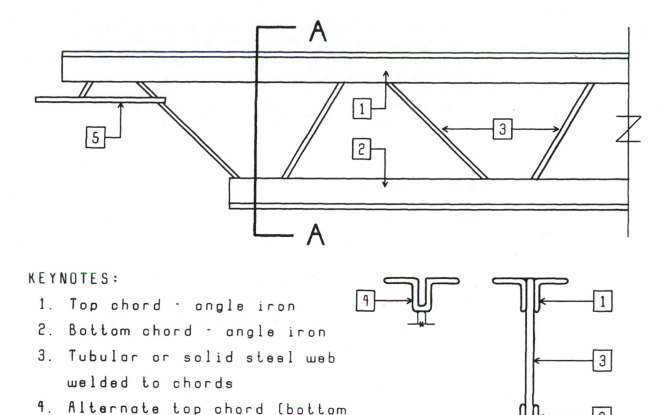

KEYNOTES:

1. Top chord - angle iron

2. Bottom chord - angle iron

3. Tubular or solid steel web
    welded to chords

4. Alternate top chord (bottom
    similar but opposite)

5. Gusset plate welded to web

SECTION A-A

FIGURE 7-4
Miscellaneous Steel: Open Web Joist

Newer types of steel joist construction are now in existence. One is the modular steel joist system, which is bolted and/or welded to other modular joists to make a solid exposed system for under roofs.

Also included in the category of miscellaneous steel products are special entry decorative steel structures, metal railings, fences, stairwells, balusters, banisters, window guards, gates, and other decorative tubular or malleable wrought-iron work.

Expansion Controls

The expansion controls for structural steel are not to be confused with expansion and contraction joints discussed in Division 3, chapter 4, or sheet metal and flashings found in Division 7, chapter 7. Expansion control is necessary where the varying coefficients of expansion require more than a small neoprene control as used in concrete. Metal is used because its coefficient of expansion is less than that of concrete or masonry and can, therefore, withstand temperature changes more readily and prevent breakdown of the materials being controlled.

Metal plates, bars, and other special shapes are used for expansion control where dissimilar materials or substrates occur in heavily trafficked areas requiring structural stability. Connections at bridge points are the most common examples. Concrete floor and roof decks may also require such controls, especially where seismic control is necessary in large structures of steel, glass, and concrete. Some of the control connections may be of standard, prefabricated construction. However, they are more frequently customized fabrications designed and engineered for the specific job.

Use of Division 5

It is not unusual to find Division 5 eliminated in specifications for residential or small commercial construction. The division is often listed as "not used." In such instances, other divisions include the sections of Division 5, as follows:

Division 3, Concrete: rebar, welded wire fabric, and other embeds

Division 4, Masonry: rebar and other embeds

Division 6, Carpentry: beam hinge connectors, tubular and pipe steel columns

Division 9, Finishes: light-gauge metal framing

SCOPE OF WORK

The steel support beams (under-floor) are the only steel construction included in the base bid. In appendix IV, Division 5, the specifications are as follows:

Division 5 Metals

05000 Scope of Work

Division 1 and the General Conditions shall be considered a part of this division. Provide all labor, material and equipment necessary to complete the structural and miscellaneous steel work indicated on the drawings. All materials to meet ASTM requirements. Provide all steel embeds, anchors and accessories as shown on plans or as required for a complete installation. Submit shop drawings for all structural steel components.

05100 Structural Metal Framing

Support beams shall be W8×28 (W20.32 cm × 12.73 kg) wide-flange structural steel beams spanning from wall to wall in both an east/west and north/south direction. A 4″ (10.16 cm) embedment (bearing) shall be installed in the wall at each end. Beams shall be fastened together with 3″× 3″× 1/4″× 6″ long (7.62 cm × 7.62 cm × 0.64 cm × 15.25 cm) clip angle stiffeners, bolted and welded at both sides of all junctions of all web joints. All welding, burning, scarfing and painting of metal shall be done on the job site. Bolts shall be minimum 5/8″ (1.59 cm) DIA × 2″ (5.08 cm) long with nut and lock washer. Bolts shall be tack-welded to prevent loosening. Weld at perimeter of stiffeners shall be minimum 1/4″ (0.64 cm) continuous fillet. Flange surface joints

shall be "V" shaped with weld to fill "V" to a minimum 1/8"
(0.32 cm) above surface of flange. Surface weld shall be scarfed
smooth. Paint all exposed surfaces with rust-inhibiting primer.

End of Division

THE ESTIMATE

See figure 7–5. The type of spreadsheet to summarize the estimate is the choice of the estimator or contractor. The sheet shown in figure 7–5 is one of the many varieties available.

Structural Steel Beams

See Plans, Sheet S–1, Foundation Plan. The specifications for a W8×28 (W20.32 cm ×12.73 kg) beam are shown in cross section in figure 7–1. The plan for the Medical Clinic indicates the steel beams are placed over the concrete piers and embedded into the foundation walls. The size of the pier is determined by the type of construction being supported above. The beam rests on a 2×8 (5.08 cm × 20.32 cm) treated sill plate (PTMS) at all walls and on the piers. There is a 2× (5.08 m×) plate fastened to the top of the beam. The indent in the foundation wall for the beam to rest is 11" (27.94 cm) high × 4" (10.16 cm) deep × 6 1/2" ± (16.51 cm) wide. Other materials that may be considered in lieu of the 2× sill plate are corrosion-resistant products designed to protect the beam from the concrete foundation wall. These may include anticorrosive paints or other chemical protection. If one of these is used in lieu of the 2×, the height of the embedment must be changed to 9 1/2" (24.13 cm). The owner or engineer must make this decision prior to the installation of the foundation wall to correct the height of the embedment.

The lengths of beam may be broken down in three ways:

1. The east/west beams may be the main beams cut to fit from wall to pier and from pier to pier, with the shorter north/south beams continuous.
2. The application may be reversed.
3. All the beams may be cut to fit from wall to pier and from pier to pier in both directions.

See chart 7–1. The third method is used in the example in chart 7–1. The walls are 41'-0" × 58'-0" × 10" (12.50 m × 17.68 m × 25.4 cm). The embedments are 4" (10.16 cm) deep at the walls on each end. All wall-to-pier spans in both directions are the same length. The pier-to-pier spans vary due to the spacing of the piers.

Labor

See figure 7–6a and *figure 7–6b, Composite Crew Schedule.* A 4-person crew and a foreman are required to install the steel beams. It takes the crew 2 1/2 days to complete the installation. The following shows how to calculate the labor cost estimate.

QUANTITY SURVEY

PROJECT: Medical Clinic, Caliente, Nevada

ACCOUNT: _____

ACCOUNT	DESCRIPTION	QUANTITY						
	Foundation beam:							
	W8x28	12 ea						
	W8x28	4 ea						
	W8x28	6 ea						
	Stiffeners (4 ea per connection):							
	4 ea x 8 =	32 ea						
	(¼"x6"x3½" clip angles)							
	Bolts nuts and washers:12 ea per connection point:							
	5/8"x4" bolts	96 ea						
	5/8" nuts	96 ea						
	5/8" washers	96 ea						
	Treated lumber (alternate):							
	2x8	12 lf						
	2x6	288 lf						
	(See Division 9, Finishes for light gauge structural steel)							

FIGURE 7-5
Spreadsheet

134

North/south beams:
Total beam span:
    41 lf − (0.83 lf × 2) + (0.33 lf × 2) =
    41 lf − 1.66 lf + 0.66 lf =
    41 lf − 1 lf = **40 lf**

    12.50 m − (0.25 m × 2) + (0.10 m × 2) =
    12.50 m − 0.50 m + 0.20 m =
    12.50 m − 0.30 m = **12.20 m**

East/west beams:
Total beam span:
    58 lf − (0.83 lf × 2) + (0.33 lf × 2) =
    58 lf − 1.66 lf + 0.66 lf =
    58 lf − 1 lf = **57 lf**

    17.68 m − (0.25 m × 2) + (0.10 m × 2) =
    17.68 m − 0.50 m + 0.20 m =
    17.68 m − 0.30 m = **17.38 m**

Wall-to-pier—all walls (wall embedment to center of pier):
    11.25 lf + 0.33 lf − 0.83 lf = **10.75 lf**
    3.43 m + 0.10 m − 0.25 m = **3.28 m**

Pier-to-pier (north/south):
    40 lf − (11.25 lf × 2) =
    40 lf − 22.5 lf = **17.5 lf ea**

    12.19 m − (3.43 m × 2) =
    12.19 m − 6.86 m = **5.33 m ea**

Pier-to-pier (east/west):
    58 lf − (11.25 lf × 2) =
    58 lf − 22.5 lf = 35.5 lf
    35.5 lf ÷ 3 (pier spaces) = **11.83 lf ea**

    17.68 m − (3.43 m × 2) =
    17.68 m − 6.86 m = 10.82 m
    10.82 m ÷ 3 (pier spaces) = **3.61 m**

Total beam quantity:
    Wall-to-pier: 12 ea × 10.75 lf   = 129.00 lf
    N/S pier-to-pier: 4 ea × 17.5 lf   =   70.00 lf
    E/W   "   "   " : 6 ea × 11.83 lf =   70.98 lf

    Total lf: **269.98 lf**

    12 ea × 3.28 m = 39.36 m
    4 ea × 5.33 m = 21.32 m
    6 ea × 3.61 m = 21.66 m

               82.34 m

Weight of steel (W8 × 28):
    (269.98 lf × 28 lb/lf) ÷ 2,000 lb =
    7,559.44 lb ÷ 2,000 lb = **3.78 T**

    (82.34 m × 12.70 kg/0.305 m) ÷ 907.18 kg =
    1,045.72 kg ÷ 907.18 kg = **1.15 metric T**

CHART 7—1
Structural Steel Estimate

CREW	HOURLY + BURDEN WAGE	% TIME ON JOB/HR	HOURLY RATE
Foreman	$16.65 + $ 5.20	16%	= $ 3.50
Oper. Engr.	$16.45 + $ 3.40	35.5%	= $ 7.05
Ironworker	$16.15 + $ 5.20	11%	= $ 2.35
Oiler	$13.24 + $ 3.40	2%	= $ 0.33
Laborer	$11.75 + $ 3.74	35.5%	= $ 5.50
Composite Crew Rate:		100%	$18.73/MH

FIGURE 7–6a
Composite Crew Schedule

CREW	HOURLY WAGE + BURDEN
Foreman	$16.65 + $ 5.20
Oper. Engr.	$16.45 + $ 3.40
Ironworker	$16.15 + $ 5.20
Oiler	$13.24 + $ 3.40
Laborer	$11.75 + $ 3.74
	$74.24 + $20.94 = $95.19
Composite Crew Rate:	$95.18/5 = $19.04

FIGURE 7–6b
Composite Crew Schedule

FIGURE 7–7
Equipment Schedule

EQUIPMENT	USE TIME	UNIT COST	TOTAL
Truck w/ Welder	2.5 days	@ $175/day	= $ 437.50
Crane	2.5 days	@ $250/day	= $ 625.00
P/U & Delivery			= $ 180.00
Equipment Total:			$1,242.50

The productivity rating is determined to be 66%. The productivity factor is calculated as follows:

70% ÷ 66 % = 1.06

The calculations for the labor cost are as follows:

Method 7-6a:
$18.73/MH × 1.06 = $19.85/MH
$19.85/MH × 8 hr = $158.80/MD
$158.80/MD × 5 crew members = $794.00/CD
$794.00/CD × 2.5 days = $1,985.00

Method 7-6b:
$19.04/MH × 1.06 = $20.18/MH
$20.18/MH × 8 hr = $161.44/MD
$161.44/MD × 5 crew members = $807.20/CD
$807.20/CD × 2.5 days = $2,018.00

Equipment

See figure 7–7. The equipment required for the installation of the steel beams for the Medical Clinic includes a welding machine and a crane to assist in placement of the beams. A mobile, truck-mounted boom crane is sufficient for the work. The crane cost is $250 per day. The calculations for the equipment, including pickup and delivery, are shown in figure 7–7.

CHAPTER EXERCISES

1. What size and length of clip angle are needed for the steel beam connections?

2. How many bolts, nuts, and washers are required for the clip angle connectors?

3. How many lineal feet of welding is necessary for the beam and clip angle connectors?

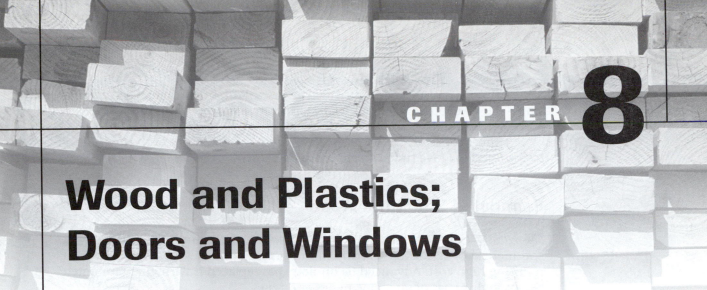

CHAPTER 8

Wood and Plastics; Doors and Windows

Divisions 6 and 8

A carpenter is a part of many trades involved in building construction—from layout and formwork for excavating, grading, and concrete, to metal stud, drywall, and window and door installations, as well as rough and finish wood framing. Division 6, Wood and Plastics, and Division 8, Doors and Windows, are both included in this chapter since a carpenter is called upon to do most of the installations. The chapter, therefore, is divided into three separate subsections. The first section deals with **rough carpentry,** the second with **finish carpentry,** and the last with **doors and windows.**

ROUGH CARPENTRY

See plans, Sheet A–1, Architectural Floor Plan, and Sheets S–1 through S–8, Structural Plans. See also appendix IV, The Project Manual, Division 6, Carpentry, and appendix V for wood classifications, types and uses. The structural framing plans, which include plates (sill, sole, and top), floor joists, subflooring, wall framing, ceiling joists, structural roof construction, and roof sheathing are part of rough carpentry (or rough framing). All accessories that aid in these installations also become a part of the procedures and materials of rough carpentry. Grades and types of lumber, nailing requirements, splicing procedures, and fasteners are indicated in the specifications for a project.

Heavy Timber Construction

Heavy timber construction is most commonly used in caustic environments such as shoring for mines, rail ties, poles for power line construction, and supports for wooden bridges and trestles. The smallest milled member included in heavy timber is a 6×6 (15.24 cm × 15.24 cm). Some building installations such as barns or barnlike structures use heavy timber beams and columns.

Heavy timber is also used to provide the rustic look in commercial construction such as exposed decorative support beams and vegas (used in Spanish-style architecture).

Timber construction has been greatly reduced as a result of the dwindling forest reserves, government regulation, and costs.

Fabricated Structural Wood

See figure 8–1. As just mentioned, heavy timber is not commonly used today in commercial or residential construction because of its lack of availability and resulting high cost. Advanced technology has replaced it with glue-laminated beams and trusses of several varieties and types.

Glue-Laminated Wood Beams.   The replacement for large timber beams and buttresses are called **glue-laminated beams** (glu-lams or GLBs) made from laminated and glued 2× select lumber. A smooth-finished exposed glu-lam beam is called an **architectural beam.** An unexposed semi-smooth-finished glu-lam is referred to as a **structural beam.** Both types are of the same structural quality. The only difference between them is appearance.

A smaller laminated beam made of 1/10" (0.25 cm) or 1/8" (0.32 cm) plywood veneers glued together in parallel grain patterns up to 1 3/4" (4.45 cm) thick is called a **Micro-Lam®**. This beam is used in light commercial and residential construction for floor joists, residential garage door header beams, and so on. Dependent upon the design and strength required for the truss, the Micro-Lam® also doubles as a truss.

Truss Beams and Joists.   *Refer to figure 8–1. See appendix V, Truss Joist TJI Series.* Solid truss construction is more common to residential construction. The TJI Series truss is made with a top and bottom wood chord of single or double 2× (5.08 cm×) lumber with a plywood or OSB® web similar to the Micro-Lam® beam. Another type of truss, called a **Parallam®**, is made of compressed wood and adhesives similar to OSB® board; however, in appearance, it is similar to the plywood truss.

The open-web joist, manufactured much like the steel open-web joist, is also referred to as a truss. The strength of the wood joist is less than the steel joist; therefore, wood joists can be used only in shorter spans and where less stress is placed on the joist. The open-web joist may be manufactured using metal tubular steel web or wooden 2× web construction. As with the open-web steel joist, the wood joist may be used for flat commercial roof or floor joist applications, as well as for new barn and open-shed construction and carports.

Wood Treatment

The location of the project and the specific use of the lumber determine the type of protection that may be required for the wood. There are three classifications of wood treatment with which lumber is impregnated: (1) fire-retardant, (2) termite protection, and (3) moisture-resistant.

Fire-retardant lumber is impregnated with a chemical called **pentachlorophenol (penta).** Another fire-retarder is **creosote.** Creosote is used as a lumber treatment for all three purposes: fire-retardant, termite protection,

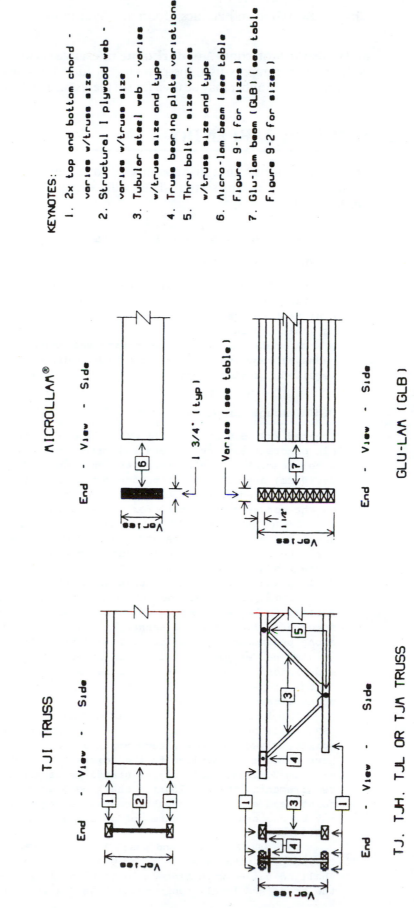

KEYNOTES:

1. 2x top and bottom chord - varies w/truss size

2. Structural I plywood web - varies w/truss size

3. Tubular steel web - varies w/truss size and type

4. Truss bearing plate variations

5. Thru bolt - size varies w/truss size and type

6. Micro-lam beam (see table Figure 9-1 for sizes)

7. Glu-lam beam (GLB) (see table Figure 9-2 for sizes)

MICROLLAM®

End - View - Side

1 3/4" (typ)

Varies

GLU-LAM (GLB)

End - View - Side

Varies (see table)

1 1/2"

Varies

TJI TRUSS

End - View - Side

Varies

TJ. TJH. TJL OR TJA TRUSS

End - View - Side

Varies

FIGURE 8–1
Glue-Laminated Beams and Trusses

141

and moisture protection. A **waterborne preservative** called "Wolmanizing" is the most commonly used insect retardant found in construction materials. "Wolmanized" lumber may be used for sill plates (mudsills) instead of redwood.

SCOPE OF WORK: ROUGH CARPENTRY

The specifications found in Appendix IV for rough framing for the Medical Clinic are given in this section. They will be used in making the rough carpentry estimate.

Division 6: Wood and Plastics

06000 Scope of Work

Division 1 and the General Conditions are to be considered a part of this division. Furnish all labor, materials, tools and equipment necessary to complete all work under this division and as indicated on drawings.

Provide and maintain temporary enclosures, fences and barricades as required by local codes and ordinances and OSHA. If required, provide temporary door and window enclosures.

06100 Rough Carpentry

Treated 2×8 (5.08 cm × 20.32 cm) sill plate shall be placed on all concrete surfaces (piers and walls) prior to installation of steel beam. Sill plate may be attached using 1/2″ × 10″ (1.27 cm × 25.40 cm) anchor bolts or powder actuated shot and pin. If anchor bolts are used, the carpentry contractor shall supply the anchors to the concrete contractor for installation.

2×8 (5.08 cm × 20.32 cm) HF (Hemlock Fir), utility grade, shall be installed on the structural steel beams as per plans and shall be fastened with powder actuated shot and pin. The fasteners shall be spaced 4′-0″ O/C (1.22 m). The lumber shall be drilled and fastened with countersunk nuts and washers.

Floor joists shall be 2×10 (5.08 cm × 25.40 cm) DF (Douglas Fir) #1 or better. Spacing and lengths shall be as indicated on structural floor plan. A header (rim joist) shall be installed along perimeter of floor to close and hide stub ends of floor joists. Header joists shall be fastened with 4 16d nails at each end. Interior floor joists shall be fastened with joist hangers of the proper size. Metal cross bridging shall be installed where spans exceed 8′-0″ (2.44 m).

Standard 3/4″ (1.91 cm), 5-ply, underlayment, or 1″ (2.54 cm) OSB, shall be used for the subflooring applied over the floor joists. Plywood or OSB sheets applied over the floor joists shall have an adhesive applied to the joists and shall be nailed with minimum 8d shank nails as per standards of the trade and local requirements. The subflooring shall be placed with staggered joints and clips at the butt ends where required or underlayment may be cut and fit to center of joists and nailed at 9″ O/C (22.86 cm).

1/2″ (1.27 cm) plywood shall bear the DFPA stamp, type CDX or CCX, 5-ply, with exterior glue, UNO, for exterior use at roof and shall be nailed with minimum 8d shank nails as per standards of the trade and local requirements. The CCX shall be applied along the eaves with the smooth side exposed to the underside. The remainder of the roof shall be filled with CDX material. All joints to be staggered with clips at the butt ends as required.

Exterior walls and interior bearing walls are 2×6 (5.08 cm × 15.24 cm) studs at 16″ (40.64 cm) O/C. Plumbing walls shall be staggered 2×4 (5.08 cm × 10.16 cm) studs on 2×6 plate at 24″ (60.96 cm) O/C. Partition walls shall also be 2×4 (5.08 cm × 10.16 cm) studs at 24″ (60.96 cm) O/C. All studs shall be DF, construction grade. Sole plate and double top plate shall be 2×6 (5.08 cm × 15.24 cm) HF utility grade for exterior bearing walls and interior bearing walls and 2×4 (5.08 cm × 10.16 cm) HF utility grade for nonbearing interior partitions. All walls shall extend 9′-0″ (2.74 m) A.F.F. Where code requires 2×6 (5.08 cm × 15.24 cm) or 2×4 (5.08 cm or 10.16 cm), fire blocking shall be installed to match the wall size.

All exterior corners shall have a diagonal let-in brace applied so that the brace extends from sole plate to double top plate at an angle of no more than 60° at the sole plate. An alternate 3/8″ (0.95 cm) CDX plywood or OSB shear panel may be installed in lieu of the diagonal bracing. Additional let-in bracing shall be installed for every 25 lf of uninterrupted wall space between corners.

A fire wall shall be constructed above the interior East and West bearing walls. The fire wall shall extend from the top plate of the interior bearing walls to the underside of the roof structure and shall be constructed with 2×6 (5.08 cm × 15.24 cm) construction grade studs at 16″ O/C (40.64 cm). Where code requires, fire blocking shall be installed at mid-height of the walls.

3 2×6 (5.08 cm × 15.24 cm) DF construction grade studs or a 6×6 (15.24 cm × 15.24 cm) DF #2 or better post shall be installed in the Restroom/Break Room common wall and 3 2×4 (5.08 cm × 10.16 cm) DF construction grade studs or a 4×6 (10.16 cm × 15.24 cm) DF #2 or better post shall be installed in the Break Room/Reception Room common wall. The posts shall be placed directly below the double ceiling joists. Two (2) sets of 3 2×6 (5.08 cm × 15.24 cm) construction grade studs or two 6×6 (15.24 cm × 15.24 cm) DF #2 or better posts shall be installed in the Reception Room/Waiting Room common wall. One post shall be installed on each side of the Reception Room window opening.

All furred-down ceiling areas shall be constructed of 2×2 (5.08 cm × 5.08 cm) DF common with vertical members spaced at 24″ O/C (60.96 cm). Where required, 2×2 (5.08 cm × 5.08 cm) or 2×4 (5.08 cm × 10.16 cm) furring shall be used for backup for GWB installations.

Ceiling joists shall be 2×6 (5.08 cm × 15.24 cm) DF #2 or better spaced as indicated on the plans. All joists shall be fastened with joist hangers of proper size at end connections where abutting double joists and header joists. Double joists shall be installed over all bearing walls. Header joists shall be installed to hide exposed joist ends and for fastening of joist hangers. Frieze blocking shall be installed along perimeters parallel to the joists at plate line where header joists are not required.

Conventional roof framing shall include 2×6 (5.08 cm × 15.24 cm) DF #2 or better for rafters and double 2×8 (5.08 cm × 20.32 cm) or a 4×8 (10.16 cm × 20.32 cm) DF #1 or better for hip and ridge beams. Rafters shall be attached at the plate line with

Simpson Strong Tie anchors #A34, #A35, or equal, and with Simpson
skewed joist hangers, or equal, at all hip and ridge connections
as per manufacturer's recommendation.

The conventional roof framing shall be supported by
installing 3 2×6 (5.08 cm × 15.24 cm) studs or 6×6 (15.24 cm ×
15.24 cm) posts over the interior bearing walls where there is no
fire wall, spaced at 4'-0" O/C (1.22 m). These posts shall have
2×4 (5.08 cm × 10.16 cm) collar ties extending transversely from
post to post at the juncture with the post and the roof
structure. 2×4 (5.08 cm × 10.16 cm) purlins shall be run continuously parallel with the post construction supporting the collar
ties at the posts.

A rough-sawn (R/S) fascia board shall be 2×8 (5.08 cm ×
20.32 cm) DF #2 or better and nailed to ends of rafter and hip
tails with 2 8d shank nails at each connection.

THE ROUGH CARPENTRY ESTIMATE

The Estimate/Order Form

See figure 8–2. A form like the one shown in figure 8–2 is commonly used by
carpenters, by lumber yards, and by some mills and mill brokers. The estimator may be required to use metric measurements, where applicable. This estimate sheet should include the following information:

Column 1: Number of pieces

Column 2: Nominal size, sheet (plywood) size, or manufacturer's
designation

Column 3: Lineal feet or thickness of sheet

Column 4: Description of material

Column 5: Usage (for what purpose and/or location)

Column 6: Board feet or square feet required (extended quantities)

Column 7: Itemized unit price

Column 8: Itemized cost extensions, taxes, markup (if any), and total
cost of materials

When estimating materials, the estimator must take into account two items:
the **length of lumber** and the **waste factor**. The length of lumber should always be in even lengths. The waste factor varies from product to product and
from contractor to contractor. *A 5% waste factor is used throughout this text.*

Foundation Framing

See Plans, Sheet S–1, Foundation Plan: See also chart 8–1. The estimator builds the
estimate just as the framer builds the structure, starting at the foundation and
finishing with the roof.

Sill Plate.   Wherever wood meets masonry or concrete or where wood is used
below grade, a sill plate is required. It may be redwood or pressure treated lumber. The sill plate specified for the Medical Clinic is a 2×8 (5.05 cm × 20.32 cm)
PTMS (*Pressure-Treated MudSill*).

DATE OF ESTIMATE	ARCHITECT	OWNER
10/30/92	Christie & Assoc.	Southwest Marble and Mirror Co.

CONTRACTOR	OWNER'S ADDRESS
Mar-Ja International, Inc.	1000 75th Ave., Bethlehem, PA

ADDRESS	JOB LOCATION
6592 Fairlynn Blvd.	359 Washington Blvd. No.

CITY	STATE	ZIP		
Bethlehem	PA	10987		Bethlehem, PA

TELEPHONE (123)456-7890

SHEET No. 1 of 3

Acct#	#	PIECES	SIZE	LENGTH (LINEAL)	DESCRIPTION		USAGE	TOTAL FEET	UNIT PRICE	AMOUNT
	1	20	2x4	16	PTMS/Redwood	S4S	sill plate	213.33 BF	0.15	$ 32 00
	2	36	2x6	16	" "		" "	576.00	0.17	97 92
	3	40	2x4	16	DF cannon/HF utility		plate (T&B)	426.67	0.13	55 47
	4	72	2x6	16	"		" "	1152.00	0.15	172 80
	5	R/L	2x4	152			blocking	101.33	0.13	13 17
	6	R/L	2x6	88			"	88.00	0.15	13 20
	7	26	2x6	12	Select Structural #2 or #3		studs	312.00	0.21	65 62
	8	175	2x4	10	Stud Grade		"	1166.67	0.19	221 67
	9	5	2x10	14	(16/4 lf) DF #2 or better		header	53.33	0.19	10 13
	10	5	2x10	14	DF #2 or better		ledger	116.67	0.26	· 30 33
	11	6	3x10	16	" " " "		"	240.00	0.30	72 00
	12	25	11⅞"	x32'-8"	TJI/25 Series truss joists		roof truss	816.75 LF	4.65	3797 88
	13	1		x16'-0"				16.00		74 40
	14	1		x12'-0"				12.00		55 80
	15	4		x 3'-8"				14.67		68 22
	16	1	5⅛"	x20'-0"	GLB (architectural)	S4S	beam	20.00	9.70	194 00
	17	52	4x8	x ½"	CDX plywd Structural 1		sheathing	1664.00 SF	0.18	299 52
	37				NOTE: Freight included in pricing					0 00

COMMENTS:		
Prices firm for 3 months. Add 2% to Grand Total at that	FORWARD	5273 73
for anticipated increase. Get escalation clause in con-	SUB-TOTAL	421 90
tract if project start is beyond 1/2/93.	TAX @ 8%	0 00
	TOTAL	5695 63

FIGURE 8–2
Spreadsheet/Bill of Materials

(All lumber lengths are to the nearest even lineal foot with a waste factor of 5% included.)

Foundation walls:

(58 lf × 2) + (41 lf × 2) × 1.05 =	(17.68 m × 2) + (12.50 m × 2) × 1.05 =
(116 lf + 82 lf) × 1.05 =	(35.36 m + 25 m) × 1.05 =
198 lf × 1.05 = 207.9 or **208 lf**	60.36 m × 1.05 = 63.38 or **64 m**

Piers (top of pier 8" × 8" [20.32 cm × 20.32 cm]):

8 piers × 0.67 lf × 1.05 =	8 piers × 0.20 m × 1.05 =
5.36 lf × 1.05 = 5.63 or **6 lf**	1.6 m × 1.05 = 1.68 or **2 m**

Total sill plate:

208 lf + 6 lf = **214 lf of 2×8 PTMS**	64 m + 2 m = **66 m of 5.08 cm × 20.32 cm PTMS**

CHART 8–1
Sill Plate Estimate

(All lumber lengths are to the nearest even lineal foot with a waste factor of 5% included.)

Total length of 2×8 (5.08 cm × 20.32 cm) HF utility grade lumber on beams:

270 lf × 1.05 = 283.5 or **284 lf**	82.34 m × 1.05 = 86.46 m or **87 m**

Shot-and-pin @ 4'-0" (1.22 m) O/C:
North/south beams (4):

(40 lf ÷ 4 lf) + 1 = 11 shot-and-pin per beam	(12.19 m ÷ 1.22 m) + 1 = 10.91
	or 11 shot-and-pin per beam

11 × 4 = **44 shot-and-pin**

East/west beams (2):

(57 lf ÷ 4 lf) + 1 = 15.25 or 16 shot-and-pin	(17.37 m ÷ 1.22 m) + 1 = 15.24 or 16 shot-and-pin

16 × 2 = **32 shot-and-pin**

Total shot-and-pin:
(44 + 32) × 1.05 = **79.8 or 80 shot-and-pin**

CHART 8–2
Utility Plate Estimate: Steel Beam and Shot-and-Pin

Wood Plate for Steel Beam

See chart 8–2. Also refer to chart 7–1. The beam plate stock for the Medical Clinic is 2×6 (5.05 cm × 15.24 cm) HF utility grade. The total lineal feet or metric units, in random lengths, may be considered. The material needed for the beam plate is equal to the total length of the steel beams estimated in chapter 7.

Shot-and-Pin. *See chart 8–2.* The number of shot-and-pin units needed to fasten the wood plate stock depends upon the spacing of the shot-and-pin and the length of the steel beam. The normal spacing is from 2 lf (0.61 m) to 4 lf (1.22 m). The Specifications for the Medical Clinic state that 4 lf (1.22 m) spacing is required. From the information above, the lengths of the beams and the total lineal feet or metric units are known. The number of shot-and-pin should be broken down into the number per beam, and then totaled.

Floor Framing

See Plans, Sheet S–2, Structural Floor Plan. Floor framing includes the installation of the floor joists and the subflooring.

(All lumber lengths are to the nearest even lineal foot with a waste factor of 5% included.)

Number of joists @ 2'-0" (0.61 m) O/C (east/west ends):

(41 lf ÷ 2 lf) + 1 = **21.5 or 22 joists**   (12.50 m ÷ 0.61 m) + 1 = **21.49 or 22 joists**

Add 1 for double joist @ room wall above:

22 + 1 = **23 joists**

Length and number of 2×10 (5.05 cm × 30.48 cm) joists (east/west):

11.25 lf + 0.67 lf − 0.125 lf = 11.8 or 12 lf ea   3.43 m + 0.20 m − 0.04 m = 3.59 m

12 lf × 23 pc × 1.05 = 289.8 lf   3.59 m × 23 pc × 1.05 = 86.70 m

289.8 lf ÷ 12 lf ea = **24.15 or 24 joists**   86.70 m ÷ 3.66 m = **23.69 or 24 joists**

North/south 2×10 (5.08 cm × 30.48 cm) header (rim) and interior double joist perpendicular to floor joists – 3 joists total:

41 lf × 3 × 1.05 = **129.15 or 130 lf**   12.50 m × 3 × 1.05 = **39.38 or 40 m**

Bridging:

23 joists; end joists have minimal space, therefore:

21 spaces × 2 lf × 1.05 = **44.1 or 44 lf**   21 spaces × 0.61 m × 1.05 = **13.45 or 13.5 m**

CHART 8–3
Floor Joist Estimate: Playroom/Waiting Room Floors

Floor Joists. *See chart 8–3.* The Specifications for the Medical Clinic call for 2×10 (5.05 cm × 25.40 cm) floor joists spaced as per plan. The floor joists are placed utilizing the shortest practical span possible for structural flexural strength. They are spaced at both 1 lf (30.48 cm) and 2 lf (0.61 m) intervals. The closer spacing is for the purpose of providing additional strength in areas where extra loads are applied. These areas include the restroom, break room, X-ray laboratory, ambulatory operating room, and the processing and records room. All joists may be fastened by nailing alone or with framing anchors (clips and hangers).

A simple mathematical verification of the number of joists can also determine the accuracy of the drawing (Sheet S–2). For example, the waiting room/playroom area along the east wall of the Medical Clinic can be determined by using the Framing Ratio Table, found in appendix IV. The building is 41 lf (12.50 m) along the east wall, and the spacing is 2'-0" O/C (0.61 m). Code also demands that floor joists parallel with a bearing wall must be doubled. There is one bearing wall parallel to the joists. The number of joists by the count-up method is identical to the number of joists shown on Sheet S–2 and the math in the first column of chart 8–3; namely, 22.

The next step is to estimate the length of the floor joists. The length from the west wall to the center of the beam supporting a floor joist is 11'-3" (3.43 m). The floor joist abuts the **header** (rim) joist on the east end and rests on the north/south steel beam at the interior end, abutting the double joists that are fastened parallel to the beam. The nearest even length of lumber is 12'-0" (3.66 m). See chart 8–3.

Header Joists. The header (rim) joist is a continuous member extending out-to-out along the perimeter of the east wall. The joist is used to hide, protect, and stiffen the interior joists abutting it. The length of the members may be random lengths. They are butted together for both appearance and strength. See north/south rim and double joists in chart 8–3.

Joist Hangers. All of the joists perpendicular to the headers and interior double joists are fastened with joist hangers. The hanger size is determined by the

---

(All lumber lengths are to the nearest even lineal foot with a waste factor of 5% included.)

¾" (1.91 cm) subflooring (underlayment):

Area (east/west ends):

　　41 lf × 11.25 lf = **461.25 sq ft**　　　　　　　　　　12.50 m × 3.43 m = **42.88 m²**

Number of sheets 4'× 8' × ¾" (1.22 m × 2.44 m × 1.91 cm) underlayment:

　　(461.25 sq ft ÷ 32 sq ft) × 1.05 =　　　　　　　　　(42.88 m² ÷ 2.97 m²) × 1.05 =

　　14.41 × 1.05 = **15.13 or 15 sheets**　　　　　　　　14.44 × 1.05 = **15.16 or 15 sheets**

CHART 8–4
Subflooring Estimate: Playroom/Waiting Room

size of the joist. There are 2 hangers required for each joist. The double joists may also be fastened to the header joists by means of joist hangers.

Bridging. The bridging is not indicated on the plans for the Medical Clinic. Most building code requirements state that there is to be bridging supplied for all joists where the span is greater than 8 lf (2.44 m). The bridging may be 2 × 10 (5.08 cm × 25.40 cm) solid blocking (to match the joist size), 2× wood cross bridging, or metal cross bridging. The Specifications call for the installation of the metal cross bridging. If solid bridging is to be used, chart 8–3 indicates the quantity calculation.

Subflooring (Underlayment). *See chart 8–4.* The Specifications for the Medical Clinic call for a 4'×8' × 3/4" (1.22 m × 2.44 m × 1.91 cm) plywood underlayment installed over the floor joists for the subflooring. The underlayment is glued and nailed to the supporting joists. The sheets may be clipped at the butt ends where they do not meet over a joist, or the plywood may be cut to fit over the joists and the butt ends nailed directly to the joists.

Wall Framing

See Plans, Sheet A–1, Architectural Floor Plan; Sheets S–3 and S–4, Wall Framing Plans. Also see Sheet S–7, Longitudinal and Transverse Structural Sections. The exterior walls and interior bearing walls are framed with 2×6 (5.08 cm × 15.24 cm) studs. The interior plumbing wall is framed with 2×4 (5.08 cm × 10.16 cm) studs staggered on 2×6 (5.08 cm × 15.24 cm) plate. The remaining nonbearing (partition) walls are 2×4 (5.08 cm × 10.16 cm) studs. All walls are 9 lf (2.74 m) high. This requires an estimate and/or order for specially cut studs or for 10 lf (3.05 m) studs to be cut on the job. The estimator must consider the most cost-effective method. The sample estimate uses 10 lf (3.05 m) studs. An estimate for wall framing may be made by the **lineal-foot method,** the **count-up method,** or the **count-up/ratio method.** The west exterior wall of the Medical Clinic and one of the interior partition walls between Examination Rooms #1 and #2 are used as examples for the estimates in chart 8–5, 8–6, and 8–7.

Lineal-Foot Method. *See chart 8–5.* The lineal-foot method is the simplest and quickest. This method is simply to add the lineal footages of the walls and count the total footage as equal to the number of studs. It does not take into

---

(All lumber lengths are to the nearest even lineal foot with a waste factor of 5% included.)

Lineal-foot method:

Exterior west bearing wall (this wall has studs spaced at 16" [15.24 cm] O/C):

    41 lf = 41 pc of **2×6 × 10 lf CG studs**

Interior common partition wall @ examination rooms #1 & #2 (this wall has studs spaced at 24" [20.32 cm] O/C):

    10 lf = 10 pc of **2×4 × 10 lf CG studs**

For the quantities in metrics, calculations must be performed, where 0.30 m = 12":

Exterior west bearing wall:

    12.50 m ÷ 0.30 m = 41 pc of **5.08 cm × 20.32 cm × 3.05 m CG studs**

Interior common partition wall:

    3.05 m ÷ 0.30 m = 10 pc of **5.08 cm × 10.16 cm × 3.05 m CG studs**

CHART 8—5
Wall Framing Estimate, Using Lineal-Foot Method: West Wall and Examination Room

---

West exterior wall:
By counting, there are 37 studs:
    2 corner studs
    2 abutting wall studs
    6 drywall-backing studs
  <u>27 studs @ 16" O/C</u>
37 of 2×6 (5.08 cm × 15.24 cm) studs

Interior office wall:
By counting, there are 8 studs (excluding exterior wall)
    1 stud at hall
    2 drywall-backing studs
  <u>5 studs @ 24" O/C</u>
8 of 2×4 (5.08 cm × 10.16 cm) studs

CHART 8—6
Wall Framing Estimate, Using Count-up Method: West Wall and Interior Office Partition

---

(See appendix IV, Framing Ratios per Stud Spacing.)

West exterior wall; studs @ 16" (15.24 cm) O/C:
Per table, 16" O/C = 75%
41 lf × 0.75 = 30.75 or 31 studs
  31 studs
  <u>6 drywall-backup studs</u>
37 2×6 (5.08 cm × 15.24 cm) studs

Interior office partition; studs @ 24" (60.96 cm) O/C:
Per table, 24" O/C = 50%
10 lf × 0.50 = 5 studs
  2 drywall-backup studs
  <u>1 additional hall stud</u>
8 2×4 (5.08 cm × 10.16 cm) studs

CHART 8—7
Wall Framing Estimate, Using Count-up Ratio Method: Exterior West Wall and Interior Office Partition

---

consideration the spacing of the studs or the wall openings. It will be seen that there are weaknesses with this estimate by comparing it to either of the other two methods discussed below.

Count-up Method.   *See chart 8–6.* The count-up method is ideal, but has some major drawbacks. In this method, all studs must be counted individually, including any trimmers, king studs, backing studs for wall finish, and so on. This may entail making deductions for openings and identifying cripple walls.

(All lumber lengths are to the nearest even lineal foot with a waste factor of 5% included.)

West exterior wall plate stock:

2×6 (5.08 cm × 15.24 cm) sole plate:

    41 lf × 1.05 = **43.05 or 44 lf**   12.50 m × 1.05 = **13.13 or 13 m**

2×6 (5.08 cm × 15.24 cm) double top plate:

    44 lf × 2 = **88 lf**   13.41 m × 2 = **26.82 m**

Interior common partition wall (office/exam room):

2×4 (5.08 cm × 10.16 cm) sole plate:

    10 lf × 1.05 = **10.5 or 12 lf**   3.05 m × 1.05 = **3.20 or 3 m**

2×4 (5.08 cm × 10.16 cm) double top plate:

    12 lf × 2 = **24 lf**   3.66 m × 2 = **7.32 m**

CHART 8–8

Plate Estimate: Exterior West Wall and Interior Office Partition

The count-up method is tedious, and errors are easily made as a result of loss of concentration, perhaps from interruptions by co-workers, the telephone, lunch break, and so on. In addition, the method is accurate only if the structural wall elevations are accurate.

Count-up/Ratio Method.   *See chart 8–7.* The count-up/ratio estimate is quite accurate and is the best method to use. This method is faster because the studs are calculated using a ratio (or percentage) to determine the standard number of studs. The count-up is done only at areas that require additional studs, such as the additional drywall backup studs, the abutting wall studs, and corner studs.

The west wall of the clinic is 41 lf (12.5 m). The studs are spaced at 16″ O/C (15.24 cm). According to the **ratio** table in appendix IV, Framing Ratios per Stud Spacing, the multiplier is 75% (0.75). This will indicate the number of uninterrupted studs in a wall. The extra **count-ups** are made for studs required on each side of abutting walls along the west wall for drywall (GWB) backing, one more stud than spaces, and one extra stud at each end for the corner frame.

Plate.   (See *chart 8–8.*) Estimates are needed for the sole plate and double top plate for the wall framing. The lumber used for the sole plate is equal to the total sill plate, 208 lf (63.4 m), including waste. The lumber used for the sole plate and the double top plate is HF utility or common stock. The lumber is calculated in lineal feet and ordered in random lengths.

Lintels.   The lintel (also known as a header) in nonbearing partitions may be a single flat piece or a double piece of stud material. In bearing walls, or wherever additional load support is needed, the lumber used may be double or triple pieces of larger stock. A "rule of thumb" states that a window or door opening that is 4′-0″ (1.22 m) wide in a 2×6 (5.08 × 15.24 cm) bearing wall should have 3 2×6s (5.08 cm × 15.24 cm) or a 6×6 (15.24 cm × 15.24 cm) DF #1 or #2 lintel. A lintel 6′-0″ to 8′-0″ (1.83 m to 2.44 m) wide should be installed with 3 2×8s (5.08 cm × 20.32 cm) or a 6×8 (15.24 cm × 20.32 cm) DF #1 or #2. The specifications may require even larger sizes dependent upon the load the lintel supports.

King and Trimmer Studs.   Wherever an opening in a wall occurs, there are two king studs and two trimmer studs. The **king stud** is the full-height stud immediately adjacent to an opening. The **trimmer stud** supports the lintel (header) and is cut to fit to the bottom of the lintel. These studs constitute additional count-ups to be included in the estimate.

Any partial wall above and/or below an opening is called a **cripple wall.** The stud count for these walls *may be deducted* from the total count and the lengths of the cripples added. The number of studs required to make the cripple stock is added to the total number for the wall. *It is simpler not to calculate the cripples*. They should be measured as though they were full length studs. This allows for extra material for fire blocking, and so on.

Diagonal Bracing or Shear Wall.   The purpose of diagonal bracing or shear paneling is to give additional strength to a structure, as well as to maintain a true and straight alignment of the walls.

The let-in brace may be 1×4 (2.54 cm × 10.16 cm) HF utility or common stock cut into the studs and nailed to each stud in which the embedment is made. A standard metal let-in brace may be used instead of the 1×4 (2.54 cm × 10.16 cm) HF.

The alternate 3/8" (0.95 cm) shear panel indicated in the Specifications is made of 4×8 (1.22 m × 2.44 m) sheets and nailed from bottom plate to top plate on both sides of the exterior corner.

Fire Blocking and Additional Bracing.   The waste lumber from the wall framing and/or the utility stock long enough to fit the stud spacing may be used for the blocking. Codes stipulate that fire blocking may be necessary at 4'-0" (1.22 m) A.F.F. and 8'-0" (2.44 m) A.F.F. Some areas require blocking only at the 8'-0" (2.44 m) or 10'-0" (3.05 m) level. This should be determined by the estimator from the local building department authorities or fire marshal.

Additional bracing is required to support and position the exterior bearing walls until the ceiling joists or trusses are installed. This bracing is usually added to the estimate as 20'-0" (6.10 m) lengths of 2×4 HF utility stock, at least 2 pieces per wall. When the ceiling or roof support is completed, the bracing can be used for fire blocking.

Interior Wall Framing.   *See Plans, Sheet A–1, Architectural Floor Plan; Sheet S–4, Interior Wall Framing Plan, Hall 1—East Wall. See also chart 8–9*. The same procedures for estimating the exterior framing can be used to estimate the interior framing.

Posts for Joist Support.   *See Plans, Sheet A–1, Architectural Floor Plan.* Under the middle east-west double ceiling joists, there are 4×6 (10.16 cm × 15.24 cm) or 6×6 (15.24 cm × 15.24 cm) posts or 3-2×4 (5.08 cm × 10.16 cm) or 3-2×6 (5.08 cm × 15.24 cm) studs for support of the double joist. Read the Specifications for the Medical Clinic carefully and note where they are indicated on the plans.

Fire-Wall Assembly.   The Specifications for the Medical Clinic indicate that a fire wall is to be constructed over the interior bearing wall on both the east and west ends to the underside of the roof structure. The framing matches the framing of the bearing wall below with horizontal fire blocking at a maximum of 4 lf (1.22 m) above the double top plate as per code.

The estimate for the fire wall is a count-up procedure only. The framing immediately under the hips may be a double 4×6 (10.16 × 15.24 cm) post. All studs in-between the hips are the same length. The studs between the hips and the plate are shortened to fit and are estimated as follows:

(All lumber lengths are to the nearest even lineal foot with a waste factor of 5% included.)

Interior framing - hall #1, east wall:

2×4 (5.08 cm × 10.16 cm) sole and top plate:

([11.25 lf × 2] − 1.0 lf) + 9.5 lf = 31 lf	([3.43 m × 2] − 0.30 m) + 2.90 m = 9.46 m
31 lf × 3 × 1.05 = 97.65 or 98 lf	9.46 m × 3 × 1.05 = 29.80 or 30 m

2×4 (5.08 cm × 10.16 cm) studs (ratio/count-up method):

31 lf × .50 = 15.5 or 15 studs	(9.46 m ÷ 0.30 m) × .50 = 15.76 or 15 studs
2 corner studs	2 corner studs
6 drywall-backup	6 drywall-backup
1 king stud	1 king stud
2 trimmers	2 trimmers
26 studs*	**26 studs***

(* includes 1 for cripple; 1 king stud is a regular stud; excludes 2×6 studs at exterior and bearing walls)

2 2×4 (5.05 cm × 10.16 cm) or 4×4 (10.16 cm × 10.16 cm) header @ door opening:

Opening = 3'-0"	Opening = 0.91 m
add 4" for trimmer support = **3'−4"**	add 0.10 m for trimmer support = **1.01 m**

CHART 8–9
Interior Wall Framing Estimate: Hall #1, East Wall

The longest stud nearest the hip and shortest stud nearest the plate line are equal to the length of the studs between the hips. The next longest stud and the next shortest are also equal to the longer studs between the hips. This procedure continues until all combinations of longer and shorter studs are counted. Upon completion of the count-up, waste is added; the extra material is used for fire blocking, if necessary.

Ceiling and Roof Structures

See Plans, Sheet S–5, Structural Ceiling Plan; Sheet S–6, Structural Roof Plan. As mentioned above, the walls are held in place by bracing, which remains in place until the walls are stiffened and strengthened with the installation of the ceiling joists. The structure is further strengthened by the roof structure and sheathing.

Ceiling Joists.   *See chart 8–10.* The ceiling joists for the Medical Clinic are spaced as per plan. The ceiling joists over the east and west walls are spaced at 24″ O/C (0.61 m). Solid blocking or frieze blocking is installed between the rafter tails in place of the rim joists. There are double ceiling joists constructed parallel to and over the bearing walls perpendicular to the ceiling joists at both the east and west ends.

Header (Rim) Joists or Frieze Blocking.   The quantity is the same as that for the **rim joist** at the floor structure, 208 lf 2×6 (63.4 m of 5.08 cm × 15.24 cm) DF #2 or better. See chart 8–10.

Frieze blocking is common to the southern areas of the country to aid air circulation in attic spaces. If used, the quantity is determined by the number of spaces between the rafters. A frieze-block may be a 1× or a 2× material, common stock, OSB, or plywood. The length of the block is equal to the space between rafter tails.

(All lumber lengths are to the nearest even lineal foot with a waste factor of 5% included.)

2×6 (5.08 cm × 15.24 cm) ceiling joists @ 24" (0.61 m) O/C (east end of building, west end similar):

(41 lf × 0.50) ÷ 1 = 21 joists	([12.50 m ÷ 0.30 m] × 0.50) + 1 = 21 joists
21 joists × 2 = **42 joists**	21 joists × 2 = **42 joists**

Length of joists:

same as floor joists in chart 8-3 = 12 lf	same as floor joists in chart 8-3 = 3.59 m
42 × 12 lf × 1.05 = **529.2 or 530 lf**	42 × 3.66 m × 1.05 = **161.41 or 161 m**

Double 2×6 (5.08 cm × 15.24 cm) ceiling joists perpendicular to above joists and over bearing walls (each end):

41 lf × 4 × 1.05 = **172.2 or 174 lf**	12.50 m × 4 × 1.05 = **52.5 m**

2×6 (5.05 cm × 15.24 cm) header (rim) joist:

41 lf × 2 × 1.05 = **86.1 or 86 lf**	12.50 m × 2 × 1.05 = **26.5 m**

2×6 × 1'-10½" (5.08 cm × 15.24 cm × 57.15 cm) freize blocking:

2 lf O/C − 0.125 lf (1½")* = 1'-10½"	0.61 m − 0.04 m* = 0.57 m
	21 joists + 1 = 22 spaces
	22 × 2 = **44 pc**

(*thickness of joist or rafter)

Hangers (2 per joist):

    42 joists × 2 = **84 hangers**

CHART 8–10
Ceiling Joist Estimate: East and West Ends

Ceiling Joist Hangers. The ceiling joists abut the double bearing joists; therefore, as with the floor joists, the hangers are necessary. There are two hangers for each joist spanning from the exterior rim joist and the interior perpendicular double joists.

Rafters. *See appendix V, Roof Slope Table. Also see chart 8–11.* The plan indicates the roof structure is a **hip roof.** This presents a slightly more difficult estimate than a straight gable roof. The rafters are of the same size and type material as the ceiling joists, 2×6 (5.08 cm × 15.24 cm) DF #2 or better. There is a gable roof between the junction of the hips and ridge. The hip rafters on the east and west end are the same. Two types of rafters are installed in the roof structure, the **common rafter** and the **jack rafter.** A common rafter extends from the ridge to the plate without interruption. A jack rafter is interrupted somewhere between the ridge and plate line, such as by a chimney, dormer, or hip beam.

The estimator must consider the length of the common rafter, the jack rafter, and the slope of the roof. The structural roof plan gives the *flat plane length* of the common rafter from the point where the hip meets the ridge to the plate line. The actual lengths of the rafters must be determined.

Common Rafter. The total length of the roof is 62 lf (18.9 m). The length of the ridge is 17 lf (5.18 m). The length of the common rafter at the hip is the same as the common rafter on the gable roof.

Jack Rafters. On a true (45°) hip, *the rafter next to the common rafter and the shortest rafter at the end* are equal to the length of the common rafter. Continuing this method, the *next largest and the next smallest jack rafters* are equal to the common rafter length, and so on, until all combinations are counted. The rafter

(All lumber lengths are to the nearest even lineal foot with a waste factor of 5% included.)
2×6 (5.08 cm × 15.24 cm) rafters @ 24" (0.61 m) O/C, roof structure (5/12 slope):

Flat measurements:

(58 lf + [2 lf × 2]) × (41 lf + [2 lf × 2]) =   (17.68 m + [0.61 m × 2]) × (12.50 m + [0.61 m × 2]) =
62 lf × 45 lf   18.90 m + 13.72 m

Gable area common rafters:

(Hips are true 45° angles at flat area: this means that the length of the legs of the right triangle formed are equal.)

∴ 45 lf ÷ 2 = 22.5 lf   ∴ 13.72 m ÷ 2 = 6.86 m
   62 lf − 45 lf = 17 lf   18.90 m − 13.72 m = 5.18 m
   17 lf ÷ 2 = 8.5 or 9 rafters ea side   (5.18 m ÷ 0.30 m) ÷ 2 = 8.63 or 9 rafters ea side

$$9 \times 2 = \textbf{18 rafters}$$

Length of common rafters:

By roof table:

   22.5 lf × 1.08 = **24.3 or 26 lf**   6.86 m × 1.08 = **7.41 or 7.5 m**

By proportion and theorem: **5/12 slope = 1.52/3.66**

5 lf ÷ 12 lf = x ÷ 22.5 lf (run)   1.52 m ÷ 3.66 m = x ÷ 6.86 m
12 lf × x = 22.5 lf × 5 lf   3.66 m × x = 6.86 m × 1.52 m
x = (22.5 lf × 5 lf) ÷ 12 lf x = (6.86 m × 1.52 m) ÷ 3.66 m
x = 112.5 lf ÷ 12 lf x = 10.43 m ÷ 3.66 m
x = **9.38 lf (rise)** x = **2.85 m**

$c^2 = a^2 + b^2$ $c^2 = a^2 + b^2$
c^2 = (22.5 lf × 22.5 lf) + (9.38 lf × 9.38 lf) c^2 = (6.86 m × 6.86 m) + (2.85 m × 2.85 m)
c^2 = 506.25 sq ft + 87.98 sq ft c^2 = 47.06 m² + 8.12 m²
c^2 = 594.23 sq ft c^2 = 55.18 m²
c = **24.38 or 26 lf** c = **7.42 or 8 m**

Jack rafters @ hips only:

By count-up there are 10 rafters per each half of hip (excluding the common rafter):

∴ 10 rafters × 4 (2 halves/hip) = **40 jack rafters**

Combinations of jack rafters to equal common rafter:

largest + smallest = common rafter
next largest + next smallest = common rafter
   "   "   + "   "   =   "   "
   "   "   + "   "   =   "   "
   "   "   + "   "   =   "   "

There are 5 combinations per half hip:

∴ 5 × 4 = **20 common rafters at hips**

Total common rafters:

20 combinations + 2 common hips + 18 common rafters at gable = 40   **2×6 × 26 lf
(5.08 cm × 15.24 cm × 7.92 m)**

CHART 8–11
Rafter Estimate: Hip Roof

quantity is estimated as common rafters. They are cut for proper installation per the plan. There are 10 jack rafters on each half of a hip. See chart 8–11.

Rafter (Joist) Hangers.   The roof rafters also require hangers. The difference between the ceiling joist hangers and the hangers used for the rafters is in design. All of the rafter hangers for sloped roofs are **skewed hangers.** Skewed hangers are sloped at the bottom, twisted off center, or from a right angle. Skewed hangers may have several designs. Examples are 30° sloped hangers and 30° left and right skewed. The angle of slope is dependent upon the roof slope; for example, where the roof slope is 7 / 12 or greater, a 45° hanger is used.

(All lumber lengths are to the nearest even lineal foot with a waste factor of 5% included.)
Double 2×8 (5.08 cm × 20.32 cm) or one 4×8 (10.16 cm × 20.32 cm) beam for hips and ridge:

Hips:

Flat plane length of hip beam by Pythagorean theorem:

$c^2 = a^2 + b^2$ $\qquad\qquad\qquad\qquad\qquad$ $c^2 = a^2 + b^2$

$c^2 = (22.5 \text{ lf} \times 22.5 \text{ lf}) \times 2$ $\qquad\quad$ $c^2 = (6.86 \text{ m} \times 6.86 \text{ m}) \times 2$

$c^2 = 506.25 \text{ sq ft} \times 2$ $\qquad\qquad$ $c^2 = 47.06 \text{ m}^2 \times 2$

$c^2 = 1{,}012.5 \text{ sq ft}$ $\qquad\qquad\qquad$ $c^2 = 94.12 \text{ m}^2$

$c = $ **31.82 lf** - flat plane length $\qquad$ $c = $ **9.70 m** - flat plane length

Sloped length by proportion and theorem: $\qquad$ **⁵⁄₁₂ slope = 1.52/3.66**

$5 \text{ lf} \div 12 \text{ lf} = x \div 22.5 \text{ lf}$ (run) $\qquad$ $1.52 \text{ m} \div 3.66 \text{ m} = x \div 6.86 \text{ m}$

$12 \text{ lf} \times x = 22.5 \text{ lf} \times 5 \text{ lf}$ $\qquad\quad$ $3.66 \text{ m} \times x = 6.86 \text{ m} \times 1.52 \text{ m}$

$x = (22.5 \text{ lf} \times 5 \text{ lf}) \div 12 \text{ lf}$ $\qquad$ $x = (6.86 \text{ m} \times 1.52 \text{ m}) \div 3.66 \text{ m}$

$x = 112.5 \text{ lf} \div 12 \text{ lf}$ $\qquad\qquad$ $x = 10.43 \text{ m} \div 3.66 \text{ m}$

$x = $ **9.38 lf** (rise) $\qquad\qquad\qquad$ $x = $ **2.85 m**

$c^2 = a^2 + b^2$ $\qquad\qquad\qquad\qquad\qquad$ $c^2 = a^2 + b^2$

$c^2 = (31.82 \text{ lf} \times 31.82 \text{ lf}) + (9.38 \text{ lf} \times 9.38) \text{ lf}$ $\quad$ $c^2 = (9.70 \text{ m} \times 9.70 \text{ m}) + (2.85 \text{ m} \times 2.85 \text{ m})$

$c^2 = 1{,}012.51 \text{ sq ft} + 87.98 \text{ sq ft}$ $\qquad$ $c^2 = 94.09 \text{ m}^2 + 8.12 \text{ m}^2$

$c^2 = 1{,}100.49 \text{ sq ft}$ $\qquad\qquad\qquad$ $c^2 = 102.21 \text{ m}^2$

$c = $ **33.17 or 36 lf** $\qquad\qquad\qquad$ $c = $ **10.11 or 11 m**

Sloped length by roof table:

$31.82 \text{ lf} \times 1.08 = $ **34.37 or 36 lf** $\qquad$ $9.70 \text{ m} \times 1.08 = $ **10.48 or 11 m**

Ridge:

$62 \text{ lf} - 45 \text{ lf} = $ **17 or 18 lf** $\qquad\qquad$ $18.90 \text{ m} - 13.72 \text{ m} = $ **5.18 or 5.5 m**

4'×8' (1.22 m × 2.44 m) CDX or CCX plywood or OSB sheathing:

$([62 \text{ lf} \times 45 \text{ lf}] \times 1.08) \times 1.05 = $ $\qquad$ $([18.90 \text{ m} \times 13.72 \text{ m}] \times 1.08) \times 1.05 = $

$(2{,}790 \text{ sq ft} \times 1.08) \times 1.05 = $ $\qquad\quad$ $(259.31 \text{ m}^2 \times 1.08) \times 1.05 = $

$3{,}013.2 \text{ sq ft} \times 1.05 = 3{,}163.86 \text{ sq ft}$ $\qquad$ $280.05 \text{ m}^2 \times 1.05 = 294.05 \text{ m}^2$

$3{,}163.86 \text{ sq ft} \div 32 \text{ sq ft} = $ **98.87 or 99 sheets** $\quad$ $294.05 \text{ m}^2 \div 2.98 \text{ m}^2 = $ **98.67 or 99 sheets**

CHART 8–12
Hip and Ridge Beam Estimate/Roof Sheathing Estimate

The sloped hangers are used for the common rafters at the ridge. The left and right skewed hangers are used at the hips. One hanger should be estimated for each rafter. The number of sloped hangers, the number of left skewed hangers, and the number of right skewed hangers need to be designated. There are also anchor clips (hurricane clips) at the plate line (one per rafter) referred to as A34s, A35s, or A36s.

Hips and Ridge.   *See chart 8–12.* The final portion of conventional structural roof framing are the hips and ridge. The hips and ridge are double 2×8s (5.08 cm × 20.32 cm). The ridge may be a 4×8 (10.16 cm × 20.32 cm) DF #2, but double 2×s are recommended. The ridge length is already known. The length of the hips may be determined by use of the Pythagorean theorem or the Roof Slope/Pitch Table in appendix IV.

Structural Roof Accessories.   Additional members used to support the roof raftering are the double 2×4 (5.08 cm × 10.16 cm) or 2×6 (5.08 cm × 15.24 cm) king posts, 2×4 (5.08 cm × 10.16 cm) **purlins,** collar ties, and vertical braces. **King posts** indicated in this area are structural members used to support the ridge beam. The posts are placed directly under the beam and spaced equally along its length. In the drawings for the Medical Clinic, the king posts are spaced at 4'-0" O/C (1.22 m). The horizontal bracing, called a **collar tie,** is fastened to the rafters and the **vertical braces,** which are centered between the king post and the plate line on either side of the king post. The continuous horizontal members perpendicular to the collar ties at the braces are the purlins.

Roof Sheathing.   The roof sheathing is specified as a 4'×8" × 1/2" (1.22 m × 2.44 m × 1.27 cm) CCX or CDX plywood. The CCX, if used, is placed along the eave line for appearance, and the CDX is installed on the remainder of the roof. When CCX is not used, CDX may be installed throughout the whole roof area. See chart 8–12 for the roof sheafing estimate for the Medical Clinic.

Alternate Estimate

See Appendix IV, the Project Manual, Division 1, Section 01030, Alternatives/ Alternates. The alternates included in the framing estimate are the 6×8 (15.24 cm × 20.32 cm) DF #1 or better girder beam and the truss roof system. The specifications are as follows:

Alternate #4

An alternate structural floor support beam and alternate truss roof system shall read as follows:

06100 Rough Carpentry. A wood support beam may be used in lieu of the steel support beam. The wood beam shall be constructed and installed per the recommendations of the Western Wood Products Association.

   The beam shall be supplied from 6×8 (15.24 cm × 20.32 cm) DF #1 or better. The beam shall be installed in the same manner as the steel beam with embedment in the foundation walls and centered on the concrete piers.

   The beams shall be supported at the piers with a specially constructed saddle support to meet all local code and ordinance structural specifications. The saddles and beams shall be fastened with 3/4" (1.91 cm) through bolts and tightened in place with 3/4" (1.91 cm) nuts, washers and lock washers on both sides of the connection. The nuts shall be spot-welded sufficiently to guarantee that they shall not come loose.

   Special inspections of the saddles and the beam construction are required.

06170 Prefabricated Structural Wood. An alternate truss roof system may be used in lieu of conventional roof framing.

   Prefabricated wood trusses, 5/12 slope, shall be manufactured by Trus-Joist/MacMillan, or equal, and installed in lieu of ceiling joists and roof rafters. Trusses shall be constructed with a 2×6 (5.08 cm × 15.24 cm) top chord and 2×4 (5.08 cm × 10.16 cm) bottom chord. The trusses shall be constructed so as to provide the hip configuration as indicated on the structural framing plan, and longitudinal and transverse sections. All common and jack trusses, blocking and accessories shall be supplied by the manufacturer. The truss shall include a rafter tail to extend 2'-0" (0.61 m) beyond the plate line at all eaves.

Girder Beam. *See Plans, Sheet S–1, Structural Foundation Plan.* The girder beam is called out in the alternate specification as a 6×8 (15.24 cm × 20.32 cm) timber. The estimate for the girder beam is similar in procedure to the steel beam. The exception is the connections at the piers and the total materials needed.

The first thing to include in the alternate estimate is a *deduction for the steel beam, beam plate stock, and the shot-and-pin,* since these materials are not needed for the wood framing.

The beam is 6" (15.24 cm) wide. The estimator must determine the most economical layout for cost effectiveness. The estimator may choose one of the following methods to keep the lengths of the beams as short as possible for freighting and to fit them together for the most support:

1. Cut all lengths from the north/south foundation walls to the piers the same.
2. Cut all lengths from the east/west walls to the piers the same.
3. Cut the 4 interior north/south lengths the same.
4. Cut the 6 interior east/west lengths the same.

Caution must be taken in the cuts so that the pieces fit properly at each pier. A special metal support called a **saddle** must be used. The saddles are four-way saddle. If the four-way saddles are not available from one of the accessory manufacturers, they must be custom-made to the specifications required by local codes.

Truss Roof.   *See Plans, Sheet S–7, Longitudinal Section.* Also noted on the structural sections are a common truss and/or a jack truss. These are shown as alternates to the conventional framing. Just as in conventional framing, the common truss extends from plate to plate on the exterior bearing walls in the transverse section. The jack truss represents one of the trusses that make up a hip roof. The largest jack truss is shown (equal to a common rafter in length). The **top chord** (sloped) is the equivalent of the rafter. The **bottom chord** is the equivalent of the ceiling joist. The bracing is a part of the structural strength of a truss. The truss is held together with **gang plates** in lieu of nails. It is prefabricated in jigs at the truss manufacturer and shipped to the project as a unit.

There is one major change between a conventional frame and a truss. There are no ridge or hip beams. The trusses are connected together with pre-cut blocking supplied as part of the truss system. The frieze blocking is also a part of the truss supplies.

The accessories required for a truss system are framing ties and hurricane clips to hold the system together. At each connection with the ridge or hip blocking, one or two metal ties are used to fasten them together. The hurricane clips are used to anchor the truss and the frieze blocking to the plate.

It is usually the responsibility of the truss manufacturer to estimate the required amount of trusses and truss accessories (excluding the ties and anchors) and tender a bid directly to the owner or owner's representative.

Labor

The rough framing includes several phases of work in which members of the same crew may be used; for example, a laborer may be needed to assist on the floor and wall framing. The work on rough carpentry overlaps, since the wall

CREW	HOURLY + BURDEN WAGE	% TIME ON JOB/HR	HOURLY RATE
Foreman	$16.90 + $ 3.32	8%	= $ 1.62
Carpenter (2)	$16.40 + $ 3.32 × 2	80%	= $31.55
Laborer (2)	$11.75 + $ 3.74 × 2	12%	= $ 3.72
Composite Crew Rate:		100%	$36.89/MH

FIGURE 8–3a
Composite Crew Schedule

CREW	HOURLY WAGE + BURDEN
Foreman	$16.90 + $ 3.32
Carpenter (2)	$16.40 + $ 3.32 × 2
Laborer (2)	$11.75 + $ 3.74 × 2
	$73.20 + $17.44 = $90.64
Composite Crew Rate:	$90.64/3 = $30.22

FIGURE 8–3b
Composite Crew Schedule

framing crew can start before the floor underlayment is completed. This is also true of the ceiling joist and roof rafter construction. A number of composite crew schedules are used because of variations in wages for different crews. The productivity factor has been calculated at 1.06 for all phases of the work.

Floor Structure Labor. *See figures 8–3a and 8–3b, Composite Crew Schedule: Rough Carpentry—Floor.* For the Medical Clinic, a 5-person crew installs the sill plate, beam plate, floor joists, and sub-floor. The time installation is 3 days. The labor cost is calculated as follows:

Method 8–3a:

$36.89/hr × 1.06 = $39.10/MH

$39.10/MH × 8 hr = $312.80/MD

$312.80/MD × 5 crew persons = $1,564.00/CD

$1.564.00/CD × 2 days = $3,128.00

Method 8–3b:

$30.22/hr × 1.06 = $32.03/MH

$32.03/MH × 8 hr = $256.24/MD

$256.24/MD × 5 crew persons = $1,281.20/CD

$1,281.20/CD × 2 days = $2,562.30

CREW	HOURLY + BURDEN WAGE	% TIME ON JOB/HR	HOURLY RATE
Foreman	$16.90 + $ 3.32	5%	= $ 1.01
Carpenter (2)	$16.40 + $ 3.32 × 2	70%	= $27.61
Laborer (2)	$11.75 + $ 3.74 × 2	20%	= $ 6.20
Forklift Operator	$11.75 + $ 3.74	5%	= $ 0.78
Composite Crew Rate:		100%	$35.60/MH

FIGURE 8–4a
Composite Crew Schedule

CREW	HOURLY WAGE + BURDEN
Foreman	$16.90 + $ 3.32
Carpenter (2)	$16.40 + $ 3.32 × 2
Laborer (2)	$11.75 + $ 3.74 × 2
Forklift Operator	$11.75 + $ 3.74
	$84.95 + $21.18 = $106.13
Composite Crew Rate:	$106.13/4 = $26.54

FIGURE 8–4b
Composite Crew Schedule

Exterior and Interior Wall Framing Labor. *See figures 8–4a and 8–4b, Composite Crew Schedule: Rough Carpentry—Wall Framing.* The erection of the walls is separated into operations. The exterior walls and the interior bearing walls are constructed first. The interior partition walls are constructed after the ceiling joists have been installed. It takes a 6-person crew nine (9) days to complete all of the walls. The labor cost is calculated as follows:

Method 8–4a:

$35.60/hr × 1.06 = $37.74/MH

$37.74/MH × 8 hr = $301.92/MD

$301.92/MD × 6 crew members = $1,811.52/CD

$1,811.52/CD × 9 days = $16,303.68 or $16,304.00

Method 8–4b:

$26.54/hr × 1.06 = $28.13/MH

$28.13/MH × 8 hr = $225.04/MD

$225.04/MD × 6 crew members = $1,350.24/CD

$1,350.24/CD × 9 days = $12,152.16 or $12,152.00

Ceiling Joist Labor.　*Refer to figures 8–4a and 8–4b.* A 6-person crew is necessary to complete the installation of the celing joists in five (5) days. The labor cost is the same as for the wall-framing group. The calculations are as follows:

Method 8–4a:
$35.60/hr × 1.06 = $37.74/MH
$37.74/MH × 8 hr = $301.92/MD
$301.92/MD × 6 crew members = $1,811.52/CD
$1,811.52/CD × 5 days = $9,057.60 or $9,058.00

Method 8–4b:
$26.54/hr × 1.06 = $28.13/MH
$28.13/MH × 8 hr = $225.04/MD
$225.04/MD × 6 crew members = $1,350.24/CD
$1,350.24/CD × 5 days = $6,751.20 or $6,751.00

Roof Structure Labor.　*Refer to figures 8–4a and 8–4b.* The same crew and productivity factor estimated for the ceiling joists are used for the roof structure. Time consumed in construction is 7 days. The labor cost is calculated as follows:

Method 8–4a:
$1,811.04/CD × 7 days = $12,677.28 or $12,677.00

Method 8–4b:
$1,350.24/CD × 7 days = $9,451.68 or $9,452.00

Labor Total.　The total labor cost is as follows:

	Method 8–4a:		Method 8–4b
Floor Joists	=	$ 3,128.00	$ 2,562.00
Walls	=	$16,304.00	$12,152.00
Ceiling Joists	=	$ 9,058.00	$ 6,751.00
Roof Structure	=	$12,677.00	$ 9,452.00
Total Labor:		$41,167.00	$30,917.00

Equipment

See figure 8–5. The equipment necessary for the installation includes personnel and material transportation, a truck crane, an extended lift ("Pettibone"), a table saw, and a powder-actuated gun.

FIGURE 8–5
Equipment Schedule

Equipment	Use Time	Unit Cost	Total
Pers. Trans.	23 days	@ $ 10/day	= $ 230.00
Material Transport	23 days	@ $ 30/day	= $ 690.00
Truck Crane	8 days	@ $185/day	= $1,480.00
Extended Lift (forklift)	23 days	@ $150/day	= $3,450.00
Table Saw	23 days	@ $ 75/day	= $1,725.00
Powder Actuated Gun	1 day	@ $ 15/day	= $ 15.00
Equipment Total:			$7,590.00

FINISH CARPENTRY

Finish carpentry is the portion of the carpentry contractor's work that is exposed, such as baseboard, door and window trim work, and cabinetry.

See Plans, Sheet A–1, Architectural Floor Plan; Sheet A–6, Architectural Sections; Sheets A–7 and A–8, Door, Window, and Finish Schedules. The finish carpentry work specified for the Medical Clinic includes installation of interior and exterior wood trim. Interior trim includes the interior window and door trim, baseboard, moldings, and so on. The exterior trim includes items such as siding, decorative carpentry details, and exterior window and door trim. The exterior trim, except for siding, may be installed after the exterior finish (siding, stucco, and so on) work is completed and may be considered plant-ons inasmuch as they are installed, or "planted," over the exterior finish. Door and window trim includes any special finished wood not a part of the standard door and window jambs or casings. This includes all the face trim placed over the exterior framing and is commonly used for aesthetic reasons to hide the rough work beneath.

All built-in cabinetry, stairwells (finished and exposed treads and risers), banisters, newel posts, railings, chair rails, paneling, and moldings are also considered as finish carpentry. This work may be specified in Division 6 or Division 12, Furnishings.

The plastics used for skylights, impact-resistant decorative items such as room divider screen walls, posts and shelving, atrium and patio roof covers, and corrugated plastic are specified as finish carpentry. The plastics are usually prefabricated and come with instructions for installation. Other structural plastic fabrications include laminated plastic countertops for kitchen and bath cabinetry, for laboratory and commercial cabinets, and for special doors that are lightweight yet sturdy enough to take abuse, such as warehouse interior doors and restaurant kitchen/dining entries. Nonstructural fabrications include those made for decorative use in lieu of wood or concrete plant-ons.

SCOPE OF WORK: FINISH CARPENTRY

See Plans, Sheets A–7 and A–8, Door, Window, and Finish Schedules. The Specifications, finish schedule, and plans for the Medical Clinic indicate the types of materials for finish carpentry and where they are to be used. The finish schedule indicates the materials to be used on floors, walls, and ceilings of the Clinic. This schedule must be closely followed by not only the finish carpenter but other trades referred to in later chapters. As per appendix IV, Project Manual, the specifications for finish carpentry are as follows:

06200 Finish Carpentry

A "Slimline" oak veneer wood trim shall be installed surrounding all windows on the interior side of the exterior walls. In addition, a 1/2" (1.27 cm) to 3/4" (1.91 cm) thick return (match the thickness of the "Slimline" material) of the same finish shall be applied to both sides and head of each window immediately adjacent to the interior side of the window. Where a window exists on the interior only, both sides of the window shall be similarly trimmed. An apron and stool shall be applied to the interior side of the exterior windows and on both sides of the interior window. The interior windows include the Waiting Room/Playroom window and the Waiting Room/Reception Room window. The Waiting Room/Reception Room window shall have a 3/4" × 18" (1.91 cm × 45.72 cm) wide, select pine, shelf, with apron both sides, centered on the wall the full length of the window opening. All nailing shall be with 6d finish nails, maximum 1 1/2" (3.81 cm) long. The nails shall be slightly punched for application of a finish putty over each nail head. All joints shall be smooth and even.

A 2×4 (5.08 cm × 10.16 cm), select DF, R/S finish, exterior trim shall be applied to the exterior wall framing surrounding each window with a 1×4 (2.54 cm × 10.16 cm) return to the window of the same material. A water table shall be applied at the head of each window and a sloped stool extending 3/4" (1.91 cm) beyond an apron, 1 1/2" deep (3.81 cm), R/S, 2×4 (5.08 cm × 10.16 cm), select DF, supporting the stool. All exterior trim shall be installed prior to the wall finish installation.

THE FINISH CARPENTRY ESTIMATE

Interior Trim

See figure 8–6 and chart 8–13. The summary/purchase order form shown in figure 8–6 is a combination for interior finish trim, doors, and windows. It shows some of the major items in a finish carpentry estimate.

The finish schedule for the Medical Clinic, Plans, Sheets A–7 and A–8, indicates a pine wood with an oak veneer, 2" (5.08 cm) wide, slimline style, which is available in lengths from 6 lf (1.83 m) to 20 lf (6.10 m).

Baseboard.   *See chart 8–13.* The finish schedule, Plans, Sheet A–8, calls for a slimline oak veneer baseboard to be located in the waiting room. The room is 29'-0" (8.84 m) by 10'-6" (3.20 m). The estimator may determine the total baseboard by using either of two methods. The first method (shown in chart 8–13) does not deduct for openings; therefore, waste is not important because the equivalent of one additional length is already included. There are two openings 3'-0" (0.91 m) wide (hall door and cased opening) and one opening 6'-0" (1.83 m) wide (main entry). The second method deducts for openings and includes the waste factor.

Window Trim.   *See chart 8–13.* The interior trim used for the baseboard is also called for around the 4'-0" by 2'-8" (1.22 m × 0.81 m) window at the nurse's office and includes the two sides and head with returns. The sill portion of the

THE A.C. HOUSTON LUMBER CO.

"Lumbermen Since 1884"

CUSTOMER	ORDERED BY	CUST. P.O. NUMBER	DELIVERY ADDRESS	SALESMAN	OPER. #	WORK ORDER #

JOB NAME - #	PRODUCTION DATE	DELIVERY DATE	LT.	BK.	MODEL NAME	ELV.	STD.	REV.	INVOICE #	DATE ORDERED

WOOD DOOR HANDING		PERMA DOOR HANDING		HINGE STDS.	BORE STDS.	BACKST STDS.	BORE PLCMT.	DESCRIPTIONS	DOORS	FRM. & JAMB	MOULDINGS	A
RIGHT	LEFT	RIGHT	LEFT	⅝ RUS 4	F.B. 2⅛"	INT. 2⅜"	44" FROM TOP		H/C - HOLLOW CORE	R/E - RABT. EXT.	S/M - STUCCO	APPLD. EXT. MLDG.
				8 3½"					S/C - SOLID CORE	I/J - INT. JAMB	B/M - BRICK	
				4 4"	DB 5½" O.C.	P.D. 2¾"			D/E - EMBOSSED	F/J - FING. JNT.	R/W - REDWD.	
									D/G - DUAL GLAZE	C/R - CLEAR	P/C - PRIMECOAT	

EXT. DRS. FRMS. & PKT. FRM

SKU #	QTY.	WIDE	HIGH	8	4	DOOR TYPE	FRM IN.	TYPE SPECIES	L H	R H	B/S 8 4 D. B.	EXT. MLDG. DESCRIPT.	A	MISC. INSTRUCTIONS		

CASING SPECS	2"	F/J		2"	C/R		2½" #711	F/J		2½" #711	C/R	EXT.		INT.	

INT. P/H. DOORS & SLABS

SKU #	QTY.	WIDE	HIGH	8	4	DOOR TYPE	JB IN.	TYPE SPECIES	L H	R H	MISC. INSTRUCTIONS		

WARDROBE DOORS

SKU #	QTY.	WIDE	HIGH	WARDROBE DESCRIPTION	MISC. INSTRUCTIONS		

INT. FINISH TRIM & MISC. HARDWARE

SKU #	QTY.	FINISH MATERIAL	DESCRIPTION	SPECIFIC INT. MILLWORK INSTRUCTIONS		
19412		1 x 12 PART. BRD.				
17812		CLOSET POLE				
		HOOK STRIP				
		BASE				
17829		ROSETTES				
17827		SHELF SUPPORTS				

FIGURE 8–6
Summary/Spreadsheet for Trim

163

(All lumber lengths are to the nearest even lineal foot with a waste factor of 5% included [UNO].)

Baseboard (10 lf [3.05 m] lengths) - waiting room:

Method 1:

(29 lf + 10.5 lf) × 2 =   (8.84 m + 3.20 m) × 2 =
39.5 lf × 2 = **79 or 80 lf**   12.04 m × 2 = **24.08 or 24 m**

Method 2:

([29 lf × 2] + [10.5 lf × 2]) − ([3 lf × 2]   ([8.84 m × 2] + [3.20 m × 2]) − ([0.91 m × 2]
    + 6 lf) × 1.05 =   + 1.83 m) × 1.05 =
([58 lf + 21 lf] − 12 lf) × 1.05 =   (17.68 m + 6.40 m) − (1.82 m + 1.83 m) × 1.05 =
(79 lf − 12 lf) × 1.05 =   (24.08 m − 3.65 m) × 1.05 =
67 lf × 1.05 = **70.35 or 70 lf**   20.43 × 1.05 = **21.45 or 21.5 m**

Interior window trim at nurse office, 4 lf wide by 2'-8" high (1.22 m wide by 0.81 m high):

Trim—3 sides:

4 lf + (2.67 lf × 2) =   1.22 m + (0.81 m × 2) =
4 lf + 5.34 lf = 9.34 lf   1.22 m + 1.62 m = 2.84 m
9.34 lf × 1.05 = **9.81 or 10 lf**   2.84 m × 1.05 = **2.98 or 3 m**

Stool—2³/₄" (6.99 cm) wide:

(4 lf + 1.25 lf) × 1.05 =   (1.22 m + 0.38 m) × 1.05 =
5.25 lf × 1.05 = **5.51 or 6 lf**   1.60 m × 1.05 = **1.68 or 2 m**

Apron - 1¹/₂" (*3.81 cm) wide:

4 lf × 1.05 = **4.2 or 4 lf**   1.22 m × 1.05 = **1.28 or 1.5 m**

Reception office window, 10'-0" × 2'-0" (3.05 m × 0.61 m) w/18" (0.45 m) wide shelf:

Trim—3 sides, both sides:

(10 lf + 4 lf) × 2 × 1.05 = **29.4 or 30 lf**   (3.05 m + 1.22 m) × 2 × 1.05 = **8.97 or 9 m**

Shelf:

10 lf long × 18" wide   **3.05 m long × 0.45 m wide**

Apron - 1¹/₂" wide, both sides:

10 lf × 2 = **20 lf**   3.05 m × 2 = **6.1 m**

CHART 8–13
Trim and Baseboard Estimates

window calls for a stool and apron. The width of the window trim is 2"+ (5.08 cm+) and the same thickness as the thickest part of the slimline. The finish matches the slimline trim (oak veneer).

Aprons, Stools, and Window Shelving. All of the windows except the waiting room/reception office window require stools and aprons. The width of the stool is 3/4" (1.91 cm) wider than the returns to allow for a "lip" extending beyond the apron. The apron is the same thickness as the returns and 1 1/2" (3.81 cm) wide. The reception office window is 10'-0" by 2'-0" × 1" (3.05 m × 0.61 m × 2.54 cm). The window requires an 18" (0.45 m) shelf centered on the wall with the same style apron to help support it on both sides.

DOORS AND WINDOWS

See Plans, Sheet A–8, Door, Window, and Finish Schedules. Refer also to figure 8–7. As previously discussed, doors and windows are included with this chapter because the framer installs them. They are included on the finish carpentry estimate form.

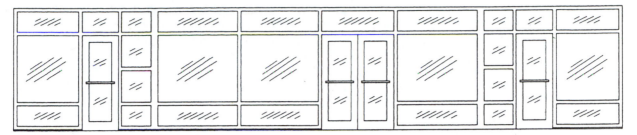

FIGURE 8–7
Storefront

Doors

The major classifications for doors are **panel, flush** or **slab,** and **combinations of panel** and **flush with glass** called **lights (lites).** Doors may be manufactured in steel, wood, plastic, a combination of steel and wood, or a combination of wood and plastic. Doors may be further designated as **inside swing, outside swing, double-swing, gate (Dutch),** or **sliding.**

Metal Doors.   Doors made of steel, with steel frames and casings, are known as **hollow-metal doors and frames (HM).** The hollow-metal door and frame are made from 16-gauge or heavier cold-rolled steel. The door frames are welded together as a single unit by the manufacturer. They are installed during the rough framing or masonry installations. The doors themselves may be installed later. The purpose of the HM frame and accompanying steel door is twofold: security and fire protection. These doors are manufactured in standard sizes. Special customized construction is uncommon.

Another kind of steel frame, a **knock-down hollow-metal (KDHM),** is manufactured from 18- or 16-gauge cold-rolled steel. This frame may be used for installations with steel or wood doors. KDHM frames are sometimes used in exterior door construction but are primarily used for interior door installations. The KDHM frame is installed after the rough framing and drywall are completed. The parts of the frame are snapped together into a snug, smooth fit.

Both types of doors—HM and KDHM—are common wherever a metal stud frame is used such as on multistory, multiunit applications (apartments, condominiums, hotels) and commercial or industrial applications. The purpose of the KDHM frame is to provide freedom from maintenance and protection from damage.

Structural aluminum or steel prefabricated, custom-made units—preassembled or ready for assembly—and oversize units for commercial entries (other than standard storefronts), as well as custom entries for residential construction, are specialty items usually installed by the manufacturer. These specialty items are often combinations of both windows and doors.

Wood and Plastic Doors.   There are several varieties of wood and plastic doors. The wood doors are the most common in residential construction and as interior doors for offices, hotels, and other commercial construction. A door manufactured from a combination of light-gauge metal and wood, referred to as a metal-clad door, is commonly used as an entry door in residential and light commercial construction. Wood doors are manufactured in standard sizes or may be readily customized.

Plastic doors or plastic-clad wood doors are used for many commercial applications such as double-swing doors for heavy warehouse traffic and between the kitchen and dining areas in restaurants. Small modular offices and partitions may be manufactured from structural plastics with plastic doors and lites. Many doors, installed for safety protection, have plastic rather than glass windows as an integral part of the door construction.

Just as with the metal combinations mentioned above, there are prefabricated, custom-made units—preassembled or ready for assembly—as well as oversize units for commercial entries (other than standard storefronts) and residential construction. These, too, are often combinations of both windows and doors. The materials used may be any combination of metal, wood, or plastic.

Windows

The classifications of windows include **fixed glass, sliding glass, single-** or **double-hung, awning, hopper, casement, projected, jalousie,** or combinations of them. For example, the windows between the waiting room and the reception room of the Medical Clinic and the exterior windows of the waiting room use two of the varieties mentioned, the fixed window and slider. The 4'-0" × 4'-0" (1.22 m × 1.22 m) windows are designated as fixed windows (4040FX or 1.22 m × 1.22 m FX). The reception office window is a 10'-0" × 2'-0" (3.05 m × 0.61 m) combination sliding/fixed glass (100200XXO or 3.05 m × 0.61 m OXXO). The "OXXO" means that a portion of the window, the "X," slides and a portion, the "O," is fixed; therefore, the window is fixed-open-open-fixed.

Metal Windows

As with doors, some windows are manufactured with steel or aluminum frames and casings. The steel hollow-metal framed window is made from 18-gauge or heavier cold-rolled steel. The window frame, like the door frame, is also welded as a single unit by the manufacturer. The steel windows are installed in the same manner as the steel door frames. The glazing is installed after the walls are finished.

The aluminum-framed window is prefabricated with the glazing (glass) included. Many of the types of windows mentioned above may have aluminum frames. Aluminum-framed windows are installed prior to the finish material applications. Aluminum-framed windows are common where wood or metal stud frames are used.

Wood and Plastic Windows.   Several varieties of wood and plastic windows are available. Like the doors, wood windows are the most common for residential construction. Metal-clad wood windows and frames are also common.

Entrances and Storefronts

See figure 8–7. Small, one-story structures such as commercial and retail frontages use combinations of aluminum, steel or wood, and glazing called **storefronts.** The storefronts include doors and windows in single units separated only by the steel, aluminum, or wood mullions. **Entrances** are smaller storefront units, with a single entry and sidelights. They are used for a single commercial structure such as a free-standing bank building or a hotel or motel entrance. A sidelight (sidelite) is a glass or plastic window adjacent to a door used for both light and aesthetics.

Hardware and Specialties

See Scope of Work below. See also Plans, Sheet A–1, Architectural Floor Plan; Sheets A–7 and A–8, Door, Window, and Finish Schedules. The schedule for all hardware and hardware specialty items may appear in the Specifications, in the plans, or both. The Medical Clinic plans show identification **letters** or **numbers** at the door and window openings called **marks.** The mark on the schedule matches the mark on the plans. The schedules indicate the types and sizes of units referenced by the mark. The information given identifies not only the door or window, but the hardware or any other items to be used.

Glazing

Glazing includes all glass used for doors, windows, and mirrors in all types of structures. The glazing may be plate glass, tempered plate glass, or both for structural strength and safety, and fire resistance. The glass may be tinted, may have double thickness with air space (insulating glass), or may be regular glass, as commonly used in residential construction. The type of glass required is indicated in the plans, in the door and window schedules, or in the specifications of a project. Plastic windows are also considered a part of the glazing requirements.

SCOPE OF WORK: DOORS AND WINDOWS

Per appendix IV, the Project Manual, the specifications for the Medical Clinic doors, windows, and hardware are as follows:

Division 8: Doors, Windows Glazing

08000 SCOPE OF WORK

Division 1 and the General Conditions are to be considered a part of this division. Furnish all labor, materials and equipment necessary to complete all work under this division and as indicated on drawings.

08100 Metal Doors and Frames & 08200 Wood and Plastic Doors

Exterior doors are to have hollow-metal (HM) frames. Interior doors are to have hollow-metal knock-down (KDHM) frames. Main entrance exterior doors shall be of metal-clad wood construction.
        The door schedule is as follows:

Mark	Size	Frame	Description	Remarks
1	pr 3'×6'8" (0.91 m × 2.03 m)	HM	Wd, m/c, birch, 3-panel, 1¾" (4.45 cm)	mfr paint
2	3'×6'8" (0.91 m × 2.03 m)	HM	2-panel HM, 1¾" (4.45 cm)	mfr paint

Mark	Size	Frame	Description	Remarks
3	3'×6'8" (0.91 m × 2.03 m)	KDHM	flush, wood, birch, 1³/₈" (3.49 cm), h/c	stain (typ)
4	3'×6'8" (0.91 m × 2.03 m)	KDHM	flush, wood, birch, 1³/₈" (3.49 cm), s/c	lead-lined
5	pr 2'×6'8" (0.61 m × 2.03 m)	KDHM	flush, wood, birch, 1³/₈" (3.49 cm), h/c	6"×18" lite
6	3'×6'8" (0.91 m × 2.03 m)	KDHM	flush, wood, birch, 1³/₈" (3.49 cm), h/c	pocket
7	2'×6'8" (0.61 m × 2.03 m)	KDHM	flush, wood, birch, 1³/₈"(3.49 cm), h/c	stain (typ)
8	3'×6'8" (0.91 m × 2.03 m)	KDHM	cased opening	

All interior doors are to have sound insulation fill (STC 60) in the door cores.

08250 Door Opening Assemblies

All door hardware is to be supplied by one manufacturer. The hardware shall be Schlage. The following is the hardware schedule for all doors:

Front Entry - Schlage entry latch w/thumb latch handle and deadbolt, w/matching key, antique brass. Schlage handle to match latch. 1 1/2 sets hinge butts, antique brass, each leaf.

Side Exterior Doors - Schlage emergency kit hardware only (no special knowledge). 1 1/2 sets hinge butts, antique brass.

Doctor Office, Accounting Office, Nurse Office, Reception, Record Storage, Restroom - Schlage privacy latch, antique brass, 1 1/2 sets hinge butts, antique brass.

Interior Halls, Break Room and Examination Rooms - Schlage passage latch, antique brass, 1 1/2 set hinge butts, antique brass.

Operating Room and X-Ray Laboratory - Schlage antique brass handle w/push plate both sides, each leaf. 2'-6" × 1'-6" (0.76 m × 0.46 m) at X-Ray Laboratory and 3'-0" × 1'-6" (0.91 m × 0.46 m) at Operating Room, antique brass kick plate both sides, each leaf and 1 1/2 set hinge butts, antique brass, each leaf.

08500 Metal Windows

Windows shall be aluminum framed and manufactured to fit into the frame or masonry wall openings, depending on owner's exterior wall choice. Windows shall be of such construction so that the mullions are installed at the mid-point width of the framing stud or the masonry unit.

All glazing for the exterior windows shall be integrally tinted, gray, dual pane insulated glass, 1/8" (0.32 cm) thick, with 1/2" (1.27 cm) air space between panes. The interior windows shall be installed with clear 1/4" (0.64 cm) tempered plate glass. Windows are to be installed as per plans and details.

The window schedule is as follows:

Mark	Size	Frame	Description	Remarks
A	4'×4' (1.22 m × 1.22 m)	Alum	FX GL, insulpane	
B	4'×2'8" (1.22 m × 0.81 m)	Alum	FX GL, insulpane	
C	6'×2'8" (1.83 m × 0.81 m)	N/A	4×8×8 GL BLK	Solar Decor
D	4'×2'8" (1.22 m × 0.81 m)	N/A	4×8×8 GL BLK	Solar Decor
E	4'×5' (1.22 m × 1.52 m)	Alum	FX Tempered GL	¼" (0.64 cm) thk
F	10'×2'6" (3.05 m × 0.76 m)	Alum	OXXO Sliding GL	

End of Division

THE DOOR AND WINDOW ESTIMATE

Refer to figure 8–6. The estimate form shown in figure 8–6 for finish carpentry may be used for doors and windows if the doors are of the type used for the Medical Clinic.

Doors and Windows

Estimating doors and windows are nothing more than count-ups or copying from the specification and/or schedule, including the hardware with each item listed.

Labor

See figure 8–8. The labor for trim work is determined by the lineal foot of material a carpenter is capable of applying. Labor for doors and windows is determined by the time it takes to install one unit (door or window). In most instances, one carpenter and one helper or apprentice will suffice to do a

CREW	HOURLY + BURDEN WAGE	% TIME ON JOB/HR	HOURLY RATE
Foreman	$16.45 + $ 3.32	50%	= $ 9.86
Laborer	$11.75 + $ 3.74	50%	= $ 7.75
Composite Crew Rate:		100%	$17.61/MH

FIGURE 8–8a
Composite Crew Schedule: Finish Carpentry–Doors and Windows

CREW	HOURLY WAGE + BURDEN
Carpenter	$16.40 + $3.32
Laborer	$11.75 + $3.74
	$28.15 + $7.06 = $35.21
Composite Crew Rate:	$35.21/2 = $17.61

FIGURE 8–8b

Composite Crew Schedule: Finish Carpentry—Doors and Windows

complete installation on a project the size of the Medical Clinic. The productivity rate is 75%; therefore, the productivity factor is calculated as follows:

$$70\% \div 75\% = 0.93$$

The crew is able to install the following quantities:

Baseboard @ 300 lf (91.44 m)/day
Window/door trim @ 50 lf (15.24 m)/hr
Door installation @ 1/hr
Window installation @ 1/0.75 hr

The total trim labor cost for the waiting room is calculated as follows:

Baseboard:
79 lf ÷ 300 lf/day = 0.26 day or 2 hr
(24.08 m ÷ 91.44 m/day = 0.26 day or 2 hr)

Window and door trim:
376.35 lf ÷ 50 lf/hr = 7.5 hr
(114.71 m ÷ 15.24 m/hr = 7.5 hr)

Doors, 1 pr + 1:
3 doors × 1/hr = 3 hr

Windows, 5 ea:
5 × 0.75 hr = 3.75 hr

Total hours:
2 hr + 7.5 hr + 3 hr + 3.75 hr = 16.25 hr

Methods 8–8a and 8–8b are equal in this case:

$17.61/MH × 0.93 = $16.38/MH
$16.38/MH × 2 persons = $32.76/CH
$32.76/CH × 16.25 hr = $532.35 or $532.00

Equipment

There is no equipment estimate necessary for door and windows because all materials are freighted by the suppliers to the project. Personal hand tools are all that the crew requires.

CHAPTER EXERCISES

1. Determine the material quantities needed for rough framing the whole Medical Clinic. Include shear panels, fire blocking @ 4'-0" (1.22 m) and 8'-0" (2.44 m) intervals vertically, the king posts, braces, collar ties, and purlins. Indicate sizes and quantity of each material required.

2. Estimate the number of floor joist hangers, ceiling joist hangers, and straight, sloped and skewed (left and right) rafter hangers for the Medical Clinic.

3. Per the finish door and window schedules for the Medical Clinic (Plans, Sheets A–7 and A–8), indicate what materials are used for trim for the processing and storage room, the administration office, and the nurse's office.

4. Perform a quantity survey of paneling and all trim necessary to complete the doctor's office. The panels are 4'×8"× 1/4" (1.22 m × 2.44 m × 0.64 cm) oak veneer sheets. See the finish schedule (Plans, Sheets A–7 and A–8).

5. Estimate the materials necessary for the alternate wood girder beam installation. Break the estimate down into specific lengths of beam.

6. Per an alternate, determine the number of common and jack trusses necessary to complete the roof structure. Include anchors, spacer blocks, and frieze blocking.

7. The owner makes the decision to change the roof structure from a 5/12 slope tile roof to a 1/2"/ft (1.27 cm/30.48 cm) slope for a BUR system per Alternate #5, Division 1, Section 1030, of the appendix III. This alternate forces a change in the roof structure. Estimate the roof, ceiling and bearing wall framing. The specifications for the framing change are as follows:

Alternate #5. Built-up Roofing System in Lieu of Tile Roofing.

06100 Rough Carpentry. The slope of roof shall change from 5/12 slope to a 1/2"/ft (1.27 cm/30.48 cm) slope gable-framed roof structure. Conventional framing techniques shall be used with 2×6 (5.08 cm × 15.24 cm) rafters and ceiling joists spaced at 24" O/C (0.61 m). A double 2×8 (5.08 cm × 20.32 cm) ridge shall be installed full length of roof. The overhang shall remain at 2'-0" (0.61 m) on all sides. All king posts, braces and purlins shall be eliminated. 2×6 (5.08 cm × 15.24 cm) staggered solid blocking shall be installed between rafters and ceiling joists and shall be centered 10'-3" (3.12 m) between the plate and ridge on both sides.

Walls shall be constructed so that all bearing walls shall extend to the bottom of the roof structure. All partition walls shall remain at 9'-0" (2.74 m) A.F.F. There shall be no fire wall construction.

Thermal and Moisture Protection

Division 7

GENERAL INFORMATION

Protection against water, weather, heat, and cold are included in Division 7. The title—Thermal and Moisture Protection—is correct in that the term *moisture protection* is preferred over the terms *waterproofing* or *dampproofing*. The term *proof* is a misnomer because, technically, there is no product that will water*proof* or damp*proof*. Materials will only *resist* or *retard* water or dampness penetration. The longevity of a protection system's ability to resist or retard water and moisture depends upon the materials, installation procedures and maintenance, and the location of the system—whether it is below grade or on the roof of a structure.

Materials

Moisture protection is accomplished through the use of asphalt-based materials, concrete additives, and plastics such as polyethylene, polyurethane, and elastomeric polymers. Such materials are manufactured in sheet, roll, or liquid form. Thermal protection includes products offering resistance to heat such as mineral wool, fibrous materials, minerals, fiberglass, cementitious mixtures, polystyrene, polyester, or combinations of them, formed into rigid, foam, loose fill, batt, and blanket products.

The most common moisture-retardant products are derived from two sources. One is **asphalt,** which is found in a natural state ("tar" pits) or is refined from petroleum. The other is **pitch,** a coal by-product. These products are classed as **bitumens** and are used directly or in combination with sheet or roll materials such as roofing felts, polyester, nylon, and fiberboard.

Products such as **gypsum, polymers,** and **cement slurry,** which are mixed with moisture-retardant additives and which harden like cement to prevent moisture penetration, are referred to as a **cementitious** material. They can be applied by spraying or hand-troweling, or they may come in the form of cement-impregnated boardlike sheets, called **composite boards.**

Several products that provide both moisture and thermal protection are available. These include the following products:

1. **Slurries,** which may be sprayed directly upon the earth to prevent moisture penetration, as well as to deter wall deterioration as the result of

aging or mud slides, and so on. The use of slurries is particularly effective where there is little space between structures, and moisture protection must be applied prior to a new foundation installation.

2. **Polyethylene** (called "Visqueen," the name given by the original manufacturer), which is available in sheets or rolls 6 mil (mm) to 20 mil (mm) thick and from 20 lf (6.10 m) to 200 lf (60.96 m) in length. It is used primarily for horizontal moisture protection under foundations.

3. **Polystyene board,** better known as "styrofoam," which is rigid insulation usable for moisture protection, for insulating purposes on the interior of concrete or masonry walls, for a backup in an EIFS (Exterior Insulating Finish Surface) system, or for rigid roof insulation. The EIFS system is discussed in chapter 10.

4. **Polyurethane foam,** which is a liquefied insulation material. It may be sprayed under pressure over existing or new roof applications or used as masonry wall fill insulation (as previously discussed).

Below-Grade Moisture Protection

See appendix V, Asphaltic Below-Grade Moisture Protection; see also figure 9–1. There are several types of below-grade bituminous protection against moisture. One of the most common is the **hot-mop** application, where asphalt or pitch is heated into a semiliquid state and applied to walls or slabs by mopping, spraying, or spreading over felts, cloth, or fiber mesh.

Another application is the **cold-applied** method, which uses an **emulsified asphalt,** also in a semiliquid state, available in cans and drums. The emulsion is not heated; it is cold-applied by trowel and/or broom (brush) directly from the container. Special applications allow for liquefying the emulsion for a spray-on installation. The specific quantities required are identified in the table in appendix V.

Another bituminous product is a self-adhering sheet or roll product that is a combination of rubber and asphalt or pitch, such as **neoprene** or **butyl.** These sheet and roll products are extremely moisture resistant when properly protected and cared for. Self-adhering sheet or roll products have become popular for below-grade, on-grade, and roofing applications.

Protection Board.   All below-grade moisture protection systems should have *additional protection against damage and abuse.* Most damage and abuse to moisture protection systems occurs during backfilling procedures. Rock, stone, crushed gravel, and other deleterious materials in the earth break, tear, or puncture the membranes and allow moisture to penetrate as if no protection system were installed. This is the purpose of the **protection board.** Prior to any backfilling against a new moisture protection system, some form of protection board, such as fiberboard or polystyrene board, should be installed. The board is adhered by asphalt mopping, other adhesive materials, or fasteners. The backfill is then placed against the board, thus preventing damage to the system.

Thermal Insulation

See Plans, Sheet S–6, Longitudinal Section; Sheet S–1B, Masonry Wall Alternate. Any material that retards the transmission of heat or sound through any part of a

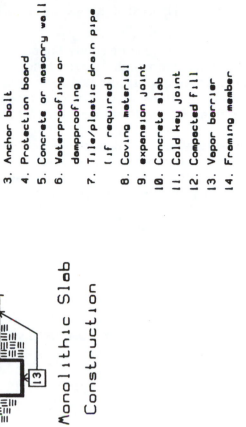

KEYNOTES:

1. Finish grade
2. Sill plate
3. Anchor bolt
4. Protection board
5. Concrete or masonry wall
6. Waterproofing or dampproofing
7. Tile/plastic drain pipe (if required)
8. Coving material
9. expansion joint
10. Concrete slab
11. Cold key joint
12. Compacted fill
13. Vapor barrier
14. Framing member

Monolithic Slab Construction

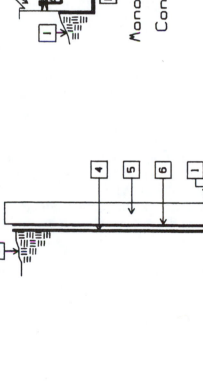

Retaining Wall

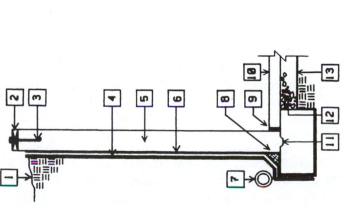

Foundation Wall

FIGURE 9–1
Below-Grade Moisture Protection

175

structure has insulating ability. Sound insulation is studied in chapter 10. The thermal insulation rating for resistance to heat and cold is called the **R-factor.** The most commonly installed insulations are rated at R-7, R-9, R-11, R-19, and R-30. The most recent energy requirements include R-19 in exterior walls and R-30 in ceilings or the underside of roofs.

Batt Insulation.   Insulation sheets of fiberglass or rockwool, called batts, may be with or without building paper, kraft paper, or foil backing. They are applied directly to or between studs, floors joists, or ceiling joists. The nominal sizes of batt insulation are as follows:

12″ (30.48 cm) wide by 8′-0″ (2.44 m) long

16″ (40.64 cm) wide by 8′-0″ (2.44 m) long

24″ (60.96 cm) wide by 8′-0″ (2.44 m) long

Blanket (Roll) Insulation.   Blanket insulation is identical to the batt insulation except that it is manufactured in longer lengths and packaged in roll form. The nominal sizes of blanket insulation are as follows:

12″ (30.48 cm) wide by 24′-0″ (7.32 m) long

16″ (40.64 cm) wide by 24′-0″ (7.32 m) long

24″ (60.96 cm) wide by 24′-0″ (7.32 m) long

Loose-Fill Insulation.   The four types of loose-fill insulation are **perlite, vermiculite, cellulose,** and **rockwool.** These materials were previously described in the discussion of masonry wall insulation in chapter 5. As mentioned, loose-fill insulations are available in bags. The materials may be blown under pressure or poured into wall or ceiling cavities.

Rigid Insulation.   Insulation manufactured into boardlike shapes is referred to as rigid insulation. The boards are combinations of any of the previously mentioned insulating materials. The materials are mixed together, compressed into boards, and covered with surfacing products. The most commonly used insulation materials are fiberglass, polystyrene, and **cementitious composite boards.**

Polyurethane Foam.   Polyurethane foam is used for insulating existing and new roof applications, as well as for masonry wall cavities. The cured foam, when used for roofing, must be coated with an acrylic elastomer for moisture and ultraviolet ray protection.

Roofing

The term *roofing* means any covering of the structural roof used for moisture and/or thermal protection. The standard measurement of roofing is a square. One square = 100 sq ft (9.29 m^2). The many varieties of roofing materials are discussed below.

Shingle Roofing.   There are three classifications for shingles: the composition asphalt shingle, the wood shingle, and the shake shingle.

The **composition shingle** most commonly installed is the three-tab shingle available in four weight categories, 235 lb (106.59 kg), 255 lb (115.67 kg), 285 lb (129.27 kg), and 378 lb (171.46 kg). The 235 lb (106.59 kg) shingle is packaged so that there are **three bundles** per square. The 255 lb (115.67 kg), 285 lb (129.27 kg), and 378 lb (171.46 kg) shingles contain four bundles per square. The three-tab shingle is 36" (91.44 cm) long or 39.37" (1 m) long. The standard exposure for a three-tab shingle is 5" (12.7 cm). Most of the three-tab shingles are self-sealing.

Most **wood shingles** are made of western red cedar cut 18" (45.72 cm) long and sawn both sides in widths from 3" (7.62 cm) to 14" (35.56 cm) with a butt (exposed end) thickness of 3/8" (0.95 cm). Wood shingles contain four bundles per square. Specially made **shingle trim** covers approximately 33 lf (10.06 m) per bundle, or three bundles per square.

Most **wood shakes** are also made from western red cedar cut 24" (60.96 cm) long and vary in width from a minimum of 1 1/2" (3.81 cm) up to 12" (30.48 cm) wide, with the **butts** ranging in thickness from 1/2" (1.27 cm) to 5/8" (1.59 cm) for medium shakes and from 3/4" (1.91 cm) to 1 1/2" (3.81 cm) for heavy shakes. Wood shakes may be split one side and sawn one side or may be split both sides. One square of shakes contains five bundles. Special **trim** for **medium shake** roofing contains four bundles per square, or 25 lf (7.62 m) per bundle. There is no special trim for **heavy shakes;** therefore, an additional bundle of shakes must be included for every 25 lf (7.62 m) on each side of the hip and/or ridge.

Tile Roofing. There are several types and styles of tile roofing. Tile roofing includes clay-based, cement-based, and combinations of cement-based and organic or inorganic materials. The clay-tile materials may have a natural clay (terra cotta) or a flashed, burnt finish. Concrete tiles may appear with a natural concrete color (gray) or may be integrally colored, color-coated, or colored and glazed.

Tile styles vary from the Spanish architecture mission and "S"-shaped tiles to a variety of flat tiles made to appear like shake shingles. The estimator must be aware of the number of tiles per square because the weight and size produced by each manufacturer varies.

Mission tile is a two-piece clay tile in the form of a barrel, which is used for both the tops and pans. The tiles may be red (terra cotta), flash-burnt, variegated "earth" colors, or brilliantly painted, or they may have a glazed finish. There are approximately 180 pieces per square (90 tops and 90 bottoms).

"S" tile is a one-piece tile that may be manufactured from clay (with an appearance similar to barrel tile) or from cement (with a low-profile "S" appearance). The clay "S" tiles are also red (terra cotta), flash-burnt, "earth"-colored, or glaze finished. The concrete tiles may be many different colors, with or without a glazed finish. Depending upon the size, weight, and manufacturer, "S" tile may contain anywhere from 75 to 80 pieces per square for clay tile and 90 to 110 pieces per square for concrete tile.

Flat tile, like "S" tile, may also be manufactured from clay or concrete. Some concrete tiles are molded to appear similar to wood shake shingles. The clay tiles are usually smooth and flat similar to slate tiles. The flat clay tiles are an import from Europe, especially France. Flat tile usually contains from 170 to 190 pieces per square, depending on size and shape.

Slate tile, although not common in the western part of the country, is used extensively in northeastern areas. Slate is a flat piece of shale cut to lengths similar to shingles and sawn on both sides to lie flat and smooth. There are approximately 190 pieces per square.

"**Shake**" **tile** (not to be confused with the concrete "shake" tile mentioned above) is manufactured from a mix of cement, sand, and perlite or vermiculite molded and scored to look like a heavy shake. The colors are usually natural cement gray or tinted dark brown or white. This tile contains 10 bundles per square with 10 to 12 pieces per bundle.

Each style of tile mentioned, with the exception of the concrete shake and slate tiles, requires a **rake trim.** The rake of a roof structure is also known as the barge or gable end. The manufacturer determines the size, style, and number of pieces of rake trim necessry.

The manufacturers of tile roofing also make special **hip and ridge trim.** Like the rakes, the manufacturer determines the size, style, and number of pieces of hip and ridge trim.

Panelized Preformed Roofing and Siding.   Panelized preformed roofing and siding include synthetic wood, plastic, and metal panelized materials. They may be found in both commercial and residential applications. The panelized systems may be butt applied or may be interlocking units. They may also have a baked enamel finish in a variety of colors.

Wood and synthetic wood panels, such as tempered pressed wood (for example, Masonite) may be formed to appear as wood shingle, wood shake, or T-1-11 siding. The panels may or may not include backing of rigid insulation adhered to the panel. The panels are available in $2' \times 4'$ (0.61 m × 1.2 m) up to $4' \times 8'$ (1.22 m × 2.44 m) sizes.

Plastic preformed panels, where used for sloped roofing, are molded over rigid insulation. One panel may vary in size from 8 sq ft (0.74 m^2) to 48 sq ft (4.46 m^2). The styles vary from a shingle or shake roof look-alike to an "S" tile design. Sealants, caulking, or asphalt emulsions are used to adhere the panels to one another and to seal the roof to prevent possible moisture problems.

Where a low range of temperatures exist, such as the winter temperatures of the North, the plastic panel may cause problems because it may become brittle and crack from exposure to the cold. The extremely warm climates can cause the material to warp or become brittle. Because of these potential problems caused by weather, care should be taken when determining location and use.

Standing seam roofing may be premanufactured and placed in panels on roofs or on walls or may be fabricated on the job with special portable forming equipment. Premanufactured panels may be obtained in 10 lf (3.05 m) and 20 lf (6.10 m) lengths by 2 lf (0.61 m), 3 lf (0.91 m), or 4 lf (1.22 m) wide. The panels made on the job may be formed in one continuous length from eave to ridge.

Corrugated cold-rolled steel is in common use for commercial and industrial metal buildings and for rural outbuildings. The metal may be used for roofing, siding, or both on one building. Corrugated metal forms were discussed in chapter 7.

Basic Information about Roofs.   All of the materials discussed above are used on sloped roofs. The roofs must be a **minimum 3:12** slope and installed over a minimum 43 lb (19.50 kg) felt on solid sheathing. All hips, valleys, and ridges require an additional 73 lb (33.11 kg) or 90 lb (40.82 kg) felt, 18″ (45.72 cm) to 24″ (60.96 cm) wide. In colder areas where snow and ice are prevalent, an additional layer of 43 lb (19.50 kg), or heavier, felt is also required along the eave and gable ends. These requirements are dependent upon local codes and ordinances.

Felt underlayments for wood shingles and shakes are 18″ (45.72 cm) wide, with lines to aid in aligning the butts. Felts for composition shingles and tile roofing are the standard 36″ (91.44 cm) wide. All of the underlayments are applied horizontally by nailing or stapling. In cases where the slope is *7:12 or steeper, the 36″ felts may be applied vertically* with proper approval. Where high-wind conditions exist, hot-mopping may also be required on all slopes.

Built-up roofing (BUR) is required for all flat roofs. A roof is considered **flat** where no slope exists up to, and including, a 3:12 slope. Built-up roofing is the term used for the combination of bituminous materials such as asphalt or coal-tar, pitch, and roofing felts. Many varieties of roofing felts and procedures are found in BUR. The felt weights vary from 15 lb (6.80 kg) to 90 lb (40.82 kg) per square. The installation procedures vary from a **single-ply** (one-layer) application such as an EPDM (a mixture of *E*thylene, *P*ropylene, and *D*iene *M*onomer) or SBS (a modified bitumen sheet made of three layers) to a **multi-ply** system, with as many as five plies of standard roofing felts (regular asphalt felts and asphalt/fiberglass-impregnated felts).

Each manufacturer identifies its product by a special combination of letters and/or numbers. Catalogues are available directly from the manufacturer or from the local roofing material supplier.

Traffic Toppings.   In certain areas where foot traffic may be excessive, for example, from a roof access point to rooftop equipment or an equipment penthouse, a traffic topping may be used. A traffic topping may consist of two or three additional layers of roofing felts or **traffic pads** laid as a walkway applied to the surface of the BUR. Some roof applications allow a lightweight concrete stepping-stone to be used.

Accessories.   Sheet metal flashings required for a complete roof installation include products such as **reglets** (used in parapet wall construction to separate the roofing materials from the wall materials), **expansion joints, crickets, pipe jacks, pans, scuppers, downspouts, gravel stops,** and **drip edges.** Special equipment-mounting supports, called **curbs,** may also be made from sheet metal. Some of the parts are premanufactured standard materials. Others may be specially formed for the specific project. Either the roofing contractor or a specialty sheet metal shop may manufacture the parts. Often the HVAC contractor with the equipment to make sheet metal parts will manufacture the materials.

Specialty accessories such as **skylights** and **roof hatches** are also a part of the roof installation. The skylight and roof hatch installations may be included in the contract of the framer or the roofing contractor. Also included for a complete roofing estimate should be special fasteners (such as **anchors** for bosun-chair or portable hanging scaffold), **cant strips, nailer boards,** and **scuppers,** sheet metal flashing, or any item not a part of the roofing system but which are required for a complete roofing installation.

SCOPE OF WORK

The specifications for the roofing application per appendix IV, the Project Manual, Division 7, are as follows:

Division 7: Thermal and Moisture Protection

07000 Scope of Work

Division 1 and the General Conditions are to be considered a part of this division. Furnish all labor, materials and equipment necessary to complete all work under this division and as indicated on drawings.

07100 Below-Grade Moisture Protection

The exterior face of the foundation wall and the footing shall be protected against moisture penetration by the use of a 36″ (91.44 cm) wide roll of self-adhering, self-sealing, bituminous sheet material by Koppers Co., Inc., or equal. The manufacturer's (Koppers) specification is as follows:

1 coat primer (1 gal/sq = 1 lb/sq) @ 15 lb/sq
(1 coat primer [3.79 liter/9.29 m^2 = .45 kg/9.29m^2] @ 6.80 kg/9.29 m^2)
1 rubberized, asphalt/polyethylene laminated membrane, 43″ × 33″ @ 80 lf/sq
(1 rubberized, asphalt/polyethylene laminated membrane, 1.09 m × 10.06 m @ 24.38 m/9.29 m^2)
3″ cant strip (continuous) @ 300 lf/bundle
(7.62 cm cant strip [continuous] @ 91.44 m/bundle)
Webbing for sealing corners and laps @ 300 lf/roll
(Webbing for sealing corners and laps @ 91.44 m/roll)
4′×8′ × 1/2″ fiberboard for protection board @ 32 sq ft/board
(1.22 m × 2.44 m × 1.27 cm fiberboard protection board @ 2.97 m^2/board)

An emulsified primer shall be applied to the wall prior to the installation of the bituminous sheet material. An extra 8″ (20.32 cm) wide layer of the same material shall be applied at all corners and all joints. A 3″×3″ (7.62 cm × 7.62 cm) wood or fibrous continuous cant strip shall be installed along the whole perimeter of the foundation wall at the juncture of the foundation wall and the top of the footing. An extra 16″ (40.64 cm) wide layer of the sheet material shall be applied over the cant strip, 4″ (10.16 cm) up the wall and extending 4″ (10.16 cm) down over the exterior top corner of the footing. All applications shall be applied so that there are no wrinkles or breaks in the material.

A layer of 1″—3.5# (2.54 cm—1.59 kg) density polystyrene foam or 1/2″ (1.27 cm) fibrous protection board shall be placed over the finished bituminous materials from the top of the foundation wall to the base of the footing prior to any backfilling of the walls. Sand or a fine aggregate shall be backfilled against the protection board to at least 1/2 the height of the foundation wall and Type II soil shall be backfilled into the remainder of the space. All backfilling shall be compacted in 8″ (20.32 cm) lifts.

07200 Insulation

Install 2'×4'×2"—3.5# (0.61 m × 1.22 m × 5.08 cm—1.59 kg) density, polystyrene foam board, or 2'×4'×2" (0.61 m × 1.22 m × 5.08 cm) rigid fiberglass insulation board, on the interior side of the foundation wall from the top of the wall to the top of the footing over 1×4 (2.54 cm × 10.16 cm) furring strips fastened w/8d concrete nails and adhesive, spaced 2'-0" O/C (0.61 m) horizontally. The insulation shall be nailed at 9" O/C (22.86 cm) along the perimeter of each piece of insulation w/wide-head 6d × 2 1/2" (6.35 cm) insulation nails. A top and bottom furring strip may be used horizontally the length of the walls.

The exterior stud walls and interior bearing stud walls shall have 6" thick × 16" wide (15.25 cm thick × 40.64 cm wide) R-19, kraft-backed tabbed insulation. All interior stud walls, bearing and partition, shall have a combination thermal and sound insulation, 4" thick × 24" wide (10.16 cm thick × 60.91 cm wide), UNO, kraft-backed paper full height, and staggered full height in the plumbing wall. The insulation shall be sound rated at 60 STC, with the exception of the wall between the Restroom and Utility Room.

Ceilings shall have R-30 loose blanket batt insulation installed as per plans.

07300 Roofing Tiles

Roofing shall be a one-piece clay "S" tile, terra cotta in color, as manufactured by Life Tile Systems, or equal. Underlayment shall be a 43# (19.50 kg), 36" (91.44 cm) wide, 5-square felt laid horizontally on the roof sheathing starting from the bottom (eave line). The felts shall have a minimum 4" (10.16 cm) lap.

A wire-tie system shall be installed per manufacturer's recommendations and specifications. Each tile shall be fastened to the tie system. The tile shall be laid with a 15" (38.10 cm) exposure. All tiles shall be laid in a straight and true horizontal line. No broken tiles shall be used. All broken tiles shall be replaced prior to final inspection of the roof.

A prefabricated plastic or metal ridge vent shall be installed along the ridge and hips in lieu of the standard 2×6 (5.08 cm × 15.24 cm) trimmer placed on edge at these areas. (See Section 07600, Sheet Metal.)

Manufacturer shall supply a ten (10) year warranty covering workmanship and material. A certificate of acceptance by the manufacturer shall be submitted to the owner prior to release of retention payment.

07600 Sheet Metal

All sheet metal flashings and accessories for the roof shall be supplied by the sheet metal contractor, to be installed by others as needed. All sheet metal shall be a minimum 26-gauge galvanized steel or aluminum material with the exception of the valleys and pipe jacks, which shall be manufactured in 1/16" (0.16 cm) thick lead and formed in the same manner as the galvanized flashings.

A prefabricated ridge vent shall be used along all ridges and hips in lieu of the 2×6 (5.08 cm × 15.24 cm) edgewise.

```
07900 Sealants and Caulking
```

```
The contractor shall provide for installation of joint sealants
and caulking at all control joints. Caulking shall also be
provided around all exterior doors and windows.
```

```
End of Division
```

THE ESTIMATE

See figure 9–2. The specifications for the Medical Clinic indicate that there is below-grade moisture protection, thermal insulation below grade, thermal and sound insulation in the walls, and tile roofing. The estimate sheet/summary sheet shown in figure 9–2 includes space for all of the necessary information for a complete estimate, plus space for additional information if it is necessary.

Below-Grade Moisture Protection

See Plans, Sheet S–1, Foundation Plan; Sheet S–8, Wall Sections. Also see chart 9–1. A study of the plans of the Medical Clinic indicates that the foundation wall is 3′-0″ (0.91 m) high from the top of the footing to the sill plate and 10″ (25.40 cm) thick. The footing is 2′-0″ × 1′-0″ (0.30 m × 0.61 m). The plan also indicates the walls are 58′-0″ × 41′-0″ (17.68 m × 12.5 m). The below-grade moisture protection includes a primer of cold-applied emulsion and a continuous self-adhering bituminous membrane, to be applied vertically from the top of the wall to the bottom of the footing, with a fiberboard protection cover. A continuous 3″×3″ (7.62 cm × 7.62 cm) fiber cant strip is placed at the junction of the base of the wall and the top of the footing. All corners, laps, cant strip, and outer edge of the footing at the top are to be covered by a matching webbing.

Below-Grade Insulation

See Plans, Sheet S–1, Foundation Plan; Sheet S–8, Wall Sections. Also see chart 9–2. The specifications and drawings indicate 2″ (5.08 cm) rigid insulation board (fiberglass or polystyrene) installed on the interior side of the wall. The insulation board may be adhered directly to the concrete or over 1×4 (2.54 cm × 10.16 cm) **furring strips.** The specifications and plans call for furring strips to be installed. The strips serve a dual purpose: They provide for an air gap between the wall and insulation as an additional thermal and moisture barrier, and they allow the board to be more easily fastened. The furring is placed 2 lf O/C (0.61 m) with an additional strip at each end of the wall.

The estimator may choose either a 2′×4′ (0.61 m × 1.22 m) or 2′×3′ (0.61 m × 0.91 m) insulation board. The cost effectiveness of the combined material and labor involved will determine which choice to make. The waste in the 2′×4′ (0.61 m × 1.22 m) board can be cut and the pieces used to fill another space. No deductions are made for wall openings when insulation is estimated. It is standard practice that no opening shall be deducted unless it is 100 sq ft (9.29 m²) or more; therefore, no waste factor is included for the Medical Clinic estimate.

DATE: mo day yr	MATERIALS	QUANTITY	UNIT PRICE	EXTENSION
Bid Date				
Job Name				
Contractor				
Phone #				
Rep				
Address				
City				
Owner				
Address				
City				
Job Location				
City				
Areas:				
Labor Charges				
		Misc. Material __ %		
		Material Subtotal		
Labor Total:		Labor Subtotal		
Equipment Charges		Tax: ____ %		
		Subsistence:		
		Miscellaneous:		
		_____		
		_____		
Equipment Total:		Equip. Subtotal		
Special Instructions:		Hard Cost Total		
		____ % Overhead		
		Subtotal		
		____ % Profit		
		GRAND TOTAL		
Square feet:	Unit Price/sq ft:			

FIGURE 9–2
Estimate Sheet/Summary Sheet

Area:
Footing:

1 lf - turndown to bottom of footing	0.30 m - turndown to bottom of footing
7" - wide top of exposed footing each end	0.18 m - wide top of exposed footing each end
(41 lf + (0.58 lf × 2) = 42.17 lf - length of footing	12.85 m - length of footing
A = (1 lf + 0.58 lf) × 42.17 lf	A = (0.30 m + 0.18 m) × 12.85 m
A = **66.63 sq ft**	A = **6.17 m²**

Wall:

A = 41 lf × 3 lf	A = 12.50 m × 0.91 m
A = **123 sq ft**	A = **11.38 m²**

Total area:

66.63 sq ft + 123 sq ft = **189.63 sq ft**	6.17 m² + 11.38 m² = **17.55 m²**

Primer:

189.63 sq ft × 15 lb ÷ 100 sq ft =	17.53 m² × 6.8 kg ÷ 9.29 m² =
2844.45 ÷ 100 lb = 28.4 lb	119.2 ÷ 9.29 kg = 12.83 kg
28.4 lb ÷ 5 gal = **5.7 or 6 5-gal pails**	12.83 kg ÷ 3.79 liter = **3.39 or 4 3.79-liter pails**
	or 3 4-liter pails

Bituminous membrane:

43" (3.58 lf) wide by 33'-0" long	1.09 m wide by 10.06 m long
(3.58 lf × 33 lf) ÷ 100 sq ft = 1.18 sq or 1 sq roll	(1.09 m × 10.06 m) ÷ 9.29 m² = 1.18 sq or 1 sq roll
189.63 sq ft ÷ 100 sq ft = **1.89 or 2 rolls**	17.53 m² ÷ 9.29 m² = **1.89 or 2 rolls**

Cant strip (3" ×3"):

(41 lf × 1.05) ÷ 300 lf/bundle =	(12.50 m × 1.05) ÷ 91.44 m/bundle =
43.05 lf ÷ 300 lf/bundle = **0.14 bundle**	13.11 lf ÷ 91.44 m/bundle = **0.14 bundle**
(approx. ¹/₈ bundle)	(approx. ¹/₈ bundle)

Webbing (sealer strips):
Vertical:

(41 lf + 42.17 lf) ÷ 2 = 41.59 lf	(12.50 m + 12.85 m) ÷ 2 = 12.68 m
41.59 ÷ 3.58 lf = 11.62 or 12 laps	12.68 m ÷ 1.09 m = 11.63 or 12 laps
4.58 lf (wall + footing) × 12 laps = **54.96 lf**	1.40 m (wall + footing) × 12 laps = **16.80 m**

Horizontal (top and bottom of wall + footing):

(41 lf × 2) + 42.17 lf =	(12.50 m × 2) + 12.85 m =
82 lf + 42.17 lf = **124.17 lf**	25.00 m + 12.85 m = **37.85 m**

Total webbing (300 lf/roll):

(54.96 lf + 124.17 lf) × 1.05 =	(16.80 m + 37.85 m) × 1.05 =
179.13 lf × 1.05 =188.09 lf	54.65 m × 1.05 = 57.38 m
188.09 lf ÷ 300 lf/roll = **0.63 or 1 roll**	57.38 m ÷ 91.44 m/roll = **0.63 or 1 roll**

Protection board (4' ×8' [1.22 m × 2.44 m] foam board):

(189.63 sq ft ÷ 32 sq ft) × 1.05 = **6.22 or 7 sheets**	17.55 m² ÷ 2.97 m²) × 1.05 = **6.20 or 7 sheets**

CHART 9–1
Estimate for Below-Grade Moisture Protection: East Wall

Wall Insulation

See Plans, Sheet A–1, Architectural Floor Plan; Sheet S–7, Longitudinal Section. Also see chart 9–3. A variety of insulating materials from blown loose-fill insulation to a fibrous or mineral blanket material may be used. The common fiberglass batt is specified for the Medical Clinic. Either 8 lf (2.44 m) batts or 24 lf (7.32 m) blankets can be used. The walls are 9 lf (2.74 m) high with studs spaced at 16" O/C (at exterior walls and interior bearing walls) or 24" O/C (interior partition walls, UNO) (15.24 cm or 60.96 cm); therefore, it is best to use the blan-

Furring (1×4 @ 2'-0" [2.54 cm × 10.16 cm @ 0.61 m] O/C w/top and bottom strips):
Inside wall measurement:

58 lf - (0.83 lf + 0.83 lf) = **56.34 lf**   17.68 m − (0.25 m + 0.25 m) = **17.18 m**

Furring (3'-0" [0.91 m] wall + 2" [5.08 cm] sill plate):

56.34 lf ÷ 2 lf = 28.17 or 28 spaces	17.18 m ÷ 0.61 m = 28.16 or 28 spaces
28 + 1 = 29 strips	28 + 1 = 29 strips
([29 × {3.17 lf - 0.33 lf}] + [56.33 lf × 2]) × 1.05 =	([29 × {0.97 m − 0.10 m}] + [17.17 m × 2]) × 1.05 =
([29 × 2.84 lf] + 112.66 lf) × 1.05 =	([29 × 0.87 m] + 34.34 m) × 1.05 =
(82.36 lf + 112.66 lf) × 1.05 =	(25.23 m + 34.34 m) × 1.05 =
195.02 lf × 1.05 = 204.77 lf	59.57 m × 1.05 = 62.55 m
204.77 lf × 2 = **409.54 or 410 lf**	62.55 m × 2 = **125.10 or 125 m**

Insulation board:
2'×4' (0.61 m × 1.22 m):

(56.34 lf × 3.17 lf) ÷ 8 sq ft	(17.18 m × 0.97 m) ÷ 0.74 m² =
178.60 sq ft ÷ 8 sq ft	16.66 m² ÷ 0.74 m² =
22.33 × 1.05 = **23.44 or 24 pc**	22.51 × 1.05 = **23.64 or 24 pc**

Cut material:

4 lf − 3.17 lf = 0.83 lf	1.22 m − 0.97 m = 0.25 m
3.17 lf ÷ 0.83 lf = 3.82 or 4 pc	0.97 m ÷ 0.25 = 3.88 or 4 pc

24 pc ÷ 4 pc = 6 pc less
24 pc − 6 pc = **18 pc**

Alternate - 2'x3' (0.61 m × 0.91 m):

178.57 sq ft ÷ 6 sq ft = **29.76 or 30 pc**   16.66 m² ÷ 0.56 m² = **28.72 or 29 pc**

CHART 9–2
Estimate for Below-Grade Rigid Insulation: North/South Walls

Wall area:

A = (41 lf × 9 lf) × 2	A = (12.50 m × 2.74 m) × 2
A = 369 sq ft × 2	A = 34.25 m² × 2
A = **738 sq ft**	A = **68.50 m²**

Blanket insulation (24 lf × 16" [7.32 m × 0.41 m]):

A = 24 lf × 1.33 lf	A = 7.32 m × 0.41 m
A = 31.92 sq ft or 32 sq ft	A = 3 m²
738 sq ft ÷ 32 sq ft = **23 blankets**	68.50 m² ÷ 3 m² = **22.83 or 23 blankets**

CHART 9–3
Estimate for Batt Insulation: East and West Frame Walls

kets. The Specifications require an R-19 for all walls (exterior and interior) and an R-30 in the ceiling.

Alternate Wall Insulation.   *Refer to Plans, Sheet S–1B, Alternate Masonry Wall Plan.* There are two types of insulation used, **loose fill** in the wall and **rigid polystyrene board** on the interior face of the wall. Information regarding loose fill has been given in chapter 6.

Rigid polystyrene insulation can be installed on the face of a masonry wall by directly adhering it, applying it over furring strips, or by installation of the **"Styrostud"** or **"Insulstud" systems.** Both systems use specially formed aluminum retainers installed as studs to which the insulation is fastened.

The use of furring strips was discussed in the below-grade insulation estimate. The directly adhered method requires only the quantity of insulation and the adhesive to be estimated. The problem with this method is that the gypsum wallboard (GWB) placed over the insulation must also be fastened to the masonry wall. This can cause breakage in both the insulation and the GWB.

The specifications for the insulation are found in *appendix IV*, Alternate #2, division 1, Section 1030, of the Project Manual. It is not unusual to find the specifications for masonry wall insulation included in Division 4, Masonry, as indicated in the alternate as follows:

> ***04210 Insulation.*** All materials of one type shall be from one manufacturer. No substitutes will be allowed. The materials selected by the contractor shall be approved in writing prior to any installations per Division 1, Section 01300, Submittals.
>
> Two types of insulation shall be installed in conjunction with the masonry construction. There shall be an expanded mineral fiber loose-fill insulation placed within the wall cavities where no grouting exists and there shall be polystyrene foam board insulation installed on the interior side of the masonry walls.
>
> The loose-fill insulation shall be applied during masonry wall construction by the masonry contractor. At each grout lift, prior to the grout-stop installations for the horizontal bond beams, the insulation shall be poured into the cells that are to have no grout. The masonry contractor shall be responsible to see that the cells are filled completely before the grout-stop is installed. The general contractor's quality control inspector on the project shall make a special inspection to assure proper installation. No cells shall be left unfilled.
>
> 2″ (5.08 cm) polystyrene insulation board (foam board), 3.5# (1.59 kg) density, shall be installed on the interior side of the masonry walls. The "Styrostud" system shall be used with either the aluminum "Z" stud or the channel "stud" to support the insulation. The board shall be directly adhered with an adhesive recommended by the manufacturer. The board shall be 2′×9′ (0.61 m × 2.74 m). The studs shall be 9′-0″ (2.74 m) long.
>
> A 2×4 (5.08 cm × 10.16 cm) wood furring strip shall be installed at the floor and ceiling levels and at each interior corner of the walls to be used as a base upon which to fasten the drywall.

See chart 9–4. There are two types of insulation for the masonry cells, the specified expanded loose fill and a liquefied polyurethane foam. As previously mentioned, one sack (bag) of the loose fill contains enough material to occupy 68 sq ft (6.32 m^2) of wall cavity in an 8″ (20.32 cm) CMU wall.

Foam may be used in lieu of loose fill. The foam is estimated either by the square foot, cubic foot, or gallon. The liquefied foam is obtained in 50-gal drums and is forced into the wall cavities by use of a propellant (for example, compressed air).

See chart 9–5. The specifications call for the "Styrostud" system for face insulation installed on the interior side of the masonry walls. The system may be constructed in either of two ways. One system utilizes a 22-gauge aluminum stud (called a "Z" stud because it is similar in shape to the letter "Z" in cross section), 1 1/2″ (3.81 cm) to 2″ (5.08 cm) wide, spaced 2 lf O/C (0.61 m), matching the board thickness and width. The board and studs are available in lengths of 8 lf (2.44 m), 9 lf (2.74 m), 10 lf (3.05 m), or 12 lf (3.66 m).

Wall area:
A = (41.33 lf × 9.33 lf) × 2	A = (12.60 m × 2.84 m) × 2
A = 385.61 sq ft × 2	A = 35.78 m² × 2
A = **771.22 sq ft**	A = **71.56 m²**

Expanded loose-fill insulation @ 67% of wall capacity (68 sq ft/bag or 6.32 m²/bag):
771.22 sq ft × 0.67 = 516.72 sq ft	71.56 m² × 0.67 = 47.95 m²
(516.72 sq ft ÷ 68 sq ft) × 1.05 =	(47.95 m² ÷ 6.32 m²) × 1.05 =
7.58 × 1.05 = **7.96 or 8 bags**	7.59 × 1.05 = **7.96 or 8 bags**

Liquefied polyurethane (foam) insulation @ 67% of wall capacity (2 lb/cu ft or 0.91 kg/0.03 m³):
V = (771.22 sq ft × 0.67 lf) × 0.67	V = (71.56 m² × 0.20 m) × 0.67
V = 516.72 cu ft × 0.67	V = 14.31 m³ × 0.67
V = **346.20 cu ft**	V = **9.59 m³**
346.20 cu ft ÷ 2 lb/cu ft = 173.1 lb	9.59 m³ ÷ 4.4 kg/0.03 m³ =
173.1 lb ÷ 8 lb = **21.64 gal or 22 gal**	319.66 ÷ 4.4 kg = 72.65 kg

CHART 9—4
Estimate for Alternate Insulation—Exterior Wall: East and West Walls

Interior wall length - 9'-4" (2.84 m) high walls:
41.33 lf − 1.33 lf = **40 lf**	12.60 m − 0.41 m = **12.19 m**

Wall area:
A = (40 lf × 9.33 lf) × 2	A = (12.19 m × 2.84 m) × 2
A = 373.2 sq ft × 2	A = 34.61 m² × 2
A = **746.4 sq ft**	A = **69.22 m²**

2×4 (5.08 cm × 10.32 cm) furring (perimeter):
([40 lf × 2] + [{9.33 lf − 0.33 lf} × 2]) × 2 =	([12.19 m × 2] + [{2.84 m − 0.10 m} × 2]) × 2 =
(80 lf + 18 lf) × 2 =	(24.38 m + 5.48 m) × 2 =
98 lf × 2 = 196 lf	29.86 m × 2 = 59.72 m
196 lf × 1.05 = **205.8 or 206 lf**	59.72 m × 1.05 = **62.71 or 63 m**

Insulation board 2'x10' (0.61 m × 3.05 m):
Method 1:
(746.4 sq ft ÷ 20 sq ft) × 1.05 =	(69.22 m² ÷ 1.86 m²) × 1.05 =
37.32 sheets × 1.05 = **39.18 or 40 sheets**	37.22 sheets × 1.05 = **39.08 or 40 sheets**

Method 2:
(40 lf ÷ 2 lf) × 2 = **40 sheets**	(12.19 m ÷ 0.61 m) × 2 = **39.96 or 40 sheets**

"Z" or channel studs:
([40 lf ÷ 2 lf] − 2) × 2 = **36 studs***	([12.19 m ÷ 0.61 m] − 2) × 2 = 35.96 or **36 studs***

*The studs are not required on the ends of each wall because of the furring.

CHART 9—5
Estimate for Alternate (Stryostud) Insulation—East and West Walls

The other stud system is identical to the "Z" stud system except that the "stud" is formed in the shape of a 22-gauge aluminum channel, 1 1/2" (3.81 cm) to 2" (5.08 cm) wide with 1/2" (1.27 cm) return legs. The insulation board, with grooves to fit the channel, and channels are available in the same sizes as the "Z" stud system.

Roof area (squares) - ⁵⁄₁₂ slope (slope factor 1.13):

A = 62 lf × 45 lf

A = 2,790 sq ft × 1.13

A = 3,152.7 sq ft ÷ 100 sq ft

A = **31.53 or 32 sq tile**

A = 18.89 m × 13.72 m

A = 259.17 m² × 1.13

A = 292.86 m² ÷ 9.29 m²

A = **31.52 or 32 sq tile**

Underlayment - 43#, 5 sq roll:

31.53 sq ÷ 5 sq = **6.31 or 7 rolls**

Trim (including waste factor - 5%):

Ridge and hip (1 piece/ft):

Ridge = 17 lf

Rafter = 24.3 lf

Hip = 34.68 lf

(17 lf + [34.68 lf × 4]) × 1.05 =

(17 lf + 138.72 lf) × 1.05 =

155.72 lf × 1.05 = **163.51 or 164 pc trim**

Ridge = 5.18 m

Rafter = 7.41 m

Hip = 10.57 m

(5.18 m + [10.57 m × 4]) × 1.05 =

(5.18 m + 42.28 m) × 1.05 =

(47.46 m ÷ 0.30 m) × 1.05 = **166.11 or 166 pc trim**

Starter:

([62 lf × 2] + [45 lf × 2]) × 1.05 =

(124 lf + 90 lf) × 1.05 =

214 lf × 1.05 = **224.7 or 225 pc starter**

([18.89 m × 2] + [13.72 m × 2]) × 1.05 =

(37.78 m + 27.44 m) × 1.05 =

(65.22 m ÷ 0.30 m) × 1.05 = **228.27 or 229 pc starter**

Alternate birdstop (10'-0" [3.05 m] long):

224.7 lf ÷ 10 lf = **22.47 or 23 lengths**

2×6 (5.08 cm × 15.24 cm) nailer or ridge vent:

same as hip and ridge trim = **120 lf or 36.56 m**

Field vents in lieu of ridge vents (1 per 10 sq or fraction thereof):

32 sq = **4 vents**

Wire-tie system:

Average lengths of roof:

(62 lf + 17 lf) ÷ 2 = 39.50 lf ea side

45 lf ÷ 2 = 22.50 lf ea end

Tile spacing = 17" (1.42 lf)

Rafter length = 24.30 lf

([39.50 lf + 22.50 lf] × 2) ÷ 1.42 lf =

(62 lf × 2) ÷ 1.42 lf =

124 lf ÷ 1.42 lf = 87.33 or 88 ties horizontal

24.30 lf × 88 ties = 2,138.4 lf

2,138.4 × 1.05 = **2,245.32 or 2,246 lf tie wire**

(18.89 m + 5.18 m) ÷ 2 = 12.04 m ea side

13.72 m ÷ 2 = 6.86 m ea end

Tile spacing = 0.43 m

Rafter length = 7.41 m

([12.04 m + 6.86 m] × 2) ÷ 0.43 m =

(18.9 m × 2) ÷ 0.43 m =

37.8 m ÷ 0.43 m = 87.9 or 88 ties horizontal

7.41 m × 88 ties = 652.08 m

652.08 m × 1.05 = **684.68 or 685 m tie wire**

Alternate 1×4 (2.54 cm ×5.08 cm) wood battens:

(24.30 lf ÷ 1.25 lf) × (39.50 lf + 22.50 lf) =

19.44 lf × 62 lf = 1,205.28 lf

1,205.28 × 1.05 = **1,265.54 or 1,266 lf**

(7.41 m ÷ 0.38 m) × (12.04 m + 6.86 m) =

19.5 × 18.90 m = 368.55 m

368.55 m × 1.05 = **386.98 or 387 m**

CHART 9–6

Roofing Estimate: With "S" Tile, 5:12 Slope

Roofing

See Plans, Sheet A–5, Roof Plan; see also chart 9–6. The specifications for the Medical Clinic state that an "S" tile is required for the roof. Ridge and hip trim, nailers, vents, tile ties, and starter (booster) pieces or aluminum birdstop are also necessary. Ridge vents are required in lieu of the nailer board at the ridge.

A quick estimate for hip and ridge trim is figuring *one piece of trim per lineal foot* determined from the rafter, hip, and ridge lengths. The alternate method is to determine the exposure of the trim tile and count the number of pieces required for each hip and the ridge.

Starter Tiles versus Birdstop.   The number of starter pieces is determined by the width of the "S" tile. This tile is 17" (43.18 cm) wide. Starters are half-length tiles that are installed along the eaves under the full tile. The starter helps to raise the first course of tile to match the field tiles as they are installed. More than one course of starter may be used (one on top the other) for Spanish design. The tiles are then "mudded in" with a mortar mix.

Aluminum or galvanized cold-rolled steel (GI) angle strips, called bird stop, with one side of the angle cut to match the "S" tile are used in lieu of starter tiles. The strips are usually available in lengths of 10 lf (3.05 m). The purpose of these strips is to align the starter tiles with the field tiles as well as to prevent birds from nesting under the tiles.

Nailers versus Ridge Vent.   Nailers are 2×6 (5.08 cm × 15.24 cm) random lengths of lumber set on edge to which the ridge and hip trim are fastened. The trim is usually nailed to the nailer board. The lineal feet of nailer is the same as the lineal feet of ridge and hip trim. Where nailer boards are used, venting must be placed in the roof field area. These vents are made of aluminum, galvanized cold-rolled steel, or lead. Code requires one vent per each 10 sq (92.9 m^2) of roofing, or fraction thereof.

Ridge vents may be galvanized cold-rolled steel, aluminum, or plastic. The materials are very porous to allow the ridge or hip to "breathe." When the metal or plastic venting is used, the trim must be fastened with ties that clip to the vent top. Where the vent is used, the ridge nailer is to be deducted.

Wire-Tie System   The wire-tie system requires one tie hook per tile; therefore, the number of hooks equals the number of tiles. The twisted wire system to which the hooks are fastened is measured vertically with the same spacing as the distance between exposed barrels of the tile.

The tiles for the Medical Clinic are fastened in 19 courses. The width of the tile is 17" (43.18 cm); therefore, the spacing from barrel to barrel is the same. The first wire-tie is spaced to align with the first barrel hole on the left and the last barrel hole on the right. The roof is a hip roof, which means that many of the tiles will be cut and there is no fixed hole position for them. The quickest method of calculation is to "open" the roof plane and assume one long flat line.

Alternate Battens.   Wood batten strips, 1×4 (2.54 cm × 10.16 cm) utility grade lumber, may be used to fasten the tiles to the roof sheathing in lieu of the wire-tie system. The battens are spaced the same as the length of the tile except the first course. The first course at the eave line is spaced to allow a minimum 1" (2.54 cm) overhang of tile beyond the edge of the sheathing at the nailing point in the tile. The tile overhang is done to allow for drainage from the roof without the moisture backing up into the sheathing under the underlayment. The battens are nailed or stapled horizontally to the sheathing through the underlayment.

Each manufacturer of battens has a different design resulting in variations of the size of the tile and/or hole position for nailing the tile. The estimator must again determine the manufacturer's recommendations and estimate the lengths accordingly. The tiles estimated for the Medical Clinic are 18" (45.72 cm) long with two holes spaced 1" (2.54 cm) from the top, centered on the barrel and on the pan. The batten for the first course is placed 15″ (38.10 cm) from the eave line. Each successive course is spaced so that there is a minimum 3″ (7.62 cm) overlap allowing a 15″ (38.10 cm) exposure. The roofer is allowed by code to "cheat" a bit on exposures if there is a problem with the spacing. In this case, a half course is made up in 19 courses.

Additional General Roof Accessory Information.   One carton of nails will cover approximately 25 sq (232.25 m^2) of roofing for composition shingles or wood shingles and shakes. Nailing has been calculated for one or two nail(s) per tile. This varies with local building code and manufacturer requirements. The nailing of every tile may be required in high-wind problem areas. Other areas may require nailing only every third, sixth, ninth, and so on, courses. Some areas may only require the first three and last three courses nailed. Codes and ordinances in each locale need to be checked to determine proper procedures.

   Metal drip-edge may be required for *all roofing*. The edge may be aluminum or galvanized iron with or without a baked enamel finish. The strips are from 1″ (2.54 cm) to 1 1/2″ (3.81 cm) wide and available in lengths of 10 lf (3.05 m). The edging is placed along the perimeter of the roof; that is, the eaves and barges (rakes).

Alternate Built-up Roofing (BUR).   *See* appendix IV, *Alternate 5, Division 1, Section 1030, the Project Manual. See also plans, Sheet A–5, Alternate Roof Plan.* Alternate #5 specifies installation of a BUR system in lieu of the tile roofing. The slope is 1/2″/ft (1.27 cm/30.48 cm). There is no parapet surrounding the roof. The specification is as follows:

> **Alternate #5.**
>
> This alternate is for a built-up roofing system in lieu of tile roofing.
>
> *07200 Insulation.* The roof deck shall be covered with one layer of 1″ (5.08 cm), 3′×4′ (0.91 m × 1.22 m) rigid isotherm insulation board and a second layer of rigid perlite composite board 1″ (2.54 cm) thick. Manufacturer shall be GAF. The first layer shall be adhered to the roof deck with a "spot" mopping. The joints shall be staggered and tape sealed. The second layer shall be fastened with typical insulation fasteners a minimum 2 1/2″ (6.35 cm) long. The joints shall be staggered and opposite the joints of the first layer and tape sealed. Insulation shall be supplied by GAF.
>
> *07500 Membrane Roofing* An alternate built-up roofing system shall be submitted in lieu of the proposed tile roof system. A three-ply BUR system, specification I-2-1-MGP by GAF, is hereby specified over insulated wood deck.
>
>   Asphalt shall be supplied in cartons of 50# each. All felt materials shall be supplied by the same manufacturer. All asphalt shall be supplied by the same manufacturer. The asphalt shall be approved for use with the BUR system. The system shall be applied as follows:
>
> 1″ Isotherm insulation (spot mopped)   @ 15# (6.80 kg)

```
1" Perlite base composite board

Type III asphalt (3 coats)                @ 75# (34.02 kg)

Gafglas Ply 6 sheet (2 plies)             @ 20# (9.07 kg)

Ruberoid MP membrane                      @100# (45.36 kg)

Total weight                               210# (95.25 kg)
```

07600 Flashing and Sheet Metal. A 1 1/2" (3.81 cm) 29 ga white enameled galvanized iron gravel stop shall be installed along the eaves on both sides of the roof. An edge metal matching the gravel stop shall be installed along the barges.

The BUR system specifies a hot-mopped *three-ply roof with cap sheet* applied over rigid insulation over the roof sheathing. The insulation is applied in two layers. The roofing specification chosen by the owner is the I-2-1-MPG system by GAF. The number and letter system of the manufacturer is described as follows:

I   =   insulated deck
2   =   two Type 6 ply sheets
1   =   "Ruberoid" cap sheet
MPG   =   gravel cap sheet surface

Asphalt is available in preheated tank truckloads of from 500 gal (1,895 liter) to several thousand gallons or can be obtained in 50 lb (22.72 kg) or 100 lb (45.36 kg) cartons for smaller projects.

Accessories. The accessories required for the BUR include a 1 1/2" (3.81 cm) gravel stop installed along the eave line to hold back the gravel from falling from the roof, roof jacks for all pipe penetrations (waste vents and so on), gutter and downspout or diverters for drainage protection over the entries, and a drip edge along the rakes (barges). The gravel stop and drip edge are available in 10 lf (3.05 m) and 20 lf (6.10) units.

Labor

The installers of below-grade moisture protection and roofing are both classed as "roofers." Some companies do both below-grade moisture protection and roofing while others specialize in one or the other. The crew size varies with each of these trades. It is important to remember that the work is different for each trade and that a separate composite crew schedule should be prepared for each.

Below-Grade Moisture Protection. *See figure 9–3.* Whether the below-grade moisture protection is applied by hot-mopping or by the cold process for an emulsion, a 3-person crew can install 10 sq/day (all materials). The productivity rate of the crew is calculated at 69%. The productivity factor is calculated as follows:

70% ÷ 69% = 1.01

CREW	HOURLY + BURDEN WAGE	% TIME ON JOB/HR	HOURLY RATE
Foreman	$12.25 + $ 3.74	50%	= $ 8.00
Laborer (3)	$11.75 + $ 3.74 × 3	50%	= $23.24
Composite Crew Rate:		100%	$31.24/MH

FIGURE 9–3a
Composite Crew Schedule

CREW	HOURLY WAGE + BURDEN
Foreman	$12.25 + $ 3.74
Laborer (3)	$11.75 + $ 3.74 × 3
	$47.50 + $14.96 = $62.46
Composite Crew Rate:	$62.46/2 = $31.24

FIGURE 9–3b
Composite Crew Schedule

The labor cost for the below-grade moisture protection on the east and west walls is:

Method 9-3a and 9-3b are both the same:

$31.24/MH × 1.01 = $31.55/MH

$31.55/MH × 8 hr = $252.40/MD

(2 sq × 2) ÷ 10 sq = 0.4 or 0.5 day

$252.40/MD × 3 persons × 0.5 day = $378.60 or $379.00

Below-Grade Insulation. Specialty contractors are used for thermal installations in all cases where the insulation is not an integral part of another trade application (such as stucco). The labor rates and personnel are usually affiliated with the carpentry trades.

Below-Grade Insulation. See figure 9–4a and figure 9–4b, Composite Crew Schedule: Below-Grade Insulation. A 2-person crew takes 2 days each to install the insulation on the north and south walls. The productivity rate is 79%. The productivity factor is calculated as follows:

70% ÷ 79% = 0.89

The labor cost is:

Method 9–4a and 9–4b are both the same:

$17.61/MH × 0.89 = $15.67/MH

$15.67/MH × 8 hr = $125.36/MD

$125.36/MD × 2 workers × 4 days = $1,002.88 or $1,003.00

CREW	HOURLY + BURDEN WAGE	% TIME ON JOB/HR	HOURLY RATE
Carpenter	$16.40 + $3.32	50%	= $ 9.86
Laborer/Helper (2)	$11.75 + $3.74	50%	= $ 7.75
Composite Crew Rate:		100%	$17.61/MH

FIGURE 9–4a
Composite Crew Schedule

CREW	HOURLY WAGE + BURDEN
Carpenter	$16.40 + $3.32
Laborer/Helper	$11.75 + $3.74
	$28.15 + $7.06 = $35.21
Composite Crew Rate:	$35.21/2 = $17.61

FIGURE 9–4b
Composite Crew Schedule

CREW	HOURLY + BURDEN WAGE	% TIME ON JOB/HR	HOURLY RATE
Laborer (3)	$11.75 + $3.74 × 3	13%	= $ 6.04
Roofer (2)	$16.40 + $3.32 × 2	87%	= $34.31
Composite Crew Rate:		100%	$40.35/MH

FIGURE 9–5
Composite Crew Schedule

Wall Insulation.   *Refer to figure 9-4a and 9-4b.* The insulation required for framed walls may be either batt or loose fill (blown). Batt insulation is normally installed in new construction. The composite crew installer/foreman and a helper/laborer. The 2-person crew requires 8 days to install all of the insulation. The same composite crew is used for building walls as were used for the below-grade insulation. The productivity factor is 0.97. The labor cost is calculated as follows:

Methods 9–4a and 9–4b:

$17.61/MH × 0.97 = $17.08/MH

$17.08/MH × 8 hr = $136.64/MD

$136.64/MD × 2 persons × 8 days = $2,186.24 or $2,186.00

Roofing.   *See figure 9–5.* Two roofers are each capable of applying 5 sq of tile/day. This includes the installation of the underlayment and the tile-ties.

There are 31.53 sqs (32 sqs) of tile. The only other labor to consider is the loading of the roof. A 3-person crew is used to load the roof. The loading takes 1/2 day.

The times consumed by 2 workers in the installation of the tile is calculated as follows:

32 sq ÷ 10 sq = 3.2 or 3.25 days

The loading takes 1/2 day. Labor for loading the tile is calculated as follows:

0.5 day × 3 workers = 1.5 days

The total time for the loading and installation of the tile is as follows:

3.25 days + 1.5 days = 4.75 days

The productivity rate is calculated at 82%. The productivity factor is calculated as follows:

70% ÷ 82% = 0.85

The total labor is determined as follows:

$40.35/MH × 0.85 = $34.30/MH
$34.30/MH × 8 hr = $274.40/MD
$274.40/MD × 5 workers × 4.75 days = $6,517.00

Equipment

Each trade is in need of its own equipment. Each crew requires personnel transportation.

See figure 9–6. The equipment for the below-grade moisture protection includes a kettle and pump and miscellaneous hand equipment.

See figure 9–7. The insulation installers require a forklift and power tools.

See figure 9–8. The roofers and loaders require freight transportation (lift truck), a forklift, and power tools.

EQUIPMENT	USE TIME	UNIT COST	TOTAL
Transportation	1 day	@ $ 10/day	= $ 10.00
Kettle and Pump	1 day	@ $175/day	= $175.00
Miscellaneous (brooms, etc.)			= $ 25.00
Equipment Total:			$210.00

FIGURE 9–6
Equipment Schedule: Below-Grade Moisture Protection

EQUIPMENT	USE TIME	UNIT COST	TOTAL
Transportation	4 days	@ $10/day	= $ 40.00
Forklift	4 days	@ $90/day	= $360.00
Staple Gun (2)	4 days	@ $25/day	= $100.00
Equipment Total:			$500.00

FIGURE 9–7
Equipment Schedule: Insulation

EQUIPMENT	USE TIME	UNIT COST	TOTAL
Transportation	4 days	@ $10/day	= $ 40.00
Freight Transport	1 day	@ $35/day	= $ 35.00
Forklift	4 days	@ $90/day	= $360.00
Nailer Gun (2)	4 days	@ $25/day	= $100.00
Staple Gun (2)	4 days	@ $25/day	= $100.00
Equipment Total:			$635.00

FIGURE 9–8
Equipment Schedule: Roofing

CHAPTER EXERCISES

1. Determine the total squares of below-grade moisture protection for the Medical Center.

2. The total lineal feet of cant strip at the footing is _____.

3. Without considering reuse of pieces of insulation, determine how much 2′×4′×2″ polystyrene board will be required for the whole crawl space. See Plans, Sheet S–1.

4. Estimate the quantities of insulation for all of the walls (interior and exterior) and the ceiling of the Medical Clinic. R-11 for all interior partition walls, R-19 for all exterior and interior bearing walls, and R-30 for the ceilings.

5. The clinic owner cannot make up his mind. Another addendum is forwarded to all roofing contractors requesting a proposal for wood shingle or wood shake roofing. The materials include the following:

   Shingles   @ $88/sq
   Medium shakes   @ $97/sq
   Underlayment   @ $3.75/roll
   Shingle trim   @ $15/bdl
   Shake trim   @ $18/bdl
   Carton nails   @ $44/ctn

   Determine the quantities and total cost of the shingles.

6. Using the information in problem 5, determine the quantities and total cost of the shakes.

7. One person can lay either shingle or shake at the rate of 18 sq/day. Determine the number of days needed if a 2-person crew is used.

8. The wage rate for the crew is paid by the square instead of by the hour. One worker lays 44% of the material. The second worker lays 56%. Determine the amount of labor paid to each worker at the rate of $33.00/sq.

9. Complete the "Styrostud" insulating system for the masonry walls (either system). *See chart 9–5.*

10. From the information supplied in the chapter, perform a quantity survey of the BUR system

Finishes

Division 9

CHAPTER 10

GENERAL INFORMATION

The most diversified specifications are found in Division 9. The division is called "Finishes" because it includes the trades such as **lath and plaster** (interior and exterior), **drywall, acoustical ceilings, floor covering, wall-coverings,** and **painting** that cover up all of the "rough-in" trades from concrete to electrical. The exception is **light-gauge metal framing,** since it is, like rough carpentry, a *support system,* not a finish system. It is the *support system* on which the finish materials are applied.

Lath and Plaster

The term **plaster** is used in the general sense for both **gypsum,** which is used for interior surfaces, and **cement** (stucco), which is normally used for exterior surfaces. Both gypsum and cement plasters are used for weather and fire protection as well as for aesthetic reasons. Both interior and exterior plastering require many of the same materials such as building paper or plastic moisture barrier, lath, fasteners, and protection materials.

The vapor barrier for exterior plaster may be installed by other trades prior to the application of the lath or may be an integral part of the lath. The lath, which is the fundamental support for the plaster, includes the following types: **wire mesh, expanded metal lath,** and **hi-rib lath.** There are also a wide range of accessories for exterior and interior plaster, the most common of which are **base screed, "J" metal, corner bead, control joints,** and **fasteners.**

There are four exterior cement plaster systems commonly in use: the one-coat, two-coat, and three-coat systems, and the Exterior Insulation and Finish System (EIFS).

1. *One-Coat System.* The one-coat system is applied to wood- or metal-stud framed structures only. Included in the system are the building paper, 1" 20-gauge (2.54 cm-20 ga) mesh or expanded metal lath. The installation is completed with a 3/8" (0.95 cm) thick cement plaster brown coat and a 1/8" (0.32 cm) thick natural gray or integrally colored cement plaster finish coat. The system may also include 1"-1.5# (2.54 cm-0.68 kg) or 1"-3.5#

197

(2.54 cm-1.59 kg) polystyrene insulation board applied over exterior sheathing prior to the installation of the building paper with mesh or expanded metal.

2.   *Two-Coat System.*   This system is applied directly over masonry walls. The two coats include the brown and finish coats just as in the one-coat system, but without building paper or mesh. The masonry, after properly setting, is wet down for the brown coat. The brown coat is sprayed or troweled and left to cure. The finish coat is then applied and allowed to cure.

3.   *Three-Coat System.   See Plans, Sheets A–2 and A–3, Exterior Elevations.* The three-coat system is specified for the Medical Clinic. This system is not only a finishing product but may also be integrated into the structural shear-wall system. If so, the walls would be so identified in the shear-wall schedule. The three-coat system includes building paper, lath, a 3/8″ (0.95 cm) scratch coat, a 3/8″ (0.95 cm) brown coat, and a 1/8″ (0.32 cm) finish coat for a maximum 3/4″ (1.91 cm) specification or 1/4″ (0.64 cm) finish coat for a maximum 1″ (2.54 cm) specification. Insulating board is optional.

4.   *Exterior Insulation and Finish System (EIFS).*   A fourth exterior finish system that has become very popular in recent years is the EIFS system. It is similar to the one-coat stucco system with several minor variations. The same basic procedures are followed with the exception that the brown coat and an elastomeric surfacing material, integrally colored, are used to complete the system. The thickness of the system (excluding the insulation) is approximately 1/4″ (0.64 cm). The elastomeric surface material is from 5 mil (millimeters) to 10 mil thick. A nylon or polyester mesh is used (in lieu of the metal wire lath) to which the finish surface material is adhered.

Lath and plaster are also used for fire protection surrounding steel beams, columns, and other structural components not exposed to view. The lath is wrapped around the components and sprayed with either gypsum (normally used) or cement plaster mixed with fiberglass or some other fire-retardant material.

Plaster Accessories.   Base screed is a cold-rolled galvanized steel or aluminum strip approximately 2″ (5.08 cm) to 6″ (15.24 cm) wide with a 3/4″ (1.91 cm) to 1″ (2.54 cm) deep "V" shaped protrusion along the center of the strip with perforations spaced evenly along the underside of the "V." It is used with many types of siding, but particularly with exterior cement plaster. The screed is a counterflashing fastened parallel to the exterior of the sill plate and deep enough to cover the top of the moisture protection. The purpose of the screed is to allow any moisture accumulated within the wall cavity to escape and to allow the wall to "breathe." A variation of the screed is the counterflashing used for termite protection in many areas of the country where infestation is prevalent.

"Milcor" (a trade name of the Milcor Corp.) is a "J"-shaped cold-rolled steel or aluminum strip used as an edge where dissimilar materials meet. The strip may be found wherever the plaster meets an exterior masonry or concrete wall, roof, plate line, or it is used as a surround at doors and windows to hold back the plaster from the opening. The smaller side of the "J" metal is exposed to the exterior. The strip is available in 8 lf (2.44 m), 9 lf (2.74 m), or 10 lf (3.05 m) strips. The hook is 3/4″ (1.91 cm) or 1″ (2.54 cm) wide to match the stucco thickness.

Corner bead is the reinforcement for cement plaster installations used at all corners. It is an angle strip of 1″ (2.54 cm) 20-gauge mesh, solid or perforated galvanized steel, or aluminum. The most commonly used bead for plaster is the 1" (2.54 cm) 20-gauge mesh. The solid or perforated styles are more likely to be installed where interior plastering, cement or gypsum, is used. There are two types of corner bead. The most common is the outside corner bead, referred to as **corneraid,** applied at all outside corner angles. Some manufacturer and code specifications also require the inside corner bead, referred to as **cornertite,** for the inside corner angles. Both types of beads are available in 10 lf (3.05 m) pieces and are placed the full vertical height of the plastered wall at the corners.

The **control joint** is a cold-rolled galvanized steel, stainless steel, aluminum, or plated or painted strip used to control feathering and cracking of the exterior plaster. The formed joint may be a "U," "V," or "W" shape. Control joints are installed vertically on all walls, horizontally for walls over 10 lf (3.05 m) high, or for every 400 sq ft (37.16 m²) of clear wall area each way. The joints are also installed vertically from the top corner of a wall opening to the top plate and from the bottom corner of a wall opening to the base screed.

Contraction joints, in the form of a troweled "V" in the finish coat, are frequently used at the openings in residential construction in lieu of the control joint. This is not a recommended procedure although its use is widespread.

Fasteners such as cap nails (wide head with or without plastic or fiber washer), screws, or staples are required to hold the lath, building paper, and/or insulation backing in place for the application of the plaster.

Exterior Cement Plaster Soffits and Ceilings.   *See figure 10–1.* The drawing in figure 10–1 could be used as an alternate entry cover for the Medical Clinic. The cement plaster exterior ceilings may be constructed from any of the cement plaster systems. Cement plaster is applied to the walls and columns, as well as the ceiling and soffit. Either of the latter two areas may require a suspension system or support wires and framing, as in the soffit in figure 10–1. The suspension system includes 1 1/2" (3.81 cm) "C" channel (black metal), 7/8" (2.22 cm) or 1 1/2" (3.81 cm) furring (hat) channel to which the hi-rib lath and building paper are attached, and #9 AWG wire and eye hooks into which the wire is fastened. Venting and control joints may also be included with the system.

Light-Gauge Metal Framing

See appendix V, Structural Light-Gauge and Light-Gauge Metal Stud Framing. See also Plans, Sheet A–1, Architectural Floor Plan; Sheet A–6, Architectural Longitudinal Section; Sheet S–7, Structural Longitudinal and Transverse Sections; Sheet S–8, Partial Wall Sections. See also figure 10–2.

Metal stud framing is used extensively in commercial and industrial construction applications and is coming into more use in residential construction. There are two types of metal framing: structural light-gauge framing and light-gauge metal stud. Structural light-gauge framing is normally included in Division 5, Steel. Where there is little or no other steel in a project, the structural framing may be included in Division 9, along with the nonstructural light-gauge metal.

The difference between structural light-gauge metal framing and light-gauge metal is noted in the table in the appendix. Structural metal studs and joists are heavier and more rigid. The metal framing used in the Medical Clinic project is considered light-gauge framing, making use of 20-gauge, 22-gauge, and 25-gauge galvanized cold-rolled steel.

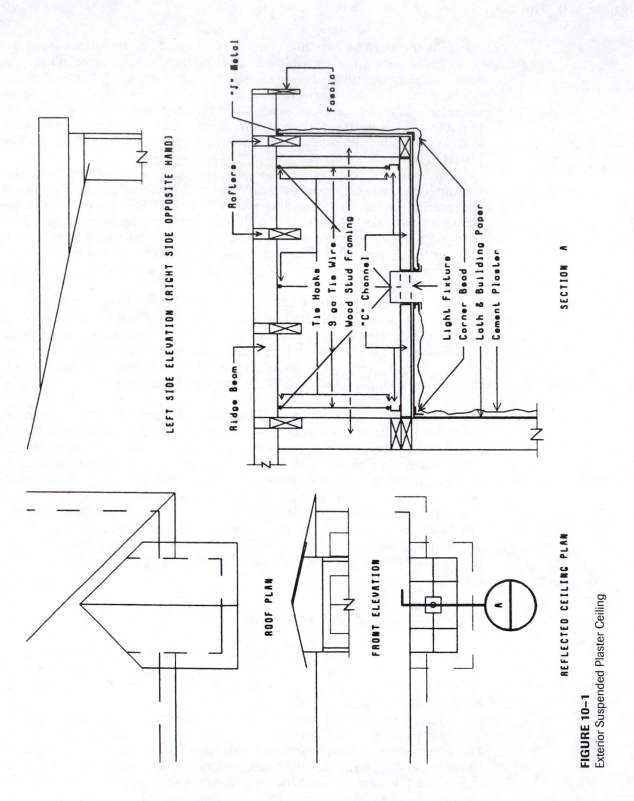

LEFT SIDE ELEVATION (RIGHT SIDE OPPOSITE HAND)

"J" Metal

Fascia

Rafters

Ridge Beam

Tie Hooks

9 ga Tie Wire

Wood Stud Framing

"C" Channel

Light Fixture

Corner Bead

Lath & Building Paper

Cement Plaster

SECTION A

ROOF PLAN

FRONT ELEVATION

REFLECTED CEILING PLAN

A

FIGURE 10–1
Exterior Suspended Plaster Ceiling

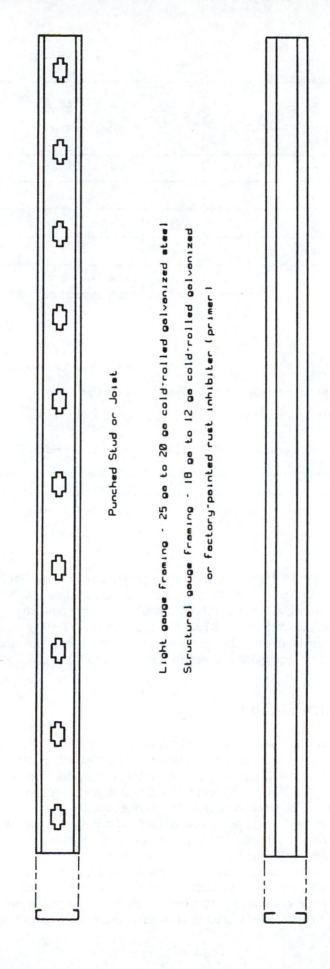

Punched Stud or Joist

Light gauge framing - 25 ga to 20 ga cold-rolled galvanized steel

Structural gauge framing - 18 ga to 12 ga cold-rolled galvanized
or factory-painted rust inhibiter (primer)

Wide-flanged Unpunched Joist

FIGURE 10-2
Cold-Rolled Light-Gauge Metal Stud and Joist

201

BOARD THICKNESS	BOARD SIZE				BOARD TYPES				
	8'	9'	10'	12'	Reg	MR**	WR***	"c"	"x"**
1/4" GWB	×			×	×				
3/8" GWB	×			×	×	×	×		
1/2" GWB	×	×	×	×	×	×	×	×	×
5/8" GWB	×	×	×	×	×	×	×	×	×

REMARKS:

* Fire-resistant Gypsum Board - 1/2" "C" - 3/4 hr rating
                              5/8" "X" - 1 hr rating

** MR Board - Moisture-resistant for exterior use.

*** WR Board - Water-resistant for interior wet area use.

Standard sizes available as indicated.

Other sizes may be obtained upon special order.

FIGURE 10–3
Gypsum Wallboard Sizes and Types

A variety of specially shaped metal studs are also available for certain applications such as a larger (wider) channel-shaped stud, an "H" stud, or an "L"-shaped stud used as a combination sound barrier and drywall installation for elevator shafts, and so on. Metal soffit or suspended ceiling installations make use of an angle iron, often called "black metal" because of the black anodized finish applied to it, and galvanized channel steel, called "hat channel," for attachment.

Gypsum Wallboard

See figure 10–3. Gypsum wallboard (GWB), better known as drywall or Sheetrock (a trade name of United States Gypsum), is used for closing up the roughed-in walls. Sheetrock is available in lengths from 4 lf (1.22 m) to 8 lf (2.44 m) by 2 lf (0.61 m) wide. The board is perforated and used primarily as a lath (in lieu of wood or steel) for interior gypsum plastered walls.

The common gypsum board used today is the drywall system. The board is already finished to look like a smooth plastered wall and is applied directly to the rough framing. As figure 10–3 indicates, GWB is available in several sizes, thicknesses, and fire-rated categories. Some manufacturers make special sheets of drywall for specific purposes such as sound attenuation or radiation shielding. Also available are completely finished panels with integral wallcoverings and connection fittings, which are used for aesthetic reasons and/or sound attenuation.

Drywall Accessories. The accessories include a moist premixed all-purpose compound (called "mud"), dry mixed compound (called "spackle"), paper and self-adhering nylon mesh joint tapes, corner bead, "J" metal strips, and fasteners.

The moist premixed all-purpose compound is used for taping and texturing walls and for acoustical treatment for ceilings. The compound is available in pint, quart, and gallon or liter containers (up to 10 gallon or 4.5 liter), or in 25 lb (11.34 kg) and 50 lb (22.68 kg) cartons. The compound can be made into a wetter, thinner mix and placed in a small pump and sprayed on the walls for texturing.

Spackle (also called "plaster of Paris") is obtained in sacks or cartons from 1 lb (0.45 kg) to 25 lbs (11.34 kg) and is mixed as required with water to make a paste similar to the premixed compound.

Tape, made of paper or self-adhering nylon mesh, is used with the compound or spackle and seals the board joints and nails or screws, horizontally and vertically, to give the wall a smooth finished appearance. The tape is manufactured in 2" (5.08 cm) wide by 150 lf (45.72 m) long self-adhering rolls and 300 lf (91.44 m) paper rolls.

Other accessories used with drywall are the following:

1. Corner bead, a solid or perforated 3/4" (1.91 cm) wide angle, 26-gauge galvanized steel or aluminum
2. "J" metal, identical to the cement plaster type but in sizes to accommodate drywall
3. Fasteners such as 7/8" (2.22 cm) to 1 1/4" 6d (3.18 cm) nails or 7/8" (2.22 cm) to 1 1/2" (3.81 cm) #6 drywall screws

Exterior GWB Soffits and Ceilings. *Refer to figure 10–3.* Exterior grade, moisture-resistant drywall (MR board), with protective coatings such as epoxy and acrylic paint may be used in lieu of the cement plaster system on the suspended ceiling portion of the stoop. The installation and materials for the suspension system are identical to the cement plaster system.

Interior GWB Soffits and Ceilings. *See Plans, Sheet A–4, Reflected Ceiling Plan; Sheets A–7 and A–8, Door, Window, and Finish Schedules.* Suspended ceilings are common where there is some equipment placed in the structure above, where an air plenum for air-conditioning return air is desired, or when other materials such as additional plumbing or electrical are installed and need to be hidden from view. The ceilings may also be suspended for aesthetic appearance or for accommodation of cabinet heights. Interior GWB suspended systems, 1/2" (1.27 cm) or 5/8" (1.59 cm) thick board, are installed with the same suspension materials as the cement plaster ceiling.

Tile

Several kinds of tiles are commonly used as finishes.

Quarry tile, used primarily for floor covering, is a kiln-dried clay (terra cotta) material available in sizes from 8" (20.32 cm) to 12" (30.48 cm) square. The tiles may be installed in a bed of mortar, approximately 1/2" (1.27 cm) thick, applied to the substrate, with grout between the tiles to seal the joints, which are a maximum of 1" (2.54 cm) wide.

Glazed, vitreous tiles, better known as **ceramic tile,** may be used for either floor or wall tiles. The tiles may be clay- or cement-based and are available in a variety of colors and designs. The sizes range from 1″ (2.54 cm) squares, 1″ (2.54 cm) squares applied in 12″ (30.48 cm) square sheets, or larger tiles from 4″ (10.16 cm) to 12″ (30.48 cm) square. The same application procedures are used for ceramic tiles as for quarry tiles. They may be installed over a lath when applied on walls, where mortar and grout are required.

Terrazzo, often classed as a tile, is made from several natural materials such as rock, slate, shale, granite, and marble. These materials are crushed and mixed with crushed seashells, nut shells, and/or glass, and then mixed with concrete to produce special surfaces or to form aesthetic designs in concrete patios, plazas, sidewalks, and entries. Terrazzo may be precast or CIP (cast in place), installed on a sand cushion, or applied with an epoxy adhesive. In some areas, pavers, such as natural or cut pieces of slate, granite, or marble embedded in mortar and grouted between the joints, are also called terrazzo.

Acoustical Treatment

Materials used for acoustical treatment (referred to as **sound enhancement** or **attenuation**) vary from the self-adhering acoustical tiles to combinations of insulation and wallboard (such as drywall in combination with batt, or other types of insulation and/or fiberboard), or specially manufactured panels.

Sound enhancement treatment is the ability to *increase and clarify sound,* such as used for theaters, opera houses, lecture halls, and churches. Enhancement is accomplished by special wall and ceiling design and rigid or moveable paneling that allows the sound to reverberate, or echo, as desired.

Sound attenuation is the ability to *decrease unwanted sound.* This is accomplished by use of combinations mentioned above in walls placed between the areas. Attenuation is the desired acoustical treatment required for the Medical Clinic.

See figure 10–4. Both enhancement and attenuation are calculated in terms of the **sound transmission coefficient (STC).** The value given this coefficient is a decibel (dB). Continuing sound transmission rated at 85 dB or higher is unacceptable in most instances. In many workplaces where sound cannot be reduced, workers need to wear earmuffs or earplugs. Many blueprints include wall details that not only indicate the materials to be used on both sides but may also give an STC rating to the wall system. The wall in figure 10–4 has a rating of STC 30. This means that no more than 30 dB of sound may be heard on the side with the rating. If a noise level of 90 dB is applied to the opposite side of the wall, the transmission must be reduced by:

90 dB − 30 dB = 60 dB

A wall with the insulation in figure 10–4 is a combination sound and thermal barrier capable of maintaining temperature control and reducing the dB level as may be desired.

Specially manufactured acoustical wall panels, portable or fixed, using variations of the insulations mentioned above with cloth or finish wood veneer are common in large offices where "sound cubicles" are desired. These may be specified in this section but are more likely to be found in Division 10, Specialties, or Division 12, Furnishings.

Directly adhered acoustical treatment includes two systems: One is the same premixed, all-purpose compound used for drywall taping, and the

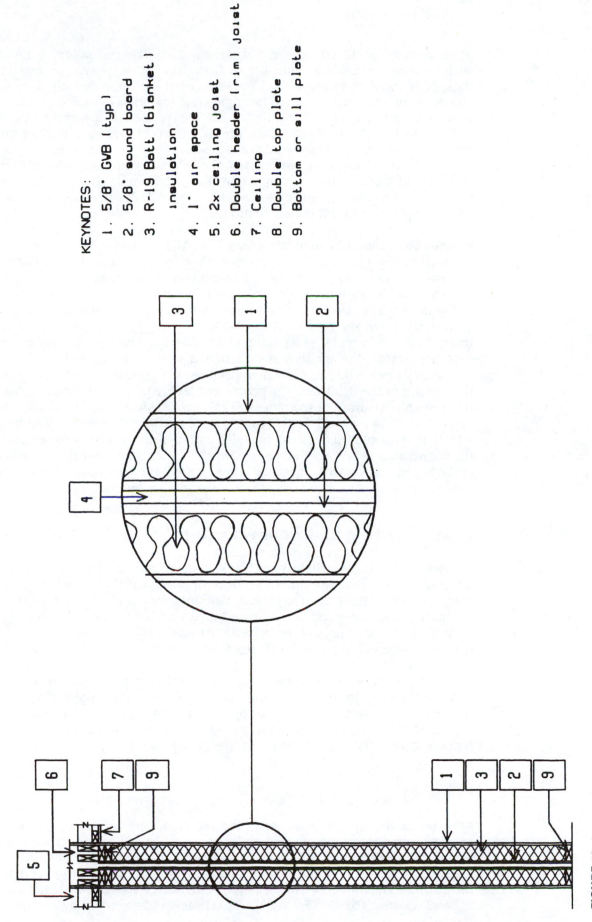

KEYNOTES:

1. 5/8" GWB (typ)
2. 5/8" sound board
3. R-19 Batt (blanket) insulation
4. 1" air space
5. 2x ceiling joist
6. Double header (rim) joist
7. Ceiling
8. Double top plate
9. Bottom or sill plate

FIGURE 10–4
Sound-Attenuation Wall Construction

other consists of directly adhered acoustical tiles. The compound is mixed with loose-grain perlite, vermiculite, or fiberglass and is sprayed on the ceilings. It is most commonly used for residential ceilings. Directly adhered acoustical tiles are manufactured from the same materials as used for composite board or fiberglass insulations but are compressed and formed into 8″ (20.32 cm) to 12″ (30.48 cm) squares from 1/8″ (0.32 cm) to 1/4″ (0.64 cm) thick. The tiles may require an adhesive base or may be self-adhering.

There are two types of **suspended acoustical** ceilings installed in commercial and institutional construction: (1) adjustable suspended paneling or ceiling for sound enhancement and attenuation and (2) suspended acoustical tile ceilings (ACT) for sound attenuation.

Interior Suspended Acoustical Ceiling Tile (ACT).   *Refer to Plans, Sheet A–4, Reflected Ceiling Plan; Sheets A–7 and A–8, Door, Window, and Finish Schedules.* Acoustical suspended (lay-in) tiles for sound attenuation vary in style ranging from a smooth finish texture to deep-fissured designs and are manufactured in a wide range of colors, sizes, and thicknesses. The normal tile sizes are 2′× 2′ (0.61 m × 0.61 m) and 2′× 4′ (0.61 m × 1.22 m) by 1/2″ (1.27 cm) to 1″ (2.54 cm) thick. Tiles that are 3/4″ (1.91 cm) and 1″ (2.54 cm) thick are manufactured with fire-retardant materials and are assigned a one-hour fire rating.

ACT suspended systems are manufactured with runners in a "T" shape for the placing of the field tiles. The perimeter tiles are placed into both the runner and an edge angle of the same size and gauge. Most runner and edge angles are 1″ (2.54 cm) to 1 1/2″ (3.81 cm) wide and are obtained in lengths of 10 lf (3.05 m) and 20 lf (6.10 m). Included with the runners and edge angle are the runner fastener clips. These are placed at the junction of the main and secondary (perpendicular) runners and at the runners and edge angles to hold the runners in place. Also necessary are #9 AWG wire and hooks.

Finish Flooring and Floor Coverings

Finish floor materials include wood plank, parquet, resilient sheet flooring and tile (VCT for *Vinyl Composition Tile*) flooring, and carpeting as well as special materials and coatings such as asphalt planking (similar to roof pads), plastic-laminated floor coverings, epoxy-based mixes such as crushed gravel, elastomeric liquid coatings, and resin-based materials. Many of the coatings and materials are especially popular for use as finish decking for exterior balconies and arcades.

Industrial floor applications for heavily trafficked areas in manufacturing and warehousing locations typically use combinations of epoxies, cementitious materials, steel-protective coatings, and coatings that are static resistant, slip resistant, abrasion resistant, fire resistant, and chemical resistant. The types of floor finishes are included in the specifications.

Painting

All exterior and interior coatings such as epoxies, acrylics, latexes, lacquers, varnishes, and stains not covered elsewhere in the specifications come under the heading of painting. The materials classified under this heading are primarily used for exterior and interior finishes other than floor protection and furnishings. The products may be sprayed on, rolled on, or brushed on. Caulking and sealants, Division 7, may also be estimated by the painting contractor.

Wallcovering

Any material applied to interior walls other than plaster or paint is considered a wallcovering. Wallcoverings may include wallpaper, cloth or other woven materials applied in the same way as wallpaper, "tambour" or other decorative wood wallcoverings, and paneling. Insulated sound-attenuation padding may also be considered as a wallcovering. Accessories that are a part of wallcoverings are sizing, paste, and exposed clear plastic protective corners similar to corner bead.

SCOPE OF WORK

The finishes required for the Medical Clinic are a part of the basic specifications with the exception of light-gauge metal framing, which is part of the Alternates/Alternatives, Division 1, Section 01030, the Project Manual, appendix IV. The base specifications are:

Division 9: Finishes

09000 Scope of Work

Division 1 and the General Conditions are to be considered a part of this division. Furnish all labor, materials and equipment necessary to complete all work under this division and as indicated on drawings.

09200 Lath and Plaster

All metal accessories are to be supplied by one manufacturer. Install accessories such as base screed and control joints; J-metal at all window and door jambs, heads and sills, and at all dissimilar materials abutting the plaster; corneraid and cornertite; and any other accessories as may be necessary for a complete job. Lath shall be 8'-0" × 36" (2.44 m × 0.91 m), 22 ga expanded metal sheets w/building paper backing.

   Apply 3/8" (0.95 cm) scratch coat over lath. Scratch coat shall be in accordance with manufacturer's recommendations and local codes and ordinances. Allow to cure for a minimum 3 days, wetting walls with fog spray daily. Apply 3/8" (0.95 cm) brown coat over freshly moistened scratch coat. Allow to cure for a minimum 7 days, wetting walls with fog spray daily. Wet walls just before application of finish coat. Finish coat is to be 1/8" (0.32 cm) thick, natural gray color, or, at the discretion of owner, with an integral color in lieu of painting.

   It is the responsibility of the plaster contractor to make certain that all exposed metal, glazing or other materials are protected and/or thoroughly clean, making sure that there is no damage to the other finished trades around the work. Clean up job site and remove debris upon completion.

09250 Gypsum Board

All GWB shall be 5/8" (1.59 cm) "X" (Firecode) by USG, or equal, as required by local codes and ordinances. Boards shall be laid horizontally with the long side perpendicular to the framing on both walls and ceilings. The sheets shall be placed so that all vertical joints on walls and the ends on the ceilings are staggered. Staggered joints shall be centered on the adjacent sheets.

GWB shall be fastened with minimum 11/8" (2.86 cm) drywall screws spaced at 6" O/C (15.24 cm) along the perimeter of each sheet and 9" O/C (22.86 cm) in the field. The screws shall be applied with sufficient force to slightly indent the GWB.

All joints on walls and ceilings shall be sealed with paper or self-adhering tape and multi-purpose compound. The first application shall be left to dry and is sanded smooth. A second application is applied to the taped joint, allowed to set, and sanded smooth to match the GWB for application of paint or wall-covering. All exposed screw heads shall also be embedded in multi-purpose compound, sanded and smoothed to match the GWB surface. See Finish Schedule for textures. All drywall ceilings are 9'-0" A.F.F. (2.74 m), UNO.

09300 Tile

See Finish Schedule for location and other information regarding ceramic wall tile to be installed. Tile shall be "Dal-Tile," or equal, 4×4 (10.16 cm × 10.16 cm), color to be selected by owner from standard ranges. Bullnose tile shall be applied at all exposed ends of tile.

Tile shall be applied using a thinset cement wall application and grouted with a color-matching grout between tiles as per manufacturer's recommendations.

09500 Acoustical Treatment

See Reflected Ceiling Plan for locations of ACT system. The ACT shall be Armstrong Acoustical Tile, 2'×4' (0.61 m × 1.22 m), 3/4" (1.91 cm) thick, treated wood fiber, fissured, fire retardant (1-hour rated). All ACT ceilings are to be 8'-0" (2.44 m) A.F.F. Install 1" (2.54 cm) wall angle along perimeter of all supporting walls. Install 1" (2.54 cm) main "T" runners spaced 2'-0" O/C (0.61 m) with secondary cross runners spaced at 4'-0" O/C (1.22 m). Center the main runners in each area for aesthetic appearance. In areas where the walls are 4'-0" (1.22 m) apart only the wall angle and main "T" runners shall be used. All joints shall be fastened with corner clips at the walls and at the cross joints.

The ceiling shall be suspended with 9 ga tie wire fastened to the wood joists by a screw eye and to the runners with a clip fastener at the corners of the mains and cross secondary members. Tie wires shall be installed so as to offer support every 9 square feet (0.83 m^2) of ceiling area or as necessary for proper support. Additional tie wire shall be added at each corner of the "T" bar ceiling structure where an electrical fluorescent fixture is to be installed. Add seismic support as may be required by local code and ordinance.

09650 Resilient Flooring

See Finish Schedule for location of resilient flooring. Resilient flooring may be either sheet vinyl flooring or 12"×12" (30.48 cm × 30.48 cm) vinyl tiles. Where sheet flooring is applied, an under-layment of 7 1/2 lb (3.40 kg) felt is adhered to the subfloor as a cushion for the sheet vinyl. The felt is smoothed and left to set. The sheet vinyl is applied over the felt, smoothed and allowed to set for twenty-four (24) hours.

Vinyl composition tile (VCT) flooring shall be installed with an adhesive directly to the subfloor. Tile shall be placed so that it is properly centered on the floor in each area where it is used.

The sheet and tile flooring shall have a 4" (10.16 cm) base coving, color selected by owner to match flooring, and is applied along the perimeter of all resilient floors. An alternate coving may be applied along the perimeter of the floor. The alternate coving is backed by a 1 1/2" (3.81 cm) concave quarter-round wood member.

The contractor shall allow for leftover material, sufficient for repairs, to remain on the project.

09680 Carpet

See Finish Schedule for location of carpet installation. Carpeting shall be DuPont, commercial grade, heavy traffic, with a rubber pad. Installation shall be by a reputable carpet contractor. Seams shall be kept to a minimum. Seams shall be installed so that the webbing or joint does not show after installation. A guarantee shall be supplied to the contractor and owner by manufacturer as to workmanship and material. A copy of the manufacturer's accreditation shall be in the hands of the owner prior to final payment and retention.

09900 Painting

See Finish Schedule for location of all interior painting. Colors to be selected by owner from standard color ranges.

Acceptable paint manufacturers for standard paints are:

Sinclair Paints   Sherwin—Williams Paints

Decatrend   Frazee Paints

Acceptable manufacturer for exterior wood paints shall be by Olympic Stain, or equal.

The painting shall be applied as follows:

Exterior Walls and Trim:

> Exterior Plaster
>> 1 coat of primer
>> 2 coats latex paint
>> Sprayed, rolled or brushed
>> Standard colors selected by owner
>
> Exterior Wood Trim
>> Oil based stain
>> Standard colors selected by owner
>
> Underside of Overhang
>> 1 coat primer
>> 2 coats latex paint
>> Match cement plaster color

Interior Walls:
> 1 coat sealer
> 1 coat primer
> 1 coat semi-gloss epoxy

09950 Wallcovering

Additional wallcoverings shall be selected by owner and shall be
directed by change order after contract is signed.

End of Division

THE ESTIMATE

The specifications and finish schedule for the Medical Clinic furnish all the information necessary for floor coverings, wall base attachments, wallcoverings, and ceiling types.

Spreadsheet

See Plans, Sheet A–8, Door, Window, and Finish Schedules; see also figure 10–5.   A 13-column sheet, part of which is shown in figure 10–5, is a good type of spreadsheet to use. With the variety of materials to be estimated, it is recommended that a separate backup sheet be used for each phase of the estimate; that is, one for plaster, one for drywall, one for floor coverings, and so on.

Cement Plaster Materials

Lath and Cement Plaster (Stucco).   *See Plans, Sheets A–2 and A–3, Exterior Elevations; Sheet A–4, Reflected Ceiling Plan. Also see chart 10–1.*   A three-coat, 7/8″ (2.22 cm), system is specified for the exterior walls of the Medical Clinic. The materials necessary for cement plaster include cement, lime, and sand in addition to the lath and accessories.

The stucco may be estimated in several different ways: by the square foot, by the square yard, or by a breakdown of materials. The breakdown for the stucco is in 500 sq ft (46.45 m²) increments. The materials necessary include the following: Expanded metal lath, made from 22-gauge or 26-gauge cold-rolled galvanized steel or aluminum sheets perforated throughout, may be installed with or without a building paper affixed to the metal and is used for exterior wall and ceiling construction. The building paper may be kraft paper, asphalt felt, or plastic moisture resistant sheet material. The lath is available in fixed 8 lf × 36″ (2.44 m × 0.91 m) sheets or in rolls up to 36 lf × 36″ (10.97 m × 0.91 m).

Accessories.   *See chart 10–1.*   The accessories required for a complete installation of the stucco include the base screed, "Milcor," corner bead, control joints, and fasteners.

Labor for Cement Plastering

See figure 10–6a and figure 10–6b.   One stucco crew can complete 90 sq yds per coat a day. Using the figures in chart 10–1, there are 92 sq yds per coat estimated

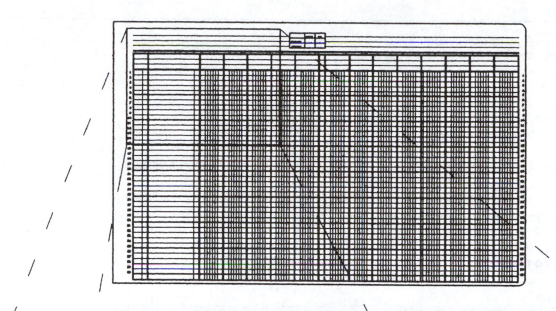

Medical Clinic – Caliente, NV   Date: 6/1/92
General Contractor – Janus Corp. (333)555-1111
Architect – Christle & Assoc. (333)555-2222
Bid Date:7/8/92 Set Date: 10/5/91 Job #92-12

	Acct#	Room	L x W x H	Area Walls	Area Ceiling	4x10 sheets 5/8" "X" CWB Walls	
1		Play Rm	10² x 10² x 9	369.0	105.0	10	pc
2		Waiting Rm	29 x 10² x 9	706.5	297.25	18	pc
3		Exam Rms (3)	10 x 10² x 9	1093.5	307.5	28	pc
4		Reception Rm	16⁴ x 10 x 9	474.0	163.3	12	pc
5		Accounting	10 x 10 x 9	360.0	100.0	9	pc
6		Doctor Office	10 x 10 x 9	360.0	100.0	9	pc
7		Nurse Office	8¹ x 10 x 9	325.5	81.7	8	pc
8		Breakroom	9² x 10 x 9	354.0	96.7	9	pc
9		Restroom	9² x 10 x 9	364.0	96.7	9	pc
10		Records	13 x 10² x 9	418.5	136.5	11	pc
11		X-ray Lab	13² x 10² x 9	427.5	139.13		
12		Oper Room	13¹ x 10² x 9	424.5	137.34	11	pc
13		Hall #1	40 x 4 x 9	432.0	160.0	11	pc
14		Hall #2	31 x 4 x 9	594.0	124.0	15	pc
15		Hall #3	20² x 4 x 9	408.0	82.68	10	pc

FIGURE 10–5
Columnar Estimate Sheet

Breakdown method—3-coat system:
500 sq ft (46.45 m²) of material basis per coat:
    1 sack hydrated lime = 85 lb or 38.56 kg
    1 sack cement   = 95 lb or 43.09 kg
    Sand   = 405 lb or 183.70 kg

Hydrated lime:
    500 sq ft ÷ 85 lb = **5.88 lb/sq ft**   46.45 m² ÷ 38.56 kg = **1.20 kg/m²**

Cement:
    500 sq ft ÷ 95 lb = **5.26 lb/sq ft**   46.45 m² ÷ 43.09 kg = **1.08 kg/m²**

Sand:
    500 sq ft ÷ 405 lb = **1.23 lb/sq ft**   46.45 m² ÷ 183.70 kg = **0.25 kg/m²**

Wall areas - 41'-0" × 10'-0" (12.50 m × 3.05 m):
    A = (41 lf × 10 lf) × 2   A = (12.50 m × 3.05 m) × 2
    A = 410 sq ft × 2   A = 38.13 m² × 2
    A = **820 sq ft**   A = **76.26 m²**

Quantities:
Hydrated lime:
    820 sq ft ÷ 5.88 lb/sq ft = 139.46 lb   76.26 m² ÷ 1.20 kg/m² = 63.55 kg
    139.46 lb ÷ 85 lb = **1.64 or 2 bags**   63.55 kg ÷ 38.63 kg = **1.64 or 2 bags**
Total lime:
                        2 bags × 3 coats = **6 bags**

Cement:
    820 sq ft ÷ 5.26 lb/sq ft = 155.89 lb   76.26 m² ÷ 1.08 kg/m² = 70.61 kg
    155.89 lb ÷ 95 lb = **1.64 or 2 bags**   70.61 kg ÷ 42.18 kg = **1.67 or 2 bags**
Total cement:
                        2 bags × 3 coats = **6 bags**

Sand:
    820 sq ft ÷ 1.23 lb/sq ft = 666.67 lb   76.26 m² ÷ 0.25 kg/m² = 305.04 kg
    666.67 lb ÷ 2,000 lb = **0.33 T**   305.04 kg ÷ 907.18 kg = **0.34 T**
Total sand:
                        0.33 T × 3 = **1 T**

Cement plaster accessories - 3-coat system:
Building paper-backed expanded metal lath - 8 lf × 3 lf (2.44 m × 0.91 m):
    (820 sq ft ÷ 24 sq ft) × 1.05 =   (76.18 m² ÷ 2.23 m²) × 1.05 =
    34.17 sheets × 1.05 = **35.87 or 36 sheets**   34.16 sheets × 1.05 = **35.87 or 36 sheets**

Pigment (integral color) - 1 lb (2.2 kg) per 10 bags cement:
                2 bags ÷ 10 bags = **0.2 lb or 0.09 kg**

Screed (base metal) - 10 lf (3.05 m) lengths:
    (41 lf × 2) × 1.05 =   (12.50 m × 2) × 1.05 =
    82 lf × 1.05 = **86.1 or 90 lf**   25.0 m × 1.05 = **26.25 m**

Corner bead (corneraid) - 10 lf (3.05 m) lengths:
    ([10 lf × 4] + [16 lf × 4] + 18.67 lf) × 1.05 =   ([3.05 m × 4] + [4.88 m × 4] + 5.69 m) × 1.05 =
    (40 lf + 64 lf + 18.67 lf) × 1.05 =   (12.2 m + 19.52 m + 5.69 m) × 1.05 =
    122.67 lf × 1.05 = **128.8 or 130 lf**   37.41 m × 1.05 = **39.28 or 39.5 m**

"J" Metal - 10 lf (3.05 m) lengths:
    (82 lf + 122.67 lf) × 1.05 =   (24.99 m + 37.39 m) × 1.05 =
    204.67 lf × 1.05 = **214.9 or 220 lf**   62.38 m × 1.05 = **65.50 m**

Staples:
    820 sq ft ÷ 225 sq ft = **3.64 or 4 cartons**   76.18 m² ÷ 20.90 m² = **3.64 or 4 cartons**

CHART 10—1
Cement Plaster Estimate: East and West Exterior Walls

CREW	HOURLY + BURDEN WAGE	% TIME ON JOB/HR	HOURLY RATE
Foreman	$15.53 + $ 2.92	24%	= $ 4.43
Plasterer	$15.03 + $ 2.92	38%	= $ 6.82
Laborer (2)	$11.75 + $ 3.74 × 2	38%	= $11.77
Composite Crew Rate:		100%	$23.02/MH

FIGURE 10–6a
Composite Crew Schedule

CREW	HOURLY WAGE + BURDEN
Foreman	$15.53 + $ 2.92
Plasterer	$15.03 + $ 2.92
Laborer (2)	$11.75 + $ 3.74 × 2
	$54.06 + $13.32 = $67.38
Composite Crew Rate:	$67.38/3 = $22.46

FIGURE 10–6b
Composite Crew Schedule

for the east and west exterior walls of the Medical Clinic (that is, 820 sq ft). The time required for the three coats specified for the job is calculated as follows:

(92 sq yd × 3) ÷ 90 sq yd = 3.06 or 3 days

([76.92 m² × 3] ÷ 75.25 m² = 3.07 or 3 days)

The 4-person plaster crew can install the exterior cement plaster to the west wall in 3 days (1 day per coat). The crew stays on the same project; therefore, the labor is calculated by the crew hour. The productivity factor is 0.89. The labor cost is:

Method 10–6a:

$23.02/MH × 0.89 = $20.49/MH

$20.49/MH × 4 workers × 8 hr = $655.68/CD

$655.68/CD × 3 days = $1,967.04 or $1,967.00

Method 10–6b:

$22.46/MH × 0.89 = $19.99/MH

$19.99/MH × 4 workers × 8 hr = $639.68/CD

$639.68/CD × 3 days = $1,919.04 or $1,919.00

Equipment for Cement Plastering

See figure 10–7. The equipment necessary to complete the exterior plaster work includes a mixer, pump, hoses, and trowels. Some of the equipment is

FIGURE 10–7
Equipment Schedule

EQUIPMENT	USE TIME	UNIT COST	TOTAL
Mixer/Pump	3 days	@ $175/day	= $525.00
Forklift	3 days	@ $ 90/day	= $270.00
Truck	3 days	@ $ 10/day	= $ 30.00
Accessories:			
Hose (5 sections)		@ $ 15/section	= $ 75.00
Nozzle (1 ea)		@ $ 50	= $ 50.00
Shovel (2 ea)		@ $ 7.50 ea	= $ 15.00
Trowel (2 ea)		@ $ 1.95 ea	= $ 3.90
Equipment Total:			$968.90

miscellaneous one-time use materials. There are depreciated costs for equipment owned by the company, which include the pump, mixer, hoses, and nozzles.

Drywall (GWB) Materials

See Plans, Sheet A–1, Architectural Floor Plan; Sheet A–4, Reflected Ceiling Plan; Sheet A–7, Door, Window, and Finish Schedules. See also figure 10–3, Gypsum Wallboard Sizes and Types. Also see chart 10–2. The finish schedule shows that all interior walls and ceilings are 9'-0" (2.74 m) A.F.F., except the restroom and break room, with 5/8" (1.59 cm) "X" GWB applied. The restroom and break room ceilings have suspended 5/8" (1.59 cm) "X" GWB at 7'-0" (2.13 m) A.F.F. The walls are drywalled to the 9'-0" (2.74 m) height. The unexposed 2'-0" are fire-taped only.

The east and west fire wall construction over the bearing walls each have a layer of GWB installed on one side extending to the underside of the roof structure. This area is also fire-taped. Fire-taping is the application of tape and mud at the board joints without sanding or finishing. The tape is applied with one coat of mud sufficient to seal the joints.

There is one special gypsum wallboard required for the Medical Clinic. The X-ray laboratory requires shielding to prevent exposure to radiation. The GWB is made with a leaded shield adhered to one side for this protection.

The estimator should *not* delete for openings under 100 sq ft (9.29 m²). This allows for waste and for additional material to be saved for the returns at the openings.

Estimating Examination Room #1.   Examination room #1 measures 10.5' × 10'-0" × 9'-0" (3.20 m × 3.05 m × 2.74 m). All walls and ceiling are covered with 5/8" (1.59 cm) "X" GWB. The exterior bearing wall and the two interior bearing walls have studs spaced at 16" O/C (40.64 cm). The partition wall between Examination Rooms #1 and #2 has studs spaced at 24" O/C (0.61 m).

The choice of sheet sizes is determined by the labor for cutting and fitting. In other words, which is the most cost effective?

A 4'×12' (1.22 m × 3.66 m) sheet is more difficult to maneuver because it is oversize: The room is only 10'-6" (3.20 m) long. With oversize sheets, the la-

Areas - 10 lf × 10.5 lf × 9 lf (3.05 m × 3.20 m × 2.74 m):
Walls:

([10 lf + 10.5 lf] × 2) × 9 lf =   ([3.05 m + 3.20 m] × 2) × 2.74 m =
(20.5 lf × 2) × 9 lf =   (6.25 m × 2) × 2.74 m =
41 lf × 9 lf = **369 sq ft**   12.50 m × 2.74 m = **34.25 m²**

Ceiling:

10 lf × 10.5 lf = **105 sq ft**   3.05 m × 3.20 m = **9.76 m²**

Walls - 4' × 8' × ⁵/₈" (10.16 cm × 20.32 cm × 1.59 cm) "X" GWB w/waste added - 5%:

(369 sq ft ÷ 32 sq ft) × 1.05 = **12.11 or 12 sheets**   (34.25 m² ÷ 2.98 m²) × 1.05 = **12.07 or 12 sheets**

Ceilings - 4' × 10' × ⁵/₈" (10.16 cm × 20.32 cm × 1.59 cm) "X" GWB w/waste added - 5%:

(105 sq ft ÷ 40 sq ft) × 1.05 = **2.75 or 3 sheets**   (9.76 m² ÷ 3.72 m²) × 1.05 = **2.75 or 3 sheets**

Total drywall:

12 sheets 4' × 8' × ⁵/₈" + 4 sheets 4' × 10' × ⁵/₈" "X"

Drywall accessories:
Joint tape - 300 lf/roll:
Walls (6 vertical and 2 horizontal joints):

(6 × 9 lf) + (2 × 41 lf) =   (6 × 2.74 m) + (2 × 12.50 m) =
54 lf + 82 lf = **136 lf**   16.44 m + 25.00 m = **41.44 m**

Ceilings (3 tape joints and perimeter joint):

(3 × 10 lf) + 41 lf = **71 lf**   (3 × 3.05 m) + 12.50 m = **21.65 m**

Total taping:

136 lf + 71 lf = **207 lf or 1 roll**   41.45 m + 21.64 m = **63.09 m or 1 roll**

All purpose compound for taping:

1 50-lb carton

Screws or nails - 30/sheet:

16 sheets × 30 nails = **480**

CHART 10–2
Drywall Estimate: Examination Room #1

bor is more time-consuming since workers need to move the material about and cut it. Therefore, it is less cost effective.

A 4'×8' (1.22 m × 2.44 m) sheet is easier for workers to handle, but there is more waste. However, the labor may be more cost effective because of ease of handling, which may outweigh the waste factor.

A 4'×10' (1.22 m × 3.05 m) sheet produces less waste than the 4'×8' (1.22 m × 2.44 m) board, is more maneuverable than the 4'×12' (1.22 m × 3.20 m) board, and, therefore, is the most cost effective.

The stud spacing may also dictate the size of the material. A 4'×8' (1.22 m × 2.44 m) or 4'×12' (1.22 m × 3.66 m) sheet can be used where there are 16" (40.64 cm) centers. All sizes can be used where the studs are 24" O/C (0.61 m).

Labor for Drywall Installation

See figures 10–8a and 10–8b, Composite Crew Schedule: Drywall. One carpenter can install 10 sheets of 4'×8' (1.22 m × 2.44 m) or 4'×10' (1.22 m × 3.05 m) per day. The taper requires 1 1/2 days to complete the taping. The crew productivity rate is 72%. The productivity factor is 0.97.

CREW	HOURLY + BURDEN WAGE	% TIME ON JOB/HR	HOURLY RATE
Foreman	$16.90 + $3.32	6%	= $ 1.21
Carpenter	$16.40 + $3.32	41%	= $ 8.09
Taper	$16.40 + $3.32	12%	= $ 2.37
Laborer	$11.75 + $3.74	41%	= $ 6.35
Composite Crew Rate:		100%	$18.02/MH

FIGURE 10–8a
Composite Crew Schedule

CREW	HOURLY WAGE + BURDEN
Foreman	$16.90 + $ 3.32
Carpenter	$16.40 + $ 3.32
Taper	$16.40 + $ 3.32
Laborer	$11.75 + $ 3.74
	$61.45 + $13.70 = $75.15
Composite Crew Rate:	$75.15/4 = $18.79

FIGURE 10–8b
Composite Crew Schedule

The labor cost for the drywall crew is calculated as follows:

Method 10–8a:

$18.02/MH × 0.97 = $17.48/MH

$17.48/MH × 8 hr = $139.84/MD

$139.84/MD × 4 workers = $559.36/CD

Method 10–8b:

$18.79/MH × 0.97 = $18.23/MH

$18.23/MH × 8 hr = $145.84/MD

$145.84/MD × 4 workers = $583.36/CD

Time consumed for completion of the drywall installation for examination room #1 is calculated as follows:

16 sheets ÷ 10 sheets = 1.6 day (drywall installation)

1.5 day (taping)

3.1 or 3 days

The labor cost for the installation of drywall is calculated as follows:

Method 10–8a:

$559.36/CD × 3 days = $1,678.08 or $1,678.00

FIGURE 10–9
Equipment Schedule

EQUIPMENT	USE TIME	UNIT COST	TOTAL
Pump	1 day	@ $25.00/day	= $25.00
Truck	3 days	@ $10.00/day	= $30.00
Equipment Total:			$55.00

Method 10–8b:

$583.36/CD $\times$ 3 days = $1,750.08 or $1,750.00

Equipment for Drywall Installation

See figure 10–9. The contractor may supply the spray pump for texturing of the drywall and personnel transportation. The supplier usually tries to stack the sheets in convenient areas; therefore, a forklift is not necessary. Most all other tools used by the drywall installer are the property of that individual.

Ceramic Tile Materials

See Plans, Sheet A–1, Architectural Floor Plan; Sheet A–8, Interior Elevations and Finish Schedule. See also chart 10–3. Ceramic tile is indicated for the walls of the break room, restroom, X-ray laboratory, and operating room in the Medical Clinic. The tiles are estimated in the same way as masonry (see the discussion of the piece count-up method in chapter 6) because of the various shapes used for specific purposes; for example, bullnose (one side -1/s; two sides -2/s; or one side, one end -1/s, 1/e) along with the standard tile. The tile specified is a 4″ square (25.81 cm^2) unit. There is no lath; therefore, the tiles are directly adhered using an adhesive base.

The Restroom Estimate.   The tile for the restroom of the Medical Clinic is installed to a height of 6′-0″ (1.83 m) A.F.F. The restroom is 10′-0″ × 6′-8″ (3.05 m × 2.03 m). There are two doors opening into the room. Each is 3′-0″ (0.91 m) wide. Some contractors tender bids on a square-foot basis. Using the square feet calculated in chart 10–3, the contractor could readily tender such a bid. A waste factor may or may not be used. In this case, a 5% waste factor is used. First, the area of a tile is calculated as follows:

4″ × 4″ = 16 sq in

(10.16 cm × 10.16 cm = 103.23 cm^2)

16 sq in ÷ 144 sq in = 0.1111

(103.23^2 cm^2 ÷ 929 cm^2 = 0.1111)

The quantity of tile needed is calculated as follows (143.28 sq ft is the net area for tile installation; see chart 10–3):

143.28 sq ft ÷ 0.1111 × 1.05 = 1,354.1 or 1,355 pc

([13.33 m^2 × 10.76] ÷ 0.1111 × 1.05 = 1,355.5 or 1,356 pc)

(Note: In the calculation above, 10.76 = 10.76 sq ft = 1 m^2)

(Restroom walls are to be 6'-0" (1.83 m) A.F.F.)

Gross area:

([{7.33 lf × 2} + {10 lf × 2}] × 6 lf) −
  (3 lf × 6 lf × 2) =
([14.66 lf + 20 lf] × 6 lf) − 36 sq ft =
207.96 sq ft − 36 sq ft = **171.96 sq ft**

([{2.23 m × 2} + {3.05 m × 2}] × 1.83 m) −
  (0.91 m × 1.83 m × 2) =
([4.46 + 6.10] × 1.83 m) − 3.33 m^2 =
19.32 m^2 − 3.33 m^2 = **15.99 m^2**

Net area:

171.96 sq ft − ([6 lf × 3 lf] + [4 lf × 2.67 lf]) =
171.96 sq ft − (18 sq ft + 10.68 sq ft) =
171.96 sq ft − 28.68 sq ft = **143.28 sq ft**

15.99 m^2 − ([1.83 m × 0.91 m] + [1.22 m × 0.81 m]) =
15.99 m^2 − (1.67 m^2 + 0.99 m^2) =
15.99 m^2 − 2.66 m^2 = **13.33 m^2**

Tiles: (tile factor for 4"x4" (10.16 cm × 10.16 cm) tile = 0.1111)

143.28 sq ft ÷ 0.1111 = **1,290 tiles**

(13.33 m^2 ÷ 0.093 m^2) ÷ 0.1111 = **1,290.12 or 1,290 tiles**

Bullnose tiles:

([7.33 lf + 10 lf] × 2) − (4 lf + [3 lf × 2]) =
(17.33 lf × 2) − 10 lf =
34.66 lf − 10 lf = 24.66 lf
(24.66 lf ÷ 0.33 lf) × 1.05 = **78.46 or 79 pc**

([2.23 m + 3.05 m] × 2) − (1.22 m + [0.91 m × 2]) =
(5.28 m × 2) − 3.04 m =
10.56 m − 3.04 m = 7.52 m
(7.52 m ÷ 0.10) × 1.05 = **78.96 or 79 pc**

Field tiles:

1,290 pc − 79 pc = **1,211 pc**

Grout - 1 lb/300 sq ft (0.45 kg/32.29 m^2):

143.28 sq ft ÷ 300 sq ft = **0.48 or 0.5 lb**

(13.33 m^2 ÷ 32.29 m^2) × 0.45 kg = **0.19 or 0.2 kg**

Mortar - 1lb/25 sq ft (0.45 kg/2.69 m^2):

143.28 sq ft ÷ 25 sq ft = **5.73 or 6 lb**

(13.33 m^2 ÷ 2.69 m^2) × 0.45 kg = **2.23 kg**

CHART 10–3
Ceramic Tile Estimate: Restroom

The estimate could stop at this point, but the actual types of tiles being used are not taken into account. For this reason, it is always best to do the piece count. The piece method is the same as that applied to the masonry estimate. The bullnose, one side (1/s), is needed for the top course. Chart 10–3 gives an example of a piece count estimate, with the number of bullnose tiles included in the estimate.

The owner may use a cove-base tile in lieu of the vinyl base specified. The cove-base tile is estimated by the piece method as was the bullnose.

Labor for Ceramic Tile Installation

See figure 10–10a and 10–10b, Composite Crew Schedule: Ceramic Tile. A 3-person crew can install the tile in the restroom in 2 days. The productivity factor is 0.97. The labor cost based on the crew hour is calculated as follows:

Method 10–10a:

$17.74/MH × 0.97 = $17.21/MH

$17.21/MH × 8 hr = $137.68/MD

$137.68/MD × 3 workers = $413.04/CD

$413.04/CD × 2 days = $826.08 or $826.00

CREW	HOURLY + BURDEN WAGE	% TIME ON JOB/HR	HOURLY RATE
Foreman	$16.90 + $3.32	10%	= $ 2.02
Carpenter	$16.40 + $3.32	42%	= $ 8.28
Laborer	$11.75 + $3.74	48%	= $ 7.44
Composite Crew Rate:		100%	$17.74/MH

FIGURE 10–10a
Composite Crew Schedule

CREW	HOURLY WAGE + BURDEN
Foreman	$16.90 + $ 3.32
Carpenter	$16.40 + $ 3.32
Laborer	$11.75 + $ 3.74
	$45.05 + $10.38 = $55.43
Composite Crew Rate:	$55.43/3 = $18.48

FIGURE 10–10b
Composite Crew Schedule

Method 10–10b:

$18.48/MH $\times$ 0.97 = $17.93/MH

$17.93/MH $\times$ 8 hr = $143.33/MD

$143.33/MD $\times$ 3 workers = $430.32/CD

$430.32/CD $\times$ 2 days = $860.64 or $861.00

Equipment for Ceramic Tile Installation

See figure 10–11. The only company-supplied equipment for ceramic tile installation is either a tile saw or tile cutter and personnel transportation. The remainder of the tools are personally owned by workers.

Flooring Materials

Refer to Plans, Sheet A–1, Architectural Floor Plan; Sheet A–8 Door, Window, and Finish Schedule. See also chart 10–4. The flooring indicated for the Medical Clinic is either vinyl sheet flooring (linoleum), as specified for the examination rooms, or tiles (VCT), as specified for all of the other areas requiring resilient flooring. The adhesive required for installing the tiles and the base coving is included with the floor covering estimate.

Sheet vinyl flooring is approximately 3/32″ (0.24 cm) thick, 12 lf (3.66 m) wide and may be obtained in rolls up to 30 lf (9.14 m). The material is applied with an adhesive. The sheet is then pressed by hand or roller until it is flat and smooth. Building paper underlayment may be installed as a cushion prior to

FIGURE 10–11
Equipment Schedule

EQUIPMENT	USE TIME	UNIT COST	TOTAL
Truck	1 day	@ $10.00/day	= $10.00
Cutter	1 day	@ $ 2.50/day	= $ 2.50
Equipment Total:			$12.50

(Examination Room #1 is 10 lf × 10.5 lf [3.05 m × 3.20 m]):

Area:

([10 lf × 10.5 lf] ÷ 9 sq ft) × 1.05 =   (3.05 m × 3.20 m) × 1.05 =
(105 sq ft ÷ 9 sq ft) × 1.05 = **12.25 sq yd**   9.76 m² × 1.05 = **10.25 m²**

Standard 4" (10.16 cm) base (4 lf [1.22 m] strips):

(10.5 lf × 2) + (10 lf × 2) =   (3.20 m × 2) + (3.05 m × 2) =
41 lf ÷ 4 lf = **10.25 or 11 strips**   12.50 ÷ 1.22 m = **10.25 or 11 strips**

Adhesive (300 sq ft/gal or 32.29 m²/3.79 L):

110.25 sq ft ÷ 300 sq ft = **0.37 gal or 1 gal**   (10.25 m² ÷ 32.29 m²) × 3.79 L = **1.20 liter**

Underlayment (felt):

110.25 sq ft ÷ 100 sq ft = **1.1 sq or 1 sq**   10.25 m² ÷ 10.76 m² = **0.95 sq or 1 sq**

Alternate vinyl sheet flooring - monolithic (including 4" (10.16 cm) coving):

([10.5 lf + {0.33 lf × 2}] × [10 lf +   ([3.20 m + {0.10 m × 2}] × [3.05 m +
  {0.33 lf × 2}]) × 1.05 =   {0.10 m × 2}]) × 1.05 =
([10.5 lf + 0.66 lf] × [10 lf + 0.66 lf]) × 1.05 =   ([3.20 m + 0.20 m] × [3.05 m + 0.20 m]) × 1.05 =
(11.16 lf × 10.66 lf) × 1.05 =   (3.40 m × 3.25 m) × 1.05 =
118.97 sq ft × 1.05 = **124.92 sq ft**   11.05 m² × 1.05 = **11.60 m²**

Base coving w/reverse ¼-round:

([10.5 lf × 2] + [10 lf × 2]) × 1.05 =   ([3.20 m × 2] + [3.05 m × 2]) × 1.05 =
(21 lf + 20 lf) × 1.05 =   (6.40 m + 6.10 m) × 1.05 =
41 lf × 1.05 = 43.05 lf   12.50 m × 1.05 = 13.13 m
43.05 lf ÷ 10 lf = **4.31 or 5 10-lf pc**   13.13 m ÷ 3.05 m = **4.30 or 5 3.05-m pc**

CHART 10–4
Vinyl Sheet Flooring Estimate: Examination Room #1

the application of the sheet vinyl. Adhesive must be used for both layers for a smooth finish.

VCT flooring is estimated in the same way as the quarry or ceramic tiles. The tiles for the Medical Clinic are 12"×12" (30.48 cm × 30.48 cm). The style and colors are not known. These are to be selected by the owner from standard colors and sizes.

An alternate estimate is also explained on the chart for a monolithic resilient sheet floor covering that includes the coving; this may be installed in lieu of the standard resilient sheet flooring and separate base cove.

Playroom Estimate. *See chart 10–5.* The following estimates are calculated for the playroom. The room size is 10.5 lf × 10.5 lf (3.20 m × 3.20 m). The floor estimate is for vinyl composition tile. The accessories necessary include adhesive and underlayment.

Area and tiles - 12" × 12" (30.48 cm × 30.48 cm):

10.5 lf × 10.5 lf = 110.25 sq ft   3.20 m × 3.20 m = 10.24 m²

110.25 sq ft × 1.05 = **115.76 sq ft**   10.24 m² × 1.05 = **10.75 m²**

115.76 sq ft = **115.76 or 116 tiles**   10.75 m² ÷ 0.09 m² = **119.44 or 120 tiles**

Adhesive (300 sq ft/gal or 32.29 m²/3.79 L):

115.76 sq ft ÷ 300 sq ft = **0.39 or 1 gal**   (10.75 m² ÷ 32.29 m²) × 3.79 L = **1.26 liter**

Underlayment (felt):

115.76 sq ft ÷ 100 sq ft = **1.16 sq or 1 sq**   10.75 m² ÷ 10.76 m² = **1 sq**

CHART 10—5
Vinyl Composition Tile: Playroom

CREW	HOURLY + BURDEN WAGE	% TIME ON JOB/HR	HOURLY RATE
Carpenter	$16.40 + $3.32	55%	= $10.85
Laborer	$11.75 + $3.74	45%	= $ 6.97
Composite Crew Rate:		100%	$17.82/MH

FIGURE 10–12a
Composite Crew Schedule

Base.   A 4 lf × 4" (1.22 m × 5.08 cm) rubber/plastic strip is installed for the base. The strip is available in cartons of 24 pieces/carton. The material can be estimated exactly as the baseboard for the wood trim. Openings may be "nonexistent" or may be deducted in the same manner as shown in chart 8–13. The quantity difference is minimal because the purchase is made by the carton.

Alternate Base Coving.   Coving is a curved turnup at the floor and is similar to the base calculated above. The curve is made using reverse 1/4-round wood or metal. The coving is measured in lineal feet and may be self-adhering or may use the same adhesive as the flooring. Both base and base coving are provided in cartons of 20 4'-0" (1.22 m) strips. Less than one carton is necessary for the playroom. Small quantities of coving may be purchased in 10 lf (3.05 m) to 24 lf (7.32 m) rolls.

Labor for Floor Covering

See figures 10–12a and 10–12b, Composite Crew Schedules: Vinyl Sheet Flooring. There are 2 workers capable of applying both the sheet vinyl and the VCT each in 1 day. The labor rate is the same as the tile installer rate. The productivity factor is 0.91. The cost for the labor for the sheet vinyl floor covering is calculated as follows:

Method 10–12a:

$17.82/MH × 0.91 = $16.22/MH

$16.22/MH × 2 workers × 8 hr = $258.24 or $258.00/CD

CREW	HOURLY WAGE + BURDEN
Carpenter	$16.40 + $3.32
Laborer	$11.75 + $3.74
	$28.15 + $7.06 = $35.21
Composite Crew Rate:	$35.21/2 = $17.61

FIGURE 10–12b
Composite Crew Schedule

CREW	HOURLY + BURDEN WAGE	% TIME ON JOB/HR	HOURLY RATE
Carpenter	$16.40 + $3.32	45%	= $ 8.87
Laborer	$11.75 + $3.74	55%	= $ 8.52
Composite Crew Rate:		100%	$17.39/MH

FIGURE 10–13a
Composite Crew Schedule

CREW	HOURLY WAGE + BURDEN
Carpenter	$16.40 + $3.32
Laborer	$11.75 + $3.74
	$28.15 + $7.06 = $35.21
Composite Crew Rate:	$35.21/2 = $17.61

FIGURE 10–13b
Composite Crew Schedule

Method 10–12b:

$17.61/MH × 0.91 = $16.03/MH

$16.03/MH × 2 workers × 8 hr = $256.48 or $256.00/CD

See figures 10–13a and 10–13b, Composite Crew Schedules: Vinyl Sheet Flooring. There are 2 workers capable of applying both the sheet vinyl and the VCT each in 1 day. The labor rate is the same as the tile installer rate. The productivity factor is 0.91. The cost for the labor for the sheet vinyl floor covering cost is calculated as follows:

Method 10–13a:

$17.39/MH × 0.91 = $15.82/MH

$15.82/MH × 2 workers × 8 hr = $253.12 or $253.00/CD

Area:
    (16.42 lf × 10 lf) × 1.05 =   (5.00 m × 3.05 m) × 1.05 =
    164.2 sq ft × 1.05 = 172.41 sq ft   15.25 m² × 1.05 = **16.01 m²**
    172.41 sq ft ÷ 9 sq ft = **19.15 or 20 sq yd**

Edge tack strips:
    ([16.42 lf × 2] + [10 lf × 2]) × 1.05 =   ([5.00 × 2] + [3.05 m × 2]) × 1.05 =
    (32.84 lf + 20 lf) × 1.05 = **55.48 or 56 lf**   (10.00 m + 6.10 m) × 1.05 = **16.91 or 17 m**

CHART 10—6
Carpeting Estimate: Reception Office

Method 10–13b:

$17.61/MH × 0.91 = $16.03/MH

$16.03/MH × 2 workers × 8 hr = $256.48 or $256.00/CD

Equipment for Floor Covering

There is no special equipment necessary for the installation of vinyl sheet or VCT. The material and personnel transportation are usually included in the labor costs.

Carpeting

Refer to Plans, Sheet A–1, Architectural Floor Plan; Sheet A–8, Door, Window, and Finish Schedules. See also chart 10–6. The finish schedule indicates that there is carpeting located in the waiting room, reception office, doctor's office, nurse's office, administration office, and all of the halls. Included in a carpet installation are the edge tack strips, seam webbing, the pad, and the carpet. In areas where dissimilar materials abut the edge of a carpet, a threshold is installed. The threshold may be a thin aluminum folded strip in anodized chrome, bronze, or polished brass finish. In some instances, a ceramic or plastic strip matching the tile flooring abutting carpet may be used as the threshold. The accessories are estimated by the lineal foot.

Most carpet estimates and installations are made by the manufacturer or supplier. The cost of installation includes all of the materials mentioned. Carpeting is figured in square yards or square meters. The only major variation in carpet costs is the carpet quality.

An experienced carpet estimator determines the most practical manner by which to lay the carpet with the least amount of cutting and seams. This may sometimes increase the waste in material, but most often what is used is very close to the amount required. The carpet padding is installed with a spot adhesive applied to the substrate to hold the pad in place during the carpet installation.

Carpeting is figured by multiplying the total square yards of material with the cost of the type and style of carpet selected. The estimator must make certain that the cost/sq yd includes the carpet, pad, adhesive, edge tack nailers, threshold strips (metal, ceramic, plastic, and so on) and the seam webbing. Most carpet prices also include the labor for installation. The estimator for the

(Specified is 4'x10'x5/8" [7.22 m × 3.05 m × 1.59 cm] "X" GWB.)

Area and quantity:

(7.33 lf × 10 lf) × 1.05 =	(2.23 m × 3.05 m) × 1.05 =
73.3 sq ft × 1.05 = 76.97 sq ft	6.80 m² × 1.05 = 7.14 m²
76.97 sq ft ÷ 40 sq ft = **1.92 or 2 sheets**	7.14 m² ÷ 3.72 m² = **1.92 or 2 sheets**

1¹/₂" × 10 lf (3.81 cm × 3.05 m) edge angle:

([7.33 lf × 2] + [10 lf × 2]) × 1.05 =	([2.23 m × 2] + [3.05 m × 2]) × 1.05 =
(14.66 lf + 20 lf) × 1.05 = **36.39 or 40 lf**	(4.46 m + 6.10 m) × 1.05 = **11.09 m or 11 m**

1¹/₂" × 10 lf (3.81 cm × 3.05 m) "C" channel in 4'x4' (1.22 m × 1.22 m) grid:

([10 lf × 2] + [7.33 lf × 3]) × 1.05 =	([3.05 m × 2] + [2.23 m × 3]) × 1.05 =
(20 lf + 21.99 lf) × 1.05 = 44.09 lf	(6.10 m + 6.69 m) × 1.05 = 13.43 m

Add for light fixture support:

([4 lf + 8 lf] × 1.05) + 44.09 = **56.69 or 60 lf**	([1.22 m + 2.44 m] × 1.05) + 13.43 = **17.27 or 17.5 m**

1¹/₂" × 10 lf (3.81 cm × 3.05 m) furring (hat) channel:

(10 lf ÷ 2 lf) + 1 = 6	(3.05 m ÷ 0.61 m) + 1 = 6
(6 × 7.33 lf) × 1.05 = **46.18 or 50 lf**	(6 × 2.23 m) × 1.05 = **14.05 or 14 m**

#9 AWG tie wire (3 lf or 0.91 m):

(73.3 sq ft ÷ 9 sq ft) × 1.05 = **8.55 or 9 ties**	(6.80 m² ÷ 0.84 m²) × 1.05 = **8.5 or 9 ties**

Eye hooks (2/wire):

9 ties × 2 = **18 hooks**

CHART 10–7
Suspended Ceiling Systems: Restroom Ceiling

carpet manufacturer and/or supplier must consider each of these items prior to the establishment of a square yard price and must also be able to determine the best method of applying the carpet with the least number of seams and least amount of waste.

Suspended Ceiling Systems

Refer to Plans, Sheet A–1, Architectural Floor Plan; Sheet A–4, Reflected Ceiling Plan; Sheet A–8, Door, Window, and Finish Schedules. Also see chart 10–7. Two types of suspended ceilings are indicated: the drywall and the acoustical ceiling tile (ACT).

GWB Suspended Restroom Ceiling. The restroom ceiling for the Medical Clinic is a suspended drywall ceiling. The measurements for the ceiling are 7'-4" × 10'-0" (2.23 m × 3.05 m). The Specifications and plans indicate that 4'×10'× 5/8" (1.22 m × 3.05 m × 1.59 cm) "X" GWB, 1 1/2" × 1/16" (3.81 cm × 0.16 cm) edge angle, and "C" channel (black iron), 1 1/2" (3.81 cm) furring (hat) channel, #9 AWG tie wire, and eye hooks are required for completion of the ceiling.

"C" Channel. "C" channel 1 1/2" (3.81 cm) in size is used to form a grid to which the hat channel and the drywall are attached. The grid layout may be in increments of 2 feet (0.61 m) or 4 feet (1.22 m) in each direction. A 4 sq ft (0.37 m²) pattern is installed in the restroom ceiling. The grid, properly installed, is laid out from the center point of the ceiling in both directions. There is a fluorescent light fixture to be installed in the center of the ceiling. There must be some form of support for the fixture; so additional grid is installed to which the fixture is fastened. The fixture opening is 2'×4' (0.61 m × 1.22 m).

Furring (Hat) Channel. The furring is placed parallel to the shortest ceiling measurement. The lengths are each 7.33 lf (2.23 m) and are spaced 2 lf (0.61 m) apart along the 10 lf (3.05 m) wall.

Tie Wire. The support system for the suspended ceiling for the restroom is #9 AWG (9-gauge) tie wire. Per code, 3 tie wires are required for every 9 sq ft (0.83 m^2). The length of the tie wire is determined by the depth of the ceiling from the bottom of the joists to the top of the "black iron" grid. The total depth of the finished ceiling is 2'-0" (0.61 m). The ties should have a minimum of 6" (15.24 cm) on each end for looping and fastening.

Eye Hooks. The number of eye hooks may be the same or double the number of ties. The type of hook is dependent upon the material to which they are fastened. For the restroom, the ceiling joists are metal and the grid is metal; therefore, the hooks must be bolt hooks and nuts. The size of the hook may vary from 1/4"×1 1/2" (0.64 cm × 3.81 cm) to 1/2"×1 1/2" (1.27 cm × 3.81 cm).

Labor for Drywall Suspended Ceiling

See figures 10–14a and 10–14b, Composite Crew Schedule Suspended Ceiling. A 2-person drywall crew can install the ceiling in 1 1/2 days. The productivity factor is 0.97. The labor cost for the GWB ceiling is calculated as follows:

Method 10–14a:

$17.62/MH × 0.97 = $17.09/MH

$17.09/MH × 2 workers × 8 hr = $273.44/CD

$273.44/CD × 1.5 day = $410.16 or $410.00

CREW	HOURLY + BURDEN WAGE	% TIME ON JOB/HR	HOURLY RATE
Carpenter	$16.90 + $3.32	45%	= $ 9.10
Laborer	$11.75 + $3.74	55%	= $ 8.52
Composite Crew Rate:		100%	$17.62/MH

FIGURE 10–14a
Composite Crew Schedule

CREW	HOURLY WAGE + BURDEN
Carpenter	$16.40 + $3.32
Laborer	$11.75 + $3.74
	$28.15 + $7.06 = $35.21
Composite Crew Rate:	$35.21/2 = $17.61

FIGURE 10–14b
Composite Crew Schedule

Method 10–14b:

$17.61/MH × 0.97 = $17.08/MH

$17.08/MH × 2 workers × 8 hr = $273.28/CD

$273.28/CD × 1.5 day = $409.92

Equipment for Drywall Suspended Ceiling

No equipment costs need to be added to the estimate. The equipment is included with the drywall installation determined previously.

Acoustical Ceiling Tile (ACT)

Refer to Plans, Sheet A–1, Architectural Floor Plan; Sheet A–4, Reflected Ceiling Plan; Sheet A–8, Window, Door, and Finish Schedules. Also see chart 10–8. The acoustical lay-in tiles are 2′×4′ (0.61 m × 1.22 m), 1-hour rated fire-retardant, deep fissure texture, white in color with recessed runners. The runner color is not specified.

Estimating the Playroom Ceiling Tile.   The ceiling, per the reflected ceiling plan and Specifications, is installed with the exposed face 8′-0″ (2.44 m) A.F.F. The materials to be included in the installation are the tiles, the edge angle support, "T" bar, fastener clips, tie wire, and eye hooks. The playroom is 10′-6″ × 10′-6″ (3.20 m × 3.20 m). The ceiling area is calculated as follows:

10.5 lf × 10.5 lf = 110.25 sq ft

$(3.20 \text{ m} × 3.20 \text{ m} = 10.24 \text{ m}^2)$

The tiles are 2′×4′ (0.61 m × 1.22 m), or 8 sq ft (0.74 m^2). There are two methods of determining the number of tiles needed. They are the square-foot method and the piece method.

Method 1: The Square-Foot Method.   The number of tiles using the square-foot method with a waste factor of 1.05 is calculated in chart 10–8.

Method 2: The Piece Method.   With the lay-out procedure, the tiles are determined by the length of the room in each direction. The reflected ceiling plan (Sheet A–4) shows the tiles are laid with the 4 lf (1.22 m) side parallel with the east wall. To properly lay ceiling tiles, the installer should start at the middle in each direction and work to the outside. The reflected ceiling plan shows "X" areas. The "X" indicates an opening in the ceiling tiles for fluorescent light fixtures. The ACT estimator does not deduct these openings. The tiles are included as part of the waste factor. See chart 10–8.

Edge Angle.   As in the other suspended ceiling systems, there is an edge angle installed to support the perimeter of the ceiling. The angle is cold-rolled steel with an enamel or plastic finish, from 1″ (2.54 cm) to 1 1/2″ (3.81 cm) wide. The quantity required for the playroom is calculated as follows:

10.5 lf × 4 × 1.05 = 44.1 or 5 pc − 10 lf

(3.20m × 4 × 1.05 = 13.44 m or 5 pc − 3.20 m)

(The playroom ceiling is 10.5 lf × 10.5 lf or [3.20 m × 3.20 m])

Method #1 - square foot:

Tiles - 2' × 4' (0.61 m × 1.22 m):

(10.5 lf × 10.5 lf) × 1.05 = 115.76 sq ft

115.76 sq ft ÷ 8 sq ft = **14.47 or 15 tiles**

(3.20 m × 3.20 m) × 1.05 = 10.75 m²

10.75 m² ÷ 0.74 m² = **14.53 or 15 tiles**

Method #2 - layout procedure:

Cut tile sizes - parallel 2' (0.61 m) side:

10.5 lf − (4 lf × 2) = 2.5 lf

2.5 lf ÷ 2 = **1.25 lf (1'-3")**

3.20 m − (1.22 m × 2) = 0.76 m

0.76 m ÷ 2 = **0.38 m**

Cut tile sizes - parallel 4' (1.22 m) side:

10.5 lf ÷ 2 = 5.25 or 5 tiles

10.5 lf − (5 × 2 lf) = **0.5 lf**

(3.20 m ÷ 0.30 m) ÷ 2 = 5.33 or 5 tiles

3.20 m − (5 × 0.61 m) = **0.15 m**

Total tiles and sizes:

8 ea - 2'x4'

8 ea - 1.25'x2'

4 ea - 1.25'x4'

4 ea - 1.25'x1.25'

8 ea - 0.61 m × 1.22 m

8 ea - 0.38 m × 0.61 m

4 ea - 0.38 m × 1.22 m

4 ea - 0.38 m × 0.38 m

Other materials:

Edge angle - 1½" × 10 lf (3.81 cm × 3.05 m):

(10.5 lf × 4) × 1.05 = **44.1 or 50 lf**

(3.20 m × 4) × 1.05 = **13.44 or 13.5 m**

Runners:

Main runners - 1½" × 10 lf (3.81 cm × 3.05 m) (5 spaces + 1 = 6 runners):

(6 × 10.5 lf) × 1.05 = **66.15 or 70 lf**

(6 × 3.20 m) × 1.05 = **20.16 or 20 m**

Secondary runners - 1½" × 10 lf (3.81 cm × 3.05 m):

(2 × 10.5 lf) × 1.05 = **22.05 or 30 lf**

(2 × 3.20 m) × 1.05 = **6.72 or 7 m**

Total runners:

70 lf + 30 lf = **100 lf**

20 m + 7 m = **27 m**

Tie wire - 9 AWG - 3 lf (0.91 m):

(12 × 3 lf) × 1.05 = **37.8 or 38 lf**

(12 × 0.91 m) × 1.05 = **11.47 or 11.5 m**

Tie/corner clips:

4-way:

6 × 2 = **12 clips**

3-way:

(6 × 2) + (2 × 2) = **16 clips**

Eye hooks:

same as 4-way clips = **12**

CHART 10—8

Acoustical Ceiling Tile: Playroom Ceiling

Runners. The "T"-shaped bar runners are divided into two types, the main runner and the secondary runner. The main runner installation is parallel to the 4 lf (1.22 m) side of the tiles and the shortest wall-to-wall measurement. There are five and a fraction tiles laid from the north exterior wall to the examination room #1 wall. The secondary runners are parallel to the 2 lf (0.61 m) side of the tiles (perpendicular to the main runners). See chart 10–8.

Ties/Corner Clips. The installer may use clips or use the ties to reinforce the connections of main and secondary runners and the edge angle to runner connections. There are two types of clips used. The one is a four-way clip installed where the runners meet. The other is a three-way, or half clip, connecting the edge angle and runners.

CREW	HOURLY + BURDEN WAGE	% TIME ON JOB/HR	HOURLY RATE
Carpenter	$16.90 + $3.32	45%	= $ 9.10
Laborer	$11.75 + $3.74	55%	= $ 8.52
Composite Crew Rate:		100%	$17.62/MH

FIGURE 10–15a
Composite Crew Schedule

CREW	HOURLY WAGE + BURDEN
Carpenter	$16.40 + $3.32
Laborer	$11.75 + $3.74
	$28.15 + $7.06 = $35.21
Composite Crew Rate:	$35.21/2 = $17.61

FIGURE 10–15b
Composite Crew Schedule

Tie Wires and Eye Hooks.   ACT systems use tie wires at all interior connecting points to the ceiling. There is a total of 12 interior clips. The length of the wire is determined by the space from ceiling or roof joist to the top of the vertical part of the inverted "T" bar with a 6″ (15.24 cm) allowance at each end for loop ties.

The number of hooks is equal to the number of ties.

Labor for Acoustical Ceiling Installation

See figure 10–15. A two-person crew can install the ceiling for the playroom in 1 1/2 days. The productivity factor is also 0.97. The crew rate schedule is the same as for the drywall found in figures 10–14a and 10–14b. The labor costs are identical to those found in those figures as follows:

Method 10–15a:

$17.62 × 0.97 = $17.09/MH

$17.09/MH × 2 workers × 8 hr = $273.44/CD

$26 = 73.44/CD × 1.5 days = $410.16 or $410.00

Method 10–15b:

$17.61 × 0.97 = $17.08/MH

$17.08/MH × 2 workers × 8 hr = $273.28/CD

$273.28/CD × 1.5 days = $409.92 or $410.00

Painting o/cement plaster in lieu of integral color (west wall):
Area:
  (41 lf × 10 lf) × 1.05 = **430.5 or 431 sq ft**   (12.50 m × 3.05 m) × 1.05 = **40.03 or 40 m²**

Sealer - 100 sq ft/gal (9.30 m²/3.79 liter):
  431 sq ft ÷ 100 sq ft = **4.31 or 5 gal**   (40 m² ÷ 9.29 m²) × 3.79 liter = **16.32 or 17 liter**

Primer and finish coat - 175 sq ft/gal (16.26 m²/3.79 liter):
  431 sq ft ÷ 175 sq ft = **2.46 or 3 gal ea**   (40 m² ÷ 16.26 m²) × 3.79 liter = **9.32 or 10 liter ea**

Primer and trim coat o/wood - 200 sq ft/gal (21.53 m²/3.79 liter):
Rafter (24) and hip (2) tails exposed ends:
  24 × (1 lf × 2.33 lf) =   24 × (0.30 m × 0.71 m) =
  24 × 2.33 sq ft = **55.92 sq ft**   24 × 0.21 m² = **5.04 m²**

  2 × (3 lf × 1.17 lf) =   2 × (0.91 m × 0.36 m) =
  2 × 3.51 sq ft = **7.02 sq ft**   2 × 0.33 m² = **0.66 m²**

Overhang:
  ([45 lf + 41 lf] ÷ 2) × 2.33 lf =   ([13.72 m + 12.50 m] ÷ 2) × 0.71 m =
  43 lf × 2.33 lf = **100.19 sq ft**   13.11 m × 0.71 m = **9.31 m²**

2×8 (5.08 cm × 20.32 cm) fascia board:
  45 lf × 1.5 lf = **67.5 sq ft**   13.72 m × 0.46 m = **6.31 m²**

Total paint - wood trim:
  55.92 sq ft + 7.02 sq ft + 100.19 sq ft +   5.04 m² + 0.66 m² + 9.31 m² + 6.31 m² = **21.32 m²**
    67.5 sq ft = **230.63 sq ft**
  230.63 sq ft ÷ 200 sq ft = **1.2 or 2 gal ea**   (21.32 m² ÷ 21.53 m²) × 3.79 liter = **3.75 or 4 liter ea**

CHART 10—9
Painting Estimate: Exterior, East Wall

Equipment for Acoustical Ceiling Installation

Again, little or no equipment is necessary other than transportation for the workers and, perhaps, hand drills; therefore, no equipment costs are added to the estimate.

Painting Materials

See Plans, Sheets A–2 and A–3, Exterior Elevations; Sheets A–7 and A–8, Door, Window, and Finish Schedules. Also see chart 10–9. The painting contractor has possible work in more areas of the Specifications than any other contractor. The estimator must search the Specifications for all of the following: in Division 3, Concrete, for brushed, rolled, or sprayed sealers called for on slabs or walls, and for caulking and sealing of concrete expansion joints; Division 4, Masonry, for brushed, rolled, or sprayed weather conditioners to be used over masonry exteriors or masonry control joint fillers, or a paint finish filler to smooth the masonry surface for other paint finishes; Division 7, Thermal and Moisture Protection, for sealants and caulking used for moisture protection, roofing, sheet metal or for door and window openings; Division 9, Finishes, for all paint finishes not covered elsewhere in the other divisions; and Division 12, Furnishings, for painting or staining of architectural work that may be located in this division. The finish schedules, interior elevations, sections and details, and exterior elevations, sections, and details must also be studied. The estimator does not deduct for any openings.

Exterior Painting.   *See chart 10–9.* For the Medical Clinic, all exposed wood or metal including the fascia, underside of the exposed roof sheathing, and window trim require a primer and colored latex finish. A base sealer, primer, and latex finish are required for covering the stucco. Spray foam insulation caulk base (to fill cavities around doors and windows) and a paint-compatible caulk around all window and door frames and at the plate line around the perimeter of the building are also required.

Paint Sealer over Stucco.   The area of the east wall is 410 sq ft (38.09 m²). In most cases, especially over rough surfaces such as stucco, 1 gallon of sealer will cover a maximum of 100 sq ft (9.29 m²).

Primer and Finish Coats over Stucco.   For painting the stucco, 1 gallon (3.79 liter) of both the exterior primer and finish latex cover a maximum of 175 sq ft (16.26 m²) of wall. One coat of each is specified.

Primer and Trim Coat over Exterior Wood.   The primer and trim coat is used for the fascia, exposed overhang, and exterior trim. One gallon (3.79 liter) of the primer and finish coats will each cover approximately 200 sq ft (18.58 m²) of area for both metal or wood finish. The east fascia is 45 lf (13.72 m). The overhang is approximately 2'-4" (0.71 m) from plate to eave.

Sealers, primers, and finish coatings are available in 3-, 5-, or 10-gallon (11.36 liter, 18.92 liter, or 37.90 liter) pails and in 50 gallon (189.27 liter) drums.

Caulking.   Caulking and foam insulation may be obtained in cartons of 12 or 24 units. The estimator calculates the lineal feet of caulk and foam base. (See chart 10–10.) The manufacturer states the approximate length one tube will cover.

Interior Walls.   *Refer to Plans, Sheets A–7 and A–8, Door, Window, and Finish Schedules. See also chart 10–11.* The finish schedule specifies that the interior

---

Windows 4-4'-0" × 5'-0":
([4 lf × 2] + [5 lf × 2] × 4) × 1.05 =
([8 lf + 10 lf] × 4) × 1.05 =
72 lf × 1.05 = **75.6 lf**

([1.22 m × 2] + [1.52 m × 2] × 4) × 1.05 =
([2.44 m + 3.04 m] × 4) × 1.05 =
21.92 m × 1.05 = **23.02 m**

Door:
([6.67 lf × 2] + 6 lf) × 1.05 = **20.31 lf**

([2.03 m × 2] + 1.83 m) × 1.05 = **6.18 m**

Plate line, rafters and hips:
([24 × 1 lf] + [2 × 1.17 lf] + 41 lf) × 1.05 =
(24 lf + 2.34 lf + 41 lf) × 1.05 =
67.34 × 1.05 = **70.71 lf**

([24 × 0.30 m] + [2 × 0.36 m] + 12.50 m) × 1.05 =
(7.20 m + 0.72 m + 12.50 m) × 1.05 =
20.42 m × 1.05 = **21.44 m**

Total lineal feet:
75.6 lf + 20.31 lf + 70.71 lf = **166.62 lf**

23.02 m + 6.18 m + 21.44 m = **50.64 m**

Caulking - tube @ 30 lf (9.14 m)/tube:
166.62 lf ÷ 30 lf = **5.55 or 6 tubes**

50.64 m ÷ 9.14 m = **5.54 or 6 tubes**

Foam insulation - can @ 25 lf (7.62 m)/can:
166.62 lf ÷ 25 lf = **6.66 or 7 cans**

50.64 m ÷ 7.62 m = **6.64 or 7 cans**

CHART 10—10
Caulking and Insulating: East Wall

(The playroom is 10.5 lf × 10.5 lf × 8 lf [3.20 m × 3.20 m × 2.44 m])
Walls - 2 coats - 275 sq ft/gal (29.60 m²/3.79 liter):
 ([{10.5 lf × 4} × 8 lf] × 2) × 1.05 =   ([{3.20 m × 4} × 2.44 m] × 2) × 1.05 =
 (336 sq ft × 2) × 1.05 = 705.6 sq ft   (31.23 m² × 2) × 1.05 = 65.58 m²
 705.6 sq ft ÷ 275 sq ft = **2.57 or 3 gal**   (65.58 m² ÷ 29.60 m²) × 3.79 liter = **8.41 or 9 liter**

CHART 10–11
Interior Painting Estimate: Playroom

CREW	HOURLY + BURDEN WAGE	% TIME ON JOB/HR	HOURLY RATE
Foreman	$14.98 + $2.97	30%	= $ 5.39
Painter (2)	$14.48 + $2.97 × 2	70%	= $24.43
Composite Crew Rate:		100%	$29.82/MH

FIGURE 10–16a
Composite Crew Schedule

CREW	HOURLY WAGE + BURDEN
Foreman	$14.98 + $2.97
Painter (2)	$14.48 + $2.97 × 2
	$43.94 + $8.91 = $52.85
Composite Crew Rate:	$52.85/2 = $26.43

FIGURE 10–16b
Composite Crew Schedule

walls are painted with an epoxy sealer, primer, and acrylic latex finish coat. One gallon (3.79 liter) of paint is capable of covering a maximum of 300 sq ft (27.87 m²). The walls in the playroom are to be painted. See chart 10–11 for the estimate of the paint required for the playroom.

Labor for Painting

See figures 10–16a and 10–16b, Composite Crew Schedule: Painting and Wallcovering. A 3-person crew can apply 1 coat to the exterior east wall stucco in 3/4 hr, including masking all of the openings and caulking. Another 3/4 hr is estimated for painting 1 coat on the exposed overhang, fascia, and trim. The productivity rate is 72%. The productivity factor is 0.97. The labor cost is:

Method 10–16a:
$29.82/MH × 0.97 = $28.93/MH
$28.93/MH × 0.75 hr × 6 coats × 3 workers = $390.55 or $391.00

FIGURE 10–17
Equipment Schedule

EQUIPMENT	USE TIME	UNIT COST	TOTAL
Truck	1.25 day	@ $10/day	= $12.50
Sprayer	1.25 day	@ $35/day	= $43.75
Mixer or drill	1.25 day	@ $15/day	= $18.75
Brushes (4)		@ $1.75 ea	= $ 7.00
Equipment Total:			$82.00

(The nurse's office is 10 lf × 7.83 lf × 9 lf [3.05 m × 2.39 m × 2.74 m])
(NOTE: 1 roll = 16 sq ft or 1.49 m²)

([10 lf × 2] + [7.83 lf × 2] × 9 lf) × 1.05 =
(35.66 lf × 9 lf) × 1.05 = 336.99 or 337 sq ft
337 sq ft ÷ 16 sq ft = **21.06 or 21 rolls**

([3.05 m × 2] + [2.39 m × 2] × 2.74 m) × 1.05 =
(10.88 m × 2.74 m) × 1.05 = 31.30 m²
31.30 m² ÷ 1.49 m² = **21 rolls**

Sizing (100 sq ft/lb or 9.29 m²/0.45 kg):
337 sq ft ÷ 100 sq ft = **3.37 or 4 lb**

(31.20 m² ÷ 9.29 m²) × 0.45 kg = **1.51 or 2 kg**

Paste (22 sq yd/gal or 18.39 m²/3.79 liter):
(337 sq ft ÷ 9 sq ft) ÷ 22 sq yd = **1.7 or 2 gal**

(31.20 m² ÷ 18.39 m²) × 3.79 liter = **6.43 or 7 liter**

CHART 10–12
Wallcovering Estimate: Nurse's Office

Method 10–16b:

$26.43/MH × 0.97 = $25.64/MH

$25.64/MH × 0.75 hr × 6 coats × 3 workers = $346.14 or $346.00

Equipment for Painting

See figure 10–17. The equipment necessary for a painting crew includes the transportation for personnel, material, and equipment; a mixer or drill with an impeller attachment; a sprayer or rollers and handles; and paintbrushes for trimming.

Wallcovering Materials

Refer to Plans, Sheet A-1, Architectural Floor Plan; Sheets A–7 and A–8, Door, Window, and Finish Schedules. See also chart 10–12. There are three types of wallcovering for the Medical Clinic, including wallpaper (or cloth) and decorative or acoustical paneling. The decorative paneling in the doctor's office is estimated by the finish carpentry contractor. The nurse's office is to be wallpapered.

Wallpaper is figured in square yards or square meters. Caution must be used when estimating in this manner. When the paper must be "matched," the paper is estimated by the roll with extra for waste or repair. The design may take three roll widths to complete; therefore, two thirds more paper is necessary. Most commercial locations use a wallpaper that requires no matching. It

FIGURE 10–18
Equipment Schedule

EQUIPMENT	USE TIME	UNIT COST	TOTAL
Truck	1 day	@ $10/day	= $10.00
Table	1 day	@ $0.50/day	= $ 0.50
Brushes (2)		@ $1.50 ea	= $ 3.00
Equipment Total:			$13.50

is this type that is estimated for the Medical Clinic. Wallpaper is available in widths up to 36″ (0.91 m).

Labor for Wallpaper Installation

Refer to figures 10–16a and 10–16b. A 3-person crew can apply the wallpaper required for the nurse's office in 1 day. The productivity factor is 0.97. The labor cost is calculated as follows:

Method 10–16a:
$29.82/MH × 0.97 = $28.93/MH
$28.93/MH × 3 workers × 8 hr = $694.32 or $695.00

Method 10–16b:
$26.43/MH × 0.97 = $25.64/MH
$25.64/MH × 0.75 hr × 6 coats × 3 workers = $346.14 or $346.00

Equipment for Wallpaper Installation

See figure 10–18. Transportation for workers, a sizing sprayer, a spreading table, and brushes are all that are needed.

ALTERNATE STRUCTURAL AND LIGHT-GAUGE METAL FRAMING

See Plans, Sheet S-2, Structural Floor Framing Plan through Sheet S–8, Wall Sections. The scope of work required for light-gauge metal framing is found in Alternate #3, Division 1, Section 01030, Alternates/Alternatives. The alternate reads as follows:

```
Alternate #3.

An alternate shall be included for light-gauge structural and
light-gauge metal framing in lieu of wood framing. The framing
shall include floor joists, wall construction (bearing and
partition), ceiling joists and the roof structure. The specifica-
tions shall read:
```

05400 Cold Formed Metal Framing. Floor joists shall be 10"
(25.40 cm) 18-ga structural unpunched "C" studs attached with all
necessary accessories for a complete installation.

Exterior walls are 9'-0" (2.74 m) high and shall be
constructed of 6" (15.24 cm) 18-ga structural steel studs with top
and bottom 6" (15.24 cm) 18-ga track. Studs shall be placed at
24" O/C (0.61 m).

All lintels over exterior openings shall be a minimum of 2 8"
(20.32 cm) 18-ga unpunched steel studs. All ceiling joists and
roof rafters shall be 6" (15.25 cm) 18-ga unpunched steel studs.
Ridge and hip beams shall be 8" (20.32 cm) 18-ga unpunched steel
studs doubled. Spacing shall be as noted on plans.

All connections at walls, lintels, rafter, and ridge and hip
shall be welded with proper clip stiffeners. Weld shall be a
fillet weld completely surrounding clip stiffener. Self-tapping
#6 × 3/4" (1.91 cm) screws may be used to hold stiffeners and
connections in place until welded.

If structural metal stud framing is accepted, the wood
utility plate on the steel support beam is not to be installed and
the wall embedment and pier heights must be adjusted accordingly.

All materials shall be supplied by American Studco Company,
Phoenix, Arizona.

09100 Metal Support Systems. Interior bearing walls shall be
6" (15.24 cm) 2 galvanized studs and track, interior plumbing
walls shall be 6" (15.24 cm-22 ga) 22-ga studs and track, and
partition walls shall be 3 5/8" ga (9.21 cm) 25-ga galvanized
studs and track. All walls shall extend 9'-0" (2.74 m) A.F.F.

All necessary accessories shall be in accordance with the
manufacturer's recommendations, codes and local ordinances.

All materials shall be supplied by American Studco Company,
Phoenix, Arizona.

Structural Floor Framing

The specifications indicate the floor framing is 10" (25.40 cm) 18-ga cold-rolled
steel "C" studs, unpunched, spaced as per plan. The floor joists are placed utilizing the shortest practical span possible for structural flexural strength. They
are spaced at both 1 lf (0.30 m) and 2 lf (0.61 m) intervals. The closer spacing
is for the purpose of providing additional strength in areas where extra loads
are applied. These areas include the restroom, break room, X-ray laboratory,
ambulatory operating room, and the processing and records area.

The simplest estimate is to use the count-up method. A mathematical
verification that an area is correctly drawn can determine the accuracy of the
drawing and the count-up. Building codes demand that floor joists parallel
with a bearing wall must be doubled.

The east wall at the waiting room/playroom area of the Medical Clinic
is 41 lf (12.50 m). The length of the floor joist must also be determined. The
length from the east wall to the center of the beam supporting a floor joist is
11.25 lf (3.43 m). The floor joist abuts the header (rim) joist on the east end
and at the double joists on the beam below at the interior end. The out-to-out
flange depth of the header joist is 1 3/8" (3.49 cm). The floor joists may be cut
at this point or extend one more span. They are cut to fit against the double
joists over the beam for this estimate. To hold the floor joists in place, stiffeners (connectors) must be screwed or bolted and welded at each end.

The header (rim) joist is a continuous member extending out-to-out along the west and east walls. As with wood frame construction, the header joist is used to hide, protect, and stiffen the interior joists abutting it. The length of the joist along the east wall must be a total of 41 lf (12.50 cm). The length of the members may be random lengths. They, too, are butted and welded with a flat stiffener for a smooth appearance. The joists parallel with the foundation wall along the north/south perimeters are applied in the same manner.

Wall Framing

There are four types of wall framing for the Medical Clinic:

6″ ga (15.24 cm) 18-ga studs at the exterior bearing walls

6″ ga (15.24 cm) 20-ga studs at the interior bearing walls

6″ (15.24 cm) 22-ga studs at the plumbing wall

3 5/8″ (9.21 cm) 25-ga studs at the interior partition walls.

Two differences exist between metal stud and wood framing. One difference is the wood stud length is shorter than the metal stud under the same height conditions because of the additional thickness of the sole plate and the double top plate used in lieu of the track in metal stud framing. The track is the top and bottom plate of a metal stud frame wall. Track is made so that the studs can fit snugly inside and be fastened securely. The second difference is the stud spacing: normally, bearing wall metal studs are spaced at 24″ O/C (60.96 cm) and 2× wood bearing wall studs are spaced at 16″ O/C (40.64 cm).

Estimating Metal Stud Framing. The estimate procedures are identical to those used for rough carpentry in chapter 8. The estimator must remember that track is used instead of sole and top plates, and the spacing and the sizes of the studs and joists are different. These must be properly identified.

Miscellaneous materials required for a complete estimate include stiffeners for rigidity of joist connections and screws for fastening joists, track, and studs. Shot-and-pin may be necessary if there is a concrete slab on which the track and studs are erected.

Stiffeners must be bolted and/or welded at each end to hold the joists and rafters in place. There are three stiffeners required for each floor joist on the east end of the building. There are two at the rim joist and one connecting to the beam below at the opposite (interior) end. There is one stiffener required at the return joists on the corners and one or two more for the random lengths; thus, the number of stiffeners required for the floor joists on the east wall is as follows:

23 pc × 3 ea = 69

69 + 2 + 2 = 73 clip-angle stiffeners

The number of stiffeners for the ceiling joists on the east end is as follows:

3 × 4 = 92 clip-angle stiffeners

The number of stiffeners for the rafters on one half of a hip is as follows:

10 jack rafters × 2 ea = 20 clip − angle stiffeners

Add one for one half of the common rafter:

20 + 1 = 21 clip-angle stiffeners

One hip requires 2 clip-angle stiffeners at each end (plate line and ridge):

2 × 2 = 4 clip-angle stiffeners

A 1 1/4" (3.18 cm) #6 screw is used when fastening track to wood frame (underlayment and the like). The screws are spaced at 2 lf O/C (0.61 m) when the floor joist is directly under and parallel to the wall. The walls perpendicular to the floor joists are fastened in accordance with the floor joist spacing. The number of screws necessary for the east wall is as follows:

41 lf ÷ 2 lf = 20.5 or 21 screws
(12.50 m ÷ 0.61 m = 20.5 or 21 screws)

The screws for the wall framing should be a minimum 3/4" (1.91 cm) #6. Two screws are used at both the top and bottom track to connect a stud. There are 38 studs on the east wall; therefore, the number of screws needed is calculated as follows:

38 studs × 4 = 152 screws

Metal Stud Framing Labor

See figure 10–19a and figure 10–19b, Composite Crew Schedule. A 3-person crew takes 3 days to install the east wall. There are a foreman, a journeyman and a laborer. The productivity factor is 1.02. The total labor estimated by crew hour is calculated as follows:

Method 10–19a:
$17.96/MH × 1.02 = $18.32/MH
$18.32/MH × 3 workers × 8 hr × 3 days = $1,319.04 or $1,319.00

Method 10–19b:
$18.48/MH × 1.02 = $19.50/MH
$19.50/MH × 3 workers × 8 hr × 3 days = $1,404.00

CREW	HOURLY + BURDEN WAGE	% TIME ON JOB/HR	HOURLY RATE
Foreman	$16.90 + $3.32	19%	= $ 3.84
Carpenter	$16.40 + $3.32	37%	= $ 7.30
Laborer	$11.75 + $3.74	44%	= $ 6.82
Composite Crew Rate:		100%	$17.96/MH

FIGURE 10–19a
Composite Crew Schedule

CREW	HOURLY WAGE + BURDEN
Foreman	$16.90 + $ 3.32
Carpenter	$16.40 + $ 3.32
Laborer	$11.75 + $ 3.74
	$45.05 + $10.38 = $55.43
Composite Crew Rate:	$55.43/3 = $18.48

FIGURE 10–19b
Composite Crew Schedule

FIGURE 10–20
Equipment Schedule: Metal Stud Framing

EQUIPMENT	USE TIME	UNIT COST	TOTAL
Per Trans	3 days	@ $ 10/day	= $ 30.00
Material Transport	3 days	@ $ 30/day	= $ 90.00
Truck Crane	1 day	@ $185/day	= $185.00
Extended Lift (forklift)	3 days	@ $150/day	= $450.00
Table Saw	3 days	@ $ 75/day	= $225.00
Powder Actuated Gun	1 day	@ $ 15/day	= $ 15.00
Equipment Total:			$995.00

Metal Stud Framing Equipment

See figure 10–20. The equipment costs for metal stud framing are identical to the equipment costs for wood framing. The equipment cost breakdown for 3 days is given in figure 10–20.

CHAPTER EXERCISES

All costs, composite crews, labor factors, and equipment breakdowns shall be the same as those used throughout the chapter.

1. Refer to figure 10–2. Calculate the quantity of cement plaster and accessories required for an alternate entry cover indicated in figure 10–2. The roof slope is 5:12. The front face of the entry is 6 lf wide × 18" (1.83 m × 0.46 m) high plus the sloped areas. The two columns are 18" square × 10 lf (0.21 m² × 3.05 m). The cover extends 4 lf (1.22 m) beyond the main wall. There is cement plaster applied to both sides and the front face of the entry cover, to the columns, and to the ceiling as shown. Hint: Redraw the entry to scale to get proper lengths and heights.

2. Determine the amount of VCT needed for the X-ray laboratory and the operating room. Include standard base, underlayment, and adhesive.

3. The break room elevation indicates both ceramic tile and paint for walls and ceiling. Estimate the quantity of tile necessary.

4. What is the quantity of paint required for the break room?

5. Estimate the quantity of carpet required for hall #1, #2, and #3. Break down the quantity for each area.

6. How much wallpaper will be necessary to complete examination rooms #1, #2, and #3?

7. Prepare a complete quantity survey of the Medical Clinic stud framing.

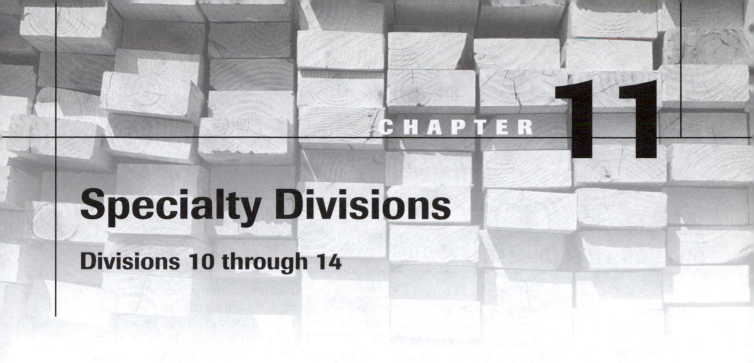

CHAPTER 11

Specialty Divisions

Divisions 10 through 14

Divisions 10 through 14 are known as the specialty divisions. They include items that are supplied directly to the owner from the manufacturers or suppliers. The manufacturers and suppliers not only supply the products but may utilize their own personnel for delivery and installation. The estimates for material, labor, and equipment are all supplied by suppliers' in-house estimators or by independent sales and estimating brokers (manufacturers' representatives).

DIVISION 10: SPECIALTIES

Division 10 includes sections for items such as chalkboards, tackboards, sound divider panels, restroom cubicles, lockers, and so on. The materials in this division are referred to as "institutional" supplies because most of them are common to school installations and other places of public occupancy.

SCOPE OF WORK

The specifications for Division 10 for the Medical Clinic are as follows:

Division 10: Specialties

10000 Scope of Work

Division 1 and the General Conditions are to be considered a part of this division. Furnish all labor, materials and equipment necessary to complete all work under this division and as indicated on drawings.

10500 Lockers

Individual personal storage lockers shall be installed for each employee and are to be located in the Restroom area. The number of employees is to be determined by owner (maximum of ten).

10800 Toilet and Bath Accessories

The contractor shall be responsible for the purchase and installation of all Restroom and Kitchen accessories including, but not limited to, mirrors, dispensers, waste depositories and grab bars per ADA requirements.

End of Division

DIVISION 11: EQUIPMENT

Large equipment found primarily in institutions or other places of public occupancy, as well as equipment for industrial and commercial use that is permanently installed in the structure, are a part of this division. Examples of such items include bank vaults and special teller equipment, built-in maintenance equipment (laundry chutes and institutional or industrial laundry equipment), commercial retail equipment, religious and educational display equipment, athletic exercise equipment, food service equipment for commercial and institutional kitchens, and medical equipment. Prison equipment and theater stage handling equipment are also a part of this division.

The medical equipment used in the Medical Clinic includes the X-ray laboratory equipment, operating room table and autoclaves, and examination room tables, as well as the accessories supplied with each.

SCOPE OF WORK

The specifications for equipment for the Medical Clinic are as follows:

Division 11: Equipment

11000 Scope of Work

Division 1 and the General Conditions are to be considered a part of this division. Furnish all labor and equipment necessary to complete all work under this division and as indicated on drawings.

11700 Medical Equipment

The owner shall select all medical equipment for this project. The contractor shall be responsible for proper installation of the equipment. Where required, coordination shall be applied by the various subcontractors responsible for specialty installations such as plumbing and/or electrical.

End of Division

DIVISION 12: FURNISHINGS

This division includes such materials and products as artwork (murals, plaques, and so on), cabinetry, window tinting, furniture, fabrics (for furniture and wallcoverings), rugs and mats (not carpeting), office equipment (desks, credenzas, chairs, file cabinets, computers, copiers, and so on), display furniture, and theater seating.

DIVISION 13: SPECIAL CONSTRUCTION

Materials needed for research and modern technology, such as clean rooms, audiometric rooms, nuclear reactors, and many of the supporting special observation equipment, are a part of this division. The division was originally established for swimming-pool construction specifications. Swimming pools are still a part of the division. The other areas now included were developed as technology demands increased.

DIVISION 14: CONVEYING SYSTEMS

Dumbwaiters, elevators, all types of material handling equipment, and the complex conveyor equipment in a bottling or canning plant are specified in this division. Also included are the controls and accessories necessary for their operation.

CHAPTER EXERCISES

1. Make an estimate for the Medical Clinic specialties: include lockers, storage shelving and all accessories for the restroom, breakroom, and examination room installations in the estimate.

2. Prepare a summary of all the equipment necessary to complete the Medical Clinic services for the operating Room, X-ray Room, and examination rooms.

CHAPTER 12

Mechanical and Plumbing

Division 15

The mechanical portion of Division 15 includes *H*eating, *V*entilation, and *A*ir-*C*onditioning (HVAC). Plumbing deals strictly with piping (for potable water) and plumbing (for waste removal). Certain types of HVAC equipment also require plumbing work. It is for this reason that both mechanical and plumbing are combined in one division. A mechanical engineer is responsible for design and development of the specifications for materials, installation, and equipment for both sections. The chapter is, therefore, divided into two separate parts of study. The first half of the chapter is concerned with the plumbing installation and the second half with the mechanical installation. There is also a close relationship between mechanical and electrical, which will be discussed later in the chapter.

Division 1 specifies conditions for all trades including Division 15, but just as structural drawings are the responsibility of a certified structural engineer, the mechanical and plumbing drawings are the responsibility of a certified mechanical engineer. The mechanical engineer supplies the technical and procedural information relating to mechanical equipment, such as that concerning placement, installation, sizing, load calculations, meters, relays, thermostats, computer controls, and any other control devices, as well as documentation referring specifically to their installations.

Mechanical and plumbing information is included in a section of Division 15 and as an adjunct to the provisions of Division 1. As the architect does in other specifications, the engineer specifies the products and acceptable manufacturers and/or suppliers for the materials. For Division 15, the architect supplies only the proposed floor plan and its measurements upon which the mechanical engineer indicates the mechanical and plumbing materials. The mechanical drawings and information take precedence over architectural design and information except for the dimensioning.

GENERAL PLUMBING INFORMATION

See figure 12–1. The size of pipe, the type of pipe, and plumbing fixtures, as well as accessories and connections to local water and waste disposal systems, are all a part of plumbing. Plumbing is a general term for the installation of

USE	LOCATION	IRON			COPPER			PLASTIC				
		Cast Iron	Galv Iron	Malleable Cast Iron	Hard L&V	Soft K&L	DWV	ABS	PVC	CPVC	PE	PB
Potable Water	above grade		*	*	*					*		*
Supply	below grade					*					*	*
Sanitary Drainage	above grade	*	*				*	*	*			
and Venting	below grade	*						*	*			
Storm Drainage	above grade	*	*				*	*	*			
Piping	below grade	*						*	*			

FIGURE 12-1
Types and Uses of Pipes

potable (drinking) water and of waste disposal, as well as their treatment. The availability, type, purification procedures, as well as the water source (river, spring, well, and so on), determine the water treatment which, in turn, is governed by local codes and ordinances. The same is true of treatment of waste water and materials and their disposal.

The plumbing trades identify water and waste as two separate categories, **piping** and **plumbing.** Piping includes any carrier of potable (drinking) water, including the fixtures and accessories from the water treatment, filtration, and purification plants. Most blueprints for residential and small commercial construction use an isometric, one-line drawing to indicate the water supply system. All of the major parts of the system (meters, valves, angle stops, and so on), excluding the fixtures, are indicated. The fixtures are listed in a schedule found in the plumbing specifications or on the architectural and/or plumbing floor plans.

Plumbing is any pipe, accessory, or fixture installed for the express purpose of waste disposal. The most common types of carriers for waste disposal are cast iron pipe or plastic (ABS) pipe. The drawing for the plumbing for use with residential and small commercial construction is also an isometric drawing. All of the major parts of the system (valves, traps, clean-outs, and so on) from the sewer connection to, but not including, the fixtures are indicated on the drawing.

Other common installations included in plumbing are fire protection systems such as sprinkler systems, automatic chemical spray systems (foam or CO_2), or combinations of them; gas and fuel-oil heating systems; and liquid-transfer heating and cooling systems associated with HVAC. All information, regulations, and codes are based upon the recommendations of the National Fire Protection Association (NFPA).

Fire Protection

Shop drawings are necessary for the planning of a fire protection system. The shop drawings are inspected not only by plan checkers, planning commissions, or other building and safety personnel but also by the fire marshall responsible for the area in which the installation is located. The drawings must indicate the type of system—for example, a dry- or wet-standpipe sprinkler system or a spray-foam type system such as used in restaurant kitchens or similar installations. The drawings must also include the pipe sizes, type of sprinkler heads, the annunciator system, and so on. The actual installation of the annunciators and other signaling devices is the responsibility of an electrical contractor (alarm device specialist).

Heating and Cooling Systems

Still larger systems for heat and power generation are included under the title of plumbing. Heat-generating systems (gas and oil fuel furnaces) are specified for residential heating as well as for commercial, institutional, and industrial applications. Specifications and installation instructions for commercial and industrial gas and fuel-oil heating and for heat and power generation systems (furnaces and boilers) include the size and type of the fuel lines, boilers, furnaces, and all appurtenant accessories (valves, safety alarms, and so on). The major portions of the plant installations for these utilities may be governed by separate codes established by and for the utility companies. Recently, many of the utility companies are converting to the construction codes (UPC, NEC, and so on) in force outside of the utilities themselves so as to eliminate the confusion caused by separate code requirements.

Portions of liquid heat-transfer systems are included under plumbing because of the special piping and plumbing installations attached to the equipment—for example, a combination cooling tower, boiler, and the individual heat-transfer units requiring plumbing necessary to connect them. *Also see the section General Mechanical (HVAC) Information.*

SCOPE OF WORK

The plumbing specifications found in appendix IV, the Project Manual, Division 15, for the Medical Clinic contain the following information:

Division 15: Mechanical

15000 Scope of Work

Division 1 and the General Conditions are to be considered a part of this division. Furnish all labor, materials and equipment necessary to complete all work under this division and as indicated on drawings.

15400 Plumbing

The plumbing contractor shall be responsible for all fee and permit costs in reference to the plumbing and piping applying to this project.

Plumbing shall include, but is not limited to, installation of all sanitary sewer, storm drainage, gas and potable water connections from off-site to, and including, the appliance or fixture shut-off valves and the appliances or fixtures themselves. Fittings not specifically mentioned shall be construed to be included to make a complete installation.

Provide and install all soil, waste, vent pipes and cleanouts for all sewer lines in accordance with local code. Provide proper drainage where necessary and ensure that all stub-outs are properly capped.

Pipe and fitting sizes shall be as per plans. Where discrepancies may occur with local codes and installation recommendations, such codes and recommendations shall prevail.

Provide and install all soil, waste, vent pipes and cleanouts for all sewer lines in accordance with local code. Provide proper drainage where necessary and ensure that all stub-outs are properly capped.

Provide and install type K copper pipe for all underground potable water service and connections. Use Type K or L copper pipe for all potable water above grade piping.

If gas is used for heating and/or hot water heat, gas piping shall be schedule 40, black steel pipe. All below-grade gas pipe and gas pipe exposed to the atmosphere shall be wrapped with a polyethylene coating.

Insulate all cold and hot water piping as required by local codes and ordinances. Hold installation to inside of building insulation to prevent freezing.

The plumbing fixture schedule is as follows:

```
Handicap Water Closet: American "Cadet" #2108.408 — 18" high
     Church #295, or equal
Lavatories: Custom-designed cultured marble one-piece
     lavatory tops w/basins integral (color and style to be
     selected by owner)
Mop Basin: Stainless Steel by Elkay, or equal
```

THE PIPING AND PLUMBING ESTIMATE

Refer to Plans, Sheet C–2, Plot Plan; Sheet A–1, Architectural Floor Plan; Sheets P–1 and P–2, Isometric Plans. A piping and plumbing estimate is somewhat more difficult than some other systems since there is no pictorial plan for dimensioning and sizing. The estimator must determine the location of entry of the piping and exit for the sewer line at the structure to be able to calculate the lengths. The point of entry or exit is then identified on the floor plan or an overlay used with the plumbing and floor plans. An estimate can be made using these locations, the isometrics, and the fixture schedules.

See figure 12–2 and chart 12–1. The estimate for the Medical Clinic in figure 12–2 is an example of a standard type estimate/summary sheet. It is again recommended that the estimator separates each category of work; that is, one section for piping work and another for plumbing work. It cannot be reiterated enough that, for the sake of clarity and for the prevention of errors, it is advisable to have various colored pencils or highlighters to mark the items and areas as they are estimated.

Piping Estimate

Refer to Plans, Sheet C–2, Plot Plan; Sheet P–1, Piping Plan. An investigation of the city records indicates that the street where the Medical Clinic is to be built is 36'-0" (10.97 m) wide. The 4" (10.16 cm) water main is centered in the street at a depth of 30" (0.76 m). The 8" (20.32 cm) sewer line is located on the side nearest the project, approximately one-fourth the width of the street at a depth of 36" (0.91 m).

The plot plan indicates that the sewer and water lines enter at or near the center of the east wall of the structure. The building setback is 40'-0" (12.19 m) from the property line. The berm between the curb and sidewalk is 5'-0" (1.52 m) and the sidewalk is 5'-0" (1.52 m) wide. The area between the sidewalk and the property line is 3'-0" (0.91 m) wide.

The potable water supply enters from the street at a point centered below and between the two center windows on the east end of the building. According to the schedule in figure 12–1, either copper, galvanized, or PVC pipe may be used. The Specifications indicate copper is to be used.

It is also important to consider the trench to be dug. The depth of the trench depends upon the depth of the frost line and the depth of the water main. If the depth exceeds 5' (1.52 m), shoring must be added. The frost line depth in Caliente, Nevada, is minimal (1'-6" or 0.46 m) and, therefore, of little concern. The primary concern is the depth of the main. According to the plans of the city, the diameter of the main is 4" (10.16 cm) and the depth is 30" (0.76 m) below finish rough grade. Therefore, the trench may slope from as shallow as 24" (0.61 m) at the structure to 30" (0.76 m) at the main. The

				MATERIALS			LABOR			
PROJECT	Caliente Medical Clinic						JOB ADDRESS	Broadway & Main Sts	DATE	9/15/92
OWNER	Dr. Robin Sims							Caliente, NV	ESTIMATE #	MC2-92
OWNER ADDRESS	50 Broadway, Caliente, NV						CONTACT	Project Mgr — McKay	SHEET #	1 of 2
ARCHITECT/ENGINEER	Mar-Jo International, Inc.						PHONE #	(333)555-2233 BID DATE 11/6/92	PLAN DATE	5/3/92

ACCT NO	DESCRIPTION	Size	MATERIALS Piece	Unit Price	Extension	Crew Size	MH/MD Rate	Extension	TOTAL
1450	Off-site Piping:								
.01	"tap	4" to 1"							
.02	"corporate cock	1"							
.03	"curb cock	1"							
.04	"meter	1" to 1"							
.05	"meter box & cover	std							
.30	"union (2 ea)	1"							
	*NOTE: all of the above items may be be supplied and installed by city								
.10	type K copper pipe	1"							
.30	solder union, 2 ea	1"							
.40	solder elbow, 6 ea	1"							
.45	solder tee	1" to 1/2"							
.50	solder valve, main	1"							
.55	solder hose bibb	1/2"							
.100	solder, flux type	1 can							

FIGURE 12-2

Piping Estimate: Potable Water

Length of trench and piping per plot plan = 140 lf or 42.67 m
Volume of trench - 140 lf (length) × 2.5 lf (average depth) × 2.0 lf (width) (42.67 m × 0.76 m × 0.61 m):

V = (lwh) ÷ 27 cu ft	V = (lwh)
V = (140 lf × 2.5 lf × 2 lf) ÷ 27 cu ft	V = (42.67 m × 0.76 m × 0.61 m)
V = (140 lf × 5 sq ft) ÷ 27 cu ft	V = (42.67 m × 0.46 m²)
V = 700 cu ft ÷ 27 cu ft	**V = 19.63 or 20 m³**
V = 25.93 or 26 cu yd	

Volume of backfill (including expansion factor - 20%):

V = 26 cu yd × 1.20 = **31.2 or 32 cu yd**   V = 20 m³ × 1.20 = **24 m³**

CHART 12—1
Piping Estimate: Trenching and Filling

trench should be 2'-0" (0.61 m) wide to make access for both the sewer drain pipe and the water pipe. The expense of the trenching, backfilling, and resurfacing of the street must be included in the labor and/or equipment costs.

It is possible that the city may install the line from the tap to, and including, the curb cock or meter. This is an issue which the estimator must address. If the city installs the line, the 18 lf of pipe and trenching from the street main must be deducted from the estimate.

The plumbing contractor must also take into consideration the removal of the excess earth. Per federal and/or state Department of Transportation (D.O.T.) regulations and city ordinances, sand or Type II fill must be used to replace the removed earth when the pipe is installed. The contractor doing the work must also always call an information hot line provided by the utility companies such as "Call Before You Dig" to confirm there are no obstructions in the line of the excavation.

The interior piping estimate is determined from measurements on the floor plan for the location of the fixtures and the isometric plan for the piping sizes and connections. The cabinetry is already estimated by the cabinetmaker. The concerns for the plumbing estimate are the piping, fittings, and fixtures to be installed in the cabinetry. The entry into the structure at the crawl space is 18" (0.46 m) below the floor (under the joists and beam support) approximately at the center of the east wall. The main valve is on the exterior side of the wall at the entry point, with a hose bibb attached. The piping then continues in a straight line to the rear of the building to the hose bibb connected at the exterior rear wall. All horizontal piping is underfloor (in the crawl space).

A possible alternate to the estimate would include the piping from the split heat-pump units in the ceiling to the compressor/condenser unit at the west wall. The line is made up of 1" (2.54 cm) type L copper pipe.

Plumbing Estimate

Refer to Plans, Sheet C–2, Plot Plan; Sheet P–2, Plumbing. Cast iron, galvanized iron, copper, or plastic (ABS) pipe may be used. The length of the drainage system is the same as the piping less the distance between the sewer main and the water main. The interior plumbing measurements are determined in the same manner as the piping, with the sizes noted.

CREW	HOURLY + BURDEN WAGE	% TIME ON JOB/HR	HOURLY RATE
Foreman	$18.49 + $4.20	10%	= $ 2.27
Plumber	$17.99 + $4.20	42%	= $ 9.32
Equipment Operator	$16.45 + $3.40	13%	= $ 2.58
Apprentice (2)	$11.75 + $3.74 × 2	35%	= $10.84
Composite Crew Rate:		100%	$25.01/MH

FIGURE 12–3a
Composite Crew Schedule

CREW	HOURLY WAGE + BURDEN
Foreman	$18.49 + $ 4.20
Plumber	$17.99 + $ 4.20
Equipment Operator	$16.45 + $ 3.40
Apprentice (2)	$11.75 + $ 3.74 × 2
	$76.43 + $19.28 = $95.71
Composite Crew Rate:	$95.71/4 = $23.93

FIGURE 12–3b
Composite Crew Schedule

Plumbing Labor

See figure 12–3a and figure 12–3b, Composite Crew Schedule: Plumbing. The crew consists of a foreman, a plumber, 2 apprentices, and a backhoe operator. The work is completed in 7 days. The productivity rate is 76%. The labor cost is calculated as follows:

70% ÷ 66% = 1.06 (productivity factor)

Method 12–3a:
$25.01/MH × 1.06 = $26.51/MH
$26.51/MH × 5 workers × 8 hr = $1,060.40/CD
$1,060.40/CD × 7 days = $7,422.80 or $7,423.00

Method 12–3b:
$23.93/MH × 1.06 = $25.37/MH
$25.37/MH × 5 workers × 8 hr = $1,014.80/CD
$1,014.80/CD × 7 days = $7,103.60 or $7,104.00

FIGURE 12–4
Equipment Schedule

EQUIPMENT	USE TIME	UNIT COST	TOTAL
Transportation	7 days	@ $10/day	= $ 70.00
Back-hoe	1 day	@ $175/day	= $175.00
Torch	3 days	@ $15/day	= $ 75.00
Chipper	5 days	@ $27.50/day	= $ 82.50
Test Equipment	1 day	@ $60/day	= $ 60.00
Equipment Total:			$462.50

Plumbing Equipment

See figure 12–4. The crew needs a back-hoe for trenching, transportation (includes personnel carrier and tools), a torch for sweating piping, hammer jack (chipper), and test equipment.

GENERAL MECHANICAL (HVAC) INFORMATION

HVAC equipment includes the units, the controls, insulation, ductwork and attachments, registers, and grilles for heating, ventilation, and cooling installations. Thermal insulation is used with any piping, ductwork, and equipment that are a part of the mechanical installation. The types and densities of insulation manufactured for refrigeration and/or air-conditioning equipment vary considerably from the types of insulation discussed in Division 7. The equipment ranges from condensers and condensing units to chillers and water towers, including liquid heat-transfer systems such as heat pumps, packaged air-conditioning units, humidifiers, and dehumidifiers.

See figure 12–5. The pictorial diagram is an example of a reversing heat-transfer unit. In one phase, the liquid is being cooled; in the other, the liquid is being heated. To better understand some of the complexities of heat exchange, consider the automobile engine. The engine can be compared to a liquid-fuel-burning boiler for a large commercial structure. The fuel heats the engine (boiler), which heats the oil used to reduce the friction in the moving parts. A coolant mixture (chiller liquid) is circulated by a pump through the engine block (the heat-transfer unit) surrounding the fuel-burning system. The coolant "absorbs" and removes the heat, passes through the radiator (chiller), and returns to the engine block (the heat-transfer unit) to remove more heat. In the process, heat is also produced for use in the passenger compartment of the automobile (office area). A secondary unit (liquid-transfer unit) is installed to supply chilled air, using the heat-transfer process between the engine (boiler) coolant and the liquefied cooling agent in the air-conditioning unit (heat-transfer unit).

See figure 12–6. Another form of heat transfer is the solar-powered heat transfer unit. The unit is a panel installed on a roof or in the open where the sun may generate its heat most of the day. This solar heat transfer unit heats the liquid (water, coolant) passing through the piping to a hot-water storage tank or heating/cooling unit. From that point, the system operates in the same manner as other liquid transfer units.

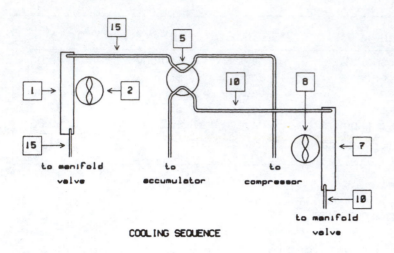

COOLING SEQUENCE

KEYNOTES:

1. (Self-contained) Condenser
   (Multi-service) Cooling tower
2. Condenser fan
3. Accumulator/Heat exchanger
   (self-contained and multi-service)
4. Liquid vapor lines
5. Reversing valve
6. Dry vapor line
7. Unit output condenser
8. Condenser fan
9. Unit compressor
10. Liquid line
11. Heating/Cooling coil
12. Filter
13. Sub-cooling control valve
14. Dual manifold check valve
15. Vapor lines

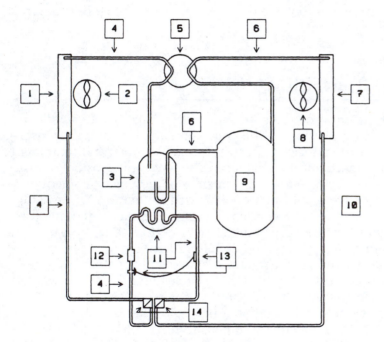

HEATING SEQUENCE

FIGURE 12–5
Heat Exchange/Heat Pump System

See Plans, Sheet M–1, Reflected Ceiling Plan—HVAC; Sheet M–2, Mechanical Schedules. See also figure 12–7. Air-handling and air distribution systems are also a part of the mechanical installation. Various types of air intake and exhaust fans, air-cleaning devices, air curtain walls, and even sound attenuators may be included. These units do not produce a change in temperature; they only move air through a structure. The unit of measure for air-handling capacities is "cubic feet per minute" (CFM). The manufacturer of a unit will indicate the rating (e.g., 250 CFM [7.08 m^3/min]). Some units are designed for air intake, while others are designed for air exhaust; some are reversible and serve both purposes as needed.

KEYNOTES:

1. Insulated panel box
2. Plate glass or plastic cover
3. Cool air flow line from return
   air system
4. Warm air flow line to appliance
5. Heat absorber
6. 3/4" copper tubing cool liquid
   flow line
7. 3/8" copper tubing riser
8. 3/4" copper tubing warm liquid
   flow line
9. Warm liquid receiving gutter
10. Parabolic reflector
11. Absorber tubing
12. Cool liquid flow line
13. Warm liquid flow line
14. Partial vacuum space

NOTES: Arrows indicate direction of
       flow. Directions vary as
       indicated depending upon
       flow line connections.
       Single solar units shown.

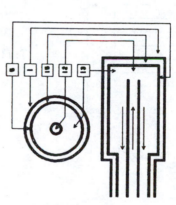

PARABOLIC REFLECTOR

EVACUATED TUBE COLLECTOR

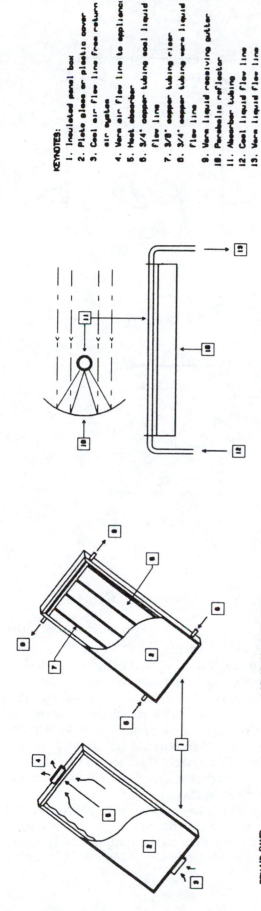

LIQUID TRANSFER PANEL

DRY AIR PANEL

TRICKLE PANEL

FIGURE 12-6
Solar Heating Panel

253

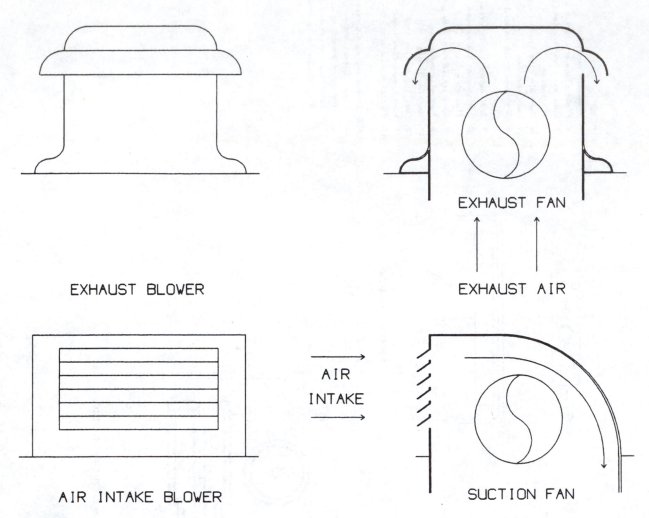

EXHAUST BLOWER

EXHAUST FAN

EXHAUST AIR

AIR INTAKE BLOWER

AIR INTAKE

SUCTION FAN

FIGURE 12–7
Air-Handling Units

HVAC systems vary in size and location within structures, according to climatic conditions. A unit installed in structures of identical size and design *primarily for heating has a smaller demand rating than a unit installed primarily for cooling* because fewer British Thermal Units (BTU) are required for heating than for cooling. The heating system required for cooler areas of the country are likely to be installed in the basement. Units required for warmer areas are likely to be installed in a special utility closet, on the roof of a structure or, as in the case of the heat pump, in an attic space. The system installed in the Medical Clinic is a type more suitable to the warmer areas of the country, which require more cooling than heating, and is installed in the attic.

There are two types of heat-pump installation: (1) the split system, which utilizes space in the interior of the structure for the heating or cooling unit while the compressor is installed somewhere next to the building on the outside and (2) a totally self-contained unit (package unit). The self-contained unit is the type installed in the Medical Clinic.

The Relationship of the HVAC and Electrical Trades

There are instances where the responsibilities of the mechanical and electrical trades may appear to overlap. The division of responsibilities must be specified for each installation. There are two ways in which the mechanical and electrical contractors may be required to interact. In most instances, the agreement is the normal relationship between the trades and is specified in a manner similar to the following:

1. The installation and maintenance of all wiring and conduit from the power supply to the disconnect controlling the HVAC unit is the responsibility of the electrical contractor.
2. The conduit installation for the thermostat cable is the responsibility of the electrical contractor.
3. The supply, installation, and maintenance of the units and internal controls and wiring, including the thermostat cable from the unit, is the responsibility of the HVAC contractor.

This is not always the case. An alternate specification may require the following:

1. The installation of the conduit and wiring from the power supply, the disconnect, and the internal wiring of the control system, including the thermostat cable, are the responsibility of the electrician.
2. The HVAC contractor is responsible only for the installation of the equipment and maintenance of the mechanical parts within the unit.

If no division of responsibility is specified, it is up to the owner and contractors to establish such responsibility prior to contract.

SCOPE OF WORK

The Project Manual, appendix IV, Division 15, mechanical specifications are as follows:

Division 15: Mechanical

15000 Scope of Work

Division 1 and the General Conditions are to be considered a part of this division. Furnish all labor, materials and equipment necessary to complete all work under this division and as indicated on drawings.

15050 Basic Mechanical Materials and Methods

In addition to the requirements stated in Section 15000, the mechanical contractor shall be governed by the regulations established by professional engineers who have designed the installation and material requirements. The mechanical contractor shall also be governed by the regulations of ASHRAE and OSHA and by national, regional and/or local mechanical and plumbing codes, where applicable. The materials used shall be as specified in the following sections.

15500 Heating, Ventilation And Air Conditioning

Mechanical contractor shall supply shop drawings for the installation of the HVAC system, if required. All fees and permits for the HVAC installation are at the expense of the mechanical contractor. The HVAC equipment shall be manufactured by Lennox Corporation, or equal.

The mechanical contractor shall propose a self-contained HVAC unit. The system contains two 3-ton, self-contained, heat exchangers with all accessories necessary for a complete installation, including, but not limited to, ductwork, grilles, registers and other fittings as necessary, installed in the ceiling. The thermostat controls shall operate both manually and automatically. See HVAC Plan, M-1.

Coordinate all work with the plumbing and electrical contractors where required.

End of Division

THE MECHANICAL ESTIMATE

See figure 12–8. The same type of estimate sheet used for the plumbing may be used for the mechanical estimate. The estimator may wish to separate each category of work when an estimate sheet is used, that is, one sheet for the HVAC units and ductwork and another for the piping to connect the units to an exterior compressor unit (if necessary). It is also wise, since there are several different items to be counted or calculated, to have various colored pencils or highlighters to mark the items or areas as they are estimated. In this manner, it is easy to note where there is anything missed.

Refer to Plans, Sheet A–1, Architectural Floor Plan; Sheet M–1, Reflected Ceiling Plan—HVAC Sheet M–2, Mechanical Schedules. The plan is calculated to standards established for Las Vegas, Nevada. Calculations for mechanical installations are already a part of the schedules shown on the Mechanical Plan. The estimator has only to follow the information shown for the units. There are only two schedules on the drawings. There may be several schedules dependent upon the complexity of the project.

A dual heat-pump system is indicated. Each unit handles the cooling, heating, and air exchange for one half of the building. The drawing describes the location and size of the heat pumps, the **supply and return ductwork, diffusers** for the air supply, and **grilles** for the air return. Also noted are the size of the duct and the CFM ratings at all supply outlets. The ductwork for the Medical Clinic is flexible insulated duct with special connections at the units and the air-supply outlets, called **transitions (TR),** used where duct dimensions change. The transition may be straight, a tee, or an elbow.

A shop drawing is required only for prefabricated metal ductwork. Prefabricated metal ductwork, such as structural steel detailing, requires such drawings to identify sizes and connections from the unit to, and including, all diffusers and grilles. Each part is specially fabricated and identified for installation

PROJECT **Medical Clinic**   JOB ADDRESS **Main & Broadway**   DATE **8/24/92**

OWNER **Dr. R. Stone & Assoc.**   **Caliente, NV**   ESTIMATE # **9214**

OWNER ADDRESS **50 Broadway, Caliente, NV**   CONTACT **Tepper McKey, PM**   SHEET # **1**

ARCHITECT/ENGINEER **W.T. Pender, PE**   PHONE # **(333)555-2233**   BID DATE **11/5/92**   PLAN DATE **5/3/92**

ACCT NO	DESCRIPTION	MATERIALS				LABOR			TOTAL
		Size	Piece	Unit Price	Extension	Crew Size	MH/MD Rate	Extension	
1401	Heat Pump	3-Ton	2 ea	$3,500 ea	$7,000.00				
1420	Air Devices:								
d1 8	Diffuser, Lay-in	8"x8"	4 ea	$45.85 ea	$183.40				
ds 8	Diffuser, Surface	8"x8"	5 ea	$43.75 ea	$218.75				
ds10	Diffuser, Surface	10"x10"	9 ea	$52.36 ea	$471.24				
g 24	Grille, Lay-in	24"x24"	4 ea	$38.12 ea	$152.48				
1450	Duct, insulated, flexible, round:								
d 6	"	6"ø							
d 7	"	7"ø							
d 8	"	8"ø							
d 9	"	8"ø							
d10	"	10"ø							
d12	"	12"ø							
d14	"	14"ø							
d18	"	18"ø							
1460	Transitions:								

FIGURE 12-8
Mechanical Estimate

257

CREW	HOURLY + BURDEN WAGE	% TIME ON JOB/HR	HOURLY RATE
Foreman	$18.45 + $4.20	16%	= $ 3.62
Technician (2)	$17.99 + $4.20 × 2	38%	= $16.86
Equipment Operator	$16.45 + $3.40	8%	= $ 1.59
Apprentice (2)	$11.75 + $3.74 × 2	38%	= $11.77
Composite Crew Rate:		100%	$33.84/MH

FIGURE 12–9a
Composite Crew Schedule

CREW	HOURLY WAGE + BURDEN
Foreman	$18.45 + $ 4.20
Technician (2)	$17.99 + $ 4.20 × 2
Equipment Operator	$16.45 + $ 3.40
Apprentice (2)	$11.75 + $ 3.74 × 2
	$94.38 + $23.48 = $117.86
Composite Crew Rate:	$117.86/4 = $29.47

FIGURE 12–9b
Composite Crew Schedule

location and size. Systems using metal ductwork and requiring shop drawings are prepared primarily for large commercial and/or industrial structures.

The estimator has two quantities to complete the rough estimate, the lineal feet of duct in each size, and count-ups for the specific parts. Count-ups include the heat pumps, diffusers, grilles, transitions, tees, collars (clamps for fastening the parts together), and any controls (thermostats, and so on).

There are several combinations that could be made in each area. Each estimator may see the project differently. The most cost-effective method is the one the estimator should choose.

HVAC Labor

See figure 12–9a and 12–9b, Composite Crew Schedule: Mechanical. The crew required for the installation is basically the same as for the plumbing. The crew includes the foreman, 2 plumbers, and 2 apprentices. The project is completed in 10 working days. The productivity rate is 76%. The total labor cost is calculated as follows:

70% ÷ 76% = 0.92

Method 12–9a:

$33.84/MH × 0.92 = $31.13/MH

$31.13/MH × 5 workers × 8 hr = $1,245.20/CD

$1,245.20 × 10 days = $12,452.00

EQUIPMENT	USE TIME	UNIT COST	TOTAL
Transportation	10 days	@ $10/day	= $100.00
Forklift	2 days	@ $85/day	= $170.00
Block and Fall	2 days	@ $5/day	= $ 10.00
Test Equipment	1 day	@ $60/day	= $ 60.00
Equipment Total:			$340.00

FIGURE 12–10
Equipment Schedule

Method 12–9b:

$29.47/MH $\times$ 0.92 = $27.11/MH

$27.11/MH $\times$ 5 workers $\times$ 8 hr = $1,084.40/CD

$1,084.40/CD $\times$ 10 days = $10,844.00

HVAC Equipment

See figure 12–10. A means of transportation for the crew, a forklift, or block-and-fall for lifting the units into place in the ceiling, and test equipment are the basic company-supplied tools for the HVAC crew.

CHAPTER EXERCISES

1. Match the following pipe sizes and types, and the fittings from the street to the Medical Clinic structure per the plot plan and isometric plan:

   1. Connected at structure entry
   2. Supplied by local water department
   3. 2 required at meter box
   4. Installed at front and rear exterior
   5. For hose bibb connection
   6. 75 lf (22.86 m) from street to structure
   7. Connection at street main
   8. Valve for shut-off at meter (street)
   9. Valve for meter shut-off
   10. Access for meter and valve
   11. For positioning of hose bibbs

   ____ a. 1" (2.54 cm) type K soft copper pipe
   ____ b. 4" to 1" (10.16 cm to 2.54 cm) tap
   ____ c. 1" (2.54 cm) corporate cock
   ____ d. 1" (2.54 cm) curb cock
   ____ e. meter
   ____ f. box w/cover
   ____ g. 1" (2.54 cm) main valve
   ____ h. 1/2" (1.27 cm) hose bibb
   ____ i. 1" to 1/2" (2.54 cm to 1.27 cm) tee
   ____ j. 1" (2.54 cm) elbows
   ____ k. 1" (2.54 cm) unions

2. How many and what size transitions are necessary to connect the south unit to—

Examination room #1?
Examination room #2?
Examination room #3?

3. Several transition combinations can be connected at examination room #1. Is a 9" DIA to 7" DIA (22.86 cm DIA to 17.78 cm DIA) elbow one of them? Why or why not?

4. What is the total length and size of duct necessary to complete the air supply for the south unit? Calculate in both feet and inches and metric measure.

5. Count the number of angle stops required for all the fixtures in the Medical Clinic.

6. There are _____ clean-outs in the drainage system.

7. How high are the vent stacks to extend beyond the roof? Check local codes.
   a. 6" (15.24 cm)
   b. 4" (10.16 cm)
   c. 12" (30.48 cm)
   d. 9" (22.86 cm)

8. Assuming the curb, gutter, and sidewalk were installed prior to the project, how best would the sewer and water taps be installed?
   a. Break up the concrete and trench through; then replace the curb, gutter and sidewalk, and resod or reseed the berm.
   b. Tunnel under the curb, gutter, sidewalk, and berm; then dig down in the berm area to install shut-off cocks, meter, and boxes.
   c. Tunnel under the curb, gutter, sidewalk, and berm; then place the shut-off cocks and meter in a convenient place inside the property line near the sidewalk.
   d. Dig up everything and forget replacement of the curb, gutter, and sidewalk. Let the owner and/or city replace the curb, gutter, sidewalk, and berm.
   e. Trench from the structure to the sidewalk and from the gutter to the main. Drive the pipe through the earth under the curb, gutter, and sidewalk; install corporate and curb cocks and meter inside the property line in a convenient area, and then close the trench.

9. A back-hoe and operator are hired to cut the trench. The operation takes 2 normal work days. The total cost for the work is $1,600.00. How much is the cost per hour for the back-hoe and operator? How much is the cost for the operator per hour if the rig cost is $85.00/hr?

10. The total fixture cost (including faucets) for the plumbing amounts to $8,200. Determine the average cost per fixture.

11. With the information given in questions 9 and 10, add the following additional material, labor, and equipment costs for piping and plumbing:
   a. Piping costs   = $ 4,325.00
   b. Plumbing costs   = $ 5,175.00
   c. Backfill and backfilling   = $ 100.00
   d. Labor costs (excluding trenching)   = $ 6,150.00
   e. Equipment costs (excluding trenching) = $ 450.00
      The total is   = $ _____

12. Prepare an alternate estimate for the HVAC according to the following specifications for appendix IV, Alternate #6, Division 1, Section 01310, in the Project Manual.

Alternate #6. If the owner chooses the BUR system the following specifications shall apply to the installation of the HVAC system.

15500 Heating, Ventilation, and Air Conditioning

The units shall be split units with the compressors placed on slab next to the electrical switchgear cabinet(s) and the air-handler units installed in the utility room. In lieu of return air being directed to the ceilings in both halls, all return air shall return to a plenum in the base of the walls on both sides of the utility room. All supply air shall be directed through the suspended ceilings into wall registers placed adjacent to the finish ceiling in each area. Supply requirements shall remain the same.

13. The new HVAC unit costs $10,000.00 installed. The balance of the materials cost $3,250.00. The labor cost is calculated at $35.00/lf. Equipment costs are $750.00 above the original estimate. What is the total cost for the HVAC installation?

CHAPTER 13

Electrical

Division 16

The electrical specifications include information on raceways (troughs, trays, conduit), low- and high-voltage distribution, alarms, communications equipment, special circuitry, such as emergency equipment circuitry, and isolation circuits for computer and other sensitive electronic equipment.

GENERAL ELECTRICAL INFORMATION

The primary code followed by the electrician is the National Electric Code (NEC), as established by the National Fire Protection Association (NFPA). There are separate requirements established for safety and special equipment for residential construction, large institutions, commercial buildings, industrial complexes, special occupancies (hospitals, nursing homes, mobile home parks), and hazardous locations (gas stations and volatile storage areas). The electrical code applications established locally throughout the United States are all based upon the NEC. The codes may expand upon the basic NEC requirements as fits local requirements, but they may *not* lower the NEC standards.

All code requirements refer to both indoor and outdoor installations. The term *indoor* refers to the on-site lighting and power equipment within the structure—from the entry switchgear to the light switches, receptacles, and electrical appliances. *Outdoor* deals with the site improvement lighting, power, and equipment. Off-site areas may also be included in the construction requirements.

Just as in mechanical specifications, the general requirements concerning the electrical trades for a project are established by an electrical engineer and are in addition to the requirements of Division 1. The owner and architect suggest what is needed or wanted and the engineer designs and calculates the load requirements and provides the complete layout for the project. Therefore, the electrical drawings, information, placement, instructions, sizing, and so on, *take precedence* over architectural design or information. The specific manufacturers, suppliers, materials, approvals, and guidelines for the methods of installation are written by the electrical engineer. One-line pictorials, schematics, and schedules are aids to the installation. Any deviation from the approved methods described must have prior approval from the engineer.

The following information regarding power generation, transmission, and distribution is supplied to give the student knowledge of the extent of the electrical specifications.

The provisions for power generation deal with the installation of all electrical components such as transformers, generators, motors, switchgear, metering, and disconnects. The installations are governed by the codes established by utility companies and the NEC. Electrical power and generation electrical equipment necessary to produce a circuit is supported by the mechanical and plumbing power and generation installations described in chapter 12.

The electrical installation procedures, materials, and equipment are governed by regulations of the utilities and the NEC covering the *transmission of electricity over 600 volts* from the generating station to the substation supplying the user. Structures such as switching stations and substations, towers, wire sizes and types, switchgear, metering, disconnecting means, and all accessories of the equipment are included.

The installation and materials required for power *under 600 volts* such as overhead or underground (lateral) feeders from the local transformer to the consumer switchgear or residential service entrance is referred to as **electrical distribution.** As with transmission circuitry, this category includes wire sizes and types, switchgear, metering, disconnecting means, and all accessories of the equipment. The installation procedures, materials, and equipment are also governed by regulations of the utilities and the NEC.

The following electrical information pertains to the areas that govern the electrical installation for the Medical Clinic, including interior general power and lighting, special systems, and communications.

Lighting specifications actually include general interior lighting and power, as well as exterior parking lot lighting and special entry or emergency lighting. For purposes of calculating electrical loads for distribution on a project, the NEC divides interior general lighting from special lighting circuits but includes the regular 120 VAC receptacles as a part of the circuit load calculations. The types of lamps, wire sizes, and installation techniques are also a part of this section. It is standard procedure for the engineer, when calculating these loads, to include both general lighting and power.

Systems used for emergency lighting such as uninterruptible power supply, battery power supply, or engine-driven generator supply are considered **special systems.** These systems are used primarily in institutional, hospital, clinics, and some commercial applications. The systems are installed to prevent loss of lifesaving lighting and equipment power in the event of a power failure. Also included under the classification of special systems are installation requirements for hazardous locations, mobile home parks, and signage.

The installation requirements for alarm, clock, voice (telephone, and so on), data (computers and computer networks), public address, music, television, microwave, and earth satellite station systems are all considered **communications circuitry.** The work involved with these systems is divided into two classifications:

1. The first includes the basic electrical systems supplying the raceways and power supply to them.
2. The second refers to the electronic systems necessitating specially trained technicians. Each system has its own contracting, estimating, and installation techniques.

Heating and cooling are also a part of the electrical trade specifications. *See section titled "The HVAC and Electrical Trades Relationship" in chapter 12.*

Electric resistance heating, another category of heating and cooling, includes special heating of plumbing and fuel lines to prevent freezing, such as the use of heat-resistant cables and mats, as well as baseboard, floor, space, and portable electric heating units.

Metering devices, recording devices, relays, solid-state control panels, and the boards or panels upon which they are placed are all part of the **controls and instrumentation specifications.** These may control any part of the electrical system from generation to consumer equipment control (lighting, stage equipment, motor control, emergency equipment, and so on), including schedules located within the plans. Some schematics and manufacturer instructions are also included.

SCOPE OF WORK

The Project Manual, appendix IV, Division 16, specifications for all of the electrical work for the Medical Clinic includes the following:

Division 16: Electrical

16000 Scope of Work

Division 1 and the General Conditions are to be considered a part of this division. Furnish all labor, materials and equipment necessary to complete all work under this division and as indicated on drawings.

16050 Basic Electrical Materials and Methods

In addition to the requirements stated in Section 16000, the electrical contractor shall be governed by the regulations established by professional engineers who have designed the installation and material requirements. The electrical contractor shall also conform to the latest edition of the NEC, OSHA, regional and/or local electrical codes, where applicable. The materials used shall be as specified in the following sections.

16400 Service and Distribution

Provide for an adequate service and grounding system as shown on drawings and as described in the specifications. Conduit shall be used as a continuous ground path from appliance to distribution center. A complete equipment ground conductor shall also be supplied from each appliance to the distribution center.

All materials shall be new and supplied by one manufacturer with shipping crates intact. The contractor shall be provided with proof of manufacturer's shipping record. All materials selected shall be as indicated in the specifications and/or electrical schedules. All equipment shall have a label and/or stamp from an approved testing laboratory such as Underwriters Laboratories (UL), and all motorized and switchgear equipment shall have nameplates which shall be supplied with the equipment. All disconnects shall be rated NEMA 1 enclosures.

The electrical contractor shall coordinate all installation with the local utility company and shall provide connections for service when all service is inspected and approved. The electrical contractor shall further coordinate all hookups with contractors of other trades where cooperation is necessary for speedy execution of the contract.

Acceptable manufacturers of the switchgear equipment are:

Square D   General Electric

White/Westinghouse   ITT

There shall be two (2) distribution panels as a part of the entry switchgear, one (1) for power and one (1) for lighting.

16500 Lighting (General Lighting and Power)

See Electrical Plans, E-1 and E-2. All standard lighting switches shall be Hubbell 1221-1, or equal. All duplex receptacles shall be Hubbell 5262-1, or equal. All 3-wire receptacles shall be as required for usage by Hubbell, or equal (minimum 25A, 240VAC). All GFCI receptacles shall be GE-TGTR115F, or equal.

Exterior lighting installations shall be underground using schedule 80 electrical PVC conduit.

The electrical contractor has the liberty to make the best application with the least cost and still acceptable to all codes and regulations. Sizes of conduit shall be determined by the electrical contractor with all connections, accessories and wiring to be in accordance with code. The minimum allowable size and insulation type of conductor shall be #12AWG, THHN, for power and exterior lighting circuits, and #14AWG, THHN, for interior lighting circuits.

The electrical contractor shall install an empty conduit for thermostat wiring.

16600 Special Systems

A special emergency system shall be installed for use in the event of power failure. The system shall be self-contained in an enclosure next to the main switchgear and shall include a throw-over switch, a battery supply and a gas-driven (natural or butane) generator. Proper ventilation shall be maintained for this system at all times. The generator shall be of sufficient size to maintain power and lighting for the Operating Room and X-Ray Laboratory as well as for all emergency lighting. The engineer shall supply load calculations.

16700 Communications

A special conduit and a special circuit shall be installed for an isolated computer system with additional junctions supplied in each office for networking.

The electrical contractor shall install an empty conduit for telephone communications and for intercom and fire alarm systems. The systems are to be installed by communications specialists who shall supply drawings and specifications to the owner for approval.

End of Division

THE ESTIMATE

See Plans, Sheet E–1, Electrical Plot Plan; Sheet E–2, Electrical Power Plan; Sheet E–3, Lighting Plan; Sheet E–4, Schedules. The plot plan introduces the utility easement, the supply transformer, the trenching required, the exterior power plan, and the lighting for the parking areas, driveways, and entries. The power plan includes the layout for all receptacles and special equipment connections. The lighting plan includes the interior lighting and the emergency lighting systems. The schedules indicate the special equipment and lighting specified to be used in the installation of the Medical Clinic.

It is of utmost importance that the estimator be as knowledgeable as possible of the NEC manual and that he or she knows where in the code the information is located. If additional help is required for interpretation of plans or codes, the estimator should ask for assistance from the engineer, the local building department electrical planner, or the electrical inspector.

See figure 13–1. Checklists are used to ensure that all equipment is included in the estimate. It is recommended that separate sheets be used for each phase of the project. Multistory construction, for example, would use one sheet for each phase and floor. Lighting is separate from power, motors, and so on.

The Site Improvements and Off-Sites

All materials required for power and lighting distribution outside the structure are the site improvements or off-sites, which include the transformer, trenching, conductors and cables, pole foundations, and light poles and fixtures. Some questions that the estimator should get answered are the following:

Is the utility transformer existing, or is it to be installed specifically for this project?

Is the transformer the responsibility of the utility company, or is it part of the contract?

Who installs the secondary taps at the transformer, the contractor or the utility?

Is the trenching to be done in a single operation or in two or three separate "digs"?

What are the soil conditions? Should a regular back-hoe or a hoe-ram be used?

May the main feeder trench be used for branch circuits, or are separate trenches required for them?

Trenching.   Local code requirements regarding frost line, power supply location, and backfill materials will dictate the trench necessary for the lateral feeders. The NEC determines the minimum size of the feeders dependent upon the load calculations. The local building department may also have regulations on the type of raceway (metal conduit, plastic conduit, concrete duct, or underground [USE] cable) that may be used in the trench. Per the NEC, the trench must be 24" (60.96 cm) deep and 12" (30.48 cm) wide (minimum) regardless of the type of raceway or cable installed.

Exterior Power and Lighting.   Exterior power and lighting may be fed from laterals or overheads. Where laterals are used, trenches must be dug to install

ELECTRICAL SPECIFICATION CHECKLIST

DATE _____

ELECTRICAL DIVISION: _____ PROJECT: _____

COMPLETED BY: _____ LOCATION: _____

Incoming Service: ☐ Overhead ☐ Underground

	Primary	Secondary
Voltage _____		
Units Sub-station & Size _____		
Number of Manholes _____		
Feeder Size _____		
Length _____		
Conduit _____		
Duct _____		
Concrete: ☐ No ☐ Yes		
Other _____		

Building Service: Size _____ Amps ____ Switchboard _____

Panels: ☐ Distribution _____ Lighting ____ Power _____

Describe _____

Motor Control Center: Furnished by _____

Describe _____

Bus Duct: ☐ No ☐ Yes Size _____ Amps Application _____

Describe _____

Cable Tray: ☐ No ☐ Yes Describe _____

Emergency System: ☐ No ☐ Yes Allowance _____ ☐ Separate Contract

Generator: ☐ No ☐ Diesel ☐ Gas ☐ Gasoline _____ Size _____ KW

Transfer Switch: ☐ No ☐ Yes Number _____ Size _____ KW

Area Protection Relay Panels: ☐ No ☐ Yes _____

Other _____

Conduit: ☐ No ☐ Yes ☐ Aluminum _____

　☐ Electric Metallic Tubing _____

　☐ Galvanized Steel _____

　☐ Plastic _____

Wire: ☐ No ☐ Yes ☐ Type Insulation _____

　☐ Armored Cable _____

　☐ Building Wire _____

　☐ Non-Metallic Sheath Cable _____

　☐ _____

Under floor Duct: ☐ No ☐ Yes Describe _____

Header Duct: ☐ No ☐ Yes Describe _____

Trench Duct: ☐ No ☐ Yes Describe _____

Underground Duct: ☐ No ☐ Yes Describe _____

Explosion Proof Areas: ☐ No ☐ Yes Describe _____

Motors: ☐ No ☐ Yes Total H.P. _____ No. of Fractional H.P. _____ Voltage _____

　☐ 1/2 to 5 H.P. _____ ☐ 7-1/2 to 25 H.P. _____ ☐ Over 25 H.P. _____

Describe _____

Starters: Type _____

　Supplied by: _____

FIGURE 13–1
Estimate Checklist

ELECTRICAL SPECIFICATION CHECKLIST (Continued)

ELECTRICAL DIVISION

Telephone System: ☐ No ☐ Yes Service Size _____ Length _____
    Manhole: ☐ No ☐ Yes Number _____ Termination _____
    Concrete Encased: ☐ No ☐ Yes ☐ Rigid Galv. ☐ Duct ☐ _____

Fire Alarm System: ☐ No ☐ Yes Service Size _____ Length _____ Wire Type _____
    Concrete Encased: ☐ No ☐ Yes ☐ Rigid Galv. ☐ Duct ☐ _____
    ☐ Stations _____ ☐ Horns _____ ☐ Lights _____ ☐ Combination _____
    Detectors: ☐ Rate of Rise _____ ☐ Fixed _____ ☐ Smoke _____
    Describe _____ Insulation _____ Wire Size _____
    ☐ Zones _____ ☐ Conduit _____ ☐ E.M.T. _____ ☐ Empty _____
    Describe _____ ☐ FACP Zones _____ ☐ Annunciator Panels _____

Security System: ☐ No ☐ Yes ☐ Stations ☐ Door Switches _____
    ☐ Alarm Bells _____ ☐ Key Re-sets _____ ☐ _____
    ☐ Conduit _____ ☐ E.M.T. _____ ☐ Wire _____ ☐ Empty _____
    Describe _____

Clock System: ☐ No ☐ Yes ☐ Electronic ☐ Wired ☐ _____
    ☐ Single Dial _____ ☐ Double Dial _____ ☐ Program Bell _____
    ☐ Conduit _____ ☐ E.M.T. _____ ☐ Empty _____
    Describe _____

Sound System: ☐ No ☐ Yes Type _____ Speakers _____
    ☐ Conduit _____ ☐ Cable _____ ☐ E.M.T. _____ ☐ Empty _____
    Describe _____

Television System: ☐ No ☐ Yes Describe _____
    ☐ Antenna _____ ☐ Closed Circuit _____ ☐ E.M.T. _____ ☐ Empty _____
    ☐ Learning Laboratory _____ ☐
    ☐ Conduit _____ ☐ E.M.T. _____ ☐ Wire _____ ☐ Empty _____

Lightning Protection: ☐ No ☐ Yes Describe _____

Low Voltage Switching: ☐ No ☐ Yes Describe _____

Scoreboard: ☐ No ☐ Yes Describe _____ Number _____

Comfort Systems: ☐ No ☐ Yes ☐ Electric Heat ☐ Snow Melting ☐ _____
    Describe _____

Other Systems: _____
_____
_____

Lighting Fixtures: ☐ No ☐ Yes ☐ Allowance _____ ☐ Separate Contract
    ☐ Economy ☐ Commercial ☐ Deluxe ☐ Explosion Proof ☐ _____
    ☐ Incandescent _____
    _____ Foot Candles _____
    ☐ Fluorescent _____
    _____ Foot Candles _____
    ☐ Mercury Vapor _____
    _____ Foot Candles _____
    ☐ _____ Foot Candles _____
    ☐ Step Lighting _____ ☐ Planter Lighting _____ ☐ Fountain Lighting _____
    ☐ Site Lighting _____ ☐ Poles _____ ☐ Area Lighting _____ ☐ Flood Lighting _____
    Dimming System: ☐ No ☐ Yes ☐ Incandescent ☐ Fluorescent
    Ceilings: ☐ T Bar ☐ Concealed Spline ☐ _____
    Emergency Battery Units: ☐ No ☐ Lead Acid ☐ Nickel Cadmium ☐ 6 Volt _____ 12 Volt _____
    Describe _____

Special Considerations: _____
_____

Special Items: _____
_____

Page 2 of 2

FIGURE 13–1
Estimate Checklist (Continued)

269

the wiring to and from the equipment. The type of lighting called out for the Medical Clinic are post lights; therefore, the lighting circuit trenches may be 18″ (45.72 cm) deep or less. The same trench used for the main supply feeder may be used for the branch circuits on that portion of the property. The size, type, foundation requirements, and wire size are normally provided by the manufacturer.

The size wire, the number of conductors, and any devices controlling the power and lighting must also be determined. The estimator may do the load calculations, although they are usually provided by the engineer. The load calculations help to determine the location of the overcurrent protection device (the circuit breaker or fuse) in the main switchgear panel supplied for the Clinic.

The On-Sites

The **service-entrance equipment** necessary for the Medical Clinic is a switchgear cabinet with built-in control panels for both the standard circuitry and the **uninterruptible power supply** (emergency power for the Operating Room, and so on).

The **power layout** (*see Sheet E–2*) provides information on the types and locations of all receptacles and equipment connections. Included are communications and isolation equipment devices, as well as special-purpose devices. The estimator needs only to count the number of each type of device by voltage and location.

The **lighting layout** (*see Sheet E–3*) indicates the size and type of incandescent and fluorescent fixtures and switching devices necessary for both the standard and the uninterruptible power supply emergency lighting as indicated for the Operating Room, halls, and other locations.

Raceways and Wiring.   *Refer to Plans, Sheet A–1, Architectural Floor Plan; Sheet E–2, Electrical Power Plan; E–3, Lighting Plan.* For estimates of raceways (conduit), the horizontal perimeter wall measurements are used wherever the receptacle circuits are shown. The conduit size is determined by the number of conductors installed. A 1/2″ (1.27 cm) conduit may be used for installations with 5–12 AWG conductors (a maximum of 8–12 AWG conductors are allowed). Anything over that number must be installed in a 3/4″ (1.91 cm), or larger, conduit. *Communications and isolated computer circuits should be installed in 1″ (2.54 cm) conduit.*

The type of conduit allowed may be **flexible metal conduit** ("Greenfield," "flex"), **electrical metal conduit** (EMT, "thinwall"), **intermediate metal conduit** (IMC, aluminum or steel), **galvanized rigid conduit** (GRC), or **PVC** (Polyvinylchloride), **schedule 40 plastic electrical conduit.**

The full height of the wall is used for estimates wherever a drop for a switch or receptacle is installed, where horizontal continuation is impractical (at door openings, and so on), or for a **home run.**

It is necessary that **junction boxes** are counted in the estimate. One junction box is necessary for each **light fixture,** one for every 360° of bends that may be in a conduit, or one for each continuous 20 lf (6.10 m). The plans do not indicate the number of conductors required for each run. Two conductors are required for each circuit (1 black and 1 white wire). As mentioned above, as many as 5 wires may be included in one conduit. This includes 3 wires (black, red, or blue) and 2 white wires.

The total length of conduit can be used for estimates of the wire length, with a minimum 8" (20.32 cm) to 12" (30.48 cm) added to each end of the conduit length and each junction box for each conductor.

The minimum wire size specified for lighting is #14 AWG with THHN insulation. Equipment sizes and types determine the wire size. Power circuits require a minimum #12 AWG with THHN insulation. The wire may be either solid (normally used for lighting and receptacle circuits) or stranded (normally used with motor and control circuits). The special equipment terminations are recommended by the manufacturer. The manufacturer also strictly follows the NEC requirements. The load requirements are included in the schedules. *Refer to Plans, Sheet E–4.*

The estimator may wish to enlarge the conduit to enable the use of more circuits in one conduit. This can reduce costs and simplify the estimate. For example, a 1" (2.54 cm) or 1 1/2" (3.81 cm) conduit may be run from the main switchgear panel to a junction box where several circuits may be joined. From this point, the size of the conduit and number of conductors can be reduced into branches and smaller conduit. It must be remembered that no conduit is smaller than 1/2" (1.27 cm).

The Switchgear.   The entrance enclosure for the switchgear is located on the west wall at the northwest corner of the building. The enclosure contains the main breaker with its metering and control devices, the subpanels for power and lighting, the meter base for utility company meter, a shunt disconnect for overload safety, the uninterruptible emergency transfer system, and the emergency generator and generator controls.

Electrical Labor

See figures 13–2a and 13–2b, Composite Crew Schedule. The electrical work for the Medical Clinic takes 12 days to complete. The crew includes a foreman, 1 electrical journeyman, and 2 apprentices (helpers). The productivity rate is 71%. The productivity factor and labor cost are calculated as follows:

$$70\% \div 71\% = 0.99$$

Method 13–2a:

$25.49/MH \times 0.99 = \$25.24/MH$

$25.24/MH \times 4 \text{ workers} \times 8 \text{ hr} = \$807.68/CD$

$807.68/CD \times 12 \text{ days} = \$9,692.16 \text{ or } \$9,692.00$

CREW	HOURLY + BURDEN WAGE	% TIME ON JOB/HR	HOURLY RATE
Foreman	$18.28 + $3.85	26%	= $ 5.75
Electrician	$17.78 + $3.85	34%	= $ 7.35
Helper (2)	$11.75 + $3.74 × 2	40%	= $12.39
Composite Crew Rate:		100%	$25.49/MH

FIGURE 13–2a
Composite Crew Schedule

CREW	HOURLY WAGE + BURDEN
Foreman	$18.28 + $ 3.85
Electrician	$17.78 + $ 3.85
Helper (2)	$11.75 + $ 3.74 × 2
	$59.56 + $15.18 = $74.74
Composite Crew Rate:	$74.74/3 = $24.91

FIGURE 13–2b
Composite Crew Schedule

FIGURE 13–3
Equipment Schedule

EQUIPMENT	USE TIME	UNIT COST	TOTAL
Transportation	12 days	@ $10/day	= $ 120.00
Bender	2 days	@ $10/day	= $ 20.00
Chipper	2 days	@ $15/day	= $ 30.00
Scaffold	12 days	@ $50/day	= $ 600.00
Crane w/operator	1 day	@ $150/day	= $ 150.00
Back-hoe w/operator	2 days	@ $100/day	= $ 200.00
Equipment Total:			$1,120.00

Method 13–2b:

$24.91/MH × 0.99 = $24.66/MH

$24.66/MH × 4 workers × 8 hr = $789.12/CD

$789.12/CD × 12 days = $9,469.44 or $9,469.00

70% ÷ 71% = 0.99

Electrical Equipment

See figure 13–3. The equipment used by the electricians for the Medical Clinic include a conduit bending machine, a hammer jack (chipper), mobile scaffold, a mobile truck crane (rented w/operator), and a back-hoe (rented with operator). Included in the estimate is the cost of transportation.

CHAPTER EXERCISES

1. Estimate the quantity of earth to be removed for the trenches per Plans, Sheet E–1, Electrical Plot Plan. The trench sizes are given in the chapter. The use of a hoe-ram is required for 35 lf (10.67 m) of the main trench and 50 lf (15.24 m) of one of the tributary trenches.

Now estimate the cost for the earth removal. The back-hoe is required for 2 days and the hoe-ram for 1 day. The operator and equipment costs are as follows:

Operator   @ $175/day
Back-hoe   @ $120/day
Hoe-ram   @ $150/day

2. The service lateral from the transformer to the switchgear requires 4-#4/0 USE conductors for a wye-connected service. What quantity (lineal feet, meters) of wire is required? Allow 3 lf (0.91 m) for each conductor at each end.

3. #12 and #14 AWG THW or THHN is obtainable in 500 lf (152.4 m) coils or cartons. To the next full coil or carton, determine the quantity of wire necessary for power (#12) and lighting (#14) for the Medical Clinic. (Assume only two wires per circuit.)

14

The Bid Package, Contract, and Follow-up

Up to this point everything explained in this text has been directed toward the quantity survey. The quantity survey usually takes approximately 75% of the time consumed in preparation of the bid proposal. The remaining time is used in applying the labor, material, and equipment costs to the overhead and profit, taxes, and any additional cost requirements.

A general contractor does not necessarily do a bid in the same manner described in all of the previous chapters. Just a portion of the work in a project (one or two trades) may be done for which it is licensed. It may do no work in any of the trades. Or the contractor may do a complete estimate as has been done in this text. If a complete estimate is done, it may be to ensure quality estimates from the subcontractors or to assist in a better understanding of the complete project. In all cases, the general contractor acts in the capacity of a broker for any work that is subcontracted. Specialized licensed trades people, such as a masonry contractor or a framing contractor, do their own bidding and submit a proposal to the contractor.

Another common alternate to a complete quantity survey by the general contractor may be the "quick check" method calculated in units, lineal feet, square feet, cubic yards, and so on. This method is based on information from construction estimating books or computer programs that include "quick-check" estimating costs that are periodically updated. Some of these books and computer programs indicate the method by which the values given were derived. The problem with the books and computer programs, however, is that the contractor's method may vary from the subcontractors' method and can cause problems with interpretation. An estimating cost catalogue is written for several regions of the country. Therefore, the costs may vary according to local requirements. For example, the western regional book may include costs for seismic construction. The eastern regional book may include additional requirements for hurricane (or even tornado) construction. Thus, the costs vary from region to region and these changes must be considered. Another simpler problem may be that the book may show the cost of a 10 lf × 10 lf (3.05 m × 3.05 m) stud wall with so many studs, so much drywall, and so much insulation lumped into a unit price when only the stud value was being sought.

The previous chapters also show how the computer calculates the work of an estimate. They also explain how to work a quantity survey manually in the event there is no computer available. There are some computer-estimating systems that may be even more accurate and go deeper into an estimate than this text has attempted to do. But, reiterating a previous statement, understand that *any computerized estimating program is only as good as the programmed system and the estimator supplying the input to the program.*

ETHICS OF ESTIMATING

Before getting into the bid packaging, contract documentation, and follow-up, the estimator should take a look at some of the other problems that can occur with the behavioral actions of the estimating process, the estimator, and the contractor. The problems being referred to are the problems of *ethics*. What has an *ethic* or *ethics* to do with estimating? The definitions of the words explain the necessity for *ethics*. **Ethic** is defined as *a moral or principle.* **Ethics** is defined as *the code of conduct or behavior governing an individual or group; principles; morals; standards. Ethic* and *ethics* are to be taken seriously and sincerely.

Proposal Ethics

Would you, as an estimator, seek to copy someone else's work to submit as a bid? Would you willingly make a mistake so that someone else could be the successful bidder? Would you be willing to have an owner/developer or a contractor come to you and tell you that, if you play the game, you could be notified as to who the low bidder is that would allow you to lower the bid on bid day? And this done with the promise that on the next bid you could come in high and get the work from one of them? Or would you have a contractor come to you after all bids had been accepted on bid day by the competition and ask you to give a bid at an even lower estimate when you weren't involved in the process to begin with?

The third and fourth questions are not uncommon occurrences in the construction industry. The following examples are actual fact:

A company had been making bid proposals for a period of time, and succeeded in making contracts with the party requesting the bids. The owner/developer felt that the work this company had done was satisfactory. The owner/developer sought a proposal from the bidding company and went so far as to identify the lowest bid. If the company accepts, a moral or principle is broken. The bidding company took unfair advantage of the competition, accepted the proposal from the owner/developer, and got the contract. The word got out that this had occurred. The problem that developed from this action was that, when others were requested to submit a bid on another project, the contractors contacted either refused to give a bid or deliberately bid the project well over cost (a high bid).

Another example occurred when the party seeking bids had actually gotten all the proposals in by the time of bid opening. The company did not seek to refuse all of the bids, nor did it reopen the process for fair estimating. Instead, the party receiving the bids sought another contractor that had not bid the project and asked for a lower bid. This is referred to as "back-dooring" the process. Again, the ethics of the bid process had been broken. The same thing occurred as that in the previous example.

Still another occurrence was one where the contractor seeking the work for a state's highway construction projects had been successful and made friends with an "insider" in the state's construction department. Another highway construction company moved into the area and started bidding the work. The "insider" gave the friendly contractor the low bid and that contractor proceeded to undercut the lowest bid by approximately 5%. This continued for several bids. The newer contractor started wondering and investigated. It was noted during the investigation that all of the bids were being reduced by the same percentage amount. The newer contractor "got even." The company submitted its next bid at a "break-even" level. The "insider" passed on the information and the bid went for 5% less. The result was a bankruptcy for the friendly bidder, an investigation by the state, and loss of a position for the "insider." The integrity of the contractor and the "insider" are gross examples of a lack of the code of ethics.

Still another consideration that should concern an estimator, as well as the contractor, is the extra-low bid received. This is the bid proposed by another contractor or subcontractor submitted at a cost of from 10% to 25% below the next lowest bid. The estimator, or contractor, receiving the bid did the ethical thing. He or she asked if the submitting party was satisfied with the number. This question will normally cause the bidder to pull the estimate for another look or to elect not to bid. This sort of action will let the contractor or subcontractor know that apparently there is something amiss and is thankful for the courtesy. This type of action ensures that, normally, the subcontractor will be willing to submit a bid on the next project because of the honesty of the estimator and the company.

Working with the Material and Equipment Suppliers

Making friendships with suppliers isn't a problem. The problem is maintaining a level of standards on the part of the estimator and the supplier. There are instances where suppliers will favor a contractor with lower costs because of continued purchasing from the supplier. The supplier may attempt to negotiate material or equipment costs so that the company will also be a part of the successful bid. This, too, can cause problems with the bid costs if not done with concern for the company's ethics.

Knowledge of the material and equipment suppliers is of extreme value to the estimator. The estimator must keep abreast of the latest material and equipment costs. This is best done by keeping in contact with *more than one supplier* to garner the proper information.

There are products that are being developed that can, and possibly have, replaced some of the products mentioned in this text. Making use of information of new and/or superior products can make the actual estimating process more cost effective. Upgraded information on materials and equipment may be found in the Architectural Sweet's Catalogues or may be obtained directly from the suppliers. These, too, will have a bearing on the bidding process and accuracy of the bid. Any estimated product that is not specified must be submitted for approval as an alternative with an explanation, sample, and a cost comparison.

Lastly, as previously mentioned in chapter 3, the labor costs will also vary according to available work, union contracts, increases in wages, and the like. It is the responsibility of the estimator to maintain a constant eye on any of these changes as well as for the material and equipment costs mentioned above.

Committing to Ethical Standards.   The ethical estimator and contractor will not willingly commit to poor standards. There are also several organizations of estimators that frown on such activities. They include the American Society of Professional Estimators (ASPE), the American Society of Cost Engineers (ASCE), and the Construction Specifications Institute (CSI). These organizations, as well as others, have established a code of ethics in the workings of an estimate and an estimator's responsibility.

One of the prospects and advantages of participation in such organizations is that the estimator may seek assistance from others in the organization anywhere in the country. For example, where a product is unknown in the estimator's locale, one of the estimators or specification writers from another company, or another area, may know the product and give assistance in material locations as well as the cost of the material or equipment.

PACKAGING THE BID

Bid Summary Sheet

See figure 14–1. As with all forms for construction, there are many variations of bid summary sheets. The form shown in figure 14–1 is a customized sheet used by either the general contractor or the subcontractor. The bid summary sheet usually includes space for such information as the name (or number) of the project, the names of the owner and architect, with addresses or telephone numbers available. If a subcontractor is using the sheet, the name of the general contractor should be included. A contact person that the estimator can call for questions and information should also be noted, as well as the bid date and time of bid.

Along with information given on the bid summary, the *date of the plans used for the estimate* is added even if the form has no specific location for it. This information is valuable in the event question arises about the estimate: often there are differences in the plans used in the estimate and the bid tendered from said plans as opposed to the actual project plans used for construction. The main portion of the sheet contains information regarding the division and/or section being bid. In addition, the addendum (or addenda) must be noted, as well as its (their) effect on the bid.

Bid Pricing

A bid form supplied to the subcontractor along with the plans and specifications may request a **lump sum** bid, a **unit price** bid, or a **breakdown of materials, labor, and equipment** similar to the numbers found on a survey sheet. Each of these types of bids is explained below.

The general contractor may have a similar bid form with the demand for a lump sum or a unit price. The general contractor may also be required to submit a list of subcontractors accepted for the tendered bid. This requirement is included in most institutional and governmental bids over a certain dollar amount.

Lump Sum Pricing.   The request for a lump sum bid is the most common. The bidder estimates the hard costs (labor, material, and equipment) along with the **overhead, profit, bonds, permits, fees,** and **taxes** required and totals them into a lump sum figure.

Brophy Construction

DATE _____ *10/30/92* _____ BID # ____ *92-05* ____

PROJECT __ *Medical Clinic* _____

PROJECT ADDRESS *Main & Broadway, Caliente, NV* _____

ARCHITECT *Christle & Assoc.* ____ TELEPHONE # *(300)555-5555*

CONTRACTOR *Janus Corporation* _____

CONTACT ___ *Jim Fatzinger* _____ TELEPHONE # *(333)555-2233*

BIDDING TRADE(S):

DIVISION(S)/SECTION(S): *1 thru 16 (all)*

MATERIALS:	$ 1,576,000
LABOR :	$ 630,400
EQUIPMENT:	$ 975,000
SUB-TOTAL:	$ 3,181,400
TAXES: @ 7%	$ 110,320 *(materials only)*
HARD COST SUB-TOTAL:	$ 3,291,720
OVERHEAD @ 16%:	$ 526,675
SUB-TOTAL:	$ 3,818,952
PROFIT @ 12%:	$ 458,274
TOTAL:	$ 4,277,226
BID BOND (if required): 5%	$ 213,861
P & P BOND(S) (if required): 1.5%	$ 64,158
FEES:	$ 2,500
PERMITS:	$ 3,000
GRAND TOTAL:	$ 4,560,745

UNIT PRICE (square foot): *$200.47/sq ft*

FIGURE 14-1
Customized Bid Summary

Unit Pricing.   Sometimes the unit price is all that is requested for a bid. Usually the unit price is added to the lump sum bid for reference purposes. (See the section below on the Bid Cover Sheet for more information on unit pricing.)

The unit price is requested for two reasons:

1.   The owner may insist this unit cost be added so that, should any additions or deletions to the work occur, the price can already be noted and a figure placed in a work authorization, change order, or addendum (bulletin) to the contract. A binding unit price becomes *unfair if costs have increased in the interim and no provision is allotted for such an increase.*

2.   The general contractor compares prices between subcontractors on the unit price estimate for accuracy. For example, two subcontractors submit a similar lump sum bid but the unit prices are not the same. Did one of the subcontractors make an error in the lump sum total or in the unit price? This question must be answered prior to accepting a bid.

Breakdown Pricing.   The breakdown bid is exactly the same breakdown as that appearing on the summary sheet (see figure 14–1). This is the least acceptable to, and will usually be refused by, the contractor or subcontractor because, in effect, the contractor is giving away "trade secrets."

Time and Material with Gross Maximum Price (T&M/GMP).   Where a cost is not determined, such as for a design/build project referred to in chapter 1, Types of Estimates, a T&M/GMP proposal may be used. Unlike the bid pricing in the previous paragraphs, T&M estimates should only be used where both the purchaser and the bidder understand the concerns of such cost evaluation. The bidder, ethically, will submit a proposal that is "not to exceed", known as "the gross maximum price". If the proposed dollar value is within the limits of the finances of the owner/developer, and accepted, a contract may ensue. Also, with a limitation, a closer eye can be kept on the costs and can save money for both the owner and the contractor. If a proposal is made and has no such statement of limitation, it should not be accepted.

This type of estimate is common in *tenant improvement* construction of existing structures. **Tenant improvements** are changes made to the interior of a structure to suit the requirements of the tenant occupying the structure, or being readied for occupancy by a new tenant.

Here, again, is where a farce may be made of the ethics of construction because, as noted in chapter 1, the contractor could illegitimately exceed the available financing that the owner/developer has available.

For example, a contractor has made a T&M proposal that was accepted without limits. The contractor saw that the work wasn't progressing as the company had planned. The company owned much of its equipment such as backhoes, graders, forklifts, trucks, and the like, as well as smaller equipment. The contractor, at an apropos time, moved some of the equipment (not used) on the project and billed the owner. This is not an unusual case. The superintendent for the contractor saw to it that this continued until someone during an audit caught the excesses.

In another instance of a lack of ethics, a superintendent had several non-existent employees on the payroll. The superintendent handed out the paychecks weekly and pocketed the mystery employees' checks. The mystery employees were carpenters on the payroll working on his boat! This action was also caught in audit.

Each of these actions caused considerable problems leading to liability, claims, and litigation. These problems will be discussed later in this chapter.

Added Costs

Permits.   *Refer to figure 14–1.* All permits required by the local building department are added to the cost of the proposal. Permits are required for any work in the earth such as the excavating/grading, concrete, plumbing, and electrical work. Permit cost is based upon the area to be worked; for example, the excavating/grading contractor will pay according to the total project area, whereas the plumbing or electrical contractor may be required to pay only for the building area. These costs are added to the contract total after the overhead and profit have been added.

Fees.   The owner or contractor may be required to pay certain fees that are additional governmental expenses outside the jurisdiction of the building departments. Items such as a land use fee, environmental impact fee, and water use fee are examples. The costs for these items are also an add-on to the total contract similar to the procedure for permits.

Taxes.   Any tax assessments that may be locally required are added to the total cost. Most taxes are applied to materials only, but some locales require taxes for labor and/or equipment as well. The contractor has two choices for taxation included in the estimate. The first method is to include the tax as part of the hard cost for materials, labor, and/or equipment. The second method adds the tax after overhead and profit are determined in the same manner as bonds, permits, and fees.

Other Costs

There are additional costs that vary with the geographical location of the work. They may include such items as protection requirements for saving certain flora and fauna species, atmospheric conditions, dust, asbestos abatement, other hazardous waste, and mold.

Examples of some of these problems can be found in the location where the imaginary project used for this text can be found: Dust, tortoise protection, atomic fallout, and mold. The locale is a desert community.

There are requirements there for removal, protection, and relocation of the desert tortoise. Where found, this action must be accomplished even before any construction can begin.

There is mold found in some projects due to failure to control the proper curing (drying out) of certain materials, such as drywall. Failure on the part of the manufacturer to properly cure the panels, shipping the product exposed to the elements, improper storage of the product and, lastly, installation under conditions that may leave the moisture within the drywall. Beyond that, there is the problem of air-conditioning with a humid atmosphere. This will draw moisture. The moisture, over time, produces mold that is detrimental to human health.

Dust is a major problem due to the dry desert and winds. Proper moistening of the earth during construction to reduce dust exposure is required. Note: Too much watering can add to the mold problem mentioned above.

Atomic fallout, although no longer existent, or abuse of chemicals dumped into the earth, may have penetrated into the earth causing hazardous soil conditions. This should be noted in any soils report prepared for the project.

Asbestos abatement is still a major problem throughout the country. Older buildings to be demolished, or to have tenant improvements made to them, must also be cleared of asbestos if it is found.

And, finally, soils reports should accompany any project, residential, commercial, or industrial. The owner is usually responsible for a soils report. The variations in the soils of the desert include very hard, rocky soil (caliche), sand, and clay. These soils conditions are found in various locations and in layers under the surface, and must be properly tested to determine if construction can be done without additional sub-grade construction.

What is the cost? The delays and liability due to any of these problems must be determined and can be an additional expense that should be noted in the estimate, or added as an additional fee. The costs for any of the above conditions may vary from 2% to 50% additional expense to the total cost of a proposal/contract. The estimator should look into these problems and investigate to determine responsibility for the costs.

Overhead and Profit

Bid Costs.   *Refer to figure 14–1.* The two groups of bid costs are referred to as the hard costs and corporate costs. The hard costs include the cost of materials, labor, equipment, fees, and taxes included in the quantity survey. The corporate costs include the project overhead and the corporate overhead.

Project overhead is usually incorporated in the provisions of Division 1, General Requirements. Project overhead includes the wages of administrative personnel *on the job,* such as the superintendent, assistant superintendent, project engineer, and secretary/receptionist. Other item costs such as temporary permits, project utilities, signage, project office trailer, storage facilities, and fencing are also included in Division 1. These costs are actually a part of the hard costs of a project estimate. Many of the computer estimating programs have such items and their costs included.

All costs to the contractor that are not direct construction costs are included in the **corporate overhead.** These costs include, but are not necessarily limited to, office personnel wages, administration costs, office material and equipment, rent/mortgage payments, depreciation of owned equipment, general comprehensive and liability insurance, and vehicle licensing fees. These corporate costs are broken down into percentages of overhead and profit.

The experienced contractor is able to determine these costs on an annual (historical) basis and reduce the cost to a percent of the annual gross receipts. This percentage becomes the overhead used for projected or anticipated contracts for the coming year. An example of a calculated overhead percentage is as follows:

Corporate costs per annum (yearly):

Mortgage	$ 12,000
Salaries	
Office Manager	$ 24,000

Secretary	$	18,500
Bookkeeper	$	21,600
Sales	$	23,400
Estimator	$	30,500
CPA	$	35,000
Licenses and Fees	$	12,000
Maintenance	$	15,000
Insurance	$	125,000
Taxes (excluding material, labor, and equipment)	$	43,345
Total	$	360,345

Previous annual gross receipts:

Contract #1	$	430,000
Contract #2	$	500,460
Contract #3	$	389,760
Contract #4	$	438,520
Contract #5	$	510,500
Total	$	2,269,240

The overhead percentage is calculated as follows:

$$\$360,345 \div \$2,269,240 = 0.158 \text{ or } 15.8\% \ (16\%)$$

A new contractor can estimate the same possibilities for anticipated overhead costs and gross product receipts. On the basis of costs for only one month, overhead can be projected in a similar way, by dividing costs into receipts.

Profit.   All companies work to make a profit. The profit spoken of at this point is actually the **profit margin** or the *desired profit* the company wishes to attain. Profit is determined on the basis of the *amount of money necessary to maintain operating expenses and a positive cash flow between projects*. The actual profit (or loss) of any work is not known until a complete analysis is made for the project. Analysis is discussed later in the chapter. The **actual profit** is that money remaining after all wages, taxes, fees, materials, and equipment are deducted from the gross estimate or contract price. The remaining money may mean the profit actually is as little as 2% or 3%.

Some companies, when work is slow, will bid work at a 2% or 3% profit margin just to keep from losing experienced crews. This action usually means that the company will actually operate at a "break-even" or loss position. Only companies that have a financial reserve with which to operate can afford such activity and then for only a short period of time. Any action of this type rates as very poor business practice and could cause the company to place itself in jeopardy of bankruptcy. For this reason alone, every precaution should be taken to avoid bids with low profit margins.

Other companies work on a **large volume basis** and bid at the 2% and 3% level to obtain work. Again, this works only with experienced companies that can keep a tight rein on expenses and that have experienced crews. It is in this situation that the estimator *must* be in constant contact with material and labor changes so that the margin can be maintained.

Some contractors tend to lump the overhead and profit into one percentage figure. Unless caution is used, this is an extremely poor policy. Should this have been done on the summary sheet in figure 14–1, the figures would appear as follows:

Overhead	=	16%
Profit	=	12%
Total		28%

Hard cost	=	$ 3,291,720
Hard cost × 0.28 (28%)	=	$ 921,681
Total		$ 4,213,401

The variance from the bid with the overhead and profit percentages separated is as follows:

$ 4,277,226

<$ 4,213,401>

<$ 68,825>

$ 68,825 ÷ $4,277,226 = 0.016 or 1.6% less

The contractor who insists upon using this method must actually increase the rate by 2% or more to maintain the same level of profitability as the contractor who separates the overhead and profit percentages as in figure 14–1. For example, if the contractor increased the percentage to 30%, the total would be as follows:

Hard costs	=	$ 3,291,720
Overhead/Profit (30%)	=	$ 987,516
Total	=	$ 4,279,236

This total is just slightly more than the total in figure 14–1. Only when the percentage is increased by 2% to 30% does the total amount for the bid approximate the total amount determined when overhead and profit are calculated separately.

One other item that must be considered by the contractor is the possible risk of cost overrun as the result of unforeseen problems and subcontractor inadequacy. The term used in this case is the **risk factor.** The risks have occurred with enough frequency that contractors now include a risk insurance in the hard costs of a project. Some contractors defer such risks by incorporating a **contingency allowance** included in the project corporate costs. This contingency may be an automatic inclusion in the bid or may be negotiated with the owner.

Bonds, permits, and/or fees are added after hard and corporate costs are tabulated. All this information should be noted for convenience and clarity in describing the cost of the work that the contractor is intending to perform. The summary sheet can also be used for communication in a "phone bid" on bid day.

The Bid Cover Sheet

See figure 14–2. There is a great similarity between the estimate summary sheet in figure 14–1 and the cover sheet in figure 14–2. A cover sheet may be totally

Brophy Construction

DATE _____ *10/30/92* _____ BID # _ *92-5* _

PROJECT _ *Medical Clinic* _

PROJECT ADDRESS _ *Broadway & Main Sts, Caliente, NV* _

OWNER _ *Dr. R. Stone & Assoc.* _

OWNER ADDRESS _ *1 Broadway, Caliente, NV* _

ARCHITECT _ *Christle & Assoc.* _

BIDDING

DIVISION(S): *1 thru 16* SECTION(S): _ *all* _

SUMMARY OF WORK: *Includes all phases of project from excavating and grading to electrical w/ all pertinent sections included.*

ADDENDUM (ADDENDA) NOTED: _ *#1 & #2* _

Special Information: BASE BID: *$ 4,560,745*

Owner requests base bid only at this time   ALTERNATE #1: _ *0* _
                                        (add [·XXX], deduct [(XXX)])

Anticipated project start - 2/5/93   ALTERNATE #2: _ *0* _
                                        (add [·XXX], deduct [(XXX)])

                                        ALTERNATE #3: _ *0* _
                                        (add [·XXX], deduct [(XXX)])

                                        ALTERNATE #4: _ *0* _
                                        (add [·XXX], deduct [(XXX)])

Bid Bond Included? _ *5* x
P & P Bond Included? *1.5* x
Taxes Included? _ *7* x
Won? ____ Lost? ____   ALTERNATE #5: _ *0* _
Low Bidder _____   (add [·XXX], deduct [(XXX)])
Low Bid _____

FIGURE 14–2
Bid Cover Sheet

different in design but should carry all the information pertinent to the bid on it. The difference between a bid sheet and a cover sheet is that a breakdown of costs is not included on the cover sheet. The basic general information is the same, addenda are noted, the lump sum total is noted, and bonding is noted if any is required. The additional information shown or requested is the cost for any alternates. The alternate costs are calculated in the same manner as the base bid. These alternates are included as "*adds*" to, or "*deducts*" from, the base bid.

The bid cover sheet should have space for any special information that may be pertinent to the proposal being tendered. If a unit cost is desired, it may be determined and placed on the cover sheet. This is done by dividing the cost by the total area of the property (for a general contractor, excavating/grading contractor, and so on) or by the area of the building (framers, drywallers, and so on).

The unit price for the Medical Clinic, in square feet (square meters), *based on an assumed contract price* that includes bond and fee costs, involving the total area of the property would appear similar to the following:

Property area is as follows:

175 lf $\times$ 130 lf = 22,750 sq ft

(53.34 m $\times$ 39.62 m = 2,113.33 m^2)

The contractors working on just the structure would use the cost and area of the structure similar to the following:

Building area:

58 lf $\times$ 41 lf = 2,378 sq ft

(17.68 m $\times$ 12.5 m = 221 m^2)

The framer estimates the work on the structure costs $66,584. Therefore, the cost-per-square foot is as follows:

$66,584 $\div$ 2,378 sq ft = $28/sq ft

Cost/sq ft or m^2:

$4,520,328 $\div$ 22,570 sq ft = $198,695 or $198.70/sq ft

$4,520,328 $\div$ 2,113.33 m^2 = $2,138.96/m^2

$2,138.96/m^2 $\div$ 10.764 sq ft/m^2 = $198.71/sq ft

Any increase or decrease in work to be performed that affects the whole property would be calculated using this per-square-foot value.

$66,584 $\div$ 221 m^2 = $301.29/m^2

$301.29/m^2 $\div$ 10.764 sq ft/m^2 = $27.99/sq ft or $28.00/sq ft

Other Bid Forms

See figures 14–3 and 14–4. The general contractor on bid day may use one or two other forms if the company is not using a computerized network. The use of a telephone quotation sheet and a cut-and-add sheet is common for manual bid taking on bid day. The telephone bid quotation sheet is used to write

RECORD OF TELEPHONE AND VERBAL QUOTATIONS

BIDDER: _____   TELEPHONE NO _____

PROJECT: _____   ESTIMATE NO _____
                                                     ACCOUNT _____
WORK: _____   SHEET NO _____

LOCATION: _____   PREPARED BY _____ DATE _____

BIDDING ON _____ ADDENDAS _____   CHECKED BY _____ DATE _____

CHECK LIST

1. Bond: Included. Yes ____ No ____ ☐	5 Bid Data: Firm Bid Yes ☐ No ☐
2. Sales Tax: Included Yes ____ No ____ ☐	
To be added Yes ____ No ____ ☐	Discount _____
3 Delivery data. Erected or installed _____ ☐	Any exceptions to plans and specifications.
F O B. jobsite _____ (other) ☐	None ☐ See below ☐
See remarks _____ ☐	
4. Schedule: Starting Date _____	6 Bid taken by
Complete in _____ days	Date / Hour

QUOTED BY: _____   CONTRACTORS LICENSE No. _____

ITEM NO.	DESCRIPTION, QUALIFICATIONS, REMARKS, ETC.	QUANTITY	UNIT BID	TOTAL BID
	ENTER ALTERNATE BID BELOW:			

REQUEST CONFIRMATION BY MAIL

FIGURE 14–3
Telephone and Verbal Quotation Sheet

CUT AND ADD SHEET

Prepared by _____

Approved by _____

PROJECT _____   BID OPENING DATE

Account	Description			In Estimate @	New Price	Cut	Add	Comments

SUMMARY OF LISTED DIRECT COST ADJUSTMENTS   _____ - _____   NET CHANGE _____
OTHER COSTS AFFECTED: (1) JOB INDIRECT COSTS _____

           (2) ADMINISTRATION OF SUBCONTRACTS _____
                @ 10% _____
           (3) SALES TAX ON MATERIAL _____
                          TOTAL ORIGINAL ESTIMATE EXCLUDING PROFIT AND BONDS _____
                    ADJUSTED ESTIMATE SUB TOTAL EXCLUDING PROFIT AND BONDS _____

MANAGEMENT CONSIDERATIONS:
_____
_____
_____
                         FINAL ADJUSTED TOTAL EXCLUDING PROFIT AND BONDS _____
                         ADD PROFIT FOR GENERAL CONTRACTOR _____ %
                                         SUB TOTAL _____
               ADD PERFORMANCE AND COMPLETION BONDS _____
                   NEW TOTAL ESTIMATED CONSTRUCTION COST _____

FIGURE 14–4
Cut-and-Add Sheet

down verbal information from other contractors or subcontractors to be incorporated into the cut-and-add sheet for a final analysis. The cut-and-add sheet summarizes the subcontract bids and deletes unwanted bids from subcontractors (too high or incomplete) or adds successful bids (low bidder) until the best possible bid is available.

THE CONTRACT

The contract is the result of a successful bid on a project. It is made per the requirements of the legal documents governing the bids and the general conditions of the project. Many contracts are awarded using the special AIA Form 401 (amended), which has been established by the architectural societies and is widely used in contract documents. There are two types of bids and contracts with which the contractor must be aware, the **competitive** and the **negotiated** types.

The term *competitive* as used in the bidding process means the bid is considered an "open" bid. This form of bidding is done when the owner requests any contractor to bid the project. The bid may have been advertised through the newspaper or some construction periodical. The contract is usually awarded to the lowest bidder.

The negotiated bid is often referred to as a "closed" bid because it is restricted to contractors chosen by the owner or general contractor. The accepted general contractors vie for the contract with one another just as in competitive bidding. The successful contractor then has the sole right to request subcontract bids and award contracts at its own discretion.

Retainage (Retention)

The use of retention is common to all contracts. The problem is that the issue of retention is often ignored at contract time. It is a form of guarantee, used in addition to, or in lieu of, a payment and performance bond, that the contractor will perform the work to the successful completion of the project. The usual retention held is 10% of the total value of the contract. This can be frightening to a subcontractor whose profit margin is equal to, or less than, the retention.

Caution should be used when reading contracts, principally in relation to the retention clause. The clause may read "10% retention held for *90 days after completion and/or acceptance of the project.*" The project could last for a year or more! Can the contractor afford the amount equal to, or less than, the profit margin for this length of time? If this clause exists, the contractor and subcontractor should try to negotiate a more reasonable retention such as "10% retention for *90 days upon completion and/or acceptance of the trade.*" This is the more common acceptance negotiated between contractors.

Enforcement of the retention clause may cause some problems other than the one mentioned above. There are times when the retention may be held for an additional period because of claims of incompetence or of incomplete or poor workmanship. Each time this occurs, the retention is held for an additional 90-day period.

JOB-COST ANALYSIS

The hard costs are the primary concern of the job-cost analyst. This is not to say that the overhead, profit, taxes, and so on are not of importance. They are. Once the contract is signed and the work begins, it is the responsibility of the project superintendent, project manager, estimator, and accountant (bookkeeper) to keep constant track of the progress of the project. This is accomplished by following the trail of the materials, labor, and equipment and is referred to as the **cost analysis.** The questions raised in the process may be ones such as the following:

1. Is the supplier delivering the exact product required or is it a substitution?
2. Is the delivery on time?
3. If the product is a substitution, is it of the same quality and value?
4. Is the substitution acceptable according to contract?
5. What is the cost?
6. Are field personnel working to their potential? Or are they lagging behind?

7. Is the equipment owned being kept in good repair?
8. Is the rental equipment also in good repair?
9. Is the equipment delivered on time?
10. Is there cooperation between trades so that there are no delays?

Sound familiar? In chapter 3, **daily work reports** were recommended as an aid in solving some of these problems such as **logistical supply** and **progress of the work.** Many of the answers to the questions above can be answered and appropriate action taken as a result of the daily reports.

In addition to the daily reporting, the superintendent, foreman, or lead-man, or whoever is in charge of receiving supplies on the job must make a *check of the invoices to determine that the correct material is delivered.* The invoicing is forwarded along with the work reports and the information placed in the job-cost records. These same records are forwarded to the accounting department for entry in the payable, receivable, and/or the general accounts registers.

When it is time for billing or if notice is made of something amiss in the invoicing, the contractor and supplier must verify the material quantities and the costs. If these do not match with the initial estimate or agreement with the supplier, there is immediate recognition of a problem. The field personnel and the estimator are notified and everyone is put on the alert. If the invoices have all been submitted and the records are kept daily, this should prevent major problems from arising.

The labor costs are also recorded on a daily or weekly basis, along with a progress report indicating what percentage of the project is completed. These are compared with the estimated costs. *Each of the supervisory and office personnel responsible for the progress reports must keep accurate records.* For best results, *weekly meetings should be held and the verbal progress reports made.* Any discrepancies can be aired and some solutions proposed and put into action.

The analysis done on a daily and weekly basis will also help in decisions on future work. The reports concerning good or bad communication and co-operation with trades and subcontractors determine the willingness of the contractor to work with the same groups on future projects. The actions of a supplier, by keeping costs of materials in line or raising costs as work progresses, can determine whether or not that supplier shall be used again. Equipment rental companies that have reasonable prices and provide well-maintained equipment will have their services requested for any future projects.

Control

Each of the preceding recommendations aid in the development of a good job-cost analysis. The continued record keeping and the immediate follow-up on any problem can reduce overhead costs, keep the hard costs in line, and result in completion of the project with a profit. *Each and every bit of information and referencing means that there is control of the work.*

This control is *mandatory* for good, quality work and the making of a profit as well as for protection from litigation and other claims. Misunderstandings, cost discrepancies, even jealousy and politics within the construction scheme can be the source of such claims of liability, and even litigation. Proper records will keep government organizations such as the IRS from seeking recourse.

The more thoroughly records are kept, the less chance for any action against the company. The paper trail is, in essence, the "bible" record of each project. Each detail that is properly noted in the daily reports, invoice confirmations, work progress reports, and the like, are very necessary. The estimator plays a large part in the follow-up by comparisons with the estimate to the actual construction costs incurred. The estimator is frequently responsible for verifying all written reports before they are recorded and maintaining the recorded information for future use.

In addition, the company doing any work on a project, from general contractor to subcontractor to supplier, should always make sure that all the administration personnel are thoroughly knowledgeable of the blueprints. This includes all of the project management team. This, too, is the responsibility of the contractor and the estimator or estimating team.

Historical Reference

The final tallies on the project that determine profit or loss also supply the historical record necessary to determine future costs. A project costing less than estimated means a larger return. A project poorly managed and ending in a "break-even" or loss position spells danger for the future of the company. An example of what good and bad management can accomplish may best be explained in the examples that follow.

The estimate for the Medical Clinic amounts to $4,560,745. The company that has won the contract has two options. In one instance, the company (called Company A for reference) has a good working relationship and follows the recommendations above. In contrast, the same company (called Company B for reference) does not accept these recommendations and goes its "merry" way. The results may appear as follows:

Estimated hard costs:

Materials	=	$ 1,576,000.00
Labor	=	$ 630,400.00
Equipment	=	$ 975,000.00
Taxes	=	$ 110,000.00
Total	=	$ 3,291,720.00

Actual hard costs:

	Company A	Company B
Materials	$ 1,498,000.00	$ 1,630,026.00
Labor	$ 630,010.00	$ 750,200.00
Equipment	$ 975,000.00	$ 1,000,050.00
Taxes	$ 108,577.00	$ 114,000.00
Total	$ 3,211,587.00	$ 3,494,276.00

Note that each item in this case is an overrun for Company B as a result of lack of control whereas Company A has costs under the estimate in most cases because of control. The hard cost difference is summarized as follows:

	Company A	Company B
Estimated cost	$ 3,291,720.00	$ 3,291,720.00
Actual cost	<$ 3,211,587.00 >	<$ 3,494,276.00 >
Difference	$ 80,133.00 profit	<$ 202,556.00 > loss

The original estimated profit margin is $458,274. The companies gross receipts are as follows:

	Company A	Company B
Estimated margin	$ 458,274.00	$ 458,274.00
Difference	$ 80,133.00	<$ 202,556.00>
Total margin	$ 538,407.00 gross	$ 255,718.00 gross

Here is a percentage summary of profit increase or decrease:

Company A: $538,407 ÷ $458,274 = 1.175 or 17.5% increase

Company B: $256,718 ÷ $458,274 = 0.56 or 56% decrease

The profit for Company A increased by 17.5% whereas the profit for Company B decreased by 56%. A good job-cost analysis, along with firm control, can result in more profits, perhaps not to the extent of the somewhat exaggerated example, but the analysis with follow-up substantially aids in correcting problems and in increasing productivity and, eventually, in producing good profits.

The Plan Center Concept

An estimate performed as a part of a feasibility study may be performed using a few schematic sketches and conceptual specifications. An estimate prepared for use in a construction proposal may involve hundreds of pages of drawings, specifications, reports, and addenda. Though the required level of accuracy of the estimate and the detail of the documents differ greatly in these examples, the documents remain the platform upon which the estimating process is based.

To facilitate the estimating process, the documents must be made available to the businesses that will be estimating the total project or any of its components. Owners usually provide the documents to general contractors in order to obtain total project cost estimates. Likewise, contractors provide the documents to subcontractors and suppliers to obtain cost estimates for various components of the project. Commonly, documents are either distributed directly to potential bidders, or they are placed in a central repository called a "plan center."

Distribution of bid documents can be a very expensive process. Reproduction costs alone can run into hundreds of thousands of dollars annually for owners and contractors engaging in large projects on a continuing basis. Time spent traveling to distribute or collect documents further adds to estimating overhead expense. Distribution by courier service or by mail can also be costly. A successful estimator may actually bid on 50% of the jobs he looks at, winning a contract on 30% or less, so the sheer number of documents moving between businesses can be immense. The plan center provides a location where a single set of documents can be posted for review by potential bidders. The plan center system benefits owners and general contractors who are soliciting bids by providing a low cost option to distributing multiple sets of documents to multiple potential bidders. Since a successful plan center may possess hundreds of sets of documents, the center also benefits contractors and suppliers by providing a central location where they can access potential new jobs.

Typically, the right to review documents in plan centers is a "members only" privilege. Since the service that the plan center sells to its members is centralized access to potential new jobs, most plan centers will post documents for no charge, or for a minimal fee. Most plan centers have a room or rooms equipped with several workstations for members to utilize when they visit. Estimators may actually perform estimates on a number of jobs while in the plan center or may simply look at several newly posted sets of documents to determine if a detailed review and estimate are called for. After selecting a promising new job, the estimator can request a full set of documents from the owner or from a local reprographics company. It is not uncommon for the bidder to pay the costs of reproduction.

Clearly, plan centers are a valuable resource for estimators who need to screen many jobs before selecting a few to pursue. Reduced travel and reproduction costs, reduced marketing expense, increased access to jobs, and improved communication between owners, contractors, and suppliers more than offset annual membership fees.

ON-LINE PLAN CENTERS

On-line plan centers are accessed through the Internet. Access is typically limited to plan center members and though services differ, at a minimum the on-line site will contain a list of jobs that are seeking bidders. Each listing includes a job description, bid date, and information about how to access the documents. There may also be links that allow an estimator to order documents on-line, register as a bidder, and contact plan holders. This service allows the estimator to look at a large volume of new job postings daily without leaving the office, following up on only those jobs that are of specific interest. Some on-line plan-center sites include features that allow the estimator to view the plans, specifications, addenda, and bid documents in addition to the basic job information. The most advanced sites include built-in digital tools that allow the estimator to perform quantity take-off activities on-line.

ON-LINE ESTIMATING

The term "on-line estimating" refers to the process of accessing documents and performing quantity take-off activities on the Internet. The estimator logs on to the plan center in the morning and reviews the current job postings looking for potential new jobs. If an interesting lead shows up, the estimator may open the documents for a closer look. From there, processing a new job differs little from the traditional process described in Chapter 1. Once the new job is in the system, the estimator may choose to do a quantity take-off on-line. To provide the reader with an opportunity to experiment with this type of system, the bid documents for the Medical Clinic are posted on the Builder's Exchange of Washington web site. If you have access to a high speed Internet connection, it is advisable to use it for on-line estimating. To access the documents and the on-line digital take-off tools, open your web browser and go to:

1. From the Home page, click on "Fastbid Install."
2. After "Fastbid" installation, on the home page, click "Posted Projects."
3. In "Posted Projects," click on "Contractors Private Projects."

4. You must agree to the "<u>conditions</u>."
5. Click on "<u>I Agree.</u>"

While the "Plan Center" part of the web site contains links to the documents for jobs that are actively bidding, the "Contractors Private Projects" page contains portals to dozens of private sites, most of which are password protected. Contractors find that on-line availability of the documents greatly enhances communication between construction team members after the initial bidding is over. This plan center offers private sites to contractors so they can retain documents for ongoing jobs. Because access to a contractor's private site is via password, a project team member need not be a plan center member to access the contractor's documents. The documents for the Medical Clinic are posted in the Edmonds Community College private site.

1. Click on "<u>EDCC Construction Management</u>."
2. Click on "<u>click here</u>."
3. Enter User Name "<u>const200</u>."
4. Enter Password "<u>student</u>."
5. Click on "<u>Bid Docs</u>."
6. You are now ready to access the Medical Center bid documents.
7. To get started, click on "<u>Plans</u>."

For an overview of "Fast Bid" features and techniques,

1. Click on "<u>Fast Bid Instructions</u>" (This option is also available on the Home Page).
2. Read the instructions carefully.
3. Go back to the Medical Center plans and begin practicing with the digital tools. You can calculate lengths, areas, count pieces, copy and paste quantity information to a spread sheet, access specifications and bid documents, and print selected plan and spec sheets. Some estimators use multiple monitors so that the plans, specs, and the estimating spread sheet can be viewed concurrently.

You are now working in an active commercial plan center! As you experiment with the system and the site, you will discover that there are many areas that are accessible only to members. There are, however, a few other spots where you can access documents. Go back to the home page and click on "Free Preview." Here you will find additional documents for practice use. Another group of documents is located in "Posted Projects." From the home page, go to "Posted Projects" then "Public Works." Most of these jobs are active and require no password. Since this is an Internet driven technology, the geographic location of construction teams is of little consequence to the system.

CAD DRAWINGS FOR INSTRUCTIONAL USE

To provide estimating instructors with a greater degree of flexibility we have included a set of Medical Clinic drawings on the disk in the text. Current Auto CAD software or Volo View is required to access and manipulate the CAD drawings. Volo View can be downloaded for free from autodesk.com. Any reprographics house should be able to facilitate the instructor's needs as well. Estimating instructors may want to consider the use of the CAD drawings to:

- Display plan sheets using a digital projector.
- Incorporate portions of drawings in digital presentations.
- Print a full size plan sheet for use with a roll out digitizer.
- Demonstrate Request for Information/Contract Clarification process using redlined CAD drawings.
- Demonstrate creation of an addendum containing a modified CAD drawing.
- Demonstrate communication of graphic images using e-mail and Internet platforms.
- Incorporate portions of drawings in handouts, quizzes, and examinations.

Abbreviations, Symbols, and Basic Mathematical Tables

CONSTRUCTION ABBREVIATIONS AND BASIC MATHEMATICAL TABLES

A

A	area
AB	anchor bolt
AC	alternate current
A/C	air conditioning
ACT	acoustical ceiling tile
A.F.F.	above finish floor
AGGR	aggregate
AIA	American Institute of Architects
AL, ALUM	aluminum
AMP	ampere
APPROX	approximate
ASPH	asphalt
ASTM	American Society for Testing Materials
AWG	American wire gauge

B

BD	board
BD FT (BF)	board foot (feet)
BLDG	building
BLK	black, block
BLKG	blocking
BM	board measure

C

CC	center to center, cubic centimeter
CEM	cement
CER	ceramic
CFM	cubic feet per minute
CIP	cast-in-place, concrete-in-place
CJ	ceiling joist, control joint
CKT	circuit (electrical)
CLG	ceiling
CMU	concrete masonry unit
CO	cleanout (plumbing)
COL	column
CONC	concrete
CONST	construction
CONTR	contractor

CU FT (ft^3)	cubic foot (feet)
CU IN (in^3)	cubic inch(es)
CU YD (yd^3)	cubic yard(s)

D

d	pennyweight (nail)
DC	direct current (elec)
DET	detail
DIA	diameter
DIAG	diagonal
DIM	dimension
DN	down
DO	ditto (same as)
DS	downspout
DWG	drawing

E

E	East
EA	each
ELEC	electric, electrical
ELEV	elevation, elevator
ENCL	enclosure
EXCAV	excavate, excavation
EXT	exterior

F

FDN	foundation
FIN	finish
FIN FLR	finish floor
FIN GRD	finish grade
FL, FLR	floor
FLG	flooring
FLUOR	fluorescent
FOB	free-on-board, factory-on-board
FOM	face of masonry
FOS	face of stud, flush on slab
FT	foot, feet
FTG	footing
FURN	furnishing, furnace
FX GL (FX)	fixed glass

G

GA	gauge
GAL	gallon
GALV	galvanize(d)
GD	ground (earth/electric)
GI	galvanized iron
GL	glass
GL BLK	glass block
GLB, GLU-LAM	glue-laminated beam
GRD	grade, ground
GWB	gypsum wall board
GYP	gypsum

H

HB	hose bibb
HDR	header
HDW	hardware
HGT/HT	height
HM	hollow metal
HORIZ	horizontal
HP	horsepower
HWH	hot water heater

I

ID	inside diameter
IN	inch(es)
INSUL	insulation
INT	interior

J

J, JST	joist
JT	joint

K

KG	kilogram
KL	kiloliter
KM	kilometer
KW	kilowatt
KWH	kilowatt hour

L

L	left, line
LAU	laundry
LAV	lavatory
LBR	labor
LDG	landing, leading
LDR	leader
LEV/LVL	level
LIN FT (LF)	lineal foot (feet)
LGTH	length
LH	left hand
LITE/LT	light (window pane)

M

MAT'L	material
MAX	maximum
MBF/MBM	thousand board feet, thousand board measure

MECH   mechanical
MISC   miscellaneous
MK   mark (identifier)
MO   momentary (electrical)
MO   masonry opening

N

N	North
NEC	National Electric Code
NIC	not in contract
NOM	nominal

O

O/A	overall (measure)
O.C. (O/C)	on center
OD	outside diameter
OH	overhead
O/H	overhang (eave line)
OPG	opening
OPP	opposite

P

PC	piece
PLAS	plastic
PLAST	plaster
PLT	plate (framing)
PR	pair
PREFAB	prefabricate(d)(tion)
PTN	partition
PVC	polyvinylchloride pipe

Q

QT	quart
QTY	quantity

R

R	right, radius, riser
RD	road, round, roof drain
REBAR	reinforced steel bar
RECEPT	receptacle
REINF	reinforce(ment)
REQ'D	required
RET	retain(ing), return
RF	roof
RFG	roofing (materials)
RH	right hand

S

S	South, beam type
SCH/SCHED	schedule
SECT	section
SERV	service (utility)
SEW	sewer
SHTHG	sheathing
SIM	similar
SP	soil pipe (plumbing)
SPEC	specification
SQ FT (ft²)	square foot (feet)

SQ IN (in^2)	inch(es)
SQ YD (yd^2)	square yard(s)
STA	station
STD	standard
STIR	stirrup (rebar)
STL	steel
STR/ST	street
STRUCT	structural
SUSP CLG	suspended ceiling
SYM	symbol, symmetric
SYS	system

T

T&G	tongue and groove
THK	thick
TOB	top of beam
TOC	top of curb
TOF	top of footing
TOL	top of ledger
TOP	top of parapet
TOS	top of steel
TR	tread, transition
TRK	track, truck
TYP	typical

U

UF	underground feeder (electrical)
USE	underground service entrance cable (electrical)

W

W	West
w/	with
w/o	without
WC	water closet (toilet)
WDW	window
WI	wrought iron
WP	weatherproof
WT/WGT	weight

Y

YD	yard

Z

Z	zinc

Symbols

&	and
∠	angle
@	at
#	number, pound
"	ditto, inch, -es
'	foot, feet
%	percent
ø	diameter

Decimal to Inch Equivalents

Inch = Decimal Fraction of One Foot			
Inch	Decimal	Inch	Decimal
1	0.083	7	0.583
2	0.167	8	0.667
3	0.250	9	0.750
4	0.333	10	0.833
5	0.417	11	0.917
6	0.500	12	1.000

Fraction to Decimal Equivalents

Fraction	Decimal	Fraction	Decimal
1/64	0.0156	33/64	0.5156
1/32	0.0313	17/32	0.5313
3/64	0.0469	35/64	0.5469
1/16	0.0625	9/16	0.5625
5/64	0.0781	37/64	0.5781
3/32	0.0938	19/32	0.5938
7/64	0.1094	39/64	0.6094
1/8	0.1250	5/8	0.6250
9/64	0.1406	41/64	0.6406
5/32	0.1563	21/32	0.6563
11/64	0.1719	43/64	0.6719
3/16	0.1875	11/16	0.6875
13/64	0.2031	45/64	0.7031
7/32	0.2188	23/32	0.7188
15/64	0.2344	47/64	0.7344
1/4	0.2500	3/4	0.7500
17/64	0.2656	49/64	0.7656
9/32	0.2813	25/32	0.7813
19/64	0.2969	51/64	0.7969
5/16	0.3125	13/16	0.8125
21/64	0.3281	53/64	0.8281
11/32	0.3438	27/32	0.8438
23/64	0.3594	55/64	0.8594
3/8	0.3750	7/8	0.8750
25/64	0.3906	57/64	0.8906
13/32	0.4063	29/32	0.9063
27/64	0.4219	59/64	0.9219
7/16	0.4375	15/16	0.9375
29/64	0.4531	61/64	0.9531
15/32	0.4689	31/32	0.9689
31/64	0.4844	63/64	0.9844
1/2	0.5000	1	1.0000

Metric Ratios

Plan Use	Ratio	Equivalent Meter Length
Details:		
	1:5	200 mm = 1 m
	1:10	100 mm = 1 m
	1:20	50 mm = 1 m
Floor Plans:		
	1:40	25 mm = 1 m
	1:50	20 mm = 1 m
Plot Plans:		
	1:80	13.3 mm = 1 m
	1:100	12.5 mm = 1 m
Plat Plans:		
	1:200	5 mm = 1 m
	1:500	2 mm = 1 m
City Map:		
	1:1250	0.8 mm = 1 m
	1:2500	0.4 mm = 1 m

Metric to English Equivalents

Metric		English	Metric		English
	Lineal			Area	
1 cm	=	0.3937 in	1 cm^2	=	0.15500 in^2
1 m	=	39.37 in	1 m^2	=	1,550.5 in^2
1 km	=	0.621 mi	1 km^2	=	0.386 mi^2
			1 m^2	=	10.764 ft^2
	Volume			Weight	
1 c.c. (cm^3)	=	.06102 in^3			
1 m^3	=	35.315 ft^3	1 kg	=	2.2046 pounds
1 m^3	=	1.308 yd^3	1 metric ton	=	2,204.6 pounds

Numbers and Their Squares and Approximate Square Roots

Number	Square	Sq. Root	Number	Square	Sq. Root
1	1	1.000	51	2601	7.141
2	4	1.414	52	2704	7.211
3	9	1.732	53	2809	7.280
4	16	2.000	54	2916	7.348
5	25	2.236	55	3025	7.416
6	36	2.449	56	3136	7.483
7	49	2.646	57	3249	7.550
8	64	2.828	58	3364	7.616
9	81	3.000	59	3481	7.681
10	100	3.162	60	3600	7.746
11	121	3.317	61	3721	7.810
12	144	3.464	62	3844	7.874
13	169	3.606	63	3969	7.937
14	196	3.742	64	4096	8.000
15	225	3.873	65	4225	8.062
16	256	4.000	66	4356	8.124
17	289	4.123	67	4489	8.185
18	324	4.243	68	4624	8.246
19	361	4.359	69	4761	8.307
20	400	4.472	70	4900	8.367
21	441	4.583	71	5041	8.426
22	484	4.690	72	5184	8.485
23	529	4.796	73	5329	8.544
24	576	4.899	74	5476	8.602
25	625	5.000	75	5625	8.660
26	676	5.099	76	5776	8.718
27	729	5.196	77	5929	8.775
28	784	5.292	78	6084	8.832
29	841	5.385	79	6241	8.888
30	900	5.477	80	6400	8.944
31	961	5.568	81	6561	9.000
32	1024	5.657	82	6724	9.055
33	1089	5.745	83	6889	9.110
34	1156	5.831	84	7056	9.165
35	1225	5.916	85	7225	9.220
36	1296	6.000	86	7396	9.274
37	1369	6.083	87	7569	9.327
38	1444	6.164	88	7744	9.381
39	1521	6.245	89	7921	9.434
40	1600	6.325	90	8100	9.487
41	1681	6.403	91	8381	9.539
42	1764	6.481	92	8464	9.592
43	1849	6.557	93	8649	9.644
44	1936	6.633	94	8836	9.695
45	2025	6.708	95	9025	9.747
46	2116	6.782	96	9216	9.798
47	2209	6.852	97	9409	9.849
48	2304	6.928	98	9604	9.899
49	2401	7.000	99	9801	9.950
50	2500	7.071	100	10000	10.000

Plane Trigonometric Natural Functions

		Sine and Cosine			
Angle	Sine	Cosine	Angle	Sine	Cosine
0	0.0000	1.0000	46	0.7193	0.6947
1	0.0175	0.9999	47	0.7314	0.6820
2	0.0349	0.9994	48	0.7431	0.6691
3	0.0523	0.9986	49	0.7547	0.6561
4	0.0698	0.9976	50	0.7660	0.6428
5	0.0872	0.9962	51	0.7772	0.6293
6	0.1045	0.9945	52	0.7880	0.6157
7	0.1219	0.9926	53	0.7986	0.6018
8	0.1392	0.9903	54	0.8090	0.5878
9	0.1564	0.9877	55	0.8192	0.5736
10	0.1737	0.9848	56	0.8290	0.5592
11	0.1908	0.9816	57	0.8387	0.5446
12	0.2079	0.9782	58	0.8481	0.5299
13	0.2250	0.9744	59	0.8572	0.5150
14	0.2419	0.9703	60	0.8660	0.5000
15	0.2588	0.9659	61	0.8746	0.4848
16	0.2756	0.9613	62	0.8830	0.4695
17	0.2924	0.9563	63	0.8910	0.4540
18	0.3090	0.9511	64	0.8988	0.4384
19	0.3256	0.9455	65	0.9063	0.4226
20	0.3420	0.9397	66	0.9136	0.4067
21	0.3584	0.9336	67	0.9205	0.3907
22	0.3746	0.9272	68	0.9297	0.3746
23	0.3907	0.9205	69	0.9336	0.3584
24	0.4067	0.9136	70	0.9397	0.3420
25	0.4226	0.9063	71	0.9455	0.3256
26	0.4384	0.8988	72	0.9511	0.3090
27	0.4540	0.8910	73	0.9563	0.2924
28	0.4695	0.8830	74	0.9613	0.2756
29	0.4848	0.8746	75	0.9659	0.2588
30	0.5000	0.8660	76	0.9703	0.2419
31	0.5150	0.8572	77	0.9744	0.2250
32	0.5299	0.8481	78	0.9782	0.2079
33	0.5446	0.8387	79	0.9816	0.1908
34	0.5592	0.8290	80	0.9848	0.1737
35	0.5736	0.8192	81	0.9877	0.1564
36	0.5878	0.8090	82	0.9903	0.1392
37	0.6018	0.7986	83	0.9926	0.1219
38	0.6157	0.7880	84	0.9945	0.1045
39	0.6293	0.7772	85	0.9962	0.0872
40	0.6428	0.7660	86	0.9976	0.0698
41	0.6561	0.7547	87	0.9986	0.0523
42	0.6691	0.7431	88	0.9994	0.0349
43	0.6820	0.7314	89	0.9999	0.0175
44	0.6947	0.7193	90	1.0000	0.0000
45	0.7071	0.7071			

The Contract Documents

CHRISTLE Associates
550 Broad Street
Las Vegas, Nevada
89000
(300)555-5555

October 30, 1992

You are invited to bid on a General Contract, including mechanical and electrical work, for a one-story, wood frame medical clinic, approximately 2,370 square feet. All bids must be on a lump-sum basis; aggregate bids will not be accepted.

The Architect, as owner's representative and agent, will receive bids until 3:00 o'clock PM, Pacific Standard Time, on Thursday, November 15, 1992, at 550 Broad Street, Las Vegas, Nevada. Any bids received after this time and date will not be accepted. All interested parties are invited to attend. Bids will be opened publicly and read aloud.

Drawings and specifications may be obtained from the Architect along with the Instructions to Bidders at a cost of two-hundred dollars ($200.00), non-refundable. A maximum of four (4) sets may be purchased by any one company.

Plans may also be examined at the following plan room locations:

The Plan Room	The Bid Depository
35 Atlantic Avenue	156 Pacific Avenue
Las Vegas, Nevada	Las Vegas, Nevada

A bid (security) bond valued at fifteen percent (15%) of the bid must accompany each bid submitted in accordance with the Instructions to Bidders. The Architect and Owner reserve the right to reject any and all bids or waive any irregularities due to discrepancies in the bids.

(Signed) Steven Christle
Architect and Agent for
The Medical Associates
Caliente, Nevada

ADVERTISEMENT TO BID

BID: November 15, 1992, Medical Clinic, J. and Co, Caliente, NV, Project 12726 is open for bid. Christle Associates, 550 Broad St, Las Vegas, NV, (300)555-5555, is representing the owner. Sealed bids will be received on a general contract, including mechanical and electrical work, for a wood frame structure approx 2,378 sq ft. All bids must be lump sum: no segregated bids will be accepted. Bids will be received until 3PM PST, Thurs, November 15, 1992, 550 Broad Street, Las Vegas, NV. No bids accepted after that time. Bids will be opened and read publicly. Plans and specifications may be examined at:

The Plan Room	The Bid Depository
35 Atlantic Ave	156 Pacific Ave
Las Vegas, NV	Las Vegas, NV

Copies may be obtained from the architect at a cost of $200/set, non-refundable, maximum 4 sets. Bid security in the amount of 15% of total bid proposal to be submitted with the bid in accordance with the Instructions to Bidders. Owner reserves right of refusal of any bid. By order of: The Medical Associates, Caliente, Nevada.

INSTRUCTIONS TO BIDDERS

CHRISTLE Associates
550 Broad Street
Las Vegas, Nevada
89000
(300)555-5555

October 30, 1992   Re: A Medical Clinic
Caliente, Nevada
Project 12726
TO: All Bidders.
All bids must be in accordance with these Instructions to Bidders to be considered.

Documents

Bonafide prime bidders may obtain a maximum of four (4) sets of Drawings and Specifications from the architect upon deposit of two-hundred and 00/100 dollars ($200) per set, non-refundable. No partial sets will be issued; no sets will be issued to sub-bidders (subcontractors) by the architect.

Examination

Bidders shall carefully examine the Documents and the project site to obtain first-hand knowledge of existing conditions. Contractors will not be given extra payment for any conditions determinable prior to bid by such examination of the Documents and the project site.

Questions

Submit all questions about the Plans and Specifications to the architect, in writing, at least ten (10) working days prior to the bid date. Replies shall be issued to all prime bidders of record as Addenda to the Plans and/or Specifications and will become a part of the Contract. The architect and owner will not be responsible for oral clarifications. Any questions after the ten (10) working-day period will not be accepted.

Substitutions

Unspecified products will not be accepted unless notification has been made ten (10) working days prior to bid date. Requests shall be accompanied by a description of the product, test approvals, and specifications of the product for verification by the architect. The architect, upon approval of said product, shall issue an Addendum to all bidders of record prior to bid date.

Basis of Bid

The bidder must include all unit cost items and all alternatives shown on the Bid Forms. Failure to comply may be cause for rejection. No segregated bids or assignments will be considered.

Preparation of Bid

Bids shall be prepared on the Bid Forms supplied with the Plans and Specifications. Any alteration to the Forms shall be sufficient cause for bid rejection. Fill in all blanks and submit two (2) copies. Bids shall be signed with the name typed below the signature. Where bidder is a corporation, Bid Forms must be signed with the legal name of the corporation, the name of the State of incorporation and legal signature of an officer authorized to bind the corporation to a contract.

Bid Security

Bid security shall be made payable to the architect, as representative and agent for the owner, in the amount of fifteen percent (15%) of the bid sum. Security shall be either by certified check or bid bond issued by a surety licensed to conduct business in the State of Nevada. The successful bidder's security will be retained until the contract is signed and the required Payment and Performance bonds submitted. The owner reserves the right to retain the security of the two (2) lowest bidders until the lowest bidder enters into contract or until sixty (60) days after bid opening, whichever is shorter. All other security will be returned as soon as practicable. Any bidders refusing to enter into contract with the owner shall have the security held for liquidated damages, not as a penalty. Security is to be submitted with the bid on bid day.

For the Owner:

(Signed) Steven Christle
          Architect and Agent

Copies:
      Owner:
      All bidders
      File

THE JANUS CORPORATION

1 Broad Street
Caliente, Nevada 89000
(702) 555-6666
BID FORM
A Medical Clinic
Our Project # 12726

Date _____

PROPOSAL FOR: Concrete
TO: The Janus Corporation
                1 Broad Street
                Caliente, Nevada 89000
                Attn: Brian Logsdon

Gentlemen:
The undersigned, doing business under the name of _____, having examined the Request for Bid, including all Documents referenced therein, and Addenda thereto, prepared by The Janus Corporation, and having familiarized myself/ourselves with the project, the project site and any conditions which affect the construction of the proposed project, including the availability of labor and materials, hereby agrees/agree to execute a contract to furnish all labor, material and equipment and any other miscellaneous items and services necessary to provide the proposed scope of work in accordance with the Contract Documents.

A. Base Bid Price:
    Our firm price is in the Lump Sum amount of _____
_____($_____).

Said bid price will be represented by a detailed itemization, referred to as Schedule "A". This Lump Sum amount includes all Federal, State and local taxes, including but not limited to, sales, use and excise taxes that may be imposed on materials or services provided under this proposal.

B. General Agreements:
1. In submitting this Bid, the Undersigned agrees/agree and understands/understand that this Bid is a firm offer continuing for sixty (60) days from the date and time of Bid. By submission of this bid the Undersigned agrees/agree to execute a construction contract for the work in the form provided with the Request for Bid.
2. By submission of this Bid the Undersigned agrees/agree and commits/commit to performing the work with sufficient trained personnel to complete all work within the scheduled time-frame. It is also understood that schedules, as issued, are subject to change and the Undersigned agrees/agree to keep informed of said changes and abide accordingly, notwithstanding strikes, work stoppages or labor disputes of any kind. The Undersigned shall be liable to both the Owner and the General Contractor for all costs, expenses and/or liabilities incurred by the Owner and/or General Contractor resulting from delays on the job or for any other liability due to the Undersigned's failure to perform as required by this paragraph. For purposes of this subcontract work stoppages and/or labor disputes shall not be, under any circumstances, or for any reason, construed as being beyond the Subcontractor's control.
3. The Undersigned has/have visited and examined the location of the proposed work and is/are thoroughly familiar with the drawings, Specifications and related Contract Documents.

4. The Undersigned understands/understand that The Janus Corporation reserves the right to reject any and all Bids and has no obligation to enter into a Contract for the work. In addition, it is understood that all Bids become the property of The Janus Corporation and there is no obligation to publish the results thereof.

5. The Undersigned understands/understand that The Janus Corporation will not be responsible for any errors of commission or omission incurred by the Undersigned in the preparation of this Bid. The Undersigned further understands/understand that no modification or withdrawal of this Bid will be permitted after the Bid opening has commenced.

C. Changes, Modifications and/or Revisions:

1. Changes, modifications and/or revisions that may occur in the work shall have appropriate adjustments made in the Contract price, and the Undersigned agrees/agree that the charges for extra work shall be determined in one of the following ways by The Janus Corporation:

    a. By estimate and mutual acceptance of a Lump Sum, properly itemized;

    b. Or by cost plus a percentage fee.

2. If such work is to be added or deducted by written change order of The Janus Corporation, and such work is not covered by unit prices or Alternate Bids quoted in this proposal, the cost of such changes shall be determined prior to the time the work is ordered, and, at The Janus Corporation's option, the Contract will be adjusted accordingly on the following basis:

    a. Additional Work Performed by Subcontractors:

        (1) Charges are to be the Subcontractor's estimated price for the work, agreed to by the Owner, plus ten percent (10%) for overhead and profit.

    b. Additional Work Performed by the Undersigned's Forces:

        (1) Charges shall be computed at the estimated cost for labor and material entering into the work plus ten percent (10%) for overhead and five percent (5%) for profit.

    c. Work Omitted:

        (1) Credit will be allowed in the amount of the actual savings in cost computed on the same basis as for added work but without application of the above costs covering the Undersigned's job supervision, general job expenses and the percentage for overhead and profit.

    d. Changes Resulting in Work Both Added or Omitted:

        (1) Costs covering the Undersigned's job supervision (if applicable), general job expense and the percentage for overhead and profit shall be applied to the new difference only between the cost of work added and deducted if the net result is an ADD.

    e. Additional Costs for Supervision:

        (1) There will be no adds for supervision costs if the extra work is performed concurrently with work already contracted. Should extra work extend, or be performed, after contracted work has been completed, supervision costs may then be added for that period of time from when contracted work was completed to when the extra work was completed.

        (2) Supervision costs will only be paid for once during any period of construction. At no time will the Subcontractor include these costs in Lump Sum or Time and Material change order requests unless they are permitted above, or, in case of Time and Material work in which the Superintendent actually performs the work and this is verified by the Contractor's Project Superintendent.

f.   Premium Time Costs:
- (1) When a Subcontractor has been directed to perform contracted work on an overtime basis, said Subcontractor shall submit only the premium time cost for labor, documented by signed time tickets, plus ten percent (10%) allowable mark-up for overhead. Additional mark-up for profit on already contracted work will not be permitted.

g.   Job Progress:
- (1) The Undersigned agrees/agree not to delay job progress of any work pending final determination of value for the revised scope, provided the Undersigned receives/receive written authorization to proceed from The Janus Corporation.

D. Contract Bond/Evidence of Insurance:

The Undersigned agrees/agree to execute and abide by the form of Contract provided to the Undersigned with this Bid Form, and to furnish, at the time of execution of the Contract, guaranty bonds and evidences of insurance as specified in the General Conditions.

E. Addenda:

Receipt of Addendum/Addenda numbered _____ is/are hereby acknowledged.

F. Return of Plans and Specifications:

If not the successful bidder, I/we agree to return the Plans and Specifications, Addenda and all other Contract Documents heretofore furnished to me/us as soon as the Contract is awarded to the successful bidder, including any additional copies.

G. Contractor's License:

The Undersigned is licensed to perform the proposed scope of work described herein and holds Nevada Contractor License No. _____, Classification _____, with a license limit of _____. Respectfully submitted this _____ day of _____, 19_____.

Bidder's Legal Name: _____

_____
(Signature)

_____
(Title)

_____
(Signature)

_____
(Title)

Bidder's Legal Address: _____

_____

_____

_____

_____
Telephone Number:

_____
Type of Organization:

_____
(Corporation, Partnership, Individual)

Schedule "A"

Bid Breakdown for:
Concrete

1.   3000 psi Concrete   _____ sq ft $ _____

2.   Reinforcement Bar   _____ sq ft $ _____

3.   Welded Wire Fabric   _____ sq ft $ _____

4.   Trenching   _____ sq ft $ _____

5.   Other (Itemize) _____

TOTAL CONCRETE BID: $ _____

Name of Principal Members of Firm if Partnership or Joint Venture:

_____

_____

_____

Corporation is organized under the Laws of the State of _____.

Attest: _____

         (Corporate Secretary)   (Affix Corporate Seal Here)

★ ★ ★ ★ ★ ★

Bond Rate:
       Should the Janus Corporation and/or the Owner elect to have the Subcontractor furnish a One Hundred Percent (100%) Performance and a One Hundred Percent (100%) Payment Bond the following rate shall apply:
       Add _____ %, which is equal to the sum of _____ ($_____), to the Base Bid.

_____

         (Contractor Firm Name)

Signed by: _____

Title: _____

Date: _____

Nevada Contractor's License No. _____

License Limit: _____

ADDENDUM

***CHRISTLE* Associates**
550 Broad Street
Las Vegas, Nevada
89000
(300)555-5555

Addendum #1:   November 9, 1992
A Medical Clinic   Re: Alternates
Caliente, Nevada

    This addendum shall become a part of the plans and specifications for the project known as the Medical Clinic, Caliente, Nevada. This addendum supercedes any references or changes in the plans previously considered for said structure. The Specifications for Alternate #2, Masonry, shall prevail with the following additions and/or changes:

    Concrete Reinforcement. A #5 dowel shall be placed 4'-0" O/C (1.22m) horizontally, embedded in the footing and extending 2'-0" (60.9cm) vertically above the slab.

    A #4 rebar horizontal hook shall be placed in the perimeter of the concrete slab and shall extend 4'-0" (1.22m) into the slab with a 9" (22.86 cm) hook extending into the footing. The horizontal rebar shall also be placed at 4'-0" O/C (1.22m).

    Masonry Reinforcement. All masonry shall be placed on-slab. There are no masonry stem walls. The first course placed on the slab shall be a bond beam course with 2-#4 reinforcement bars, continuous, lapped 48 diameters per code and local ordinances.

    A #5 dowel shall be placed 4'-0" O/C (1.22m) horizontally, embedded in the footing and extending 2'-0" (60.96cm) vertically above the slab.

    A #4 rebar horizontal hook shall be placed in the perimeter of the concrete slab and shall extend 4'-0" (1.22m) into the slab with a 9" (22.86cm) hook extending into the footing. The horizontal rebar shall also be placed at 4'-0" O/C (1.22m).

    Masonry. All materials, labor and equipment necessary to install a complete masonry system shall be included. The installation shall be to the best of the workmanship standards of the trade.

    Masonry rough openings for windows:
        East wall, Northeast and Southeast corners shall be
        4'-0" × 5'-0" ea (1.22m × 1.52m)
        Southwest corner shall be 6'-0" × 4'-8" (1.83m × 1.42m)
        Northwest corner shall be 6'-0" × 3'-8" (1.83m × 1.12m)
        All other window openings on North and South walls shall be 3'-4" × 3'-8" ea
        (1.01m × 1.12m)
    Masonry rough openings for doors:
        North and South openings shall be 3'-4" × 7'-4" ea (1.01m × 2.23m)
        East wall opening shall be 6'-0" × 7'-4" (1.83m × 2.23m)
    This addendum shall not alter the bid date.

(Signed) Steven Christle

Copies:

    Owner
    All Plan Holders
    File

Project Manual

Project Manual for a Medical Clinic

Caliente, Nevada

Owner: Dr. Robin Stone
dba The Medical Associates
1 Main Street
Caliente, Nevada 89008

Architect: Christle Associates
550 Broad Street
Las Vegas, Nevada 89109
Civil & Structural Engineers: Janus Corporation
1 Main Street
Caliente, Nevada 89008

Mechanical Engineer: Aquarius Mechanical & Plumbing, Inc.
375 Water Street
Las Vegas, Nevada 89121
Electrical Engineer: Brophy Electric, Inc.
935 Ampere Avenue
Las Vegas, Nevada 89119

GENERAL CONDITIONS

Definitions

For purposes of this contract The Medical Associates of 1 Main Street, Caliente, Nevada, 89008, is referred to as "the owner."

The term "project" described in this Specification is the Medical Associates Medical Clinic located at Broadway and Main Streets, Caliente, Nevada, 89008.

The term "contractor" means the person, firm or corporation, identified as such in the agreement, responsible for the execution of the work contracted with the owner.

The term "subcontractor" means, without limitation, any person, firm or corporation working directly or indirectly for the contractor, whether or not pursuant to a formal contract, that furnishes or performs a portion of the work, labor or material, according to the drawings and/or specifications.

The term "agreement" means the construction agreement between the owner and the contractor.

The term "contract" means the agreement signed by the owner and the contractor, these Specifications and all other documents listed as contract documents of this agreement.

The term "contract amount" means the dollar-value of the agreement as revised by approved contract change orders.

The term "work" includes all labor, material and equipment necessary to produce the construction required by contract.

The term "change order" is a written order to the contractor, signed by the owner, issued AFTER the execution of the contract, authorizing a change in work or an adjustment in the original contract amount as agreed upon by the owner and the contractor.

The term "contract time" is the period of time allotted in the agreement for the completion of the work as revised by approved contract change orders.

Intent of the Documents

The agreement and each of the contract documents are complementary and they shall be interpreted so that what is called for by one shall be binding upon all. Should there be any conflicts in the documents, the contractor is to bring the discrepancies to the attention of the owner at once. It shall be the owner who shall make the responsible decision as to which document is correct and all other documents shall be immediately amended by addendum.

Duplication is not intended through any of the documents and no duplication for additional cost may be claimed.

Delays and Extensions of Time

Should there be excessive delays due to the owner, an employee of the owner, or a contractor of the owner, or by changes ordered in the work, or by acts of God, or by any other cause deemed by the owner as justifying the delay, the contract shall be extended by change order. The length of the extension shall be determined by the owner.

All requests for extension of contract shall be made to owner no more than ten (10) working days after such delay occurs or they shall be otherwise waived. A continuing delay need not be put into writing unless it exceeds another ten (10) working-day period.

Extension of contract time by the owner shall be the contractor's sole remedy for the delay.

Assignments

This contract, or any rights hereunder, shall not be assigned by the contractor without the express consent of the owner.

Payment and Performance Bonds

Prior to any work the contractor, at the discretion of the owner, shall supply the owner with a payment and performance bond in the amount of one-hundred percent (100%) of the contract. The cost of such bond shall be at the expense of the contractor.

Compliance with the Law

Contractor shall be responsible for complete compliance with all laws, including OSHA, ordinances, codes or other regulations as may exist in the jurisdiction of authority in the locale of this contract.

Indemnification

The contractor shall indemnify and hold harmless the owner and all of the owner's heirs and assigns against any and all claims, damages, losses and expenses, including attorney's fees, due to the performance of the work, provided that such claims, damages, losses or expenses, causing bodily harm, illness or death due to negligence or omission of the contractor, subcontractor or anyone directly or indirectly employed by the contractor or subcon-tractor, or anyone for whose acts any of them may be liable, regardless of whether or not it is caused in part by a party indemnified hereunder, and shall further indemnify and hold harmless the owner, all of the owner's heirs and assigns from the expense of such defense against all claims for damages, losses and expenses claimed by any person, firm or corporation.

INDEX TO SPECIFICATIONS

```
      09500 Acoustical Treatment
      09650 Resilient Flooring
      09680 Carpet
      09900 Painting
      09950 Wallcovering
Division 10: Specialties
      10000 Scope of Work
      10500 Lockers
      10800 Toilet & Bath Accessories
Division 11: Equipment
      11000 Scope of Work
      11700 Medical Equipment
Division 12: Furnishings
      NIC - To Be Furnished by Owner
Division 13: Not Used
Division 14: Not Used
Division 15: Mechanical
      15000 Scope of Work
      15050 Basic Mechanical Materials & Methods
      15400 Plumbing
      15500 Heating, Ventilation and Air Conditioning
Division 16: Electrical
      16000 Scope of Work
      16050 Basic Electrical Materials and Methods
      16400 Service & Distribution
      16500 Lighting
      16600 Special Systems
      16700 Communications
```

STANDARDS

AIA	American Institute of Architects
ACI	American Concrete Institute
APA	American Plywood Association
ASHRAE	American Society of Heating, Refrigeration and Air-conditioning Engineers, Inc.
ASTM	American Society for Testing Materials
AWS	American Welding Society
CRSI	Concrete Reinforcing Steel Institute
DHI	Door and Hardware Institute
MIA	Masonry Institute of America
TCA	Tile Council of America, Inc.
UL	Underwriters Laboratories, Inc.
WWPA	Western Wood Products Association

SPECIFICATIONS

Division 1: General Requirements

01010 Summary of Work

The contractor warrants and represents that it has carefully examined all the plans and Specifications, and all of the real property upon which the work is to be conducted, and has satisfied itself as to the conditions existing and the difficulties that may be encountered in the execution of the work which should have reasonably been discovered upon such examination, will not constitute a cause for the reformation or recision of this contract, or a modification of the amount of this contract, or its termination.

The contractor shall obtain and pay for all permits, licenses, certifications, tap charges, construction easements, inspections and other approvals required, both temporary and permanent, to commence and complete the work at no additional cost to the owner.

The contractor shall be responsible for all the work on the site and the adjacent property regarding loss or damage resulting from its operations at no additional cost to the owner.

Contractor shall receive a full certificate of occupancy before the contractor can receive final payment for the work.

The contractor may have portions of the work performed by others by use of subcontract agreements. These agreements must be approved by the owner and shall in no way increase the cost of the project.

All subcontract agreements shall automatically include the General Conditions and Requirements between the owner and the contractor.

No contract between the contractor and the subcontractor shall be construed to be a contract between the owner and the subcontractor. No subcontractor has a right against the owner unless the contract has defaulted. Should this happen, the owner shall be liable only for the costs incurred in accordance with the subcontract agreement.

The contractor shall be fully responsible for any omissions, commissions or errors committed by the subcontractor, or any person, firm or corporation, or any of their respective employees, in contract with the contractor.

01020 Allowances

An allowance shall be permitted by the owner for medical equipment and lighting fixtures. The allowance for the medical equipment shall be fifty-thousand dollars and 00/100 ($50,000) and the lighting fixture allowance shall be in the amount of twenty-three hundred and 00/100 dollars ($2,300).

01025 Measurement and Payments

Each subcontractor shall submit a request for payment to the contractor as prescribed in the contract agreement. Each submission shall be made no later than the 10th day or the 25th day of each month. Requests for payment received on the 10th day shall be reimbursed on the 30th day of the same month. Requests for payment received on the 25th day of the month shall be reimbursed on the 15th day of the month following. There shall be only one payment allowed per month.

No payment shall be approved by the contractor or owner without verification of the measurement submitted with the payment request.

01030 Alternates/Alternatives

The owner has requested that the following five (5) alternates be submitted with the proposal. Should any of the materials, procedures or systems be unavailable for any reason an alternative material, procedure or system may be submitted. Should there be an alternative submitted the contractor and/or material supplier shall submit such information and change per Section 01300.

The proposal submitted to the owner shall include the following alternates:

Alternate #1. An alternate concrete slab and footing per drawings, identified as S-1A, shall be included with the bid. The concrete specifications shall read:

02100 Site Preparation. A base pad is to extend 5 lineal feet beyond the length and width of the slab and shall be 8" (20.32 cm) thick. The pad shall be with the Federal DOT Specification type E aggregate soil mix (Type II) or a sand base compacted to 95% (ASTM standard).

03200 Concrete Reinforcing. Horizontal footing reinforcement shall be 2 #4 rebar, continuous, with 48 diameter laps at all end joints.

#5 rebar dowels shall be installed horizontally at 4'-0" O/C (1.22 m), extending 2'-0" (60.96 cm) A. F. F. Dowels shall start a minimum 1'-0" each way from the corners and from each side of exterior openings. Dowels shall have a 9" (22.86 cm) hook. Dowels shall be placed not more than 3" (7.62 cm) nor less than 1 1/2" (3.81 cm), above the bottom of the footing.

#4 rebar tie hooks, 4'-0" (1.22 m) long w/1'-6" (45.72 cm) hook turned down into footings, shall be placed horizontally along perimeter of slab starting 1'-0" (30.48 cm) from the corners each way at 48" O/C (1.22 m).

03250 Concrete Accessories. Admixtures permitted include:

1. Air-entrained agent per ASTM C260.
2. Hardener and Dustproofer additive-Lapodith or equal.
3. Nonslip additive-Durafax or equal.
4. Nonshrink additive-Sika Set or equal.
5. Cure Seal additive per ASTM C309.

03300 Cast-In-Place Concrete. Concrete slab, 4" (10.16 cm) thick, as per plans, with 6×6-W1.4×W1.4 embedded 1 1/2" (3.81 cm) below finish concrete surface. WWF to be lapped 6" (15.24 cm), minimum, at all sides, ends and turndowns along perimeter.

Alternate #2. The work included in this alternate shall be for masonry exterior wall construction and masonry wall insulation in lieu of the exterior framing base bid. The Specifications shall read:

04100 Mortar and Grout. Mortar and grout shall meet specifications as indicated by the Masonry Institute of America and local codes. Solid grout shall attain a minimum strength of 2,000 psi (907.18 kg/6.45 cm^2).

04150 Masonry Accessories. All masonry accessories shall include, but are not limited to, corner units, halves, lintel block and sill block. Knock-out or deep-cut ("U") bond beam block may be used in lieu of lintel block.

04200 Unit Masonry. Concrete Masonry Units include split-face one side, load-bearing, 8×8×16 (20.32 cm × 20.32 cm × 40.64 cm), f'/m 1530, natural gray, on the East, North, and South elevations. Standard (smooth face) load-bearing, f'/m 1530, natural gray, shall be on the West elevation only.

The wall height is 9'-4" (2.84 m) from the top of slab to top of masonry. 2 #4 continuous rebar to be installed horizontally in first course, 1-#4 each course 2'-0" (0.61 m) vertically, 2 4# rebar above all openings and 2 #4 rebar at the top course. No rebar shall be heat bent.

#9 gauge truss-type horizontal joint reinforcement at 16" O/C (40.64 cm) vertically may be used in lieu of the #4 rebar except at the 4'-0" (1.22 m) level, above openings and at the top course.

1-#5 vertical rebar shall be placed at 4'-0" O/C (1.22 m) horizontally in all walls to match dowel spacing. 1-#5 rebar shall be placed vertically on each side of wall openings and 2 #4 rebar horizontally over openings in bond beam extending a minimum 1'-0" (30.48 cm) beyond each side of opening.

#4 rebar to be lapped 48 diameters and #5 rebar to be lapped 40 diameters. Rebar is lapped 2'-0" (60.96 cm) each way at all corners.

04210 Insulation. All materials of one type shall be from one manufacturer. No substitutes will be allowed. The materials selected by the contractor shall be approved in writing prior to any installations per Division 1, Section 01300, Submittals.

Two types of insulation shall be installed in conjunction with the masonry construction. There shall be an expanded mineral fiber loose-fill insulation placed within the wall cavities where no grouting exists and there shall be polystyrene foam board insulation installed on the interior side of the masonry walls.

The loose-fill insulation shall be applied during masonry wall construction by the masonry contractor. At each grout lift, prior to the grout-stop installations for the horizontal bond beams, the insulation shall be poured into the cells that are to have no grout. The masonry contractor shall be responsible to see that the cells are filled completely before the grout-stop is installed. The general contractor's quality control inspector on the project shall make a special inspection to assure proper installation. No cells shall be left unfilled.

2" (5.08 cm) polystyrene insulation board (foam board), 3.5# (1.59 kg) density, shall be installed on the interior side of the masonry walls. The "Styrostud" system shall be used with either the aluminum "Z" stud or the channel "stud" to support the insulation. The board shall be directly adhered with an adhesive recommended by the manufacturer. The board shall be 2″×9″ (0.61 m × 2.74 m). The studs shall be 9′-0″ (2.74 m) long.

A 2×4 (5.08 cm × 10.16 cm) wood furring strip shall be installed at the floor and ceiling levels and at each interior corner of the walls to be used as a base upon which to fasten the drywall.

Alternate #3. An alternate shall be included for light-gauge structural and light-gauge metal framing in lieu of wood framing. The framing shall include floor joists, wall construction, structural and partition, ceiling joists and the roof structure. The specifications shall read:

05400 Cold Formed Metal Framing. Floor joists shall be 10″ (25.40 cm) 18-ga structural unpunched "C" studs attached with all necessary accessories for a complete installation.

Exterior walls are 9′-0″ (2.74 m) high and shall be constructed of 6″ (15.24 cm) 18-ga structural steel studs with top and bottom 6″ (15.24 cm) 18-ga track. Studs shall be placed at 24″ O/C (0.61 m).

All lintels over exterior openings shall be a minimum of 2 8″ (20.32 cm) 18-ga unpunched steel studs. All ceiling joists and roof rafters shall be 6″ 18-ga unpunched steel studs. Ridge and hip beams shall be 8″ 18-ga unpunched steel studs doubled. Spacing shall be as noted on plans.

All connections at walls, lintels, rafter, and ridge and hip shall be welded with proper clip stiffeners. Weld shall be a fillet weld completely surrounding clip stiffener. Self-tapping #6 × 3/4″ (1.91 cm) screws may be used to hold stiffeners and connections in place until welded.

If structural metal stud framing is accepted, the wood utility plate on the steel support beam is not to be installed and the wall embedment and pier heights must be adjusted accordingly.

All materials shall be supplied by American Studco Company, Phoenix, Arizona.

09100 Metal Support Systems. Interior bearing walls shall be 6″ (15.24 cm) 20-ga galvanized studs and track, interior plumbing walls shall be 6″ (15.24 cm) 22-ga studs and track, and partition walls shall be 3 5/8″ (9.21 cm) 25-ga galvanized studs and track. All walls shall extend 9′-0″ (2.74 m) A.F.F.

All necessary accessories shall be in accordance with the manufacturer's recommendations, codes and local ordinances.

All materials shall be supplied by American Studco Company, Phoenix, Arizona.

Alternate #4. An alternate structural floor support beam and alternate truss roof system shall read as follows:

06100 Rough Carpentry. A wood support beam may be used in lieu of the steel support beam. The wood beam shall be constructed and installed per the recommendations of the Western Wood Products Association.

The beam shall be supplied from 6×8 (15.24 cm × 20.32 cm) DF #1 or better. The beam shall be installed in the same manner as the steel beam with embedment in the foundation walls and centered on the concrete piers.

The beams shall be supported at the piers with a specially constructed saddle support to meet all local code and ordinance structural specifications. The saddles and beams shall be fastened with 3/4″ (1.91 cm) through bolts and tightened in place with 3/4″ (1.91 cm) nuts, washers and lock washers on both sides of the connection. The nuts shall be spot-welded sufficiently to guarantee that they shall not come loose.

Special inspections of the saddles and the beam construction are required.

06170 Prefabricated Structural Wood. An alternate truss roof system may be used in lieu of conventional roof framing.

Prefabricated wood trusses, 5/12 slope, shall be manufactured by Trus-Joist/MacMillan, or equal, and installed in lieu of ceiling joists and roof rafters. Trusses shall be constructed with a 2×6 (5.08 cm × 15.24 cm) top chord and 2×4 (5.08 cm × 10.16 cm) bottom chord. The trusses shall be constructed so as to provide the hip configuration as indicated on the structural framing plan, and longitudinal and transverse sections. All common and jack trusses, blocking and accessories shall be supplied by the manufacturer. The truss shall include a rafter tail to extend 2′-0″ beyond the plate line at all eaves.

Alternate #5. This alternate is for a built-up roofing system in lieu of tile roofing.

06100 Rough Carpentry. The slope of roof shall change from 5/12 slope to a 1/2″/ft (1.27 cm/30.48 cm) slope gable-framed roof structure. Conventional framing techniques shall be used with 2×6 (5.08 cm × 15.24 cm) rafters and ceiling joists spaced at 24″ O/C (0.61 m). A double 2×8 (5.08 cm × 20.32 cm) ridge shall be installed full length of roof. The overhang shall remain at 2′-0″ (0.61 m) on all sides. All king posts, braces and purlins shall be eliminated. 2×6 (5.08 cm × 15.24 cm) staggered solid blocking shall be installed between rafters and ceiling joists and shall be centered (10′-3″) (3.12 m) between the plate and ridge on both sides.

Walls shall be constructed so that all bearing walls shall extend to the bottom of the roof structure. All partition walls shall remain at 9′-0″ (2.74 m) A.F.F. There shall be no fire wall construction.

07200 Insulation. The roof deck shall be covered with one layer of 1″ (5.08 cm), 3′×4′ (0.91 m × 1.22 m) rigid isotherm insulation board and a second layer of rigid perlite composite board 1″ (2.54 cm) thick. Manufacturer shall be GAF. The first layer shall be adhered to the roof deck with a "spot" mopping. The joints shall be staggered and tape sealed. The second layer shall be fastened with typical insulation fasteners a minimum 2 1/2″ (6.35 cm) long. The joints shall be staggered and opposite the joints of the first layer and tape sealed.

07500 Membrane Roofing. An alternate built-up roofing system shall be submitted in lieu of the proposed tile roof system. A three-ply BUR system, specification I-2-1-MGP by GAF, is hereby specified over insulated wood deck. Insulation shall be supplied by GAF. There shall be one layer of isotherm, 1″ thick, and one layer of perlite composite board, 1″ thick.

Asphalt shall be supplied in cartons of 50# each. All felt materials shall be supplied by the same manufacturer. All asphalt shall be supplied by the same manufacturer. The asphalt shall be approved for use with the BUR system. The system shall be applied as follows:

1″ Isotherm insulation	@ 15# (6.80 kg)
1″ Perlite base composite board Type III asphalt (3 coats)	@ 75# (34.02 kg)
Gafglas Ply 6 sheet (2 plies)	@ 20# (9.07 kg)
Ruberoid MP membrane	@100# (45.36 kg)
Total weight	@210# (95.25 kg)

07600 Flashing and Sheet Metal. A 1 1/2″ (3.81 cm) 20-ga white enameled galvanized iron gravel stop shall be installed along the eaves on both sides of the roof. An edge metal matching the gravel stop shall be installed along the barges.

Alternate #6. If the owner chooses the BUR system, the following specifications shall apply to the installation of the HVAC system.

15500 Heating, Ventilation, and Air Conditioning. The units shall be split units with the compressors placed on slab next to the electrical switchgear cabinet(s) and the air-handler units installed in the utility room. In lieu of return air being directed to the ceilings in both halls, all return air shall return to a plenum in the base of the walls on both sides of the utility room. All supply air shall be directed through the suspended ceilings into wall registers placed adjacent to the finish ceiling in each area. Supply requirements shall remain the same.

These alternate bids are to be submitted on the proposal as an ADD or DEDUCT from the base proposal.

01040 Coordination

It is the responsibility of the contractor to supply a Critical Path Chart to the owner, all selected subcontractors and manufacturers or suppliers so that the work can be accomplished in a timely manner without confusion or delay.

01060 Workmen's Compensation and Insurance

The contractor, at its own expense, shall be responsible for maintenance of workmen's compensation in accordance with the laws of the state in which the project is being constructed.

The contractor shall also supply the owner with liability insurance in the amount of one million and 00/100 dollars ($1,000,000) for injury or death and three million and 00/100 dollars ($3,000,000) for property damage. The owner shall be named as co-insurer.

01200 Project Meetings

It shall be the responsibility of the contractor and all subcontractors, manufacturer's representatives and/or suppliers to be available for regular project meetings to be held on-site weekly for the purposes of discussing continuity, labor, material or equipment problems, and safety. The day and time of the meeting is at the discretion of the contractor. The owner may or may not be present at these meetings.

01300 Submittals/Substitutions

The contractor shall submit to the owner, or owner's representative, for approval, all materials, equipment and procedures to be a part of the completed the project. Submittals shall be in writing and certified to be as per manufacturer's recommendations.

All "or equal" and alternative products or procedures are to be submitted in writing to the owner, or owner's representative, for approval. The reason for the "or equal" or alternative materials or procedures must be explained in the submittal. Such submittals must be available to the owner or owner's representative no less than ten (10) working days prior to the start of work on the project.

The owner has the right to reject any and all such submittals except in the event the material is no longer available or there is a delay in time in obtaining the material or the procedure must be changed due to the change in material.

01400 Quality Control

The contractor warrants that all materials and equipment supplied to the owner for the project are new unless otherwise specified. All work shall be free from any defects in material and workmanship.

All warranties or guarantees supplied by the manufacturers to the contractor or subcontractors shall be deemed as supplied to the owner as well. Prior to final payment by the owner, all copies of the warranties/guarantees shall be submitted to the owner and the said warranties/guarantees assigned directly to the owner.

01500 Construction Facilities and Temporary Controls

The contractor, at its own cost, shall be responsible that all temporary facilities such as telephones, electrical supply, personal care equipment, first aid equipment, potable water and fire prevention facilities are made available on the project.

Fire prevention facilities and services, and first aid and medical assistance must be prominently displayed so that all persons, firms or corporations employed on the project may have access to them.

01600 Material and Equipment

At the discretion of the owner, if there is sufficient room, an area may be set aside for storage of equipment and materials. If possible, a fence will be so provided for enclosure of the materials and equipment. It is the responsibility of each person, firm or corporation to make certain that the area is secure at the end of each workday.

01700 Contract Closeout

The contractor shall be responsible for maintenance of all records. A copy of such records shall be provided to the owner at the time of completion of project including manufacturers' warranties, guarantees, certifications of workmanship and material prior to final payment and/or retention. Where no manu-facturer's warranty or guaranty exists, and, regardless of such warranties or guarantees, all trades shall submit, in writing, a minimum two (2) year guarantee defects in workmanship and material which are a permanent part of the project.

The contractor, at its own expense, shall be responsible for a clean worksite. All rubbish caused by the contractor's employees, the subcontractor or its employees and the suppliers or their employees shall be removed and properly stored in containers for removal to a suitable site for dumping.

End of Division

Division 2: Sitework

02000 Scope of Work

Division 1 and the General Conditions are to be considered a part of this division. All labor and equipment for a complete instal-lation are also a part of this division.

02010 Subsurface Investigation

The owner shall provide for subsurface exploration to be conducted by a qualified soils engineering firm. The soils testing and results shall be made available, in writing, to the owner or owner's representative and the contractor and shall become a part of these Specifications.

The report shall include the type of surface soil, the type, or types, of soil for a minimum of ten (10) feet (3.05 m) below grade, obtained by test borings or core drillings, and shall make recommendations, if any, for correcting substandard soils condi-tions. During excavation and grading, soils testing shall be performed to ensure the soils meet a minimum of 3,000 psf (1,360.71 kg/0.929 m^2) design strength.

02100 Site Preparation

The contractor shall make certain that certain vegetation is marked to remain intact or to be removed, saved and transplanted. This shall be accomplished in cooperation with the owner, contractor and clearing and grubbing contractor. When all vegeta-tion to be saved is so marked, all remaining vegetation, debris and refuse is to be cleared and removed.

02200 Earthwork

Excavate as required to achieve proper grade levels, for the mass excavation of the crawl space and for working room required for laying of foundation walls and footings surrounding the mass excavation. Excavation for all footings is to be on undisturbed earth or minimum 95% compacted soil with a minimum depth as shown on drawings or otherwise governed by local codes.

Should the contractor contact caliche or large rock conditions which would require blasting, the owner will reimburse the contractor for the cost of such work.

Backfill at exterior walls shall be Type II soil, well compacted, to a subgrade 8″ (20.32 cm) below top of foundation wall. Backfill over utilities shall conform with the utility company requirements of sand and Type II soil. The remainder of the site shall be graded to assure proper drainage away from the building. Remove all excess soils from the site.

Grades not otherwise indicated on the plans shall be of uniform levels or slopes between points where elevations are given.

Contractor is to notify owner immediately if any excavation reveals fill or ground water.

02500 Paving and Surfacing

All paving is to be of asphaltic materials. All paving shall be installed in areas indicated on plans. Pavement design shall meet ten (10) year minimum design criteria for local areas as established by the Asphalt Institute. The following guide should be used as a minimum thickness required:

Soil Class	Minimum Pavement
Poor—CBR = 3.5—type, plastic when wet such as clay, fine silt, sandy loam	6″ (15.24 cm) coarse asphalt base binder (1 1/2″ [3.81 cm] asphalt aggregate) and 1 1/2″ (3.81 cm) asphalt topping (maximum 1/2″ [1.27 cm] aggregate)
Medium—CBR = 7.0—type, hard, silty sands or sand gravels containing clay or fine silt	4″ (10.16 cm) coarse asphalt base binder (1 1/2″ [3.81 cm] asphalt aggregate) and 1 1/2″ (3.81 cm) asphalt topping (maximum 1/2″ [1.27 cm] aggregate)
Good—CBR = 12—type, clean sand and sand gravel free of asphalt topping clay, silt or loam	3″ (7.62 cm) coarse asphalt base material (1 1/2″ [3.81 cm] asphalt aggregate) and 1 1/2″ (3.81 cm) asphalt topping (maximum 1/2″ [1.27 cm] aggregate)

or

6″ (15.24 cm) (compacted thickness) stone base plus 2 1/2″ (6.35 cm) asphalt topping (maximum 3/4″ [1.91 cm] aggregate)

Finish paving shall be 4″ (10.16 cm) asphalt mix at all light-trafficked areas over a 6″ (15.24 cm) cementitious base over 10″

(25.40 cm) compacted base aggregate or sand at all paved areas. The aggregate base shall be compacted to maintain an 80% compaction rate. Base shall be tested for compaction prior to application of asphalt finish. All paving surfaces shall be properly sealed from weather deterioration as per local codes and accepted workmanship of the trade.

Precast concrete parking blocks, 6'-0" (1.83 m) long and 5" (12.70 cm) high, shall be as shown on plans, or one for each two (2) parking places, spanning one half (1/2) per parking space, except at handicapped parking where the concrete block shall be 4'-0" (1.22 m) long and 5" (12.70 cm) high, one (1) per parking space, if not indicated otherwise on plans.

Curbs shall be 6" (15.24 cm) machine-formed asphaltic curbs of the same material as the heavily trafficked topping. Any curbing which becomes defective within a ninety (90) day period after final certificate of occupancy shall be replaced at no cost to owner.

02900 Landscaping

Provide all labor, material and equipment necessary to complete the seeding, sodding, landscape planting, earthwork and edging as shown on plans. Landscape bidder shall submit a proposal and drawings for approval by the owner. Proposal shall include size, type and number of plantings, and exact area to be sodded.

Landscape contractor shall be responsible for the installation of the topsoil to finish grade at all the rough grading. The area shall be free of all debris and well drained prior to any planting. Total proposal shall include all taxes where applicable.

End of Division

Division 3: Concrete

03000 Scope of Work

Division 1 and the General Conditions are considered a part of this division. All labor, material and equipment necessary to complete all concrete work including formwork, reinforcing and cement finish shall be furnished by the concrete contractor.

03100 Concrete Formwork

All labor materials and equipment necessary for the installation of footing and foundation wall formwork shall include steel stakes, 3'-0" (0.91 m) long for footing form support, 2× treated lumber or 1" (min) (2.54 cm) treated plywood for footing forms, 3/4" (min) (1.91 cm) plyform for wall forms, formties and any other accessories necessary for proper construction of the foundation walls and footings.

03200 Reinforcement

All rebar shall be grade 60 (60 kps). Rebar shall be 2-#4 laid horizontally and continuous in footings with 48 bar diameters at all laps. Rebar shall be installed on chairs 3" (7.62 cm) from bottom of footing. Corners shall have 2 #4 rebar, 4'-0" (1.22 m) long, bent 90° at the center, and shall extend 2'-0" each way from the corner. 1-#5 rebar shall be installed vertically in foundation walls at 4'-0" O/C (1.22 m) horizontally with 6" (15.24 cm) hook tied to footing rebar. Bar length shall extend to 3" (7.62 cm) below top of wall. No rebar shall be heat bent. All rebar shall be installed and inspected prior to placement of concrete.

03300 Cast-in-Place Concrete

Footings and foundation walls are to be 3,000 psi (1,360.77 kg/6.45 cm²) ready-mix concrete per ASTM C94. Type III cement shall be used. Concrete shall be tested at the expense of the owner at 3 days, 7 days and 28 days in accordance with ASTM C31 and ASTM C150. If any of the tests fail, the contractor shall, at its own expense, make all necessary repairs and/or replacements.

     Concrete components shall be Portland cement, one brand; aggregate-fine sand and maximum 3/4" (1.91 cm) DIA coarse gravel free from other deleterious substances; potable water.

     Admixtures permitted shall be:

1. Air-entrained agent per ASTM C260
2. Hardener and dustproofer—Lapodith or equal
3. Nonslip additive—Durafax or equal
4. Nonshrink additive—Sika Set or equal

03400 Precast Concrete

Piers and pier pads are to be precast concrete products that are supplied by the manufacturer to be installed by the concrete contractor. Pier pads shall have 2 #4 rebar each way. The rebar shall have a clearance of 2" (5.08 cm) from each end of the pad and shall be embedded 1 1/2" (3.81 cm) below surface of concrete. The vertical rebar shall be so placed so as to be perpendicular to the horizontal rebar. The rebar height shall end 3" (7.62 cm) below top of pier. The 6" (15.24 cm) hook shall be tied to the horizontal pier pad rebar at each vertical rebar. Piers and pier pads shall be aligned to support the beams as shown on the plans.

     The concrete contractor shall build into the concrete all materials furnished by others and shall secure same: including plumbing, electrical conduit, concrete inserts, anchors, hangers, hold-downs, sleeving for piping, etc., when and where required by the other trades.

End of Division

Division 4: Masonry — NOT USED

Division 5: Metals

05000 Scope of Work

Division 1 and the General Conditions shall be considered a part of this division. Provide all labor, material and equipment necessary to complete the structural and miscellaneous steel work indicated on the drawings. All materials to meet ASTM requirements. Provide all steel embeds, anchors and accessories as shown on plans or as required for a complete installation. Submit shop drawings for all structural steel components.

05100 Structural Metal Framing

Support beams shall be W8×28 (W20.32 cm × 12.73 kg) wide-flange structural steel beams spanning from wall to wall in both an east/west and north/south direction. A 4″ (10.16 cm) embedment (bearing) shall be installed in the wall at each end. Beams shall be fastened together with 3″×3″×1/4″×6″ long (7.62 cm × 7.62 cm × 0.64 cm × 15.25 cm) clip angle stiffeners, bolted and welded at both sides of all junctions of all web joints. All welding, burning, scarfing and painting of metal shall be done on the job site. Bolts shall be minimum 5/8″ (1.59 cm) DIA × 2″ (5.08 cm) long with nut and lock washer. Bolts shall be tack-welded to prevent loosening. Weld at perimeter of stiffeners shall be minimum 1/4″ (0.64 cm) continuous fillet. Flange surface joints shall be "V" shaped with weld to fill "V" to a minimum 1/8″ (0.32 cm) above surface of flange. Surface weld shall be scarfed smooth. Paint all exposed surfaces with rust-inhibiting primer.

End of Division

Division 6: Wood and Plastics

06000 Scope of Work

Division 1 and the General Conditions are to be considered a part of this division. Furnish all labor, materials, tools and equipment necessary to complete all work under this division and as indicated on drawings.

Provide and maintain temporary enclosures, fences and barricades as required by local codes and ordinances and OSHA. If required, provide temporary door and window enclosures.

06100 Rough Carpentry

Treated 2×8 (5.08 cm × 20.32 cm) sill plate shall be placed on all concrete surfaces (piers and walls) prior to installation of steel beam. Sill plate may be attached using 1/2″ × 10″ (1.27 cm × 25.40 cm) anchor bolts or powder actuated shot and pin. If anchor bolts are used, the carpentry contractor shall supply the anchors to the concrete contractor for installation.

2×8 (5.08 cm × 20.32 cm) HF (Hemlock Fir), utility grade, shall be installed on the structural steel beams as per plans and shall be fastened with powder actuated shot and pin. The fasteners shall be spaced 4′-0″ O/C (1.22 m). The lumber shall be drilled and fastened with countersunk nuts and washers.

Floor joists shall be 2×10 (5.08 cm × 25.40 cm) DF (Douglas Fir) #1 or better. Spacing and lengths shall be as indicated on structural floor plan. A header (rim joist) shall be installed along perimeter of floor to close and hide stub ends of floor joists. Header joists shall be fastened with 4 16d nails toe-nailed at each end. Interior floor joists shall be fastened with joist hangers of the proper size. Metal cross bridging shall be installed where spans exceed 8′-0″ (2.44 m).

Standard 3/4″ (1.91 cm), 5-ply, underlayment, or 1″ (2.54 cm) OSB, shall be used for the sub-flooring applied over the floor joists. Plywood or OSB sheets applied over the floor joists shall have an adhesive applied to the joists and shall be nailed with minimum 8d shank nails as per standards of the trade and local requirements. The subflooring shall be placed with staggered joints and clips at the butt ends where required or underlayment may be cut and fit to center of joists and nailed at 9″ O/C (22.86 cm).

1/2″ (1.27 cm) plywood shall bear the DFPA stamp, type CDX or CCX, 5-ply, with exterior glue, UNO, for exterior use at roof and shall be nailed with minimum 8d shank nails as per standards of the trade and local requirements. The CCX shall be applied along the eaves with the smooth side exposed to the underside. The remainder of the roof shall be filled with CDX material. All joints to be staggered with clips at the butt ends as required.

Exterior walls and interior bearing walls are 2×6 (5.08 cm × 15.24 cm) studs at 16″ (40.64 cm) O/C. Plumbing walls shall be staggered 2×4 (5.08 cm × 10.16 cm) studs on 2×6 plate at 24″ (60.96 cm) O/C. Partition walls shall also be 2×4 (5.08 cm × 10.16 cm) studs at 24″ (60.96 cm) O/C. All studs shall be DF, construction grade. Sole plate and double top plate shall be 2×6 (5.08 cm × 15.24 cm) HF utility grade for exterior bearing walls and interior bearing walls and 2×4 (5.08 cm × 10.16 cm) HF utility grade for nonbearing interior partitions. All walls shall extend 9′-0″ (2.74 m) A.F.F. Where code requires, 2×6 (5.08 cm × 15.24 cm) or 2×4 (5.08 cm or 10.16 cm), fire blocking shall be installed to match the wall size.

All exterior corners shall have a diagonal let-in brace applied so that the brace extends from sole plate to double top plate at an angle of no more than 60° at the sole plate. An alternate 3/8″ (0.95 cm) CDX plywood or OSB shear panel may be installed in lieu of the diagonal bracing. Additional let-in bracing shall be installed for every 25 lf of uninterrupted wall space between corners.

A fire wall shall be constructed above the interior East and West bearing walls. The fire wall shall extend from the top plate of the interior bearing walls to the underside of the roof structure and shall be constructed with 2×6 (5.08 cm × 15.24 cm), construction grade studs at 16″ O/C (40.64 cm). Where code requires, fire blocking shall be installed at mid-height of the walls.

3 2×6 (5.08 cm × 15.24 cm) DF construction grade studs or a 6×6 (15.24 cm × 15.24 cm) DF #2 or better post shall be installed in the Restroom/Break Room common wall and 3 2×4 (5.08 cm × 10.16 cm) DF construction grade studs or a 4×6 (10.16 cm × 15.24 cm) DF #2 or better post shall be installed in the Break Room/Reception Room common wall. The posts shall be placed directly below the double ceiling joists. Two (2) sets of 3 2×6 (5.08 cm × 15.24 cm) construction grade studs or 2 6×6 (15.24 cm × 15.24 cm) DF #2 or better posts shall be installed in the Reception Room/Waiting Room common wall. One post shall be installed on each side of the Reception Room window opening.

All furred-down ceiling areas shall be constructed of 2×2 (5.08 cm × 5.08 cm) DF common with vertical members spaced at 24″ O/C (60.96 cm). Where required, 2×2 (5.08 cm × 5.08 cm) or 2×4 (5.08 cm × 10.16 cm) furring shall be used for back-up for GWB installations.

Ceiling joists shall be 2×6 (5.08 cm × 15.24 cm) DF #2 or better spaced as indicated on the plans. All joists shall be fastened with joist hangers of proper size at end connections where abutting double joists and header joists. Double joists shall be installed over all bearing walls. Header joists shall be installed to hide exposed joist ends and for fastening of joist hangers. Frieze blocking shall be installed along perimeters parallel to the joists at plate line where header joists are not required.

Conventional roof framing shall include 2×6 (5.08 cm × 15.24 cm) DF #2 or better for rafters and double 2×8 (5.08 cm × 20.32 cm) or a 4×8 (10.16 cm × 20.32 cm) DF #1 or better for hip and ridge beams. Rafters shall be attached at the plate line with Simpson Strong Tie anchors #A34, #A35, or equal, and with Simpson skewed joist hangers, or equal, at all hip and ridge connections as per manufacturer's recommendation.

The conventional roof framing shall be supported by installing 3 2×6 (5.08 cm × 15.24 cm) studs or 6×6 (15.24 cm × 15.24 cm) posts over the interior bearing walls where there is no fire wall, spaced at 4'-0" O/C (1.22 m). These posts shall have 2×4 (5.08 cm × 10.16 cm) collar ties extending transversely from post to post at the juncture with the post and the roof structure. 2×4 (5.08 cm × 10.16 cm) purlins shall be run continuously parallel with the post construction supporting the collar ties at the posts.

A rough-sawn (R/S) fascia board shall be 2×8 (5.08 cm × 20.32 cm) DF #2 or better and nailed to ends of rafter and hip tails with 2 8d shank nails at each connection.

06200 Finish Carpentry

A "Slimline" oak veneer wood trim shall be installed surrounding all windows on the interior side of the exterior walls. In addition, a 1/2" (1.27 cm) to 3/4" (1.91 cm) thick return (match the thickness of the "Slimline" material) of the same finish shall be applied to both sides and head of each window immediately adjacent to the interior side of the window. Where a window exists on the interior only, both sides of the window shall be similarly trimmed. An apron and stool shall be applied to the interior side of the exterior windows and on both sides of the interior window. The interior windows include the Waiting Room/Playroom window and the Waiting Room/Reception Room window. The Waiting Room/Reception Room window shall have a 3/4" × 18" (1.91 cm × 45.72 cm) wide, select pine, shelf, with apron both sides, centered on the wall the full length of the window opening. All nailing shall be with 6d finish nails, maximum 1 1/2" (3.81 cm) long. The nails shall be slightly punched for application of a finish putty over each nail head. All joints shall be smooth and even.

A 2×4 (5.08 cm × 10.16 cm), select DF, R/S finish, exterior trim shall be applied to the exterior wall framing surrounding each window with a 1×4 (2.54 cm × 10.16 cm) return to the window of the same material. A water table shall be applied at the head of each window and a sloped stool extending 3/4" (1.91 cm) beyond an apron, 1 1/2" deep (3.81 cm), R/S, 2×4 (5.08 cm × 10.16 cm), select DF, supporting the stool. All exterior trim shall be installed prior to the wall finish installation.

End of Division

Division 7: Thermal and Moisture Protection

07000 Scope of Work

Division 1 and the General Conditions are to be considered a part of this division. Furnish all labor, materials and equipment

necessary to complete all work under this division and as
indicated on drawings.

07100 Below-Grade Moisture Protection

The exterior face of the foundation wall and the footing shall be
protected against moisture penetration by the use of a 36"
(91.44 cm) wide roll of self-adhering, self-sealing, bituminous
sheet material by Koppers Co., Inc., or equal. The manufacturer's
(Koppers) specification is as follows:

> 1 coat primer (1 gal/sq = 1 lb/sq) @ 15 lb/sq
> (1 coat primer [3.79 liter/9.29 m^2 = .45 kg/9.29 m^2] @ 6.80 kg/
>   9.29 m^2)
> 1 rubberized, asphalt/polyethylene laminated membrane, 43" ×
>   33' @ 80 lf/sq
> (1 rubberized, asphalt/polyethylene laminated membrane,
>   1.09 m × 10.06 m @ 24.38 m/9.29 m^2)
> 3" cant strip (continuous) @ 300 lf/bundle
> (7.62 cm cant strip [continuous] @ 91.44 m/bundle)
> Webbing for sealing corners and laps @ 300 lf/roll
> (Webbing for sealing corners and laps @ 91.44 m/roll)
> 4'×8'×1/2" fiberboard for protection board @ 32 sq ft/board
> (1.22 m × 2.44 m × 1.27 cm fiberboard protection board
>   @ 2.97 m^2/board)

An emulsified primer shall be applied to the wall prior to the
installation of the bituminous sheet material. An extra 8"
(20.32 cm) wide layer (4" [10.16 cm] each side) of the same
material shall be applied at all corners and all joints. A 3"×3"
(7.62 cm × 7.62 cm) wood or fibrous continuous cant strip shall
be installed along the whole perimeter of the foundation wall at
the juncture of the foundation wall and the top of the footing.
An extra 16" (40.64 cm) wide layer of the sheet material shall be
applied over the cant strip, 4" (10.16 cm) up the wall and
extending 4" (10.16 cm) down over the exterior top corner of the
footing. All applications shall be applied so that there are no
wrinkles or breaks in the material.

A layer of 1" (2.54 cm) × 3.5# (1.59 kg) density polystyrene
foam or 1/2" (1.27 cm) fibrous protection board shall be placed
over the finished bituminous materials from the top of the foundation wall to the base of the footing prior to any backfilling
of the walls. Sand or a fine aggregate shall be backfilled
against the protection board to at least 1/2 the height of the
foundation wall and Type II soil shall be backfilled into the
remainder of the space. All backfilling shall be compacted in 8"
(20.32 cm) lifts.

07200 Insulation

Install 2" (5.08 cm) thick 2'×4' (0.61 m × 1.22 m), 3.5# (1.59 kg)
density, polystyrene foam board, or 2" (5.08 cm) rigid fiberglass
insulation board, on the interior side of the foundation wall
from the top of the wall to the top of the footing over 1×4
(2.54 cm × 10.16 cm) furring strips fastened w/8d concrete nails
and adhesive, spaced 2'-0" O/C (0.610 m) horizontally. The insulation shall be nailed at 9" O/C (22.86 cm) along the perimeter of
each piece of insulation w/wide-head 6d × 2 1/2" (6.35 cm) insulation nails. A top and bottom furring strip may be used horizontally the length of the walls.

The exterior stud walls and interior bearing stud walls shall have 6″ (15.24 cm), R-19, kraft-backed, 16″ (40.64 cm) wide, tabbed insulation. All interior stud walls, bearing and partition, shall have a combination thermal and sound insulation, 4″ (10.16 cm) thick, 24″ (60.96 cm) wide, kraft-backed paper full height, and staggered full height in the plumbing wall. The insulation shall be sound rated at 60 STC, with the exception of the wall between the Restroom and Utility Room.

Ceilings shall have R-30 loose blanket batt insulation installed as per plans.

07300 Roofing Tiles

Roofing shall be a one-piece clay "S" tile, terra cotta in color, as manufactured by Life Tile Systems, or equal. Underlayment shall be a 43# (19.50 kg), 36″ (91.44 cm) wide, 5-square felt laid horizontally on the roof sheathing starting from the bottom (eave line). The felts shall have a minimum 4″ (10.16 cm) lap.

A wire-tie system shall be installed per manufacturer's recommendations and specifications. Each tile shall be fastened to the tie system. The tile shall be laid with a 15″ (38.10 cm) exposure. All tiles shall be laid in a straight and true horizontal line. No broken tiles shall be used. All broken tiles shall be replaced prior to final inspection of the roof.

A prefabricated plastic or metal ridge vent shall be installed along the ridge and hips in lieu of the standard 2×6 (5.08 cm × 15.24 cm) trimmer placed on edge at these areas. (See Section 07600, Sheet Metal.)

Manufacturer shall supply a ten (10) year warranty covering workmanship and material. A certificate of acceptance by the manufacturer shall be submitted to the owner prior to release of retention payment.

07600 Sheet Metal

All sheet metal flashings and accessories for the roof shall be supplied by the sheet metal contractor, to be installed by others as needed. All sheet metal shall be a minimum 26-gauge galvanized steel or aluminum material with the exception of the valleys and pipe jacks, which shall be manufactured in 1/16″ (0.16 cm) thick lead and formed in the same manner as the galvanized flashings.

A prefabricated ridge vent shall be used along all ridges and hips in lieu of the 2×6 (5.08 cm × 15.24 cm) edgewise.

07900 Sealants and Caulking

The contractor shall provide for installation of joint sealants and caulking at all control joints. Caulking shall also be provided around all exterior doors and windows.

End of Division

Division 8: Doors, Windows, Glazing

08000 Scope of Work

Division 1 and the General Conditions are to be considered a part of this division. Furnish all labor, materials and equipment necessary to complete all work under this division and as indicated on drawings.

08100 Metal Doors and Frames & 08200 Wood and Plastic Doors

Exterior doors are to have hollow-metal (HM) frames. Interior doors are to have hollow-metal knock-down (KDHM) frames. Main entrance exterior doors shall be of metal-clad wood construction. The door schedule is as follows:

Mark	Size	Frame	Description	Remarks
1	pr 3′×6′8″	HM	Wd, m/c, birch, 3-panel,	mfr paint
	(0.91 m × 2.03 m)		1 3/4″ (4.45 cm)	
2	3′×6′8″	HM	2-panel HM, 1 3/4″	mfr paint
	(0.91 m × 2.03 m)		(4.45 cm)	
3	3′×6′8″	KDHM	flush, wood, birch,	stain (typ)
	(0.91 m × 2.03 m)		1 3/8″ (3.49 cm), h/c	
4	3′×6′8″	KDHM	flush, wood, birch,	lead-lined
	(0.91 m × 2.03 m)		1 3/8″ (3.49 cm), s/c	
5	pr 2′×6′8″	KDHM	flush, wood, birch,	6″×18″ lite
	(0.61 m × 2.03 m)		1 3/8″ (3.49 cm), h/c	
6	3′×6′8″	KDHM	flush, wood, birch,	pocket
	(0.91 m × 2.03 m)		1 3/8″ (3.49 cm), h/c	
7	2′×6′8″	KDHM	flush, wood, birch,	stain (typ)
	(0.61 m × 2.03 m)		1 3/8″ (3.49 cm), h/c	
8	3′×6′8″	KDHM	cased opening	
	(0.91 m × 2.03 m)			

All interior doors are to have sound insulation fill (STC 60) in the door cores.

08250 Door Opening Assemblies

All door hardware is to be supplied by one manufacturer. The hardware shall be Schlage. The following is the hardware schedule for all doors:

> Front Entry-Schlage entry latch w/thumb latch handle and deadbolt, w/matching key, antique brass. Schlage handle to match latch. 1 1/2 sets hinge butts, antique brass, each leaf.
>
> Side Exterior Doors-Schlage emergency kit hardware only (no special knowledge). 1 1/2 sets hinge butts, antique brass.
>
> Doctor Office, Accounting Office, Nurse Office, Reception, Record Storage, Restroom-Schlage privacy latch, antique brass, 1 1/2 sets hinge butts, antique brass.
>
> Interior Halls, Break Room and Examination Rooms-Schlage passage latch, antique brass, 1 1/2 set hinge butts, antique brass.

Operating Room and X-Ray Laboratory- Schlage antique brass handle w/push plate both sides, each leaf. 2'6" × 1'-6" (0.76 m × 0.46 m) at X-Ray Laboratory and 3'-0" × 1'-6" (0.91 m × 0.46 m) at Operating Room, antique brass kick plate both sides, each leaf and 1 1/2 set hinge butts, antique brass, each leaf.

08500 Metal Windows

Windows shall be aluminum framed and manufactured to fit into frame or masonry wall openings. Windows shall be of such construction so that the mullions are installed at the mid-point width of the framing stud or the masonry unit.

All glazing for the exterior windows shall be integrally tinted, gray, dual pane insulated glass, 1/8" (0.32 cm) thick, with 1/2" (1.27 cm) air space between panes. The interior windows shall be installed with clear 1/4" (0.64 cm) tempered plate glass. Windows are to be installed as per plans and details.

The window schedule is as follows:

Mark	Size	Frame	Description	Remarks
A	4'×4' (1.22 m × 1.22 m)	Alum	FX GL,insulpane	
B	4'×2'8" (1.22 m × 0.81 m)	Alum	FX GL,insulpane	
C	6'×2'8" (1.83 m × 0.81 m)	N/A	4×8×8 GL BLK	Solar Decor
D	4'×2'8" (1.22 m × 0.81 m)	N/A	4×8×8 GL BLK	Solar Decor
E	4'×5' (1.22 m × 1.52 m)	Alum	FX Tempered GL	1/4"(0.64 cm) thk
F	10'×2'6" (3.05 m × 0.76 m)	Alum	OXXO Sliding GL	

End of Division

Division 9: Finishes

09000 Scope of Work

Division 1 and the General Conditions are to be considered a part of this division. Furnish all labor, materials and equipment necessary to complete all work under this division and as indicated on drawings.

09200 Lath and Plaster

All metal accessories are to be supplied by one manufacturer. Install accessories such as base screed and control joints; J-metal at all window and door jambs, heads and sills, and at all dissimilar materials abutting the plaster; corneraid and cornertite; and any other accessories as may be necessary for a complete job. Lath shall be 8'-0" × 36" (2.44 m × 0.91 m), 22-ga expanded metal sheets w/building paper backing.

Apply 3/8" (0.95 cm) scratch coat over lath. Scratch coat shall be in accordance with manufacturer's recommendations and local codes and ordinances. Allow to cure for a minimum 3 days, wetting walls with fog spray daily. Apply 3/8" (0.95 cm) brown coat over freshly moistened scratch coat. Allow to cure for a minimum 7 days, wetting walls with fog spray daily. Wet walls just before application of finish coat. Finish coat is to be 1/8" (0.32 cm) thick, natural gray color, or, at the discretion of owner, with an integral color in lieu of painting.

It is the responsibility of the plaster contractor to make certain that all exposed metal, glazing or other materials are protected and/or thoroughly clean, making sure that there is no damage to the other finished trades around the work. Clean up job site and remove debris upon completion.

09250 Gypsum Board (GWB)

All GWB shall be 5/8" (1.59 cm) "X" (Firecode) by USG, or equal, as required by local codes and ordinances. Boards shall be laid horizontally with the long side perpendicular to the framing on both walls and ceilings. The sheets shall be placed so that all vertical joints on walls and the ends on the ceilings are staggered. Staggered joints shall be centered on the adjacent sheets.

GWB shall be fastened with minimum 1 1/8" (2.86 cm) drywall screws spaced at 6" O/C (15.24 cm) along the perimeter of each sheet and 9" O/C (22.86 cm) in the field. The screws shall be applied with sufficient force to slightly indent the GWB.

All joints on walls and ceilings shall be sealed with paper or self-adhering tape and multi-purpose compound. The first application shall be left to dry and is sanded smooth. A second application is applied to the taped joint, allowed to set, and sanded smooth to match the GWB for application of paint or wall-covering. All exposed screw heads shall also be embedded in multi-purpose compound, sanded and smoothed to match the GWB surface. See Finish Schedule for textures. All drywall ceilings are 9'-0" A.F.F. (2.74 m), UNO.

09300 Tile

See Finish Schedule for location and other information regarding ceramic wall tile to be installed. Tile shall be "Dal-Tile," or equal, 4×4 (10.16 cm × 10.16 cm), color to be selected by owner from standard ranges. Bullnose tile shall be applied at all exposed ends of tile.

Tile shall be applied using a thinset cement wall application and grouted with a color-matching grout between tiles as per manufacturer's recommendations.

09500 Acoustical Treatment

See Reflected Ceiling Plan for locations of ACT system. The ACT shall be Armstrong Acoustical Tile, 2'×4' (0.61 m × 1.22 m), 3/4" (1.91 cm) thick, treated wood fiber, fissured, fire retardant (1-hour rated). All ACT ceilings are to be 8'-0" (2.44 m) A.F.F.

Install 1″ (2.54 cm) wall angle along perimeter of all supporting walls. Install 1″ (2.54 cm) main "T" runners spaced 2′-0″ O/C (0.61 m) with secondary cross runners spaced at 4′-0″ O/C (1.22 m). Center the main runners in each area for aesthetic appearance. In areas where the walls are 4′-0″ (1.22 m) apart, only the wall angle and main "T" runners shall be used. All joints shall be fastened with corner clips at the walls and at the cross joints.

The ceiling shall be suspended with 9-ga tie wire fastened to the wood joists by a screw eye and to the runners with a clip fastener at the corners of the mains and cross secondary members. Tie wires shall be installed so as to offer support every 9 square feet of ceiling area or as necessary for proper support. Additional tie wire shall be added at each corner of the "T" bar ceiling structure where an electrical fluorescent fixture is to be installed. Add seismic support as may be required by local code and ordinance.

09650 Resilient Flooring

See Finish Schedule for location of resilient flooring. Resilient flooring may be either sheet vinyl flooring or 12″×12″ (30.48 cm × 30.48 cm) vinyl tiles. Where sheet flooring is applied, an underlayment of 7 1/2 lb (3.40 kg) felt is to be adhered to the subfloor as a cushion for the sheet vinyl. The felt is to be smoothed and left to set. The sheet vinyl is to be applied over the felt, smoothed and allowed to set for twenty-four (24) hours.

Vinyl composition tile (VCT) flooring shall be installed with an adhesive directly to the subfloor. Tile shall be placed so that it is properly centered on the floor in each area where it is used.

The sheet and tile flooring shall have a 4″ (10.16 cm) base coving, color selected by owner to match flooring, and is applied along the perimeter of all resilient floors. An alternate coving may be applied along the perimeter of the floor. The alternate coving is backed by a 1 1/2″ (3.81 cm) concave quarter-round wood member.

The contractor shall allow for leftover material, sufficient for repairs, to remain on the project.

09680 Carpet

See Finish Schedule for location of carpet installation. Carpeting shall be DuPont, commercial grade, heavy traffic, with a rubber pad. Installation shall be by a reputable carpet contractor. Seams shall be kept to a minimum. Seams shall be installed so that the webbing or joint does not show after installation. A guarantee shall be supplied to the contractor and owner by manufacturer as to workmanship and material. A copy of the manufacturer's accreditation shall be in the hands of the owner prior to final payment and retention.

09900 Painting

See Finish Schedule for location of all interior painting. Colors to be selected by owner from standard color ranges.

Acceptable paint manufacturers for standard paints are:

Sinclair Paints   Sherwin-Williams Paints
Decatrend   Frazee Paints

Acceptable manufacturer for exterior wood paints shall be by Olympic Stain, or equal.
The painting shall be applied as follows:

Exterior Walls and Trim:

Exterior Plaster
  1 coat of primer
  2 coats latex paint
  Sprayed, rolled or brushed
  Standard colors selected by owner

Exterior Wood Trim
  Oil based stain
  Standard colors selected by owner

Underside of Overhang
  1 coat primer
  2 coats latex paint
  Match cement plaster color

Interior Walls
  1 coat sealer
  1 coat primer
  1 coat semi-gloss epoxy

09950 Wallcovering

Additional wallcoverings shall be selected by owner and shall be directed by change order after contract is signed.

End of Division

Division 10: Specialties

10000 Scope of Work

Division 1 and the General Conditions are to be considered a part of this division. Furnish all labor, materials and equipment necessary to complete all work under this division and as indicated on drawings.

10500 Lockers

Individual personal storage lockers shall be installed for each employee and are to be located in the Restroom area. The number of employees is to be determined by owner (maximum of ten).

10800 Toilet and Bath Accessories

The contractor shall be responsible for the purchase and installation of all Restroom and Kitchen accessories including, but not limited to, mirrors, dispensers, waste depositories and grab bars per ADA requirements.

End of Division

Division 11: Equipment

11000 Scope of Work

Division 1 and the General Conditions are to be considered a part of this division. Furnish all labor and equipment necessary to complete all work under this division and as indicated on drawings.

11700 Medical Equipment

The owner shall select all medical equipment for this project. The contractor shall be responsible for proper installation of the equipment. Where required, coordination shall be applied by the various subcontractors responsible for specialty installations such as plumbing and/or electrical.

End of Division

Division 12: Furnishings - NOT USED

Division 13: Special Construction - NOT USED

Division 14: Conveying Systems - NOT USED

Division 15: Mechanical

15000 Scope of Work

Division 1 and the General Conditions are to be considered a part of this division. Furnish all labor, materials and equipment necessary to complete all work under this division and as indicated on drawings.

15050 Basic Mechanical Materials and Methods

In addition to the requirements stated in Section 15000, the mechanical contractor shall be governed by the regulations established by professional engineers who have designed the installation and material requirements. The mechanical contractor shall also be governed by the regulations of ASHRAE and OSHA and by national, regional and/or local mechanical and plumbing codes, where applicable. The materials used shall be as specified in the following sections.

15400 Plumbing

The plumbing contractor shall be responsible for all fee and permit costs in reference to the plumbing and piping applying to this project.

Plumbing shall include, but is not limited to, installation of all sanitary sewer, storm drainage, gas and potable water connections from off-site to, and including, the appliance or fixture shut-off valves and the appliances or fixtures themselves. Fittings not specifically mentioned shall be construed to be included to make a complete installation.

Provide and install all soil, waste, vent pipes and clean-outs for all sewer lines in accordance with local code. Provide proper drainage where necessary and ensure that all stub-outs are properly capped. Pipe and fitting sizes shall be as per plans. Where discrepancies may occur with local codes and installation recommendations, such codes and recommendations shall prevail.

Provide and install type K copper pipe for all underground potable water service and connections. Use Type K or L copper pipe for all potable water above grade pipe.

If gas is used for heating and/or hot water heat, gas piping shall be schedule 40, black steel pipe. All below-grade gas pipe and gas pipe exposed to the atmosphere shall be wrapped with a polyethylene coating.

Insulate all cold and hot water piping as required by local codes and ordinances. Hold installation to inside of building insulation to prevent freezing.

The plumbing fixture schedule is as follows:

Handicap Water Closet: American "Cadet" #2108.408 – 18" high Church #295, or equal

Lavatories: Custom-designed cultured marble one-piece lavatory tops w/basins integral (color and style to be selected by owner)

Mop Basin: Stainless Steel by Elkay, or equal

15500 Heating, Ventilation and Air Conditioning

Mechanical contractor shall supply shop drawings for the installation of the HVAC system, if required. All fees and permits for the HVAC installation are at the expense of the mechanical contractor. The HVAC equipment shall be manufactured by Lennox Corporation, or equal.

The mechanical contractor shall propose a self-contained HVAC unit. The system contains two 3-ton, self-contained, heat exchangers with all accessories necessary for a complete installation, including, but not limited to, ductwork, grilles, registers and other fittings as necessary, installed in the ceiling. The thermostat controls shall operate both manually and automatically. See HVAC Plan, M—1.

Coordinate all work with the plumbing and electrical contractors where required.

End of Division

Division 16: Electrical

16000 Scope of Work

Division 1 and the General Conditions are to be considered a part of this division. Furnish all labor, materials and equipment necessary to complete all work under this division and as indicated on drawings.

16050 Basic Electrical Materials and Methods.

In addition to the requirements stated in Section 16000, the electrical contractor shall be governed by the regulations established by professional engineers who have designed the installation and material requirements. The electrical contractor shall also conform to the latest edition of the NEC OSHA, regional and/or local electrical codes, where applicable. The materials used shall be as specified in the following sections.

16400 Service and Distribution

Provide for an adequate service and grounding system as shown on drawings and as described in the specifications. Conduit shall be used as a continuous ground path from appliance to distribution center. A complete equipment ground conductor shall also be supplied from each appliance to the distribution center.

All materials shall be new and supplied by one manufacturer with shipping crates intact. The contractor shall be provided with proof of manufacturer's shipping record. All materials selected shall be as indicated in the specifications and/or electrical schedules. All equipment shall have a label and/or stamp from an approved testing laboratory such as Underwriters Laboratories (UL), and all motorized and switchgear equipment shall have nameplates which shall be supplied with the equipment. All disconnects shall be rated NEMA 1 enclosures.

The electrical contractor shall coordinate all installation with the local utility company and shall provide connections for service when all service is inspected and approved. The electrical contractor shall further coordinate all hookups with contractors of other trades where cooperation is necessary for speedy execution of the contract.

Acceptable manufacturers of the switchgear equipment are:

Square D   General Electric

White/Westinghouse   ITT

There shall be two (2) distribution panels as a part of the entry switchgear, one (1) for power and one (1) for lighting.

16500 Lighting (General Lighting and Power)

See Electrical Plans, E-1 and E-2. All standard lighting switches shall be Hubbell 1221-1, or equal. All duplex receptacles shall be Hubbell 5262-1, or equal. All 3-wire receptacles shall be as required for usage by Hubbell, or equal (minimum 25A, 240VAC). All GFCI receptacles shall be GE-TGTR115F, or equal.

Exterior lighting installations shall be underground using schedule 80 electrical PVC conduit.

The electrical contractor has the liberty to make the best application with the least cost and still be acceptable to all codes and regulations. Sizes of conduit shall be determined by the electrical contractor with all connections, accessories and wiring to be in accordance with code. The minimum allowable size and insulation type of conductor shall be #12AWG, THNN, for power and exterior lighting circuits, and #14AWG, THNN, for interior lighting circuits.

The electrical contractor shall install an empty conduit for thermostat wiring.

16600 Special Systems

A special emergency system shall be installed for use in the event of power failure. The system shall be self-contained in an enclosure next to the main switchgear and shall include a throw-over switch, a battery supply and a gas-driven (natural or butane) generator. Proper ventilation shall be maintained for this system at all times. The generator shall be of sufficient size to maintain power and lighting for the Operating Room and

X-Ray Laboratory as well as for all emergency lighting. The engineer shall supply load calculations.

16700 Communications

A special conduit and a special circuit shall be installed for an isolated computer system with additional junctions supplied in each office for networking.

The electrical contractor shall install an empty conduit for telephone communications and for intercom and fire alarm systems. The systems are to be installed by communications specialists who shall supply drawings and specifications to the owner for approval.

End of Division

(Excerpts of a Soils Report)

Soils Report

Controlled Earthwork

Do all grading, compaction, excavation and backfill within the limits of construction. Work and materials shall conform to the soils report and boring log, bound with this section of the Specifications. . . .

Observe the exposed subgrade before and during subsequent scarification for evidences of any remaining debris, old backfills, etc., requiring additional removal. . . .

All fill materials should be soils free of vegetation, debris, organic contaminants and fragments larger than six inches (6") in size. Natural site clay soils may be used for required fills beneath bituminous pavement. However, these soils may become expansive when compacted and are not recommended for fills beneath building floors and exterior concrete slabs.

Based on the results of one expansion test, the existing surface fill similarly is expansive and, therefore, not recommended for reuse beneath building floors and exterior concrete slabs.

Any import fill or backfill soils for use beneath the buildings or exterior concrete slab areas should conform with the following specification requirements:

Maximum Particle Size 6 inches[*]
Maximum Percent Expansion 1.5 %[*]
Maximum size may be reduced at Architect's direction to
        satisfy trenching or landscaping requirements, etc.

Base course materials for use beneath building floors and asphaltic concrete pavements should be well graded sand and gravel materials meeting (local government) specifications for aggregate base-course materials.

Fill materials shall be placed in horizontal lifts not exceeding six inches (6") compacted thickness.

Compaction

Compaction of subgrade soil, backfill, subbase fill and base course materials should be accomplished to the following density criteria:

Material	% Compaction (ASTM D698)
Subgrade Soil:	
Below Slabs	88 minimum - 94 maximum
Below Footings	95 minimum
Below Asphaltic Pavement	95 minimum

[*]Performed on sample remolded to 95% of the maximum ASTM D698 density and 2% below optimum moisture under 100 psf surcharge pressure.

Subbase Fill of On-Site Soils:

Below Slabs	Not Recommended for Use
Below Footings	Not Recommended for Use
Below Asphaltic Pavement	95 minimum

Imported Subbase Fill:

Below Slabs	90 minimum
Below Footings	95 minimum
Below Asphaltic Pavement	95 minimum
Miscellaneous Backfill[†]	90 minimum

Base Course:

Below Slabs	95 minimum
Below Asphaltic Pavement	100 minimum

   Provide additional material required, of top soil quality, and place as part of the work of this section.

Soil Boring Report

Boring log and site plan showing location of borings made by Thomas-Hartig and Associates, Inc., are included for information of bidders, but are not a part of the Contract Documents. Neither the Architect nor Owner guarantee the continuity of conditions indicated at the boring locations and the Contractor is responsible for any conclusions to be drawn from the boring data.

[†]Utility trench and wall backfill not used for foundation, pavement or utility line support.
Courtesy of Thomas-Hartig and Associates, Inc., Phoenix, Arizona
Note: The above Soils Report information is *not* a part of the plans used for the text. This report is displayed for demonstration only.

Basic Tables Relating to
the Construction Divisions

DIVISION 2: SITEWORK

Swell Factors for "Loose" Soil

Material	Expansion Percentage
Wet Gravel (to 2″)	15%
Dry Gravel (to 2″)	15%
Sandy Loam, Wet	10%
Sandy Loam, Dry	20%
Wet Clay	20%
Dry Clay	20%
Topsoil	30%
Well-Blasted Rock (charges close together)	20%
Average-Blasted Rock (charges spaced for medium-sized chunks)	25%
Poorly Blasted Rock (single charge spaced approx. every 100 sq ft)	50%

DIVISION 3: CONCRETE

Reinforcement Bar

Bar Size	Diameter
#2	1/4″
#3	3/8″
#4	1/2″
#5	5/8″
#6	3/4″
#7	7/8″
#8	1″
#9	1 1/8″
#10	1 1/4″
#11	1 3/8″
#14	1 3/4″
#18	2 1/4″

Welded Wire Fabric

Rolls	Sheets
6×6 - W1.4×W1.4	6×6 - W2.0×W2.0
6×6 - W2.9×W2.9	6×6 - W2.9×W2.9
6×6 - W4.0×W4.0	6×6 - W4.0×W4.0
6×6 - W5.5×W5.5	4×4 - W1.4×W1.4
4×4 - W4.0×W4.0	4×4 - W2.9×W2.9
4×4 - W2.9×W2.9	

Note: If there is a letter "D" included with the sizes, it means that the WWF is deformed similarly to rebar. The "W" designation is the wire gauge in metric denominations.

DIVISION 4: MASONRY

Masonry Unit Factors

Type Unit	Size	Factor
Brick (3c-8)	2 1/4″ × 2 1/4″ × 8″	0.1294
″	4″ × 4″ × 8″	0.2222
″	4″ × 4″ × 12″	0.3333
Concrete Masonry Unit	4″ × 4″ × 8″	0.2222
″	6″ × 6″ × 8″	0.3333
″	6″ × 6″ × 12″	0.5000
″	6″ × 6″ × 16″	0.6666
″	8″ × 4″ × 9″	0.2500
″	8″ × 8″ × 8″	0.4444
″	8″ × 8″ × 10″	0.5555
″	8″ × 8″ × 12″	0.6666
″	8″ × 8″ × 16″	0.8888
″	12″ × 12″ × 12″	1.0000

Masonry Mortar and Grout Tables

Mortar

Unit Size	Quantity	Cu Ft Mortar
8 × 16 CMU	112.5 pc	3.2 cu ft
12 × 16 CMU	75 pc	2.2 cu ft
2 1/4 × 2 1/4 × 8	674 pc	7.9 cu ft

Note: Mortar quantity per 100 ft^2 of masonry

Grout

Vertical Wall Spacing	Percentage of Wall Area Covered
16″ O/C	50%
24″ O/C	33.33%
32″ O/C	25%
40″ O/C	20%
48″ O/C	16.67%

Note: Grout quantities (yd^3) per vertical rebar spacing

Grout Wall Capacities

Grout for Reinforced Cells Only

1 cu yd will fill 90 lf of 12″ CMU wall (12×8×16).
1 cu yd will fill 135 lf of 8″ CMU wall (8×8×16).
1 cu yd will fill 180 lf of 6″ CMU wall (6×8×16).

Solid Grouted Wall

1 cu yd will fill 45 sq ft of 12″ CMU wall (12×8×16).
1 cu yd will fill 90 sq ft of 8″ CMU wall (8×8×16).
1 cu yd will fill 135 sq ft of 6″ CMU wall (6×8×16).

DIVISION 6: FRAMING

Framing Ratios per Stud Spacing		
Wall Framing		
Ratio Constant		
Stud Spacing	**Fraction**	**Decimal**
12″	1	1.00
16″	3/4	0.75
18″	2/3	0.67
20″	3/5	0.60
24″	1/2	0.50
32″	3/8	0.375
36″	1/3	0.33

Grade Designation for Dimension Lumber

Category	Grades	Sizes
Light Framing	Construction, Standard, Utility, Economy	2″ to 4″ thick 2″ to 4″ wide
Studs	Stud, Economy	2″ to 4″ thick 2″ to 4″ wide
Structural Light Framing	Select Structural Nos. 1, 2, 3, Economy	2″ to 4″ thick 2″ to 4″ wide
Appearance* Framing Appearance*		2″ to 4″ thick 2″ and wider
Structural Joists and Planks	Select Structural Nos. 1, 2, 3, Economy	2″ to 4″ thick 6″ and wider
Decking	Selected Decking Commercial Decking	2″ to 4″ thick 4″ and wider
Beams, Stringers, Posts, and Timbers	Select Structural Nos. 1, 2, 3	5″ and thicker 5″ and wider

*See Grade Designation for Douglas Fir (DF) and Pine Appearance Grade below.

Grade Designation for Douglas Fir (DF) and Pine Appearance Grade

Category	Douglas Fir (Finish Grades)	Pine (Select Grades)
Clears	C and better (Superior Finish) D Prime Finish	C and better Selects
Factory Douglas Fir Shop Grade (Material to be remanufactured into moldings, casings, base, jambs, etc.)	Molding No. 3 Clear Nos. 1, 2, 3 Shop	Molding No. 3 Clear Nos. 1, 2, 3 Shop
Boards	Select, Construction, Standard, Utility, Economy	Nos. 1, 2, 3, 4, 5

Surface Finishing Abbreviations (Yard and Structural Lumber)

Abbreviation	Definition
S1S	Smooth surface, one side
S1S1E	Smooth surface, one side, one end
S1S2E	Smooth surface, one side, two ends
S2S	Smooth surface, two sides
S2S1E	Smooth surface, two sides, one end
S2S2E	Smooth surface, two sides, two ends
S3S	Smooth surface, three sides
S3S1E	Smooth surface, three sides, one end
S3S2E	Smooth surface, three sides, two ends
S4S	Smooth surface, four sides
S4S1E	Smooth surface, four sides, one end
S4S2E	Smooth surface, four sides, two ends
R/E	Resawn (same as S1S or S1S2E)
R/O or R/S	Rough sawn (no smooth surfaces)

Glue-Laminated Timber Sizing

Width Nominal	Actual	Depth Nominal		Actual
3″	2 1/4″	8″	(6 3/4″ W)	9″
4″	3 1/8″	10″	(5 1/8″ W)	10 1/2″
6″	5 1/8″	8″	(5 1/8″ W)	9″
8″	6 3/4″	6″	(5 1/8″ W)	6″
10″	8 3/4″	6″	(3 1/8″ W)	7 1/2″
12″				10 3/4″
14″				12 1/4″
16″				14 1/4″

Note: Glu-lam depths shown are only for those widths indicated in the parentheses next to the depths. All glu-lam timbers are constructed from structural lumber only and must meet the requirements of the American Institute of Timber Construction and the U.S. Department of Agriculture.

Truss Joist T JI Series

Series Size	Flange Size (Inches) (w × t)[1]	Web Size and TYPE[2]	Web Depth (Inches)
TJI/15DF	1.5″ × 1.5″	3/8″ pp[3]OSB	9 1/2″, 11 7/8″
TJI/25DF	1.75″ × 1.5″	DO	9 1/2″, 11 7/8″, 14″, 16″
TJI/35DF	2.3″ × 1.5″	DO	11 7/8″, 14″, 16″
TJI/25	1.75″ × 1.5″	3/8″ Str # 1 PLYWD	9 1/2″, 11 7/8″, 14″, 16″
TJI/35	2.3″ × 1.5″	DO	11 7/8″, 14″, 16″
TJI/35P	DO	15/32″ Str # 1 PLYWD	11 7/8″, (14″–30″)[4]
TJI/40P	2.3″ × 1.75″	DO	DO
TJI/55P	3.5″ × 1.5″	DO	DO
TJI/35C	2.3″ × 1.5″	7/18″ OSB	DO
TJI/40C	2.3″ × 1.75″	DO	DO
TJI/55C	3.5″ × 1.5″	DO	DO
TJI/55DF	DO	7/16″ pp[3]OSB	11 7/8″, 14″, 16″
TJI/60C	3.5″ × 1.75″	7/16″ OSB	11 7/8″, (14″–30″)[4]
TJI/60P	DO	15/32″ Str # 1 PLYWD	DO
196L	2.25″ × 3.85″	5/8″ & 3/4″ Str # 1 PLYWD	26.35″ or 34.35″
196H	2.5″ × 3.85″	DO	26.85″, 34.85″, 37.1″
196H	2.5″ × 4.65″	DO	34.85″ or 37.1″

[1] Width of flange lumber × thickness of flange lumber
[2] Oriented Strand Board (OSB) or Plywood (PLYWD)
[3] "Performance Plus" OSB
[4] In 2″ increments
Courtesy of Trus Joist/MacMillan Corporation

DIVISION 7: THERMAL AND MOISTURE PROTECTION

Roof Slope/Pitch Table

Slope Ratio	Pitch Ratio	Conversion Factor Percentage		Waste Factor Percentage		Slope Factor Percentage
3:12	1/8	1.03	+	.05	=	1.08
3.5:12	7/24	1.04	+	.05	=	1.09
4:12	1/8	1.05	+	.05	=	1.10
4.5:12	9/48	1.06	+	.05	=	1.11
5:12	5/24	1.08	+	.05	=	1.13
5.5:12	11/48	1.10	+	.05	=	1.15
6:12	1/4	1.12	+	.05	=	1.17
6.5:12	13/48	1.14	+	.05	=	1.19
7:12	7/24	1.16	+	.05	=	1.21
7.5:12	15/48	1.18	+	.05	=	1.23
8:12	1/3	1.20	+	.05	=	1.25
10:12	5/12	1.30	+	.05	=	1.35
12:12	1/2	1.41	+	.05	=	1.46
18:12	3/4	2.00	+	.05	=	2.05
24:12	1	2.00	+	.05	=	2.05

Note: Factors shown in decimal equivalents

Asphaltic Below-Grade Moisture Protection

Materials

Hydrostatic Pressure (in feet)	Cold Applied Emulsion			Hot Mop Asphalt and Base Sheet			Vertical wall protection (layers)
	Primer	Fabric	Emulsion	Primer	Base Sheet	Asphalt	
1	1	1	2	1	2	3	1
2	1	1	2	1	2	3	1
3	1	1	3	1	2	3	1
4	1	1	3	1	2	3	1
5	1	1	3	1	2	3	1
6	1	1	3	1	3	4	1
7	1	2	4	1	3	4	1
8	1	2	4	1	3	4	1
9	1	2	4	1	4	5	1
10	1	2	4	1	4	5	1
12	1	2	4	1	5	6	1
15	1	3	5	1	5	6	1
20	1	3	5	1	6	7	1
25	1	4	6	1	7	8	1
30	1	4	6	1	9	10	1

DIVISION 9: FINISHES (DIVISION 5: COLD FORMED STEEL FRAMING)

**Structural Light-Gauge and Light-Gauge Metal Stud Framing
(Size and Weight/In Ft)**

Size Inches	Metal Gauge	Net Weight lb/ft
	Studs	
1 1/2″	25	0.443
1 1/2″	20	0.700
2 1/2″	25	0.509
2 1/2″	20	0.810
3″	25	0.555
3″	20	0.875
3 1/4″	25	0.575
3 1/4″	20	0.910
3 1/2″	25	0.597
3 1/2″	20	0.944
3 5/8″	25	0.608
3 5/8″	20	0.964
4″	25	0.641
4″	20	1.014
5 1/2″	20	1.240
6″	20	1.290
	Joists	
6″	20	1.486
6″	18	1.889
6″	16	2.339
6″	14	2.914
8″	18	2.215
8″	16	2.740
8″	14	3.411
10″	16	3.142
10″	14	3.908

Courtesy of American Studco Manufacturing Company

Index